Food, Culture and Identity in Germany's Century of War

Heather Merle Benbow · Heather R. Perry
Editors

Food, Culture and Identity in Germany's Century of War

palgrave
macmillan

Editors
Heather Merle Benbow
University of Melbourne
Melbourne, VIC, Australia

Heather R. Perry
University of North Carolina
at Charlotte
Charlotte, NC, USA

ISBN 978-3-030-27137-4   ISBN 978-3-030-27138-1 (eBook)
https://doi.org/10.1007/978-3-030-27138-1

© The Editor(s) (if applicable) and The Author(s) 2019
This work is subject to copyright. All rights are solely and exclusively licensed by the Publisher, whether the whole or part of the material is concerned, specifically the rights of translation, reprinting, reuse of illustrations, recitation, broadcasting, reproduction on microfilms or in any other physical way, and transmission or information storage and retrieval, electronic adaptation, computer software, or by similar or dissimilar methodology now known or hereafter developed.
The use of general descriptive names, registered names, trademarks, service marks, etc. in this publication does not imply, even in the absence of a specific statement, that such names are exempt from the relevant protective laws and regulations and therefore free for general use.
The publisher, the authors and the editors are safe to assume that the advice and information in this book are believed to be true and accurate at the date of publication. Neither the publisher nor the authors or the editors give a warranty, expressed or implied, with respect to the material contained herein or for any errors or omissions that may have been made. The publisher remains neutral with regard to jurisdictional claims in published maps and institutional affiliations.

Cover illustration: Amoret Tanner/Alamy Stock Photo

This Palgrave Macmillan imprint is published by the registered company Springer Nature Switzerland AG
The registered company address is: Gewerbestrasse 11, 6330 Cham, Switzerland

Acknowledgements

Co-editing a book in different hemispheres is a challenging task. As much as the editors were able to find scholarly common ground in a passion for understanding the role of food in the German experience of war, advancing the conversation in disparate time zones was never easy. We are therefore particularly grateful for the support of both the University of Melbourne and the University of North Carolina at Charlotte that enabled us to work together for a sustained period on the first draft of the volume in 2018. Specifically, we acknowledge the support provided by the Dyason Fellowship scheme and the McCoy Seed Fund. Heather Perry would like to thank the Department of History, the College of Liberal Arts and Sciences and the Faculty Research Grants program at UNC Charlotte for continued research funding and support. Heather Benbow would also like to thank the School of Languages and Linguistics and the Faculty of Arts at the University of Melbourne for support for this research.

The editors would also like to thank the following people who have supported the project. Firstly, thanks to those who conceived, organized and above all participated in the international meeting which inspired this volume. The three-day seminar "Nourishing the Volk: Food and Foodways in Central Europe" which met at the 2016 meeting of the German Studies Association in San Diego would not have materialized without the initial efforts of the co-organizers Gesine Gerhard, Andrew Kloiber and Heather Perry. And it would not have been a success without the participation of Heather Benbow, Michael Bryant, Mark Cole,

Friederike Emonds, Christine Fojtik, Gesine Gerhard, Andrew Kloiber, Melissa Kravetz, Heather Perry, Chad Ross, Uwe Spiekermann, Jenny Sprenger-Syeffarth, Robert Terrell and Corinna Treitel. The sustained conversations we enjoyed over those three days confirmed that there was still much to research, learn and discuss with regard to food and German identity—and we are grateful that organizations such as the GSA exist and provide a forum for workshopping international, interdisciplinary ideas. That seminar seeded the idea for this project and several participants from that initial meeting eventually contributed chapters for this volume. We also want to acknowledge Stefan Siemsen and Jana Verhoeven at the University of Melbourne for helping us with the organizing and editing of the manuscript. We could not have pulled it together without your efforts.

At Palgrave, we are indebted to Christine Pardue and Megan Laddusaw for their advice, patience and trust in us despite a number of interruptions to the volume's planned trajectory. We also thank the anonymous reviewers of the book proposal and the initial manuscript for taking time to make useful suggestions that have improved this book. Finally, we thank our authors for their constructive engagement with our feedback and their patience as we steered this project to completion. It has been a pleasure to read and engage with your work.

Contents

1 Hunger Pangs: The Contours of Violence and Food Scarcity in Germany's Twentieth-Century Wars 1
   Heather Merle Benbow and Heather R. Perry

2 Onward Kitchen Soldiers! Gender, Food and Health in Germany's Long Great War 17
   Heather R. Perry

3 Food, Drink and Hunger for World War I German Soldiers 45
   Heather Merle Benbow

4 Public Feeding in the First World War: Berlin's First Public Kitchen System 75
   Jenny Sprenger-Seyffarth

5 Coping with Hunger in the Ghettos: The Impact of Nazi Racialized Food Policy 103
   Helene J. Sinnreich

6 Bee Stings and Beer: The Significance of Food in Alabamian POW Newspapers 125
   Christine Rinne

7	The Productive *Heimat*: Territorial Loss and Rurality in German Identity at the *Stunde Null* Christine Fojtik	153
8	Postwar Food Rumors: Security, Victimhood and Fear Laura J. Hilton	177
9	The Taste of Defeat: Food, Peace and Power in US-Occupied Germany Kaete O'Connell	201
10	Cold (Beer) War: The German *Volksgetränk* in East German Rhetoric (1945–1971) John Gillespie	227
11	Brewing Global Relations During the Cold War: Coffee, East Germans and Southeast Asia, 1978–1990 Andrew Kloiber	247
Index		271

Notes on Contributors

Heather Merle Benbow is a scholar of German Studies at the University of Melbourne, Australia. She received her Ph.D. from the University of Melbourne in 2003. She has published widely on German literature, film, food, the body and the history of ideas. Her most recent book is *Marriage in Turkish German Popular Culture: States of Matrimony in the New Millennium* (Lexington, 2015).

Christine Fojtik (Ph.D., University of Wisconsin 2013) is an assistant professor of history at Saint Xavier University in Chicago. She is interested in food, gender and agriculture in postwar Germany and is currently working on an article about agricultural policy in occupied Germany. She has served as the managing editor of H-German for the past three years and is the director of the Digital Humanities program at her university.

John Gillespie is a Ph.D. student at Vanderbilt University researching questions of cultural nationalism in Central Europe during the Cold War, with a particular focus on the cultural politics of beer in the divided Germany and Czechoslovakia. He earned bachelor's degrees in history and English at Virginia Tech in 2013 and a master's degree in European history at Middle Tennessee State University in 2017. His master's thesis The People's Drink: The Politics of Beer in East Germany 1945–1971 represents the initial work in his ongoing research.

Laura J. Hilton is professor of history at Muskingum University in New Concord, OH. She earned her Ph.D. in modern European history from The Ohio State University. Her research focuses on the postwar period of Germany, 1945–1951, in particular the interactions among Germans, refugees, displaced persons and Allied occupiers. Recently, she has published articles in *German History, Jahrbuch des International Tracing Service, Holocaust and Genocide Studies* and *The History Teacher*. She is co-editor of a forthcoming collection, Understanding and Teaching the Holocaust (University of Wisconsin Press) and is currently working on a monograph centered on the rumor culture in postwar Germany.

Andrew Kloiber earned his Ph.D. at McMaster University (Canada). His work broadly examines the cultural history of modern Germany—particularly the role of material culture in shaping identity, social norms and power. His current work considers the changing landscapes of memory and commemoration surrounding the Peaceful Revolution of 1989. His work has received generous support from the German Academic Exchange Service (DAAD), the German Historical Institute, the University of Exeter and McMaster University. He is currently revising a manuscript for publication.

Kaete O'Connell is a postdoctoral fellow at the Center for Presidential History at Southern Methodist University. She received her Ph.D. from Temple University, where she wrote a dissertation that explored the political, cultural and emotional impact of US food diplomacy in postwar Germany. She is the author of "'Uncle Wiggly Wings': Children, Chocolates, and the Berlin Airlift," featured in a special issue of *Food and Foodways* and an essay on food and memory in a forthcoming volume on the Berlin Airlift and the making of the Cold War.

Heather R. Perry is associate professor of history at the University of North Carolina at Charlotte. Her research focuses on the social, cultural and medical history of the First World War, with special attention to Germany and Europe. She earned her Ph.D. from Indiana University in 2005, where she also worked at the *American Historical Review*. She currently serves as editor of the international journal, *First World War Studies*. Her book, *Recycling the Disabled: Army, Medicine, and Modernity in WWI Germany,* was published in 2014 (Manchester UP) and her current project examines gender, health and popular culture in the First World War.

Christine Rinne is associate professor of German at the University of South Alabama. She has published on the literary formations of social identity in turn of the twentieth-century writings by authors such as Sigmund Freud, material consumption in East Germany and German historical reality television. She is currently working on a manuscript that analyzes German POW newspapers written at camps in Alabama during the Second World War, of which this article is a part.

Helene J. Sinnreich is director of the Fern and Manfred Steinfeld Program in Judaic Studies and associate professor of religious studies at University of Tennessee, Knoxville. Dr. Sinnreich serves as editor in chief of the *Journal of Jewish Identities* (Johns Hopkins University Press). She has served as a fellow at the United States Holocaust Memorial Museum in Washington, DC, and at Yad Vashem in Jerusalem. She is editor of *A Hidden Diary from the Lodz Ghetto: 1942–1944* (2015). Her forthcoming monograph is a comparative study of hunger in the Lodz, Warsaw and Krakow ghettos.

Jenny Sprenger-Seyffarth is doctoral candidate in modern history at Freie Universität Berlin, Germany, and a scholarship holder of the Friedrich Ebert Foundation. Her dissertation traces the development of public feeding and the private family meal in Berlin and Vienna during the First World War. Published articles include "Public Kitchens (Germany)," in 1914–1918-online. International Encyclopedia of the First World War, edited by U. Daniel et al. Forthcoming is "'Es ist doch geradezu ein Skandal…!'—Die Berliner Volksspeisung im Ersten Weltkrieg zwischen Qualität und sozialem Stigma," in S. Steinberg and F. Jacob (eds.) Semmeln aus Sägemehl. Lebensmittelskandale des 19. und 20. Jahrhunderts als Orte des Wissens.

List of Figures

Fig. 2.1	"The Hindenburg of German Housewives"	26
Fig. 2.2	Just's *War Cookbook for Women's Relief: 50 Proven Recipes*, 1915	31
Fig. 3.1	"Nem tu dom"	64
Fig. 4.1	Map of Berlin's public feeding network during the First World War	80
Fig. 4.2	Outdoor view of Red Cross dining hall in Berlin, 1914	81
Fig. 4.3	Feeding of army reservists' children by the *Verein für Kindervolksküchen und Volkskinderhorte* (Postcard, August 1914)	82
Fig. 4.4	Chart comparing number of meals served by Berlin Red Cross kitchens between November 1914 and March 1915	84
Fig. 4.5	Graph of weekly registration figures for meal passes from the NFD, 1914–1919	85
Fig. 4.6	Relation of weekly registered meal passes and food coupons, November 1914–December 1918	86
Fig. 6.1	"Why not? You constantly come to breakfast in this getup too, dear!" cartoon from *Der Zaungast*, June 10, 1945 (*Source* Reproduced by permission of the Aliceville Museum)	133

CHAPTER 1

Hunger Pangs: The Contours of Violence and Food Scarcity in Germany's Twentieth-Century Wars

Heather Merle Benbow and Heather R. Perry

With the publication of his seminal works *Sweetness and Power* and *Tasting Food, Tasting Freedom*, the widely acknowledged "father of food anthropology" Sidney Mintz urged anthropologists and other scholars of food culture to pay closer attention to how food—foodstuffs, food preferences and food rituals—were deeply and historically rooted in structures of power, knowledge and location. The culture and meanings of food were neither immutable nor timeless; and, even more importantly, he demonstrated that with careful examination these complex food histories could be uncovered and used to illuminate new aspects of human culture and society.[1]

H. M. Benbow
University of Melbourne, Melbourne, VIC, Australia

H. R. Perry (✉)
University of North Carolina at Charlotte, Charlotte, NC, USA

© The Author(s) 2019
H. M. Benbow and H. R. Perry (eds.), *Food, Culture and Identity in Germany's Century of War*,
https://doi.org/10.1007/978-3-030-27138-1_1

For Mintz, the "large-scale and general case" of war presented an ideal opportunity for examining the different ways that power could inform food choices and meanings.[2] For instance, in one of his more well-known examples, he revealed how military planning and organizational structures combined with wartime battle conditions and soldier patriotism to fundamentally shape the emotional meanings of Coca-Cola among US soldiers in the Second World War—and afterward. The "single most powerful instrument of dietary change in human experience," Mintz argued, was war:

> In time of war, both civilians and soldiers are regimented—in modern times, more even than before. There can occur at the same time terrible disorganization and (some would say) terrible organization. Food resources are mobilized, along with other sorts of resources. Large numbers of persons are assembled to do things together—ultimately, to kill together. While learning how, they must eat together.[3]

Nevertheless, despite the growth of food studies and the rise of scholarship focusing on the social and cultural significance of food in history, historians of modern wars and conflict have been slow to embrace what Sidney Mintz saw as both important and obvious: the analytical potential of food-centered research to shed new light on modern conflicts or their aftermath. To be sure, scholars have examined the impact of food insecurity on populations at war—most notably the role food plays in international conflicts over natural resources or as the fulcrum around which home-front morale fundamentally pivots. Yet, while scholars of military strategy or wartime policy have included discussions of the origins, experiences and impacts of siege warfare on home-front food supplies or political stability, significant research lacunae on the cultural, social and emotional significance of food in warfare remain. This is even more surprising given the turn in the late twentieth century from more traditional, operational histories of war to newer research on wartime gender, culture and economy—a trend more generally understood as the study of War and Society.[4] The essays collected in this volume represent a significant step toward filling this scholarly gap through examinations of the different cultural saliencies of food and their relationships to German identity in the nation's war-torn twentieth century.

Thanks to Mintz and other scholars, the field of food studies has emerged from the ethnographic shadows of Anthropology and Folklore programs to achieve widespread recognition as a fundamental lens through which to study and understand religious, ethnic, gender and cultural identities.[5] Scholars from many disciplines have come to recognize the centrality of food and foodways in the shaping of cultural practices and imaginaries and the sub-disciplines of Food Anthropology, the Sociology of Food and Food History are well established. And, as one might expect, scholars in the early decades of the twenty-first century are increasingly heeding the call to examine how human relationships with and emotions surrounding food have been transformed and amplified—in both positive and negative ways—under conditions of conflict and resource scarcity. However, few of these focus specifically on wartime Germany.[6] Indeed, somewhat ironically, in spite of the abundance of research on Germany's bellicose twentieth century, few scholars have concentrated on developing a picture of the cultural significance or historical meanings of food across the nation's hot and cold global wars of the modern era.[7]

Beginning in the 1990s, scholars began publishing cultural histories of food in wartime with a particular focus on the First World War and a relatively small amount of cultural history research on German experiences of food and hunger.[8] Even those studies which offer cultural analyses of food experiences or meanings in Central Europe, focus rather on top-down governmental policies during a single war or particular political regime—or even gloss over the war, viewing it as a temporary disruption and not a significant focal point.[9] While Alice Weinreb looks at the geopolitics of food in the short twentieth century, including the role of the food system in the "making of war and peace," only Corinna Treitel's monograph on the history of "natural eating" and vegetarianism in modern Germany offers a glimpse of what a study of food from the "bottom up" looks like.[10] And still none of these works offer readers the opportunity that this volume does: The occasion to examine the multi-valency of Germany's food experiences across the twentieth century within the contextual pressures and changing dynamics of modern warfare.

VOLUME AIMS AND THEMATIC CONSTELLATIONS

The collection of essays in this volume examines the social, cultural and emotional significance of food and hunger in Germany's tumultuous twentieth century—with especial attention to two key forces: war and identity. The essays represent emerging research from new and established scholars and concentrate on the three German-centered conflicts which defined the twentieth century: the First and Second World Wars and the ensuing global Cold War. All of the essays analyze Germany's modern wars through food-centered perspectives and experiences "from below" that suggest broader and more significant political, social and cultural consequences of these conflicts. We examine the analytical saliency of food when studying Germany's violent and turbulent twentieth century while consciously pushing conventional temporal frameworks and disciplinary boundaries. Through the essays gathered here, our aim is to interrogate and reconsider the ways in which deeper studies of food culture in Germany can shed new light on old wars. In particular, we find that the research presented here makes the following significant contributions:

1. it looks beyond the food experiences in "hot zones" of armed conflict in order to include other important wartime food spaces such as public kitchens, occupation zones, medical encounters and reconstruction programs;
2. it considers not only "top-down" policies and practices around food provision, but also individual experiences and histories of food in wartime and postwar eras, thus yielding new syntheses of the varied meanings of food in times of conflict;
3. it uses national, transnational and cross-cultural perspectives to examine the experiences and effects of wartime eating, shortages and hunger; and finally
4. in examining the different meanings and changing German experiences of food across the three major conflicts of the twentieth century, the volume enables us to see more easily the continuities, changes—even significant ruptures—in German food culture and history that more traditional military or political frameworks obscure.

Moreover, in addition to these contributions in the study of German history and culture, we find the volume brings important new scholarly dimensions to the two broader research areas of food and culture studies and war and society studies.

In putting together this volume, we have found that a number of "thematic constellations" suffuse the experiences and practices of all three conflicts. Because they recur throughout the volume more explicitly in some places than others, we think they bear emphasizing at the outset. The first, and most obvious, is the constellation of FOOD, POWER AND AUTHORITY in wartime. The control of food resources and access to food becomes critical during times of war and can cement, disrupt, determine or challenge peacetime power relationships. This is true at a transnational and at a personal level. It is also true of the power of food as a symbolic object—hence its frequent deployment in wartime propaganda. Food, in the pressurized context of conflict, *is* power—yet it is often a power that poses a significant challenge or subversion of peacetime authority.

The power exerted over food in war often manifests in an important corollary to the above, which is our second thematic constellation: HUNGER, DEPRIVATION AND SCARCITY. The devastating consequences and enduring legacy of the Entente Blockade during the First World War informed the food and population policies that underpinned the Second and cemented itself in German cultural memory even after that second devastating conflict that deployed mass civilian starvation on an unthinkable scale. Even the lesser deprivations such as the "stretching" of basic foodstuffs caused corrosive civilian resentment with the power to turn the tide of conflict from the First World War through to the Cold War.

Analyzing Germany's twentieth-century wars through the lens of food draws our attention to its material role as an object of CONSUMPTION, TRADE AND COMMERCE—our third thematic constellation. Germany's rapid industrialization at the end of the nineteenth century had created an empire that—in spite of its rich natural and industrial resources—was not "food independent" or self-sufficient. Throughout the mechanized total wars of the twentieth century, Germany's defeat ultimately hinged more upon the nation's agricultural resources and food supplies than its military might or prowess. The focus of much existing scholarship on the German home-front deprivation and scarcity in the First and Second World Wars has also perhaps obscured the experiences of both East and West Germans during the global Cold War as they struggled to acquire land for agricultural development and food production, to cement international trade agreements, and secure steady access to the foodstuffs which could ensure the health and well-being of their populations.

The mobilization of vast, hungry armies and especially their intrusion into foreign cities, villages and countryside occasioned countless personal, often highly emotional, intimate encounters with "the other." Moreover, in the wake of the twentieth century's total wars, the humanitarian assistance and food aid that accompanied occupation armies and state-sponsored programs of pacification in Germany was an intrinsically transnational affair. Yet most studies of these phenomena (during and after the conflict) have focused on the policies and bureaucracies that implemented them—and ignored the experiences of the *humans* who imposed, suffered or benefitted from them. Thus, the sharing of meals in such INTERCULTURAL ENCOUNTERS, our fourth thematic constellation, could scarcely be avoided. Whether within the regionally and religiously diverse Imperial Army or socially stratified home front, the German nation at war was still a highly decentralized and culturally diverse nation struggling to maintain its fragile and still recent unity. Brothers-in-arms from the Austro-Hungarian and Ottoman Empires further added to the cultural mix within the fighting forces of the Central Powers.

Interactions with civilians, POWs or enemy soldiers were frequently driven by the need to secure nourishment and were characterized often by the intimacy that can accompany commensality. Reflecting on these unexpected and food-centered encounters—many times coerced, invasive and unwelcome—offers the chance to engage our final thematic constellation: FOOD, EMOTIONS AND IDENTITY. Every chapter in this volume is alert to the personal, cultural and social meanings of food in the wartime context. Unlike earlier histories of conflicts that have too often seen food narrowly in operational terms, or at best in terms of its impact on morale, the essays in this volume notice and interrogate the layered experiences of food and hunger; they seek out lesser studied, personal accounts including diaries, correspondence, rumors, advertising, POW newspapers and censors' reports and listen to the voices of individuals impacted by and participating in the tumultuous events in which food played a pivotal political role. More often than not, the authors in this volume uncover personal accounts that are surprising, contrary or enlightening perspectives on well-studied conflicts. Food is, after all, more than the administrative concern of feeding the *Volk*; it is a material object that is incorporated into the quotidian aspects of human life in ways that are both public and private, simultaneously intimate and mundane. This personal experience is not only shaped by war, but also "feeds back" to the body politic the subjective experience of war.

Volume Structure and Chapter Outlines

The book begins with Heather Perry's examination of how the Great War reshaped German popular ideas about nutrition and bodily health. Whereas other historians have focused on the failure of state authorities and bureaucrats to effectively manage food resources on the German home front, Perry focuses instead on how other "food authorities"—physiologists, nutritionists and social reformers—sought to manage information about the relationships between food, health and nutrition. Here she outlines how efforts at reeducating the general public about the relationships between food, health and nutrition ultimately created new social and cultural alliances between laboratory researchers and the nation's housewives—ones that remained long after the war ended. Through an analysis of wartime cookbooks, nutritional advice manuals, home economic schools, and public exhibits, Perry investigates the attempt to "mobilize" German women on the home front as "kitchen soldiers" whose daily choices could have significant impact on the health and welfare of the nation. In doing so, her chapter reveals how this "scientization of food" and the private kitchen that occurred during the war ultimately shifted popular notions about the responsibility of citizens—primarily the nation's housewives—toward promoting national health through food. Yet, at the same time, she reveals how regional tastes and food preferences thwarted attempts at fostering a standardized "national diet."

Taking as her departure point the commonplace observation that food plays a central role in the daily lives of soldiers and is critical for morale, Heather Merle Benbow explores the importance of food, drink and hunger in interpersonal interactions of various kinds for German soldiers in the First World War. She argues that morale is not the only story to be told about the significance of food for the German soldier, and that food enables, shapes and disrupts interpersonal relationships during the conflict. Drawing on sources including army newspapers, soldier memoirs, letters and censorship reports, Benbow observes how food (and especially drink) could be a comforting, consoling element in the wartime experience. The experience of hunger and deprivation, however, threatened those same comradely bonds. Similarly, food and drink could poignantly evoke the connections between home and fighting fronts. However, dissatisfaction due to home-front hunger—expressed forcefully in the so-called *Jammerbriefe*—made soldiers question why they were fighting. While food frequently had the potential to forge and disrupt interpersonal connections, culinary encounters are most ambiguous, Benbow suggests, when it comes to interactions between soldiers and civilians. While some soldiers recall with affection restorative and warm interactions with civilians, food and drink also attained new and threatening meanings in the context of war.

In the third chapter to deal with food and hunger in the First World War, Jenny Sprenger-Seyffarth examines the voluntary public kitchens and municipal feeding programs ("*Volksspeisung*") which were established and run through mid-1916. She demonstrates how the city of Berlin responded to the food emergency early in the war and how these improvised kitchens worked until the state stepped in and tried to reorganize and oversee these public programs in 1916. Sprenger-Seyffarth analyzes popular responses to the public meal—and reveals how socioeconomic status, class and religion influenced and shaped the variegated public attitudes toward food aid. As she points out, social standing and cultural norms could at times override hunger and desperation when it came to notions about *what specifically* one should eat and *where specifically* one should eat it. In the end, German utilization of public kitchens came down not just to hardship, but also social identity. As these chapters show us, even amidst the desperate conditions of total war, food constitutes more than simple nourishment.

Germany's disastrous food shortages in the First World War were determinative for the National Socialist regime's approach in the Second. As Helene J. Sinnreich discusses, Nazi food policy distributed food on the basis of a calculus of perceived racial value. Sinnreich looks at the ghettos in Nazi-occupied Europe and describes how their Jewish inhabitants struggled to survive amid grave food shortages. Eschewing an overarching theory of ghetto experience due to its diversity, Sinnreich looks in granular detail at individual narratives via the lens of food and hunger. Echoing a recurring theme of this volume, Sinnreich shows that social, religious, gender and economic status play out in the quotidian wartime struggles around food. Strategies employed in various ghettos include ration systems, public feeding, trade and barter, theft, smuggling, prostitution and—when food as a material substance is all but impossible to come by—"stretching" food with more-or-less inedible ingredients, "savoring" miniscule portions, food-themed art and elaborate food fantasies. The responses to food crisis in the ghettos were as diverse as their populations. Some went to extraordinary and detrimental lengths to maintain a kosher diet, while others reportedly transgressed not just religious rules but also a range of social injunctions, such as that against cannibalism. Above all, Sinnreich observes, food in the ghetto held great coercive power and was a significant element in the final stages of the Nazi campaign against Jewish life; the genocidal food shortages in the ghettos were an effective tool in persuading Jews to board the deportation trains.

Captivity or confinement is a defining wartime experience, and one in which the social, cultural, gendered or religious meanings of food are placed under pressure. The multiple functions of food in German prisoner of war newspapers during the Second World War are the focus of Christine Rinne's chapter. The publications *Der Zaungast* and *POW-Oase* emerged from two Alabama-based army bases: Camp Aliceville and Fort McClellan. Food features in the fiction, cartoons and reports on camp life within the newspapers. In these publications, writes Rinne, food functioned as a way to form interpersonal bonds and find comfort with fellow POWs as well as maintaining ties to a distant homeland. In her close reading of the trope of food in the newspapers, Rinne uncovers how the camp canteens, care packages from home and German communities elsewhere in the world, as well as the experience of growing food in camp gardens or outside the camp on local farms are all occasions for nostalgia and longing for the *Heimat*. As so often in wartime contexts, food was also a point of intercultural difference, however. While deployed on work details in the agriculture industry and in hospital kitchens, POWs experienced the local food culture. Contributors to the POW newspapers are critical of American marketing of seemingly unnatural foods like canned goods and cola. Their experience of American food culture occasioned nostalgia for Germany and its unadulterated beer. Despite shortages and alienation from their host culture, Rinne argues that the German POWs of Alabama were able to use food in various ways to create "oases" far from the conflict that helped the men prepare for a return home and postwar life.

A number of chapters turn to this precarious postwar context and the deepening food crisis that resulted. Just as shortages were most severe after the Armistice, German civilians faced years of shortages and hunger under occupation. The chapters in this volume highlight the social and political dimensions of food, feeding and hunger in this postwar context. Christine Fojtik examines how Germans struggling to rebuild after 1945 used food as the nexus around which to reconstruct both national and individual identities. After defeat in two global, industrialized wars, as well as Stalin's blockade of Berlin, many Germans were confronting a truth they had long evaded: The pastoral, German *Heimat* of small farmers and peasants was more imagined than real. As refugees and expellees from the East streamed across the Oder and back into the fatherland, many Germans feared that food insecurity would continue to plague the nation despite the war's end. How would Germany rebuild, they argued, if the government did not implement land distribution and resettlement schemes? Moreover, what would become of farmers without farmland? Fojtik demonstrates that questions about the nation's future turned uncomfortably on the tensions between the popular imaginary of Germany as a nation of peasant-farmers and the cold reality of food dependence under occupation. Thus, she argues, public conversations about food—its production, distribution and consumption—were tied as much to individual fears about dislocation and rebuilding as they were to bigger questions of national security, economic independence and political sovereignty during a period of massive change and uncertainty.

The postwar occupation is examined further from a personal and political perspective by Laura J. Hilton in her analysis of post-Second World War food rumors. The occupation powers sought to use food to "rank the worthiness of populations, pegged to their wartime experiences as victims, perpetrators or bystanders," leading to the perception by German citizens that postwar food shortages were the result of occupier vindictiveness and that Germans were themselves being victimized. Hilton's analysis of the food rumors that proliferated thus gives us a new perspective on postwar perpetrator/victim narratives that emerged after the Second World War. Collective memories of the hunger endured during the First World War under the blockade informed the sense of victimhood felt by Germans after the end of the Second World War, a feeling expressed in rumors that the Allies aimed to deliberately starve the German population. Resentments of authorities, farmers and foreigners were also vociferously expressed again, as was the case during the hunger of the First World War. Food was central to the alternative discourses that Germans developed during the postwar, Hilton argues. German civilians effectively rewrote the Second World War past through the lens of their own hunger, an experience far more immediate for them than the crimes of the Nazis.

Kaete O'Connell zooms in even further on personal interactions around food in occupied Germany. She examines what she calls the emotional and cultural consequences of food exchange in conquered and early occupied post-Second World War Germany. She points to a gap in research around the role of food in civilian–military interactions in Germany. American soldiers witnessed firsthand the effects of starvation as a weapon of war and played a part in its utilization as a tool of peace. O'Connell is alert to the often ambiguous nature of gifts in an occupation scenario in which the power differential vis-à-vis a hungry population in receipt of food aid could not be more obvious. As well as bringing to light the disdain often felt toward German civilians by occupying US soldiers, O'Connell traces the administrative struggles to understand local food and drink customs. Ignorance of the cultural and nutritional importance of beer in Bavaria, or the widespread perception of corn as mere cattle feed outside of Bavaria threatened the success of postwar food diplomacy. Looking at both sides of the exchange of food in occupied Germany, O'Connell argues that food can serve as an alternative measure of power and was "as important in the postwar as it was during the conflict."

The final two chapters of the volume look at the bifurcation of food policy, politics and representation in divided Germany during the Cold War. In a study of political discourse in the first two decades after the Second World War, John Gillespie reveals the role of beer as a political weapon in a cultural conflict that accompanied the Cold War. Much like the wrangling over other parts of German cultural heritage, the East German regime claimed to be the rightful heir to Germany's beer heritage, portraying beer as a cultural commodity better suited to their new, socialist vision of German life than to West German capitalism. Ironically, however, it was the Federal Republic, with its adherence to the ancient "purity law," that upheld the connection to Germany's beer traditions, while the Democratic Republic followed international trends toward industry consolidation and the use of non-traditional ingredients and struggled to maintain even basic quality standards on a regular basis. The GDR pursued dual aims of technological and social modernity in relation to beer, fashioned as the "worker's drink." The GDR press depicted the beer culture of the FRG as by contrast characterized by capitalist exploitation, excessive consumption and regressive social attitudes.

Andrew Kloiber looks at the German Democratic Republic's coffee crisis of 1977 and its attempt to solve it via a long-term development project in Vietnam. Kloiber's analysis looks at both the symbolic and material value of coffee for GDR citizens and the state. Coffee was incorporated into the ruling Socialist Unity Party's messages about the bright socialist future built on modernity, progress and culture. Hence, when shortages led to the provision of a product that was comprised of almost half "surrogate" ingredients, the public reaction was very negative. The product evoked among consumers memories of wartime deprivation. Just as during the "hot" conflicts of the twentieth century, this Cold War austerity impacted morale among the "troops," in this case the workers of the socialist state. The critique of the *Ersatz* coffee served up to workers was a threat to the political legitimacy of the GDR. The engagement with Vietnam and the development of its fledgling coffee industry was for the GDR part of its Cold War political strategy as well as a solution to a domestic problem. GDR support for Vietnam came to be known as its "Vietnam bonus" as the global tide of opinion turned against the war. The successful cultivation of a coffee industry in Vietnam is indicative for Kloiber that the GDR was not a passive pawn within a broader in twentieth-century game of globalization.

Throughout Germany's twentieth century of conflict, food was a means by which Germany (and the Germanies) represented itself, not only, as Kloiber shows us so deftly, in the Cold War. Food is at all times, but especially under the pressurized conditions of transnational conflict, a symbolic as well as a material substance. As a substance that does double duty, it can connect and unite people or separate and divide them.[11] The chapters in this volume bear out this important observation by showing how on the one hand food cemented strong interpersonal connections, while on the other hand could be a potent point of difference. Food formed part of the social glue that bound communities or social groups together in times of stress. But the personal experiences of food in Germany's twentieth century were refracted through its deployment as a weapon of war. Beginning with the first "total" war and the "mobilization of the kitchen" described by Perry, Germany's food supply, consumption and representation were inextricably entwined with its misadventures in large-scale international conflict throughout the century. As central to the making and enduring of war as to rebuilding and peace, food, drink and hunger provide a lens through which to view Germany's wars anew, a visceral and potent perspective on personal, collective and transnational experiences of conflict.

NOTES

1. The two canonical studies from Mintz are Sidney W. Mintz, *Sweetness and Power: The Place of Sugar in Modern History* (New York: Viking, 1985); and Sidney W. Mintz, *Tasting Food, Tasting Freedom: Excursions into Eating, Culture, and the Past* (Boston: Beacon Press, 1997).
2. Mintz, "Food and Its Relationship to Concepts of Power," *Tasting Food, Tasting Freedom*, 25.
3. Ibid.
4. For a brief introduction to this turn, see Robert M. Citino, "Military Histories Old and New: A Reintroduction," *American Historical Review* 112, no. 4: 1070–1090.
5. See for instance the journals *Food & History* (Brepols) and *Food and Foodways* (Taylor and Francis) and the scholarly organizations: Association for the Study of Food and Society; the Society for the Anthropology of Food and Nutrition; the American Folklore Society; and the Institut Europeen d'Histoire et des Cultures de l'Alimentation (IEHCA).
6. See, for instance, Rachel Duffett, *The Stomach for Fighting: Food and the Soldiers of the Great War* (Manchester: Manchester University Press, 2012); Ina Zweiniger-Bargielowska, Rachel Duffett, and Alain Drouard, *Food and War in Twentieth Century Europe* (Farnham, MD: Ashgate, 2011); Frank Trentmann and Flemming Just, *Food and Conflict in Europe in the Age of the Two World Wars* (Basingstoke: Palgrave Macmillan, 2006); Bertrand M. Patenaude, *The Big Show in Bololand: The American Relief Expedition to Soviet Russia in the Famine of 1921* (Stanford: Stanford University Press, 2002); Marcelle Cinq-Mars, *La cuisine rationnée: nourrir un peuple et une armée, 1914–1918* (Outremont, QC: Athéna éditions, 2011); Rudolf Kučera, *Rationed Life: Science, Everyday Life and Working-Class Politics in the Bohemian Lands, 1914–1918* (New York: Berghahn, 2016); and Hilda Kean, *The Great Cat and Dog Massacre: The Real Story of World War Two's Unknown Tragedy* (Chicago: The University of Chicago Press, 2017).
7. Although Mintz and Du Bois noted the general neglect of the study of food during times of war in their 2002 review of scholarship in food studies, a few notable studies of German wartime food management have since emerged. For their review, see Sidney W. Mintz and Christine Du Bois, "The Anthropology of Food and Eating," *Annual Review of Anthropology* 31 (2002): 99–119, 105. Studies of food in wartime Germany published since then include Belinda J. Davis, *Home Fires Burning: Food, Politics and Everyday Life in World War I Berlin* (Chapel Hill: University of North Carolina Press, 2000); Gesine Gerhard, *Nazi Hunger Politics:*

A History of Food in the Third Reich (Lanham: Rowman & Littlefield, 2015); Other important studies with significant chapters on food in wartime Germany are Roger Chickering, *The Great War and Urban Life in Germany: Freiburg, 1914–1918* (Cambridge: Cambridge University Press, 2007); Alice Weinreb, *Modern Hungers: Food and Power in Twentieth-Century Germany* (Oxford: Oxford University Press, 2017); and Tatjana Tönsmeyer, Peter Haslinger, and Agnes Laba, eds., *Coping with Hunger and Shortage Under German Occupation in World War II* (New York: Palgrave Macmillan, 2018).

8. Until the early twenty-first century, the leading studies on food in the First World War Germany were those by Vincent and Offer. See C. Paul Vincent, *The Politics of Hunger: The Allied Blockade of Germany, 1915–1919* (Athens, OH: Ohio University Press, 1985); and Avner Offer, *The First World War: An Agrarian Interpretation* (New York: Oxford University Press, 1989). Subsequent studies include Zweiniger-Bargielowska et al., *Food and War in Twentieth Century Europe*; Davis, *Home Fires Burning*; and Maureen Healy, *Vienna and the Fall of the Habsburg Empire: Total War and Everyday Life in World War I* (Cambridge: Cambridge University Press, 2004).

9. For cultural analyses of food in Germany, see Gerhard, *Nazi Hunger Politics*; Weinreb, *Modern Hungers*; and Corinna Treitel, *Eating Nature in Modern Germany: Food, Agriculture, and Environment, c. 1870–2000* (Cambridge: Cambridge University Press, 2017). Studies with a focus on wartime food administration and/or policy include George Yaney, *The World of the Manager: Food Administration in Berlin During World War I* (New York: Peter Lang, 1994); Keith Allen, "Sharing Scarcity: Bread Rationing and the First World War in Berlin, 1914–1923," *Journal of Social History* (Winter 1998): 371–393; as well as Davis, *Home Fires Burning*; Healy, *Vienna and the Fall of the Habsburg Empire*; and Gerhard, *Nazi Hunger Politics*.

10. See Weinreb, *Modern Hungers*, 5. Though Treitel's recent book offers an excellent examination of Germany's natural food culture, it skims only the surface of wartime experiences. See Treitel, *Eating Nature in Modern Germany*.

11. See Liza Debevec and Blanka Tivadar, "Making Connections Through Foodways: Contemporary Issues in Anthropological and Sociological Studies of Food," *Anthropological Notebooks* 12, no. 1 (2006): 5–16, 5.

Bibliography

Allen, Keith. "Sharing Scarcity: Bread Rationing and the First World War in Berlin, 1914–1923." *Journal of Social History* 32 (Winter 1998): 371–393.
Chickering, Roger. *The Great War and Urban Life in Germany: Freiburg, 1914–1918.* Cambridge: Cambridge University Press, 2007.
Cinq-Mars, Marcelle. *La cuisine rationnée: nourrir un peuple et une armée, 1914–1918.* Outremont, QC: Athéna éditions, 2011.
Citino, Robert M. "Military Histories Old and New: A Reintroduction." *American Historical Review* 112, no. 4 (2007): 1070–1090.
Davis, Belinda J. *Home Fires Burning: Food, Politics and Everyday Life in World War I Berlin.* Chapel Hill: University of North Carolina Press, 2000.
Debevec, Liza, and Blanka Tivadar. "Making Connections Through Foodways: Contemporary Issues in Anthropological and Sociological Studies of Food." *Anthropological Notebooks* 12, no. 1 (2006): 5–16.
Duffett, Rachel. *The Stomach for Fighting: Food and the Soldiers of the Great War.* Manchester: Manchester University Press, 2012.
Gerhard, Gesine. *Nazi Hunger Politics: A History of Food in the Third Reich.* Lanham, MD: Rowman & Littlefield, 2015.
Healy, Maureen. *Vienna and the Fall of the Habsburg Empire: Total War and Everyday Life in World War I.* Cambridge: Cambridge University Press, 2004.
Kean, Hilda. *The Great Cat and Dog Massacre: The Real Story of World War Two's Unknown Tragedy.* Chicago: The University of Chicago Press, 2017.
Kučera, Rudolf. *Rationed Life: Science, Everyday Life and Working-Class Politics in the Bohemian Lands, 1914–1918.* New York: Berghahn, 2016.
Mintz, Sidney W. *Sweetness and Power: The Place of Sugar in Modern History.* New York: Viking, 1985.
Mintz, Sidney W. *Tasting Food, Tasting Freedom: Excursions into Eating, Culture, and the Past.* Boston: Beacon Press, 1997.
Mintz, Sidney W., and Christine Du Bois. "The Anthropology of Food and Eating." *Annual Review of Anthropology* 31 (2002): 99–119.
Offer, Avner. *The First World War: An Agrarian Interpretation.* New York: Oxford University Press, 1989.
Patenaude, Bertrand M. *The Big Show in Bololand: The American Relief Expedition to Soviet Russia in the Famine of 1921.* Stanford: Stanford University Press, 2002.
Tönsmeyer, Tatjana, Peter Haslinger, and Agnes Laba, eds. *Coping with Hunger and Shortage Under German Occupation in World War II.* New York: Palgrave Macmillan, 2018.
Treitel, Corinna. *Eating Nature in Modern Germany: Food, Agriculture, and Environment, c. 1870–2000.* Cambridge: Cambridge University Press, 2017.

Trentmann, Frank, and Flemming Just. *Food and Conflict in Europe in the Age of the Two World Wars*. Basingstoke: Palgrave Macmillan, 2006.
Vincent, C. Paul. *The Politics of Hunger: The Allied Blockade of Germany, 1915–1919*. Athens, OH: Ohio University Press, 1985.
Weinreb, Alice. *Modern Hungers: Food and Power in Twentieth-Century Germany*. Oxford: Oxford University Press, 2017.
Yaney, George. *The World of the Manager: Food Administration in Berlin During World War I*. New York: Peter Lang, 1994.
Zweiniger-Bargielowska, Ina, Rachel Duffett, and Alain Drouard. *Food and War in Twentieth Century Europe*. Farnham: Ashgate, 2011.

CHAPTER 2

Onward Kitchen Soldiers! Gender, Food and Health in Germany's Long Great War

Heather R. Perry

The war taught us many lessons in the field of nutrition. Before the war no one racked their brains over the big pictures of 'how to organize national nutrition' or 'how to create the building blocks of nutrition'. However, during the war we learned that deprivation and scarcity of food can have a good impact for the nourishment and health of mankind.[1]

Berlin Mayor's Press Address for the Nutrition Exhibit (17 December 1927)

In the spring of 1928, the city of Berlin unveiled the most ambitious public health exposition undertaken in Germany since before the war. Housed in the expo halls on the Kaiserdamm, the exhibit entitled NUTRITION: AN EXHIBITION FOR HEALTHY AND PRACTICAL DIET [*Die Ernährung: Ausstellung für gesunde und*

H. R. Perry (✉)
University of North Carolina at Charlotte, Charlotte, NC, USA

© The Author(s) 2019
H. M. Benbow and H. R. Perry (eds.), *Food, Culture and Identity in Germany's Century of War*,
https://doi.org/10.1007/978-3-030-27138-1_2

zweckmässige Ernährungsweise], combined the latest scientific research, economic considerations and practical advice on food and how to eat it. Comprised of dozens of different installations, NUTRITION offered the public easily accessible information on the bioscience and physiology of the nascent field of nutrition; outlined the nutritional value of common foods and foodstuffs; detailed the latest developments in industrial food production and processing; and displayed cutting edge kitchen technologies. Most importantly, however, the event showcased information on how to cook and serve healthy meals—meals that would promote not only individual fitness but ultimately contribute to the long-term health and revitalization of the nation. NUTRITION aimed to take the advancements in research borne from a decade of food insecurity and economic desperation and put them in the service of those who, as far as politicians, civic leaders and health professionals could see, held the fate of the nation in their hands: the German *Hausfrau*.[2]

This chapter looks at the long-term impacts of Germany's Great War through the lenses of food and nutrition. Whereas most scholars have focused on how wartime hunger and deprivation on the German homefront contributed to military defeat, social division, female politicization or popular revolution, this chapter looks rather at how a decade of food *and* economic insecurity—two conditions which transcended the temporal parameters of Germany's experiences of war, defeat, revolution and occupation—impacted ideas about gender, health and national identity. In looking at the ways that Germany's "long First World War" reshaped both scientific and popular ideas about diet, nutrition, culinary habits and eating practices, this research suggests that the cumulative impact of scarcity embedded the sentiment among Germans that *national belonging* was deeply tied to the promotion and maintenance of national health. Moreover, this research suggests that by focusing too narrowly on the disbanding of armed forces, civilian auxiliary organizations and other wartime support groups, studies of postwar demobilization have missed the important ways that everyday Germans were encouraged—even forced—to continue following the survival strategies and culinary practices developed as part of the nation's wartime mobilization of food. Indeed, as this chapter demonstrates, due to the food shortages and resource scarcity that continued to plague Germany in the wake of the war, nutritional science and its proponents became even more significant in the continuing mobilization of women as "kitchen soldiers" in the struggling postwar nation's new nutritional order.

Rethinking Food in WWI Germany

Although the significance and impact of wartime *hunger* and *food scarcity* in Germany have generated an abundance of scholarship, historians have by and large overlooked the cultural impacts of the food crisis precipitated by the blockade of Germany during the First World War. Already in 1914, officials on both sides of the conflict were calculating whether Germany's food supply would outlast the blockade imposed upon the nation by the Allies.[3] When the war finally ended, many then turned their analyses toward evaluating the effects of the blockade and food shortages with an especial focus on the military and demographic impacts.[4] Even as the war receded from immediate memory and was supplanted by more horrific and murderous conflicts, historians in general continued to focus on more conventional analyses of resource scarcity during the First World War.

Thus, for example, military historians have concentrated on the impact of the blockade on the German Empire's war strategies and occupation regimes. Other scholars have examined the political repercussions of widespread starvation among the German populace. Political historians have been interested in how hunger and deprivation contributed to revolution and the collapse of the imperial state. They, along with social historians, examined the impact of resource scarcity—especially food—on homefront morale and linked it to the erosion of popular support for the war and eventually state authorities. Economic historians have looked at the macroeconomic impacts of food shortages and demonstrated how they contributed to price inflation and the creation of informal, gray market and barter economies during the war—two phenomena which not only carried over into the postwar period but which fundamentally stamped the early years of the Weimar Republic.[5] Arguably, even gender historians—those scholars perhaps most predisposed to cultural analyses—have focused more on the political and social changes that wartime breadlines and food riots brought to women's public lives and civic identities. Yet, despite the centrality of food to the German Empire's experience of the First World War, few studies have focused on understanding how food knowledge and culture were itself transformed by this conflict and its aftermath.[6] Thus, the first point of scholarly disruption that this chapter offers is a (re)focusing of the scholarly eye on food—and not the political, social and economic impacts circling around it.

As the introduction to this volume points out, existing studies of food in WWI Germany have examined how food scarcity contributed to domestic political unrest and social division among the German people. Social historians, Ute Daniel and Jürgen Kocka, examined how working-class experiences under draconian regulations—including food rationing regulations—first united and then ultimately exacerbated deep divisions within German society.[7] Belinda Davis and Maureen Healy have demonstrated how severe food shortages on the Berlin and Viennese homefronts, respectively, galvanized women into protest actions and eroded popular support for imperial authority. Through examinations of female experiences of both consumer and political disenfranchisement, both Davis and Healy argue that women in the Central European capitals redefined the nature of citizenship and the government's obligations to the people. For both Davis and Healy, however, food is largely the lens through which they examine their primary focal point: popular discontent and burgeoning political consciousness.[8] Others have focused rather on the administrative failures and bureaucratic relationships which evolved as the German government attempted to manage and ration its food resources.[9] Thus, in addition to focusing primarily on political, social and civic relationships—and not really *food*—these studies typically end with the fall of the empire and ignore the food conditions and experiences which continued to plague Germany through 1924.[10] This leads to the chapter's second point of disruption.

Focusing on Germany's experience of food insecurity—and the practical food and household strategies developed in response to it—significantly challenges how historians have framed the experience and impact of Germany's First World War. Whereas organized combat ended in November 1918 and the Versailles Treaty concluded the war in June 1919, the nation's food crisis lasted well into the 1920s. Food rationing continued in some areas until 1921 and American relief groups did not consider Germany to be "food secure" until 1924.[11] Indeed, both anecdotal and scholarly evidence confirm that Germany's food crisis in the immediate postwar period was significantly worse than it had been at any time during the war itself. This suggests that in order to understand better the cultural impacts of blockade, food scarcity and hunger in WWI Germany, one must first temporally reframe the experience as a full decade of food insecurity—and thereby also acknowledge that the "war in the kitchen" being fought by Germany's women lasted years longer than the war fought by the nation's men on the battlefield.[12]

Regardless of the divergent goals and methodological differences among the historians who have studied the impact of food scarcity on the wartime empire, they have all generally concentrated on how different groups developed and expressed *their fears* about the ongoing lack of food and growing concerns regarding the long-term impacts of such increasingly dire circumstances. Yet, as this chapter demonstrates, many nutritionists and other health professionals understood the initial food shortages as welcome opportunities for reforming German eating habits and culture. For them, the war was offering the possibility to bring the national diet more in line with modern ideas about food and health.

Nutritional Science at War

A highly industrialized nation with a population of 68 million, the German Empire had become increasingly reliant on foreign imports to feed her population in the decades before the war.[13] Cutoff from most of these outside sources by January 1915, the government realized that only by carefully managing Germany's domestic resources would the empire outlast and survive the British blockade. Almost immediately, the Reich government created two new offices to help with this: the War Raw Materials Office (KRA) and the Central Purchasing Company (ZEG)—offices which were largely concerned with the procurement and distribution of raw materials for munitions and military supply.[14] But as the war shifted from one of movement to one of stalemate, the increasing likelihood of a long-term blockade became a reality that few had anticipated. As soldiers on the frontlines resigned themselves to a war of trenches and attrition, Germans on the homefront became increasingly concerned with *food*—its procurement, management, distribution, storage and preparation.[15] As a looming crisis threatened the empire, an unlikely set of laboratory researchers stepped in to advise their nation at war.

Nutritional science was born in the laboratories of German research universities in the mid-nineteenth century. Through his experiments with humans and animals in the 1860s, the Munich chemist, Carl von Voit, had discovered the basic laws of metabolism thus establishing the foundations for nutritional chemistry and physiology. Indeed, Voit is still considered by many to be the "father" of modern dietetics and his pioneering studies on protein metabolism in the human body established the energy requirements of the human body—and how to measure them.[16]

By the turn of the century, his student and intellectual successor, Max Rubner had emerged as Germany's leading physiologist and nutrition expert. In 1913, he helped to found the Kaiser Wilhelm Institute for Work Physiology [Kaiser-Wilhelm-Institut für Arbeitsphysiologie] in Berlin, subsequently becoming its director, as well. In the years before the war, Rubner had been conducting research with the goal of determining the ideal diets—that is nutritional and caloric content—for optimizing the productivity of various professional and skilled workers. He was fascinated with trying to figure out how much energy the body needed, what the ideal sources for this energy were and how mental and physical work differed in their energy uses.[17] When the war broke out, Rubner saw the chance to use his knowledge in the service of his country by advising civilians on the homefront how best to maximize the food available to them.[18]

Rubner and others argued that the key to successfully stretching the nation's food supply was not simply cutting back on the overall quantities of food that Germans ate. Rather, they argued, Germans needed to eat more carefully so that they maintained their physical health and strength by consuming enough calories from each of the three calorie groups (protein, carbohydrates and fats), while also being mindful not to overeat or waste specific food items that were growing (or already) scarce.[19] And though today we may take this kind of nutritional information as common knowledge, at the turn of the century, it was still fairly rarified scientific knowledge which had not circulated much beyond the laboratories and classrooms at universities and research institutes. Thus, educating Germans on these "building blocks" of nutrition—how to recognize them, which foods contained them, how much the body needed—became Rubner's primary goal during the war. In public talks, essays, published addresses, exhibitions and magazine articles, the nation's food and nutrition experts spent the war years trying to teach their compatriots how to eat more efficiently for the fatherland.[20]

Rubner and other nutritionists argued that despite being isolated from previous imports of grain, fat and dairy products that the population did not face starvation. In fact, they argued that in the years before the war, Germans had become accustomed to eating too much; moreover, they also ate out of habit and not from actual hunger. Eliminating snacks and making conscious decisions to consume smaller quantities of more satiating foods (such as potatoes) rather than ones that were "scientifically proven" to be less satisfying (such as bread) would help Germans to eat more efficiently, while also feeling fuller on less food.[21] Additionally, learning how best to use food and ingredient substitutes while still preserving the taste and nutritional value of standard dishes was another key lesson which Germany's nutritionists were certain, if taken to heart by the nation, would help in combatting the Hunger Blockade.[22]

Focusing on ways to substitute other carbohydrate-rich foods for the imported wheat grain that Germany could no longer access, nutritionists suggested rye, potatoes and other root vegetables as alternate ingredients for breads and baked dishes. And it is from these suggestions that the potato and/or rye-based recipes for War Bread (*Kriegsbrot*) stemmed. Though rejected at first by many Germans as too dry and unappetizing, War Bread grew in popularity as citizens realized that these qualities were what enabled the bread to remain fresher and last longer than white flour loaves. In addition to substituting for wheat, Rubner urged Germans to grind the rye and barley they did have to a much finer grain—up to 96%—so that it could stretch further.[23] They enlisted other homefront authorities to help them in swaying public opinion, such as the Pastor Bernhard Dörries, who not only urged his flock to consume the bread as part of their national duty, but also reassured them that it was what God wanted the good people of Hannover-Kleefeld to do.[24] As fats became scarce, they urged citizens to substitute sugar and fruit purees for butter in baked goods and to use margarine or other butter substitutes when frying.

Nutritionists were also concerned about the protein that Germans consumed. According to one report, Germans ate far more red meat than was necessary and they were urged to cut back on its consumption so as not to waste the protein. Unlike fats and carbohydrates, they admonished the nation's citizens, excess protein could *not* be stored in the body as reserve energy, but rather was excreted from the body in urine. Thus they claimed that Germans who ate more than their bodies actually used were "wasting it". In fact, Rubner and others were very concerned that the empire's overabundance of swine was draining the population's carbohydrate resources and in 1915 urged that 9 million pigs be slaughtered in order to preserve the fodder—rye, corn and barley—which, they argued, could ultimately be used to feed twice as many Germans as the animal meat could.[25] Carl van Noorden, an expert in diabetes nutrition and regulation, argued that in recent decades protein consumption had risen drastically and that—in particular worker families tended to eat too much and should cut back. Nutritionists also campaigned to convince Germans that skim milk had the same protein and nutrients as whole milk—and thus could be used without fear for cooking, baking and even *drinking* (if you were an adult)—and not dismissed as only good enough for livestock as Germans were accustomed.[26] Mothers were urged to breastfeed infants so as to impart important nutrients to them and not rely on cow's milk for those who could still be nursed—and indeed received extra rations in order to support their body's milk production.[27] Moreover, advice urging the empire's citizens to reduce their consumption of meat was not intended as overall calorie reduction; rather in many cases, they urged the population to replace protein sources with legumes and fish—both of which were richly available and grew or reproduced quickly.[28] One even went so far as to suggest that it was more patriotic, expedient and nutritious to drink domestic wine, rather than beer, because the land used for growing barley and hops would be better used for growing wheat, while most landscape being used by Germany's vineyards was suitable for little else.

Germany's health and nutrition experts were convinced that with proper dietary advice and education, the empire's population would be able to withstand any shortages of foodstuffs that might set in as the British blockade tightened around them. According to Rubner and others, it was *not* the looming wartime food scarcity that posed such a threat to the health and welfare of the German people, but rather their own decadent eating habits and wasteful food decisions. Thus, improving through education the dietary choices and eating practices of Germans became the mission of nutritional and food experts during the war; however, it was a mission they could not accomplish alone. In order to transform fully the national diet, they needed direct access to decision-makers in private homes and thus they turned to those on the frontlines of the nation's food war—the German *Hausfrau*—and one of the empire's leading experts in household management: Hedwig Heyl.[29]

Hedwig Heyl and the League of German Housewives

The daughter of one of Germany's powerful shipping magnates, Hedwig Heyl (nee Crüsemann) was born in Bremen in 1850. At the early age of 18, she had married Georg Heyl, a chemical dye manufacturer in Berlin. After his death, Heyl turned her efforts toward social grooming, in particular educating bourgeois women in household and servant management, on child-rearing and social etiquette. She eventually moved to Berlin where she founded a school for cooking and domestic arts (*Haushaltschule*).[30] Additionally, she was the author of multiple cookbooks and advice manuals—including one of the empire's most well-known and beloved tomes. *The ABC's of Cooking* (*Das ABC der Küche*) was a hefty 900 pages and had just come out in its 11th edition the year before the war broke out.[31] Heyl was a natural ally for anyone looking to gain access to the German home.

Although bourgeois women and philanthropy groups had targeted lower-class homes for years as part of their campaigns for social and political reform, these efforts had met with mixed success—largely due to deep-class divisions.[32] And, as one might expect, the exigencies of war only emboldened and encouraged these efforts among Germany's middle and upper classes. Much has been written on Helene Lang and Gertrude Bäumer—including work on the patriotic women's auxiliary organizations, such as the *National Frauendienst*, that they founded and led during the war. However, because those scholars were focused primarily on tracing a narrative of female politicization, enfranchisement and social division, they have overlooked women on Germany's homefront, such as Heyl, who did not emerge as postwar feminist political leaders in the Weimar Republic.

In the years before the war, Heyl had advocated the recognition of housewifery as a learned profession and promoted this idea through both her school and publications. However, in March 1915 she was spurred into action to establish the League of German Housewives [*Deutscher Hausfrauenbund*] (renamed in 1917 as the League of German Housewives Associations) by the need to create a reliable and efficient network for educating women and spreading wartime advice for how best to withstand the food shortages.[33] Heyl sought to expand her practical work with Berlin women throughout the empire and actively worked to spread nutritional, cooking and household information throughout this formal network of women's housewives groups.[34] She even converted her late husband's chemical dye plants and manufactories into canning centers for preserving fruits and vegetables. In fact, Heyl's early wartime efforts at educating German women and helping them to stretch and preserve food were so instrumental that her fame carried across the Atlantic and throughout the United States. In cities including St. Louis, Baltimore, Norwich, CT and even El Paso, Americans could read articles about "the most powerful woman in Germany,"—heralded, they cried, in some circles as Germany's "food general" or the "the

Fig. 2.1 "The Hindenburg of German Housewives"

female Hindenburg"—and how she was preventing starvation among her people (see Fig. 2.1).[35] Heyl's stature and reputation as an educator of housewives made her an ideal partner and conduit for bringing the science of nutrition into the homes of average Germans.

CREATING THE KITCHEN SOLDIER

> Spades and wooden spoons, these are the two things that when the war broke out, no one thought would become so important. Spades for digging trenches; Wooden spoons for the fight against England's hunger-blockade. Of course, the battle with the wooden spoon is not nearly as life threatening as holding out in the trenches. But there is no doubt that combat with both weapons is of equal significance to Germany's ultimate victory.[36]

These were the opening words of Professor Dr. Martin Fassbender's wartime treatise on modern nutrition, *How You Should Live in Wartime!* [*So sollt ihr leben in der Kriegszeit!*] Published in 1915 as one of countless wartime food advice pamphlets circulating on the homefront, *How You Should Live*, was aimed at the German housewife with the goal of enlisting her help in reforming German foodways and eating habits. Reaching out to women through the rhetoric of patriotism and national defense, Fassbender detailed the urgency of nationwide food reform as the key to not just survival, but to a victorious war's end.

Just a few months into the war, nutritional advisors realized that it was not enough to make speeches urging families to cook and eat frugally. Despite calls across the empire for the population to "Be Sparing" and "Eat Less," urgent yet vague directives from medical and government authorities did little to regulate effectively the consumption of Germany's food resources. Rather, they realized that women needed specific and handy information on substituting foods, saving fats, recycling leftovers, cooking unfamiliar dishes and home-growing some of their own ingredients. Indeed, in the absence of regimented and clear instruction, authorities discovered that wealthier citizens "saved" by avoiding their usual costly fare and instead buying up huge quantities of cheaper food supplies. Unfortunately, this practice meant that supply stores which remained would become gradually unaffordable altogether for the less fortunate. Moreover, because they were unfamiliar with many of the new substitute ingredients or fuel-sparing preparation measures, frugal-minded housewives on the homefront were reluctant to experiment with the little food they had. It was the housewife who chose the menu, did the shopping, prepared the food and received the family's praise (or criticism) regarding the daily meals. Therefore, food reform directives were essentially useless if experts could not convince every one of the nation's 12 million households to adopt them. Thus, suggestions which included fundamentally changing daily habits, breaking with regional traditions, learning to acquire new tastes and even altering favorite family recipes stood little chance of being adopted without the help of one important segment of society on board—the German *Hausfrau* (housewife). The key to successful food reform and food economy was the reeducation of Germany's women and Fassbender's book of guidelines, *How You Should Live in Wartime!*, was one of many handbooks and manuals that flooded the German homefront as nutritionists began to team up with other social reformers to mobilize the nation's kitchens.[37]

Mobilizing the Kitchen in WWI Germany

> German Women! England has also declared war on you. She is trying to starve out you and yours by blockading imported foodstuffs. Therefore, to arms! The life and death of the Fatherland now hang no less on you, your loyal will, and your crafts and skills than they hang on victory out there in the battlefield.[38]

Health and welfare authorities quickly recognized the necessity of working with housewives and their associations to circulate guidelines and suggestions about food and diet reform. Early educational efforts were met with skepticism and derision, such as the case of the nutritionist who spoke to a women's group in Berlin and was subsequently criticized by them because he obviously "knew everything about carbohydrates and calories, but nothing about markets and kitchens." Expert scientific knowledge, these campaigners realized, was worthless if not combined with the practical knowledge and real-world experiences of everyday female consumers. Earning the trust of Germany's housewives became paramount and this was best accomplished through collaboration with their leaders.[39]

Beginning in 1915 government authorities, civic leaders, health professionals, research scientists began working in collaboration on an educational campaign that combined modern nutritional information with practical advice and tips for how best to cope with the war's food shortages. In Berlin, Heyl and others worked together with the medical community to host lectures and exhibitions on how to cook using different fats, while in Hamburg authorities organized groups which could visit the estates of wealthier Germans in order to instruct their entire household staff.[40] They urged cities around the empire to create "Home Economic Advice Centers" where women could get practical information and "Model War Kitchens," where recipes could be tested and demonstrated to local residents.[41] And above all, they combined forces to publish more handbooks, such as the one quoted above and put out by the Wiesbaden Municipal Commission for National Nutrition.

Like *How You Should Live in Wartime!*, the introduction from their 1915 *Handbook for War-Time Home Economy* emphasized the central importance of women's work in the kitchen to Germany's survival. However, whereas Fassbender's publication was largely didactic in nature and filled in places with admonitions, the advice manuals and how-to guides published by or in cooperation with housewives unions were more collegial in nature and infused with a sense of camaraderie. Whereas Fassbender scolded Germans for having fallen into a lazy diet or discontinued time-honored health customs, the Wiesbaden handbook emphasized the female "crafts and skills" (both learned and innate) that would save the fatherland from defeat—an admittedly subtle point, but one which I think deserves more attention. Thus while previous scholars have focused on the work of the *Nationaler Frauendienst* and other women's wartime organizations as patriotic organs pushing bourgeois nationalism, feminist political agendas or the government's food message, what they have tended to overlook is the *actual knowledge* which this wartime food campaign did transfer and the educational empowerment of women within it. Therefore, these existing histories have not fully captured the main point that Fassbender, the Wiesbaden Commission and others were making: The blockade was making daily decisions about food *matter* in unprecedented ways and the nation's very survival depended upon the *household skills* of Germany's women.

War Cuisine

"War Cuisine"—as the wartime tactics and strategies of frugal cooking and household management came to be called—emerged as a set of practices and body of knowledge which evolved and frequently changed as food supplies rose and dwindled over the course of the war. These shifting conditions meant that the education of housewives could not be a one-time educational task; it became rather an undertaking that required frequent updating and re-adjustment. Additionally, it became quickly apparent that one size—or recipe—did not fit all. Attempts at promoting empire-wide "national recipes" or standardized saving measures often met with resistance due to regional tastes and practices—or with simple resistance to outside interference. Here, too, food reformers saw further benefits of partnering with Germany's housewives. Aware that new and unfamiliar ideas which challenged regional food traditions would be met with wary eyes and stomachs, they partnered with housewives and their associations to marry their food saving advice and nutritional information with local tastes so that they would be more appealing. Together (usually) male nutritionists and female cookery experts put together War Cookbooks for specific regions which included recipes for dishes that were familiar to those residents and which made use of the local ingredients more likely to be available, as well.

Over the course of the war, the housewives' associations and other women's groups put out dozens of cookbooks and instructional pamphlets all designed to keep German housewives apprised of developments in nutrition, war cuisine, frugal household management and patriotic cooking.[42] Reviewing them all does not make sense here, but a few examples may suffice. In Frankfurt, for instance, the city's Food Commission engaged Henriette Fürth to put together *The Little War Cookbook: An Advice Manual for Frugal Cooking* which included not just recipes, but also an introduction from the Commission for National Nutrition which had been formed by doctors from the local chapter of the medical association.[43] In 1915, Johanna Just, the founder and director of a domestic arts school aimed at preparing upper middle-class daughters for marriage, published a *War Cookbook for Women's Relief: 50 Proven Recipes*, comprised of recipes that she had been developing at the college (see Fig. 2.2).[44] Cookbooks in Mecklenburg, Pommern and other northern areas, such as one dedicated to Germany's Baltic women and entitled, *The Little Emergency Cookbook*, usually included far more fish and dairy dishes, with appropriate substitutes, while dishes in middle and southern areas such as Bavaria might include suggestions for meat-based dishes which substituted rabbit or poultry for beef.[45] In fact, by 1915, Germany's Central Purchasing Agency (ZEG) was putting out five different regional editions of the free government-issued war cookbook: East, North, West, South and Middle-German.[46]

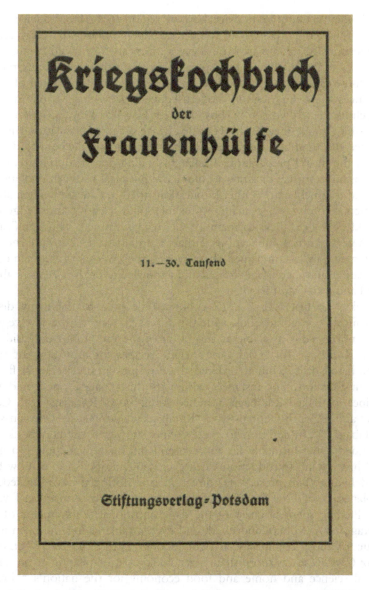

Fig. 2.2 Just's *War Cookbook for Women's Relief: 50 Proven Recipes*, 1915

Women encountered advice beyond regionally oriented advice manuals, however. For instance, some newspapers published weekly recipe suggestions to update area housewives on meals they could create from those rations available at the time. Other manuals focused on circulating more efficient preparation techniques or reminding women of older practices that relied less on modern conveniences—such as one manual which instructed women on how to use a Hay-Box Stove [*Kochkiste*] for preparing family meals. The Hay-Box Stove relied on insulation (usually packed hay or straw) to harness the heat from a partially cooked dish to finish the meal's preparation. Packing a boiling pot of soup ingredients, for instance, in hay or straw would allow the meal to finish cooking via packed thermal heat.[47] Other publications tried to educate women about particular foods—while including technical and scientific knowledge that would have been new to many of Germany's women. The significance of these and other publications is that regardless of the patriotic rhetoric that may have accompanied these works, they were primarily aimed at educating and increasing the scientific knowledge of their readers about food and proper nutrition.

Take, for instance, a 1917 cookbook devoted to the many dishes and meals one could cook with the rutabaga—one of the few vegetables more readily available at this point of the war.[48] Not only did *The New Rutabaga War Cook Book* include recipes for fifty different rutabaga-based dishes, but it ordered these recipes around regional flavors and ingredients. For instance, within its thirty pages, one could find recipes for Baked Rutabaga, Candied Rutabaga or Rutabaga with Carp, but also "South-German-style Rutabaga" and "East Prussian-style Rutabaga."[49] In addition to these recipes, however, the cookbook also included other arguably far more useful information including a general history and introduction to the vegetable, a discussion of how best to dehydrate and preserve it, directions for storing it once cooked, an explanation of how to best calculate the vegetable's nutritional value per Pfennig spent, a chart of the daily nutritional requirements of the average man, woman and child, and even a table listing the nutritional value of most commonly available foods. Thus, *The New Rutabaga War Cook Book* was more than just a cookbook; it was primer on nutritional science and home and food economy for the nation's "kitchen soldiers."[50]

In addition to publications which introduced women to modern ideas about nutrition, however, their educational and institutional spaces were often transformed, as well. Female finishing and training schools were used as collection stations for fruit stones and nuts—where women also learned how oils could be extracted from them (even if they did not learn how to do this themselves). Posters from the War Committee for Oil and Fats alerted locals in Merseburg, Berlin, and other areas that they could earn 10 pf for every kilo of cherry, apricot and plum stones they turned in or even 35 pf for each one of lemon or orange.[51] The National Women's Service [*Nationaler Frauendienst*] also posted information about how best to use or reuse what before the war had been considered kitchen waste or animal feed. They circulated flyers and posters suggesting new uses for potato peels, while others reminded them not only to dry out their allotment of rutabagas, but also included instructions on how to do so.[52]

Conclusion

Most research on the German food experience of the First World War has focused on how and why the food rationing system failed—and what the consequences of that failure were. This preliminary research suggests that there is more to this story than analyses of the effectivity or consequences of the food management system. If historians look beyond that question and instead focus on *what else* was managed and distributed during the war, there are other phenomena worthy of investigation—most notably the widespread educational campaign regarding modern nutrition and national health. In particular, this knowledge included information about nutritional science, the nutrient values of common foodstuffs, modern and hygienic food storage, mother and infant diet needs, the introduction of unfamiliar foods and other food and culinary awareness. Nutritional physiologists and other researchers, such as Max Rubner and Emil Abderhalden, were brought in specifically to lend their expertise to the enterprise of empire-wide food management and used the latest scientific information at their disposal to do so. In doing so, they brought rarified scientific knowledge about modern nutrition out of university institutions and food laboratories and into the homes of average Germans—in particular, middle- and lower-class German women. Thus, studies of food and resource management during WWI Germany should extend to an examination of how popular conceptions of healthy eating and nutrition were fundamentally influenced or transformed by the war experience.

For instance, in addition to the knowledge displayed in the public health exhibit *Nutrition*—discussed at the beginning of this chapter and which ran in Berlin for 100 days, information about vitamins, nutrition and a more scientific-based approach to eating became a staple subject in women's publications and magazines. This scientization of the kitchen and diet is a phenomenon which persisted in German culture and contributed to the cultural empowerment of housewives. After the war and well into the 1920s, newspapers such as *Land und Frau*, *Wirtschaftsfräulein* and *die Gutsfrau*, published articles on emerging ideas about nutrition, new ways to use and eat certain foods and information about vitamin research. The *Wirtschaftsfräulein* even included information and images from the *Nutrition* exhibit, itself.[53]

In addition to the longer-term impact on popular foodways and eating knowledge, however, this research adds another dimension to the story of Germany's women in the Great War. Current studies tend to center around their work in manufacturing, nursing or other positions in homefront civil society. Yet focusing on food and culture in this way suggests that there was a concerted and widespread effort to enlist women as "kitchen soldiers"—homemakers whose daily choices could help or hinder the nation at war—and that at least some of them, such as Hedwig Heyl, took this mobilization of the kitchen as a serious wartime service to the nation. Indeed, throughout the war, German women were consistently reminded how the daily choices they made when shopping, when cooking and when cleaning were key not just to supporting the war, but also to ensuring the very survival of the German nation. Yet, we have little research that takes seriously the contributions of mobilized housewives—either individual women or their mobilized networks—to food research and health reform. This is somewhat surprising because the War Ministry itself recognized the importance of their contributions when the War Foods Office (*Kriegsernährungsamt*)—created in 1916 to help better manage Germany's food supply—also included a Women's Advisory Board (*Frauenbeirat*), where Hedwig Heyl and others helped to determine domestic food and resource policies. Indeed, contemporary articles in the United States wartime press claimed that it was Heyl herself who had come up with the whole program of food rationing.[54]

Moreover, beyond their role in the war itself, there is little research on the experiences of women, nutritionists and household reformers in the crucial periods of the Armistice and Reconstruction (1919–1923)—a time when the initial availability of food and other resources was at first *far worse* than during the war. Most research on this period focuses instead on Germany's revolution and the political and social construction of Weimar society. But during a four year period in which Germany was fundamentally dependent upon international food imports and foreign charity organizations for basic sustenance, one might also ask in what ways modern ideas about nutrition, health and food economy evolved from being wartime emergency measures to routine habits.[55]

In sum, returning to the NUTRITION exhibit which opened in 1928, scholars have yet to examine fully how the decade of food insecurity informed the relationships between public health and national identity—or perhaps more specifically, *national belonging*. More than just educating and empowering women, nutritional science and knowledge became intimately linked with national health and population politics at all levels of society during the war—which is one reason why scientists and medical professionals continued to research the impacts of food shortages and nutritional deficiencies throughout the 1920s and sought to put them in the service of the nation.[56] This knowledge, too, trickled down to the general public and took on such importance that eventually government, welfare, health and school officials partnered with scientific researchers and appliance makers in 1928 to put together the most comprehensive exhibit about nutrition and food that the world had ever seen—including its centrality to national identity and survival—and stage it 10 years *after the war ended*. Thus, it seems clear that the mobilization of the kitchen during the Great War ultimately began a nationwide conversation about health and the individual responsibility—even civic duty—that *all* Germans had to cultivate and maintain it. Ultimately, perhaps the war in the kitchen was not one of "nationalism, food, and health," but rather one of "*nationalization*, food, and health"—and the start of German women's perpetual mobilization as kitchen soldiers in Germany's war-torn twentieth century.

Notes

1. "Begrüssungsrede des Herrn Oberbürgermeisters Böss," in *Ansprachen gehalten anlässlich des Empfanges der Vertreter der Behörden, der Presse und der Mitarbeiter der Ausstellung "Die Ernährung" Berlin 1928 im ehemaligen Herrenhause am 17. Dezember 1927* (Berlin, 1928), 3–4. Translation mine.
2. "Ansprache des Herrn Geh. Regierungsrat Dr. Hamel," in *Ansprachen gehalten anlässlich des Empfanges der Vertreter der Behörden, der Presse und der Mitarbeiter der Ausstellung "Die Ernährung" Berlin 1928 im ehemaligen Herrenhause am 17. Dezember 1927* (Berlin, 1928), 9.

3. Paul Eltzbacher, ed., *Die deutsche Volksernährung und der englische Aushungerungsplan* (Braunschweig: F. Vieweg & Sohn, 1914). This was translated into English with commentary in early 1915. See S. Russel Wells, ed., *Germany's Food: Can It Last? The German Case as Presented by German Experts* (London: University of London Press, 1915).
4. For a study on the immediate health impacts of Germany's food shortages, see Ernest H. Starling, "The Food Supply of Germany During the War," *Journal of the Royal Statistical Society* 83, no. 2 (1920): 225–254, https://doi.org/10.2307/2341079.
5. Here, the classic study is Gerald D. Feldman's *The Great Disorder: Politics, Economics, and Society in the German Inflation, 1914–1924* (New York: Oxford University Press, 1993).
6. See the introduction to this volume for a broader review and discussion of the work available on food and hunger in WWI Germany.
7. Ute Daniel, *Arbeiterfrauen in der Industriegesellschaft: Beruf, Familie und Politik im Ersten Weltkrieg* (Göttingen: Vandenhoeck & Ruprecht, 1986); Ute Daniel, *The War from Within: German Working-Class Women in the First World War* (Oxford: Berg, 1997); and Jürgen Kocka, *Facing Total War: German Society, 1914–1918* (Cambridge, MA: Harvard University Press, 1984).
8. See Belinda J. Davis, *Home Fires Burning: Food, Politics, and Everyday Life in World War I Berlin* (Chapel Hill: UNC Press, 2000); and Maureen Healy, *Vienna and the Fall of the Habsburg Empire: Total War and Everyday Life in World War I* (Cambridge: Cambridge University Press, 2004).
9. George Yaney's organizational study of Berlin's food administration during the war sought neither to explain failure nor to provide lessons for the future; rather his focus was simply to understand the "world of the manager" in the city's wartime crisis and the nature of bureaucratic change. In contrast, Keith Allen has suggested that Berlin city officials were not nearly as inept in their food administration as most others have argued by documenting the smooth cooperation between local government and civic leaders in resolving episodic food crises during the war. See George Yaney, *The World of the Manager: Food Administration in Berlin During World War I* (New York: Peter Lang, 1994); and Keith Allen, "Sharing Scarcity: Bread Rationing and the First World War in Berlin, 1914–1923," *Journal of Social History* (Winter 1998): 371–393.
10. Here, Feldman's work on the German inflation is arguably an exception though it concentrates primarily on the postwar period from 1918 to 1924. See Feldman, *The Great Disorder*.
11. Frank M. Surface and Raymond L. Bland, *American Food in the World War and Reconstruction Period: Operations of the Organizations Under the Direction of Herbert Hoover, 1914–1924* (Stanford: Stanford University Press, 1931). See especially the section on aid to Germany, 189–200.

12. Other scholars have re-framed the way we study the impact of war by focusing on demobilization as a continuation of violence and duress. They too focus on *the war experience* rather than official military mobilization or combat. See, for example, Adam R. Seipp, *The Ordeal of Peace: Demobilization and the Urban Experience in Britain and Germany, 1917–1921* (London: Routledge, 2016); or Richard Bessel, *Germany After the First World War* (Oxford: Clarendon Press, 1993).
13. For more on the significance of Germany's reliance on food imports before 1914, see Roger Chickering, "Imperial Germany's Peculiar War, 1914–1918," *The Journal of Modern History* 88, no. 4 (December 2016): 856–894.
14. The Zentral-Einkaufs-Gesellschaft (ZEG) was initially set up as a private entity in Hamburg in 1914 called the Reichseinkauf GmbH; however, in December it was moved to Berlin and renamed the ZEG. For more on the creation and organization of Germany's war management bureaucracies, see Gerald D. Feldman, *Army, Industry, and Labor in Germany, 1914–1918* (Princeton: Princeton University Press, 1966); for a more concise outline, see Roger Chickering, "World War I and the Theory of Total War: Reflections on the British and German Cases, 1914–1915," in *Great War, Total War: Combat and Mobilization on the Western Front, 1914–1918*, edited by Roger Chickering and Stig Förster (New York: Cambridge University Press, 2000), 35–53.
15. Avner Offer's path-breaking study on the implications of food scarcity—especially food production, consumption and distribution—effectively challenged interpretations of WWI as a predominantly industrial war, especially in the case of Germany. See Avner Offer, *The First World War: An Agrarian Interpretation* (New York: Oxford University Press, 1989).
16. For more on Voit and the history of nutritional science, see Elizabeth Neswald, "Nutritional Knowledge Between the Lab and the Field: The Search for Dietary Norms in the Late Nineteenth and Early Twentieth Centuries," in *Setting Nutritional Standards: Theory, Policies, Practices*, edited by Elizabeth Neswald, David F. Smith, and Ulrike Thoms (Rochester, NY: University of Rochester Press, 2017), 29–51, especially 32–41.
17. For more on Rubner, see Neswald, "Nutritional Knowledge," and the recently created Max Rubner Institute (MRI) in Karlsruhe—formerly known as the German Federal Research Center for Nutrition and Food (BfEL), accessed June 28, 2019, https://www.mri.bund.de/en/about-us/max-rubner/.
18. Corinna Treitel, "Max Rubner and the Biopolitics of Rational Nutrition," *Central European History* 41 (2008), 1–25.

19. See for instance Max Rubner, "Die Ernährung des Menschen" and P. Burg, "Das Fleisch und seine Verwendung im Haushalt." These were part of a lecture series on National Nutrition organized by the Prussian Minister of the Interior and held in the Berlin Abgeordnetenhaus in February 1915. They were later collected and published in *Volksernährung im Kriege: Vorträge* (Berlin: Reimar Hobbing, 1915).
20. See the lectures in *Volksernährung im Kriege*.
21. Carl Oppenheimer, "Zeitgemäße Lebenshaltung," in *Volksernährung im Kriege: Vorträge* (Berlin: Reimar Hobbing, 1915), 159–177.
22. In addition to the lectures on food, nutrition, agricultural production and animal husbandry in *Volksernährung im Kriege*, see for instance Emil Abderhalden, *Die Grundlagen unserer Ernährung unter besonderer Berückstichtigung der Jeztzeit* (Berlin: Springer, 1917); in particular see 131–139.
23. See the talk given by the Director of the Research Center for Grain Processing, M. P. Neumann, "Kriegsbrot," in *Volksernährung im Kriege: Vorträge* (Berlin: Reimar Hobbing, 1915), 144–158.
24. Bernhard Dörries, *Kriegsbrot (Predigt) mit Anhang: Lebensregeln für die Kriegszeit* (Hannover: Schlüsterschen Buchdruckerei, 1915). From Europeana 1914–1918.
25. Friedrich Naumann, "Kriegsnahrungsrede," in *Volksernährung im Kriege: Vorträge* (Berlin: Reimar Hobbing, 1915), 264–265. Unfortunately, the reasoning behind the well-known "pig massacre" of 1915 did not take into account the manure which the pigs produced—fertilizer that farmers relied upon and sorely missed when slaughtering the pigs did not result in more available foodstuffs.
26. Oppenheimer, "Zeitgemäße Lebenshaltung," 170–171.
27. Kriegsernährungsamt, *Die Kriegsernährungswirtschaft 1917*, 76.
28. See Oppenheimer, "Zeitgemäße Lebenshaltung," 170; and Hedwig Heyl, "Kriegsküche," in *Volksernährung im Kriege* (Berlin: Reimar Hobbing, 1915), 177–199, 184.
29. Oppenheimer, "Zeitgemäße Lebenshaltung," 177.
30. For more on Heyl, see Elisabeth Heimpel, "Heyl, Hedwig," in *Neue Deutsche Biographie* (Berlin: Duncker & Humblot, 1972), 83–84. See also Ann Taylor Allen, *Feminism and Motherhood in Germany, 1800–1914* (New Brunswick, NJ: Rutgers University Press, 1991), 115–120.
31. Hedwig Heyl, *Das ABC Der Küche* (Berlin: C. Habel, 1897). http://hdl.handle.net/2027/nyp.33433082244322. The eleventh edition came out in 1913.
32. Ann Taylor Allen has pointed out that bourgeois feminists and family reformers were often met with skepticism and rejection when they reached out to working-class women's groups. See Allen, *Feminism and Motherhood*, especially 150–156.

33. See "DHB—Netzwerk Haushalt" Kölner Frauenportal: Start: Frauenorganisationen: Beruf/Sebstständigkeit: DHB—Netzwerk Haushalt, accessed June 28, 2019, https://frauenportal.koeln/dhb-netzwerk-haushalt/.
34. Lora Wildenthal, *German Women for Empire, 1884–1945* (Durham, NC: Duke University Press, 2001), 159–160.
35. See for instance "The Hindenburg of German Housewives," *St. Louis Post-Dispatch* (St. Louis, MO), March 19, 1916: 60; "The Most Powerful Woman in Germany," *El Paso Herald* (El Paso, TX), June 26, 1915: 3–B. Reprinted and excerpted in *The Hattiesburg News* (Hattiesburg, MS), July 10, 1915: 9 and *Pierre Weekly Free Press* (Pierre, SD) August 5, 1915: 2; See also Wildenthal, *German Women for Empire*, 160.
36. Martin Fassbender, *So sollt ihr leben in der Kriegszeit!: ein Wort über zeitgemässe Volksernährung* (Freiburg i.B.: Herder, 1915), 3. "Spaten und Kochlöffel, das sind die zwei Dinge, die gegenwärtig eine jedenfalls bei Beginn des Krieges von der grossen Menge nicht geahnte Bedeutung gewonnen haben. Der Spaten zur Schaffung der Schützengräben, der Kochlöffel im Kampf gegen den Aushungerungsplan Englands. Gewiss ist der Kampf mit dem Kochlöffel nicht so lebensgefährlich wie das Ausharren im Schützengraben. Aber es ist nicht zu bezweifeln, dass der Kampf mit beiden Waffen für den endgültigen Sieg Deutschlands die gleiche Bedeutung beansprucht." Translation mine.
37. For more on the significance of reforming food habits and tastes, see Gertrud Bäumer, "Mittel und Wege zur Belehrung der Frauen," in *Volksernährung im Kriege: Vorträge* (Berlin: Reimar Hobbing, 1915), 199–215, especially 201–202.
38. Städtische Kommission für Volksernährung, *Anleitung zum Wirtschaften in der Kriegszeit, zugleich ein Kriegs-Kochbuch* (Wiesbaden: Heinrich Staadt, 1915), 3. Translation mine.
39. Gertrud Bäumer, "Mittel und Wege zur Belehrung der Frauen," 204–205.
40. Bäumer, "Mittel und Wege zur Belehrung der Frauen," 206–208.
41. Ibid., 208, 211.
42. In addition to the cookbooks discussed in this essay, see also Charlotte Teller, "The Best Known Woman in Germany," *The Independent* (New York City), 7 August 1916, 187–188.
43. Henriette Fürth, *Kleines Kriegskochbuch: Ein Ratgeber für sparsames Kochen* (Frankfurt: Englert and Schlosser, 1915). Fürth was a German welfare reformer and women's suffrage activist who staunchly supported the SPD.

44. See the forward written by Johanna Just in *Kriegskochbuch der Frauenhülfe: 50 zeitgemäße Rezepte* (Potsdam: Stiftungsverlag, 1915), 5–6. Johanna Just had founded the Haushaltspensionat für Töchter gebildeter Stände in 1889 in Berlin. By 1908, it had moved to Potsdam and evolved into the Königliche Handels- und Gewerbeschule für Mädchen zu Potsdam.
45. Martha Bielenstein, *Notstandskochbuchlein* (Berlin: Memel, 1916).
46. Heyl, "Kriegsküche," 197.
47. Marianne Götze, *Die Kochkiste im Dienste der Kriegskost* (Leipzig: Nauman, 1918).
48. Ida Keller, *Neues Kohlrüben Kochbuch: Praktische Anweisung zur Bereitung der verschiedensten Speisen von Kohlrüben* (Chemnitz: Robert Friese, 1917).
49. Keller, *Neues Kohlrüben Kochbuch*, 25, 20.
50. Ibid., 26–28 and appendix.
51. See for instance the posters issued by the Kriegsausschuß für Oele und Fette, "Sammelt Obstkerne zur Oelgewinnung" Poster. (Berlin: Liebheit and Thiesen, 1914) at the Deutsche Digitale Bibliothek, accessed June 28, 2019, https://www.deutsche-digitale-bibliothek.de/item/26D2OC6R6EUQ74EGGXQIOXTZNBM7J4FW.
52. See for instance the flyer "Hausfrauen dörrt jetzt Eure Steckrüben," Heimatverein Lingen: Der I. Weltkrieg in der kleinen Gemeinde Brümsel, accessed June 28, 2019, http://www.heimatverein-lingen.de/familienforschung/genealogien/der-i-weltkrieg-in-der-kleinen-gemeinde-bruemsel.htm.
53. See "Von der Berliner Ernährungsausstellung!" *Das Wirtschaftsfräulein* (Nr. 31) July 29, 1928: 487.
54. See Teller, "The Best Known Woman in Germany," 188.
55. According to the American Relief Administration's report on food relief in Europe, over the period from 1919 to 1923, Germany received 1,272,934.1 metric tons of food valued at $294,373,692.75 (1924 US dollars). See Surface and Bland, *American Food in the World War and Reconstruction Period*, 197.
56. German medical journals are regularly publishing articles on nutrition and population health research throughout the 1920s. Some examples from *Klinische Wochenschrift* are "Volksernährung und Wirtschaftsnot" "Wirtschaftlicher Abbau und Volksgesundheit"; "Die gegenwärtige Lage der Volksernärung vom Standpunkt der öffentlichen Gesundheitspflege" and many others.

BIBLIOGRAPHY

Abderhalden, Emil. *Die Grundlagen unserer Ernährung unter besonderer Berückstichtigung der Jeztzeit*. Berlin: Springer, 1917.

Allen, Ann Taylor. *Feminism and Motherhood in Germany, 1800–1914*. New Brunswick, NJ: Rutgers University Press, 1991.

Allen, Keith. "Sharing Scarcity: Bread Rationing and the First World War in Berlin, 1914–1923." *Journal of Social History* 32 (Winter 1998): 371–393.

Ansprachen gehalten anlässlich des Empfanges der Vertreter der Behörden, der Presse und der Mitarbeiter der Ausstellung "Die Ernährung" Berlin 1928 im ehemaligen Herrenhause am 17. Dezember 1927. Berlin, 1928.

Bäumer, Gertrud. "Mittel und Wege zur Belehrung der Frauen." In *Volksernährung im Kriege: Vorträge*, 199–215. Berlin: Reimar Hobbing, 1915.

Bessel, Richard. *Germany After the First World War*. Oxford: Clarendon Press, 1993.

Bielenstein, Martha. *Notstandskochbuchlein*. Berlin: Memel, 1916.

Chickering, Roger. "Imperial Germany's Peculiar War, 1914–1918." *The Journal of Modern History* 88, no. 4 (December 2016): 856–894.

Chickering, Roger. "World War I and the Theory of Total War: Reflections on the British and German Cases, 1914–1915." In *Great War, Total War: Combat and Mobilization on the Western Front, 1914–1918*, edited by Roger Chickering and Stig Förster, 35–53. New York: Cambridge University Press, 2000.

Daniel, Ute. *Arbeiterfrauen in der Industriegesellschaft: Beruf, Familie und Politik im Ersten Weltkrieg*. Göttingen: Vandenhoeck & Ruprecht, 1986.

Davis, Belinda J. *Home Fires Burning: Food, Politics, and Everyday Life in World War I Berlin*. Chapel Hill: University of North Carolina Press, 2000.

Dörries, Bernhard. *Kriegsbrot (Predigt) mit Anhang: Lebensregeln für die Kriegszeit*. Hannover: Schlüsterschen Buchdruckerei, 1915.

El Paso Herald (El Paso, TX).

Eltzbacher, Paul, ed. *Die deutsche Volksernährung und der englische Aushungerungsplan*. Braunschweig: F. Vieweg & Sohn, 1914.

Fassbender, Martin. *So sollt ihr leben in der Kriegszeit!: ein Wort über zeitgemässe Volksernährung*. Freiburg i.B.: Herder, 1915.

Feldman, Gerald D. *Army, Industry, and Labor in Germany, 1914–1918*. Princeton: Princeton University Press, 1966.

Feldman, Gerald D. *The Great Disorder: Politics, Economics, and Society in the German Inflation, 1914–1924*. New York: Oxford University Press, 1993.

Fürth, Henriette. *Kleines Kriegskochbuch: Ein Ratgeber für sparsames Kochen*. Frankfurt: Englert and Schlosser, 1915.

Götze, Marianne. *Die Kochkiste im Dienste der Kriegskost*. Leipzig: Nauman, 1918.
(The) Hattiesburg News (Hattiesburg, MS).
Healy, Maureen. *Vienna and the Fall of the Habsburg Empire: Total War and Everyday Life in World War I*. Cambridge: Cambridge University Press, 2004.
Heimpel, Elisabeth. "Heyl, Hedwig." In *Neue Deutsche Biographie*, 83–84. Berlin: Duncker & Humblot, 1972.
Heyl, Hedwig. *Das ABC Der Küche*. Berlin: C. Habel, 1897.
Heyl, Hedwig. "Kriegsküche." In *Volksernährung im Kriege: Vorträge*, 177–199. Berlin: Reimar Hobbing, 1915.
The Independent (New York, NY).
Just, Johanna. *Kriegskochbuch der Frauenhülfe: 50 zeitgemäße Rezepte*. Potsdam: Stiftungsverlag, 1915.
Keller, Ida. *Neues Kohlrüben Kochbuch: Praktische Anweisung zur Bereitung der verschiedensten Speisen von Kohlrüben*. Chemnitz: Robert Friese, 1917.
Klinische Wochenschrift (Berlin).
Kriegsausschuß für Oele und Fette, "Sammelt Obstkerne zur Oelgewinnung" (Poster) Berlin: Liebheit and Thiesen, 1914. From Deutsche Digitale Bibliothek. Accessed June 28, 2019. https://www.deutsche-digitale-bibliothek.de/item/26D2OC6R6EUQ74EGGXQIOXTZNBM7J4FW.
Kriegsernährungsamt. *Die Kriegsernährungs-Wirtschaft 1917*. Berlin, 1917.
Kocka, Jürgen. *Facing Total War: German Society, 1914–1918*. Cambridge, MA: Harvard University Press, 1984.
Kölner Frauenportal. "DHB—Netzwerk Haushalt: Geschichte." Accessed June 28, 2019. https://frauenportal.koeln/dhb-netzwerk-haushalt/.
Max Rubner-Institut. "About Us: Max Rubner." Accessed June 28, 2019. https://www.mri.bund.de/en/about-us/max-rubner/.
Neumann, M. P. "Kriegsbrot." In *Volksernährung im Kriege: Vorträge*, 144–158. Berlin: Reimar Hobbing, 1915.
Neswald, Elizabeth. "Nutritional Knowledge Between the Lab and the Field: The Search for Dietary Norms in the Late Nineteenth and Early Twentieth Centuries." In *Setting Nutritional Standards: Theory, Policies, Practices*, edited by Elizabeth Neswald, David F. Smith, and Ulrike Thoms, 29–51. Rochester, NY: University of Rochester Press, 2017.
Offer, Avner. *The First World War: An Agrarian Interpretation*. New York: Oxford University Press, 1989.
Oppenheimer, Carl. "Zeitgemäße Lebenshaltung." In *Volksernährung im Kriege: Vorträge*, 159–177. Berlin: Reimar Hobbing, 1915.
Pierre Weekly Free Press (Pierre, SD).
Städtische Kommission für Volksernährung. *Anleitung zum Wirtschaften in der Kriegszeit, zugleich ein Kriegs-Kochbuch*. Wiesbaden: Heinrich Staadt, 1915.

Seipp, Adam R. *The Ordeal of Peace: Demobilization and the Urban Experience in Britain and Germany, 1917–1921*. London: Routledge, 2016.

Starling, Ernest H. "The Food Supply of Germany During the War." *Journal of the Royal Statistical Society* 83, no. 2 (1920): 225–254.

Surface, Frank M., and Raymond L. Bland. *American Food in the World War and Reconstruction Period: Operations of the Organizations Under the Direction of Herbert Hoover, 1914–1924*. Stanford: Stanford University Press, 1931.

Treitel, Corinna. "Max Rubner and the Biopolitics of Rational Nutrition." *Central European History* 41 (2008), 1–25.

Volksernährung im Kriege: Vorträge. Berlin: Reimar Hobbing, 1915.

Wells, S. Russel, ed. *Germany's Food: Can It Last? The German Case as Presented by German Experts*. London: University of London Press, 1915.

Wildenthal, Lora. *German Women for Empire, 1884–1945*. Durham, NC: Duke University Press, 2001.

Das Wirtschaftsfräulein (Berlin).

Yaney, George. *The World of the Manager: Food Administration in Berlin During World War I*. New York: Peter Lang, 1994.

CHAPTER 3

Food, Drink and Hunger for World War I German Soldiers

Heather Merle Benbow

In his iconic novel, Erich Maria Remarque describes food as the dominant consideration in the daily life of the German World War I soldier. His stomach and digestion are areas of intense focus, accounting for "three quarters" of his vocabulary. For Remarque's soldiers, food occasions both the greatest joy and the deepest indignation.[1] This fictional assertion is borne out in letters, diaries and memoirs about the German World War I experience that is laden with discussions of food, drink and hunger as an elemental experience of World War I service. As Benjamin Ziemann has pointed out, food and drink played the "most important role in the life of the soldier."[2] Ziemann documents the impact of poor and insufficient food on the morale of German soldiers. Yet this is not all that can or should be said about the topic. This chapter examines German soldier experiences of food and hunger in World War I and shows how they were crucial in the formation, sustenance and disruption of interpersonal connections.

H. M. Benbow (✉)
University of Melbourne, Melbourne, VIC, Australia

© The Author(s) 2019
H. M. Benbow and H. R. Perry (eds.), *Food, Culture and Identity in Germany's Century of War*,
https://doi.org/10.1007/978-3-030-27138-1_3

I describe food as a vector of interpersonal connection for soldiers in World War I Germany. Food shares the properties of a vector, expressing both magnitude and direction simultaneously. Food carries cultural, social and emotional meaning and travels—both physically and symbolically—between soldiers and others, playing an important role in the formation and maintenance of interpersonal relationships. Food reflects, shapes and defines relationships of various kinds, from cursory interactions to the most intimate and enduring of connections. For German World War I soldiers, food functions as a medium of emotional expression when words fail. This chapter looks at the diverse relationships that are enabled or form around the vector of food—and hunger—for German soldiers. Relationships between *Kameraden*, between soldiers and their families as well as interactions with civilians are all played out around the consumption or exchange of food and drink. The central contention of this chapter is that food is a highly charged symbol with heightened meanings in wartime and that it plays a significant role as a vector of interpersonal interactions for soldiers.

Cultural historians have recently begun to investigate the cultural, social and emotional importance of food and hunger during wartime. For German civilians and soldiers, food went to the heart of social, cultural, religious and gender identities during the *Volkskrieg* ("people's war"). As a symbolic object, food plays an important role in identity, relationships and interpersonal communication[3]; however, in international conflagrations, "the multiple functions and meanings of food and drink [are elevated] into extreme dimensions."[4] This pertains not just to the politics of food in wartime but also to personal experiences of the effects of those politics. Food scarcity and hunger were defining German experiences during the war, and the catastrophic food situation contributed enormously to the collapse in support for the war effort on fighting and home fronts. While important research exists on the political and social dimensions of the food crisis on the home front,[5] food, drink and hunger as similarly defining experiences for German soldiers have hardly been examined.

This chapter builds upon work looking at German soldier experiences of World War I "from below." While Michael Roper's innovative study of "emotional survival" in World War I focused largely on British soldier experiences, he draws on Remarque to describe the significance of food in interpersonal bonds between soldiers. Rachel Duffett's *The Stomach for Fighting* broke new ground by placing food at the center of an analysis of British soldiers' experiences of World War I. Duffett shows that, beyond the question of nutrition, food for soldiers is "a medium through which the social and emotional experiences of military service were expressed."[6] There has been little scholarship so far that looks at the social and emotional experiences of German soldiers as expressed via food, drink and hunger.[7] Bernd Ulrich and Ben Ziemann's study of everyday experiences at the front contains surprisingly little on food, and the treatment of food is framed entirely negatively, via the rubric of hunger.[8] Ziemann's *War Experiences in Rural Germany, 1914–1923* devotes considerable attention to food, but considers it entirely in light of its impact on morale, seeing it as key to the decline in support for the war. Given these oversights, it is timely to consider German soldiers' experiences of food and hunger in their own right. Looking at German World War I soldiers' experiences of food and hunger (and not just as a matter of morale) can yield powerful insights into the everyday material and emotional experiences of World War I for German soldiers in a context in which these experiences of procuring, preparing and eating food are placed under enormous symbolic and material pressure. This chapter looks closely at German soldiers' experiences of food and hunger and examines how interpersonal connections are enabled, shaped and disrupted by food within the context of the German World War I food catastrophe.

COMRADES: FOOD AND HUNGER AMONG GERMAN SOLDIERS

When the first army's newspaper *Die Somme-Wacht* published a call in January 1917 for contributions on the topic of what to do with an empty tin can, the editors were pleased to receive a number of excellent contributions. First prize of a silver watch went to Private Ernst Scheddin for his drawing and text entitled: "Die leere Konservenbuechse bei uns als Universum."[9] Published in February of the same year, the cartoon describes in twelve images the ingenious use of an empty can in the trenches. Drawing on the notion of "making do" that was celebrated in the German army,[10] Scheddin's cartoon depicts soldiers fitting out their newly constructed trench using nothing but empty cans. In jaunty prose, the *Kameraden* are depicted constructing a chimney for a stove, a potato grater, a coffee machine for Turkish coffee and a ladle for the distribution of soup. The cans are also pressed into service as musical instruments, lighting and as warning bells. The cheerful tenor of the cartoon notwithstanding, the final image of the series is given over to hunger-induced fantasy. A weary soldier lies in bed with his boots on, hands outstretched to embrace imagined full cans of food. After all, the caption notes, soldiers far prefer these to empty cans!

The cartoon captures the tension inherent to the theme of food and drink in representations of German soldiers late in the war. On the one hand, the soldiers' preparedness to "make do" when it comes to the preparation of food and drink is celebrated as the basis of comradely belonging; however, by 1917 the soldier newspapers were under strict scrutiny by the *Feldpressestelle* (field press office) and hunger was a well-known flashpoint of discontent among the men. Thus the paper emphasizes that the men at the front are getting on with the job, making do with limited supplies and, moreover, enjoying their coffee in the style of their Turkish brothers in arms. Jason Crouthamel has observed of the German army newspapers that "through will-power and faith in comradeship, men were expected to be content and able to endure the privations of life at the front."[11] The ingenious German soldiers fashioning useful items out of tin cans inhabit a "motherless, masculine world" in which "the civilian fixity of gender roles"[12] has disappeared. The men therefore bring a tradesman-like, overtly masculine attitude to bear on the matter of food preparation.

Eating very often structured interpersonal interactions within the army. Food and drink were expressive of the affective weight of the war experience, as Duffett has amply demonstrated in relation to the taciturn British rankers. Duffett shows that for World War I British soldiers, comradeship was "for many men the only enriching aspect of their war service" and it "played out in a framework provided by eating."[13] Comradeship was one of the highest social values for German soldiers as well, as captured in Wilhelm Spengler's memoir *Wir waren drei Kameraden*. Published in 1917, the memoir contains numerous anecdotes that center around the comradely consummation of friendship over wine, the abundance of which on the Western Front is one of the war's few consolations:

> Fink was in a most exuberant mood. His steely body bore the hardships with ease. "Drink, you poor devil! Thank God that you're back, I've been worried sick about you." Beaming with joy he offered me a whole field cauldron filled with watered-down red wine. "That was much needed, Fink, I won't forget your kindness," I said and clutched his hand. In the meantime, faithful Jennrich joined our group carrying two bunches of oats.[14]

My two friends joyfully shook my hand. They'd lost sight of me because I'd been bandaging the injured and subsequently joined up with a different company. Behind a garden fence the first cork popped. Foaming wine poured out of the bottle, and arm in arm we drank to Germany's future. Cups were refilled. And as if with a single voice we called out: "We shall be friends for life!" Our eyes filling with tears, we drank up, and then, as if transported to a different world, we picked up our knapsacks and rifles and joined the company.[15]

The affective work of alcohol is as a means by which social bonds are cemented and interpersonal care is expressed. Its intoxicating effect also contributes to these functions, but such intoxication can also arise from the generally heightened emotions of battle, as we see in the following passage from Remarque when, after the death of a comrade—in a moment of intense physical awareness—Bäumer has an intimate exchange with a comrade involving food and drink:

The night crackles electrically, the front thunders like a concert of drums. My limbs move supplely, I feel my joints strong, I breathe the air deeply. The night lives, I live. I feel a hunger, greater than comes from the belly alone.

Müller stands in front of the hut waiting for me. I give him the boots. We go in and he tries them on. They fit well.

He roots among his supplies and offers me a fine piece of saveloy. With it goes hot tea and rum.[16]

The intensity of new bonds with fellow soldiers is expressed here in the language of appetite, care and the sharing of food and drink. The craving for "intimacy with other men under the guise of comradeship"[17] that Crouthamel's study has found in soldiers' correspondence is enacted via commensality. Food—especially its preparation or provision to others—offers an obvious context for feelings that depart from wartime norms of masculinity and open up possibilities for vulnerability, caring and intimacy. Food as an emotional vector plays a significant role in such behaviors.

Michael Roper discusses the role of food in comradeship in World War I and the caring role of officers when it comes to feeding. Peacetime eating is structured around family roles and framed in gendered terms of nurture and care. Roper documents movingly the extent to which some British officers took on the responsibility to nurture and feed their subordinates.[18] The caring and self-sacrifice that mothers displayed in the face of German homefront hunger have a corollary in the behavior of one officer described in Spengler's memoir. Spengler describes his captain selflessly distributing bread to his famished troops:

> In one house a man had got hold of two long loaves of white bread and brought them to our captain. Our dear captain stood among us like a father, cutting off small pieces and handing them out. "Only those who are really hungry should take some." But who among us wasn't really hungry? He gave each of us a morsel, he himself was left with nothing but the knife in his hand.[19]

Food scarcity in the German army was productive not only of the masculine trope of "Durchhalten," or making do; it also gave rise to the more feminine values of selflessness and nurturing. Incongruously, Spengler frames this scene as one of fatherly duty, yet it is also reminiscent of the mother's role in providing for her children.

While food and drink may connote comradeship in the face of adversity, and structure new and intimate bonds with comrades and others, any portrayal of food from the German perspective in the latter years of the war necessarily invokes its corollary—hunger. By the time Private Scheddin won his silver watch, the food crisis in Germany had matured to a catastrophic degree. Beginning with the privations of the "turnip winter," the year 1917 saw an intensification of the blockade as the USA entered the war and homefront rations fell to their lowest wartime levels. Hence it is a rather bitter-sweet note that the cartoon strikes in its final image of the hungry soldier dreaming—or perhaps hallucinating—about the desirability not of empty tin cans, but full ones. It is telling of the widespread perception of the food deficit in the German Imperial Army in 1917 that even this prize-winning cartoon intended to raise morale must acknowledge the experience of hunger among the troops. Alice Weinreb argues forcefully for the importance of "studying hunger alongside food" for its disruptive power to undermine "teleological models of modernity that assume an inverse relationship between processes of modernization and experiences of hunger."[20] Any study of German soldiers in World War I must necessarily acknowledge that hunger was a near universal experience and one of the most visceral elements of service.

If the criticism of the food situation in the *Somme-Wacht* is necessarily mooted, the commentary on the food situation in soldiers' correspondence is direct and scathing, censorship notwithstanding. Ulrich has described the *Feldpostbrief*, or soldier's letter as one of the most useful sources for a study of World War I soldiers' experiences, when read in context with other sources.[21] Feltmann also urges us to continue to use letters as "one of the most effective sources for determining how soldiers constructed their war experience."[22] Ulrich and Benjamin Ziemann use field post censors' reports to shed light on the contemporary reception of soldiers' letters, particularly the men's reflections on the food situation. The censor's morale report of the 5th Western Army in summer 1917 identifies "the nutrition question" as the "most important theme in the soldier's life":

> If badly and insufficiently nourished the soldier becomes less willing to serve and more inclined to criticize. That became obvious at the end of last year when the army administration began replacing the potato ration with turnips. A truly unbelievable effect was caused a few months ago by the reduction in the bread ration (March 1917). The most vehement complaints and accusations against the military authorities were lively proof of that. The effect has still not died down, quite the opposite. Every letter touches more or less temperamentally on the food question.[23]

Ziemann draws heavily on soldiers' letters in his consideration of food and morale. Complaints about insufficient rations began as early as 1915, and from 1917, he writes:

> many soldiers serving in the field army on both the Eastern and Western Front were constantly hungry. This is clearly apparent in reports by the postal surveillance offices as well as numerous soldiers' letters. Soldiers were exhausted much of the time as a result of this poor nutrition and because of the severe physical strains they were under.[24]

In the summer of 1917, the censorship office of the 8th Army on the Eastern front compiled a collection of soldier letter excerpts about the hunger situation. These letters to home reveal in crude detail the hunger the soldiers endure. The report documents soldier accounts of "Hunger so bad I could throw up; I can't bear it any longer"; "I've rather lost my enthusiasm to die a heroic death, or are we supposed to die of hunger now"; "Everyone here is yearning for peace, for the food situation can't continue like this for much longer."[25] As these and other examples documented by Ulrich and Ziemann make clear, and as Ziemann explores in more detail in his *War Experiences in Rural Germany*, there is a clear line from hunger without an apparent endpoint and the loss of fighting spirit. The case is well made that severe hunger was detrimental to the morale of German soldiers, but it bears observing that the pressure on the social function of food contributes in no small part to the loss of morale; food can, after all, bring people together as well as divide them. In situations of extreme hunger, the interpersonal connections that food can shape and enable begin to break down. So while, as discussed above, a certain level of deprivation was perhaps cause for comradely innovation, the constant, nagging hunger among the German fighting forces from 1916 on had a corrosive effect on social bonds within the army.

Roper draws on Remarque to describe the intimate social bonds forged over food, but he is alert as well to the potential of food to become the object of uncomradely disputes.[26] Spengler's memoir describes behavior at odds with the comradeliness suggested by its title:

> After our meal we got our mail. I received a small crate filled with chocolate, cigars, cigarettes, sausage, handkerchiefs, etc. It was cracked open with the bayonet and robbed of its contents. Those lying close by shared the precious things with us. I only salvaged a few of the many cigarettes, of the sausages I could only read in my dear sister's accompanying letter. Before I knew it, everything had disappeared. They all cried out: "Your mother is also our mother, so we share like brothers."[27]

The ironic invocation of brotherly bonds by Spengler's comrades is indicative of the conflation of the private with the national during the *Volkskrieg*[28] or at least the cunning use of this trope to selfish ends.

For German soldiers dealing with food scarcity for most of the duration of the war, hunger—and its uneven distribution—emphasized the social divisions between the men. Inequality between low-ranking soldiers and officers was felt viscerally around the question of food. The resentment and collapse of morale in light of this inequality are captured in a letter from a baker, Johann Brandl, who writes to a friend in May 1917:

> Here out in the field it's dire straits, food is so scarce that one can't last. The food is nothing but pig feed, but we have to eat it, there's nothing else. [...] Every third day we receive one loaf of bread, it has to last three days & we're constantly hungry. If our superior officers ate what we eat the war would long be over by now.[29]

Ziemann documents the ways in which "inequalities in provisioning"[30] led to embittered perceptions of social inequality within the army, such that, in 1916 "the quartermaster-general felt compelled to issue a decree to stop the common practice of kitchen staff preparing larger and better portions for officers, exceeding even the field rations to which they were entitled."[31] In this situation of scarcity, those who received more, such as officers, were the object of bitterness and envy. Ziemann also emphasizes another group of soldiers who were able to access surplus food, rural men in receipt of generous care packages from their farming families. Roper describes the common practice of sharing care packages among one's comrades; this generosity was not without tension, however, with some soldiers expressing resentment of this obligation, particularly when it came to food from home that was laden with emotional meaning for the recipient.[32] Echoing the homefront dynamics of urban resentment of German farmers' relatively better food situation, Ziemann notes that farmers within the army were subject to the ire of men from the cities who were not able to obtain extra food from their starving families: "their fellow soldiers commonly responded to farmers' uncomradely behavior by stealing food from them."[33]

Whereas hunger was a near universal experience in the German army, on the Eastern Front it was particularly extreme. In this context "uncomradely" behavior around food was common, as wryly explained by Kurt Bergter, a student from Darmstadt:

> Anyway, we are engaged in three battles here: against the lousy Russians, the Russian lice [...] and over the good stuff in the field cauldron. [...] There's bacon and pea soup and so the dear comrades fight over the honor to fetch the food for their group of eight men. Would you think this an act of charity? Peas and life, they're alike: the empty heads float on the top, those with a little substance get to the bottom of things, in this case the field cauldron! My buddy now returns and reports with sadness that he managed to get nothing but "thin stuff" and by way of proof lets me take a look, but he's apprehensive, I shouldn't stir. With great care, avoiding any "tremor", he pours the soup into my bowl all the time complaining that there's no "good stuff" in it. But I reach into it swiftly and grab my portion while he curses madly: "Greedy guts, uncomradely" etc. – This battle, now all the harder because we have only been receiving food at night, is played out daily, everywhere the same drama.[34]

The student soldier, whose letter is among those published in Philipp Witkop's wildly successful *Kriegsbriefe gefallener Studenten*, captures in a humorous culinary metaphor his critique of military leadership, the "Hohlköppe," or empty heads, who float to the top. The Russians in his account are but one of three main enemies; lice and hunger have equal billing in Bergter's account of soldiers engaged in a daily existential battle in which comradeship has no place, except as an accusation. Similarly, on the Western Front, Alfred Vaeth decries the failure of the war to deliver the equality among men that many were convinced it would usher in. Vaeth, a student who prides himself on his comradely relationship with working men ("My closest comrade is a bricklayer, another is a foundryman"),[35] can find no better illustration of the persistence of class distinctions in the field than in the unequal provisioning of lower ranks and officers:

> and precisely what we'd hoped for, the complete levelling of class distinction before the majesty of sacrifice and before death that is the same for all, precisely this levelling will not occur. If you don't believe me, here's an image: in the trench three people argue over a loaf a bread. The officers gather inside over wine in abundance. The heart bleeds.[36]

While the officers are able to continue to perform alimentary social rituals, the hungry men in the trenches have abandoned all sense of comradeliness. Just as the new bonds of comradeship that were formed in part around commensality were strained and broken under conditions of hunger, food and drink also served as a vector between the home and the fighting fronts.

Families and Friends: Food, Hunger and the Connection to Home

When World War I soldiers mobilize, their food routines and practices are immediately and quite drastically disrupted. For most soldiers, in their civilian lives food is tied to the home and the family, and its preparation is largely the remit of mothers and wives. As Barbara Duden has argued, women's domestic work since the eighteenth century has been framed in terms of "loving duty."[37] The food work of mothers and wives therefore carries a heavy affective payload for men. Absent the family routines that structure eating, particularly on festive occasions, soldiers perceive resonances of the emotional work of food in the field. The first Christmas of the war was a particularly poignant one for soldiers given the thwarted expectation of a quick end to the war. On the Western Front, Karl Aldag evocatively describes a wartime Christmas in which the love and care of parents have been replicated by a caring nation:

> Christmas in the field! [...] A beautiful moment as the folks stood together, the names were called out and parcels were passed out over our heads – we were all like children at Christmas, who knelt before their parcels and rifled through them in candle light [...] Everything one could wish for was there in abundance: woollen things, tobacco, Spekulatius-cookies, chocolate, sausages – gifts of love. Oh what has Germany provided for us![38]

The soldiers are figured here as children of a benevolent nation that bestows upon its "Weihnachtskinder" the traditional loving gifts of Spekulatius biscuits, chocolate and sausage. This note of gratitude to the nation stands in conspicuous contrast to the preponderance of negative commentary on food by German soldiers. More commonly, the experience of food in the field was notable for its departure from civilian norms. Spengler is haunted by the echo of civilian food rhythms as he faces the prospect of imminent hunger: "My loved ones are probably at home now eating lunch. Our stomachs are growling. When I think that we will be here possibly for another two days without bread or water! It's horrific."[39] Spengler's experience of hunger of the field intensifies his longing for his distant loved ones, as he imagines them following their peacetime routines without him.

Of course, the German home front was not beyond reach of the privations of war, but thoroughly enmeshed in the conflict. As Ziemann points out, "Domestic life and women's behavior had become increasingly nationalized in imperial Germany."[40] The mobilization of the home front was a feature of the German experience of the war, with women as well as men "expected to be mutually bound by their service to the nation, whether as mothers or as warriors."[41] Women were portrayed as dutiful *Kameradinnen* on the home front, and *Durchhalten* in times of scarcity was their motto as much as it was for front soldiers. Food shortages meant that women's food work became more onerous, as "women had to devote increasing time and energy to preparation of food."[42]

And, like the men, women experienced disruption to food routines and a loss of autonomy around food and eating as the blockade hit home. Food became politicized not just in terms of the home front, as Belinda Davis has demonstrated,[43] but also as a medium and theme of communication between soldiers and their friends and families. Robert L. Nelson writes in his study of German soldier newspapers that soldiers' connection to women as *Kameradinnen* in the war effort formed "the fundamental connection [...] between the front and the Fatherland."[44] There was a lively correspondence between German soldiers and civilians with an estimated 16.7 million letters delivered each day by the German *Feldpost*. Many of these contain references to food. Moreover, food as a material object itself traveled in care packages from the home to the fighting front. In this way, food was a particularly powerful vector between home and fighting fronts, conveying not just sustenance, but a plethora of emotional and political meanings.

Roper posits families and their care packages as an important adjunct to the army.[45] For German soldiers, particularly farmers, this was also the case; farming families were more likely to have food to spare and would even send perishable goods such as butter, eggs and meat to their sons and husbands.[46] The men enquire of their families in detail about the farm, the harvest, the prices attained for produce, whether the family's potato supplies are adequate.[47] Farming sons, knowing that their families have enough, are able to ask for extra bread to be sent to make up for shortfalls in army rations.[48] How different it was for men from urban areas in the grip of the blockade. For these men, aware of the straightened circumstances at home, receiving care packages from home could be bitter-sweet. The Berliner Hans Zelmer, for example, gently admonishes his mother in summer 1915 for sending him too much food: "It's not right that I lead such an opulent life at a time like this when black bread has such enormous value. It eats me up even if I share with my comrades."[49]

Soldiers were aware from newspapers of the blockade and its effects, but letters were the source of first-hand accounts of homefront privations. Thus even the well-fed farmers became upset at "their wives' accounts of their excessive workload, the aggressive behavior of hoarders and how the command economy was being managed."[50] So while food as a key component of care packages was used to maintain and strengthen bonds between fighting men and their wives and mothers as *Kameradinnen*, hunger—and accounts thereof—had an explosive power to damage soldier morale.

Letters in particular from urban wives and mothers that revealed in all-too-explicit detail the difficult situation at home attained the pejorative appellation of "Jammerbriefe" (wailing letters). These were vehemently discouraged by the authorities.[51] Complaints about food were a dominant theme of such letters, for example, in this letter from February 1917 in which Hedwig Lauth writes to her husband:

> My dear Julius, [...] for us bad times are beginning now. There are no more potatoes. Instead there is a pound of bread and 100grams of flour. Unfortunately, neither of these can be had and they had no bread for a whole week in the cooperative. I'm happy that I saved a few potatoes in the cellar. If only the frost would end, then one could at least buy some expensive vegetables. All thoughts center on one thing: what can we eat.[52]

This letter is written at the end of the so-called *Kohlrübenwinter* (turnip winter), as nutrition on the German home front was reaching its lowest ebb. In the same year, another woman writes to her husband as follows:

> If you were here you would be long sick of it. There is now a war kitchen and we have to get our food there: you can imagine what slop it is: if you saw it you would get an idea of what we women have to go through. Three pounds of potatoes, we have to cook for the whole week on that; 50 grams of fat per head. There's rice with bugs in it, that's the last straw for us.[53]

Ulrich and Ziemann similarly document one woman's lament that she can't send any food in a care package as there is nothing edible to buy; yet another writes that although the children have school holidays, she has no time for them due to the constant errands in search of food.[54]

It is hardly surprising that those men who were able to eat well experienced a degree of guilt about their situation relative to their families. One subaltern officer, Leutnant Hugo Frick, describes in salacious detail his epicurean life, apparently torn between a desire to share his moments of joy amid the horror of war, and the knowledge that the addressee of his letter is enduring hunger in blockade Germany:

> In contrast to the terrible things we experience, here at the rest quarters we have led a gluttonous life, apart from the daily duty; a number of hunts

provided rabbit roast and partridge which with pasta and gravy and a glass of port is rather delicious; I shouldn't even mention this to you all who are out there in the starving countryside.[55]

If the effect of the *Jammerbriefe* was to drive married soldiers "out of their minds with worry"[56] about their families, some men were at pains to avoid causing their families at home to worry for their sake. Demonstrating an acute understanding of the homefront hunger situation, one soldier writes openly to a friend on the "food question" but asks that he not share it with the soldier's wife:

I hardly need to assure you that our nutrition is very lacking. I ask you though not to say anything of this to my wife. I have namely described the situation in the best possible light for her, to reassure her and so that she won't send me anything. Of course she has nothing herself, but she would save her last bite for me and I want to avoid that for obvious reasons.[57]

Ulrich and Ziemann write that letters from soldiers to their families that were positive about the food question were understood by the censor to be coded critiques. One such letter caught the censor's eye for its conspicuous use of dashes, and no doubt due to the implausibility of its claims about the food question: "I'm satisfied with the food — Dear wife, I ask you not to worry. We here are still getting more to eat than you. I can't complain until now. — Dear wife, please don't worry any more about me, I'm still healthy and there is plenty of food."[58] The correspondence between home and fighting fronts contains forthright critique of the hunger endured in both spaces with dire effects on morale. For the rank-and-file soldiers, food was a key bone of contention with officers and military authorities, and on the home front, it was a politically explosive issue. Whether they sought to conceal their suffering, or revealed it in explicit terms, soldiers and their wives and mothers wrote prolifically on the topic of food. Food conveyed emotional and political meaning between the fronts like no other topic; it represented the longing for one's loved ones, the desire for peace and a return to civilian normality and the fading morale at home and the front. As a material object and an idea, food circulated imaginatively and literally between home and the front and its ever-worsening scarcity played a key role in breaking the emotional bonds of solidarity that underpinned the *Volkskrieg*.

Giving and Taking: German Soldiers' Culinary Encounters with Civilians

German soldiers and officers moved through vast areas of Europe, the Middle East and Africa, encountering civilians who played a crucial role in meeting soldiers' basic food needs. These culinary interactions took many forms and included purchase, coercion, theft, scavenging, billeting and sometimes gifts between soldiers and civilians in both directions. Looking at civilian–soldier interactions through the lens of food highlights the daily existential struggles that soldiers and civilians shared, across cultural, religious and national divides. This is true of both enemy and friendly populations. In these interactions, food takes on a heightened symbolic and emotional role. Encounters with women and children remind soldiers of their own distant families and their civilian lives before the war. Therefore, the transfer of food and drink that takes place between soldiers and civilian women and children has particularly emotive effects for soldiers. Sometimes these encounters can restore feelings of common humanity or highlight the universality of suffering in the war. On other occasions, the encounters entail coercion and violence, threatened or actual.

Culinary interactions between Germans and civilians who share an ethnic, linguistic or religious affiliation are sometimes described by soldiers as warm and welcoming. Spengler describes many friendly encounters with locals in Alsatia, where the soldiers and civilians often had a shared ethnic heritage. He writes of the German soldiers being showered with gifts of food by locals in Metz:

> Singing merry marching songs, we marched through the cobbled alleys. People came running carrying baskets filled with ham rolls, fruit, chocolate, bread, sugar, jams, etc. When our pockets were full we used our helmets. The entire battalion was an eating, singing, jumping, laughing train of soldiers surrounded by hundreds of local residents.[59]

Here we see food functioning as hospitality and welcome by local civilians, rather than just serving basic needs. Spengler also describes being invited into homes by Alsatian locals:

> An Alsatian woman living nearby who spoke German well twice invited me for lunch. In her clean living room, I and other comrades sat together with

the old grandmother, who was German, for another hour. Talking and smoking I spent agreeable hours there for which I am grateful to that lady to this day.[60]

The invitation to partake of a family meal and the encounters with a German grandmother create an enduring sense of gratitude for Spengler, and a few hours of normalcy within a family context, a short reprieve from the abnormal social context of war.

Spengler's Alsatian encounters can be compared to the experiences of the many Jewish German soldiers on the Eastern Front. German soldiers of Jewish faith accepted offers of hospitality from Jewish civilians in occupied areas. Steven Schouten notes that religion often transcended enmity with occupied peoples, leading to incongruous moments of intercultural hospitality.[61] Numerous such moments are described in a collection of letters by Jewish German and Austrian soldiers that were published early in the war.[62] M. v. d. W., for instance, describes his experiences in a largely Jewish Polish village on Rosh Hashanah in 1914:

> I was thirsty and asked at a house for a glass of water. A Jewish widow gave me what I asked; we conversed and when she learned that I was also Jewish, she led me into a room where the Jewish festive table was set with the two candles, apples and bread. "You must eat here with us", and it was useless to protest. I recited Kiddush, shared the delicious meal with the good woman and her two children, and if the conversation (half Yiddish, half German) was somewhat difficult, my deep emotion soon gave way to comfort.[63]

Similarly to Spengler's experiences on the Western Front, the Jewish soldier is able to enjoy a precious encounter with family life and a familiar culinary ritual. While culture and the fault lines of the war separate this soldier from this family, he is able to occupy a familiar and familial role within the scene of commensality. The Jewish villagers single out the Jewish soldier fighting for an invading army, and he is cared for enthusiastically by the Jewish villagers: "The poor market-woman who is selling apples cries: 'There he is, the Jew, God protect him', and every day I've had to accept invitations to tea, lunch and dinner."[64] Even absent a cultural or religious commonality, German soldiers claim to enjoy warm encounters with civilians that are occasioned by commensality. Ernst Jünger's memoir describes a number of culinary interactions with civilians, including quite formal hospitality in a French billet:

My billet was most agreeable; my hosts, a kindly jewellers' couple by the name of Plancot-Bourlon, rarely let me eat my lunch without sending up some delicacy or other. And in the evenings we often sat up over a cup of tea, played cards and chatted. The perennial question came up a lot, of course: Why does mankind have wars?[65]

As discussed above, the experience of hunger was something shared across fighting and home fronts. When these fronts collided in an occupation situation, hunger was a focal point of interactions that emphasized the commonality of human needs. Spengler describes such an encounter with an elderly French woman:

I sat down to rest on a bench in front of a squalid hut. Suddenly an old grandmother was standing next to me with a wooden dish full of milk and a slice of buttered bread. Without a word she passed both to me. I ate greedily as the old woman watched me pityingly and repeated: „Oh, the war! Oh, the war!" I thanked the woman with a „God bless" that I had never before meant so sincerely and deeply and, newly strengthened, I went on my way.[66]

Spengler is strengthened by this interaction not just due to the physical sustenance, but the caring gesture by a stranger whose empathy is expressed—as so often in relation to hunger during World War I—as opposition to the war. In benefiting from this act of grandmotherly caring, the soldier also presumably represents to the woman her own sons or grandsons away at the front. Her offer of sustenance to the young man is an act of humanity in barbaric times.

Soldiers describe being moved by the suffering of civilians. The trench journal of the first Battalion, *Die Sappe*, printed a piece in January 1916 in which a soldier describes pity for the suffering of Jewish civilians in Colmar: "Masses of Jews stood outside of the houses, the women and children offering cigarettes and chocolate. We were happy to buy, we felt sorry for all these poor devils looking at us so sadly wrapped in their long caftans."[67] Passing through a village on the Western Front, Spengler encounters a family hiding in their house because a woman is about to give birth and another is gravely ill. He is moved to give them his last block of chocolate: "I had bought it in Munich prior to our mobilization and firmly resolved only to eat it if I should lie wounded somewhere for more than 24 hours."[68]

Such encounters are accorded great emotional significance in soldiers' memoirs, letters and trench journals. Yet the question arises, to what extent hospitality is offered by civilians as an expression of shared humanity, and to what extent it is an act of self-preservation on the part of occupied populations. David Hamlin addresses this question in a study of occupied Romania. The presence of "armed foreigners" leads civilians in Hamlin's account to offer food as a way to attempt to re-establish "a moral community between soldier and civilian" in an effort to thwart potential violence against civilian populations.[69] This threat is clearly a factor in Spengler's rather dismissive account of the fear of a woman on the Western Front: "the woman noticed that she'd had the wrong idea about the expected barbarians. As a sign of her gratefulness ('because we had not set her house on fire and had no intention of murdering her and the child, who had nothing to do with the war') she fetched three bottles of red wine from the cellar."[70] Framing the woman's fear of the German soldiers as a mistaken impression, rather than a justified existential concern, Spengler reveals his contempt for all but the most welcoming attitudes to the invading army. Gifts of food, Hamlin argues, were a means of "constructing some limited sense of community and obligation, in such a way that it would no longer be morally possible to overstep boundaries."[71] It was crucial in these interactions that soldiers acknowledged the gift "as something other than a bribe or requisition" so that they "entered into a fuller relationship with their new subjects; a relationship in which they came to have something akin to responsibilities."[72] This effect is apparent in the scene described above, in which Spengler, seeking out hiding civilians, comes across the house with the pregnant and ill women. Apparently moved by their suffering, Spengler relinquishes his precious chocolate, an item that he states is intended to save his life should he lie wounded somewhere. This anecdote posits the soldier first and foremost as the potential victim of war. And yet, Spengler goes on to describe how he himself became the recipient of hospitality and an unwelcome guest of the same suffering civilians:

> On the steps the old farmer, crying, said: "O, monsieur, c'est la guerre, quel malheur!" In the kitchen he gave me [*schenkte mir*] milk and bread and one of the women made coffee. Then they dragged in mattresses and blankets. The old man and the two women went into a storage room in which were stacked the daily supplies of wood, potatoes, baskets,

gardening tools and other stuff, and they crouched down on the naked stone floor and cried."[73]

Hamlin notes that the wailing of women and children in Romania that is often noted in soldiers' recollections "was ultimately the terror that the usual sense of mutuality that prohibits open murder and larceny had disappeared."[74] That the soldier is sufficiently moved to offer his chocolate, and frames the coercive situation above as a "gift" ("schenkte mir"), indicates the efficacy of food as a social vector. Its social meanings are here deployed in an act of self-preservation, in a situation in which the civil norms have broken down.

The potential for sexual violence also suffuses soldier-civilian interactions in a context in which—on both Eastern and Western fronts—soldiers regularly demand food and drink at private homes. On the Eastern Front reservist, Gustav Gaß writes to his friend of his increased sexual appetite: "haven't had a woman or a girl in my arms for some time."[75] He recalls his last sexual encounter resulting, he says, from a Polish girl's infatuation with him. In the letter, he describes going into a printer to find a woman at home: "there were a few gorgeous girls [*herrliche Mädchen*] in the rooms. I sat down and demanded [*verlangte*] a glass of tea, which one can get in any house."[76] The choice of the verb "verlangen" is interesting here, connoting both a demand, but also sexual desire. It is precisely this combination of meanings that suffuses the culinary exchange described here. Gaß' visit in the homes of civilians is as much about the tea as the opportunity to experience "herrliche Mädchen" and the promise of sexual conquest.

As we have seen, in soldier–civilian encounters, hospitality was sometimes given freely, but often coerced or demanded. Other means, such as pilfering, scrounging and theft, were common methods by which German soldiers supplemented their official diet. A caricature from *Die Sappe* in February 1917 depicts a soldier running off with a goose while a startled Hungarian farmer looks on (see Fig. 3.1).[77] The theft is portrayed irreverently as a misunderstanding, with the soldier asking repeatedly in German what the goose costs and then running off gleefully when he doesn't understand the answer. The (misspelt) phrase uttered by the farmer—„nem tu dom"—means "I don't know" in Hungarian and was perhaps a familiar phrase for readers of the journal, underscoring the deceptive nature of the interaction.

Fig. 3.1 "Nem tu dom"

German soldiers' encounters with civilians were very often framed by eating and drinking. Hungry and thirsty soldiers encountered civilians with their alimentary needs and were given, purchased, demanded or took what they required. The existing emotional and social meanings of food suffused in particular interactions with women and children. The intrusion into personal spaces that the need for food and drink justified also gave rise to situations of unwanted intimacy and the threat of sexual violence; food and drink, so frequently evocative of sexuality, therefore attain new and threatening meanings in the context of war.

Conclusion

The crucial role the food situation played in the collapse of the social pact that underlay support for the war effort in World War I Germany has been widely observed by historians. As stomachs shrank, so too did social connections atrophy and break. In wartime, food—an essential requirement for life, a carrier of meaning and a means of relating to others—comes under profound symbolic and material pressure. This pressure manifests not only at a political and discursive level but is felt in the quotidian experiences of soldiers as they interact with others near and far. This chapter has considered food and drink as a vector in social interactions of three kinds: between soldiers, between soldiers and their families and between soldiers and civilians. In each case, food and drink carry material value as an essential source of nutrition and a means of survival. They also carry an array of meanings between people that can contribute to interpersonal connection. Conditions of scarcity, however, produce circumstances in which the bonds that connect people are broken and the social meanings of food are lost or disregarded. The context of war also brings with it new nuances, and intimate culinary encounters can be the context for the threat of coercion and violence. In these and other ways, food, drink and hunger are central to the social relationships that German soldiers maintain and form during World War I.

Notes

1. Erich Maria Remarque, *Im Westen Nichts Neues* (Berlin: Propylän Verlag, 1929), 14. https://archive.org/details/in.ernet.dli.2015.168305. Translation mine.
2. Benjamin Ziemann, *War Experiences in Rural Germany: 1914-1923* (London, UK: Bloomsbury Publishing PLC, 2006), 74, FN 9.
3. See Claude Lévi-Strauss, "The Culinary Triangle," *The Partisan Review* 33 (Autumn 1966): 586–596; Roland Barthes, "Toward a Psychosociology of Food Consumption," in *Food and Drink in History*, edited by Robert Forster and Orest Ranum (Baltimore: Johns Hopkins University Press, 1979), 166–173; and Mary Douglas, "Deciphering a Meal," in *Food and Culture: A Reader*, edited by Carole Counihan and Penny Van Esterik (Routledge, 1997), 36–54.
4. Katarzyna J. Cwiertka, "Sustaining and Comforting the Troops in the Pacific War," in *Food in Zones of Conflict: Cross-Disciplinary Perspectives*, edited by Paul Collinson and Helen Macbeth (New York: Berghahn Books, 2014), 134. http://ebookcentral.proquest.com/lib/unimelb/detail.action?docID=1644362.
5. See for instance Belinda J. Davis, *Home Fires Burning: Food, Politics, and Everyday Life in World War I Berlin* (Chapel Hill: The University of North Carolina Press, 2000).
6. Rachel Duffet, *The Stomach for Fighting* (Manchester: Manchester University Press, 2015), 2.
7. Notable exceptions include Steven Schouten's work on Jewish soldiers in the German army and, to some extent, David Hamlin's article on the food and the German occupation of Romania. See Steven Schouten, "Fighting a Kosher War: German Jews and Kashrut in the First World War," in *Food and War in Twentieth Century Europe*, edited by Rachel Duffet, Ina Zweiniger-Bargielowska, and Alain Drouard (Farnham, UK: Taylor & Francis Group, 2011), 41–56; and David Hamlin, "The Fruits

of Occupation: Food and Germany's Occupation of Romania in the First World War," *First World War Studies* 4, no. 1 (1 March 2013): 81–95. https://doi.org/10.1080/19475020.2012.761389.

8. Bernd Ulrich and Benjamin Ziemann, eds., *Krieg im Frieden: Die umkämpfte Erinnerung: Quellen und Dokumente* (Frankfurt/Main: Fischer, 1997), 90–93.

9. "The empty can is a universe for us." Ernst Scheddin, "Die leere Konservenbuechse bei uns als Universum," in *Die Wacht im Westen/ Somme-Wacht: Kriegszeitung d. 1. Armee — 1917 (Januar–Mai)*, Heidelberg University Library. https://doi.org/10.11588/diglit.2832 #0187. Translation mine.

10. Anne Lipp, *Meinungslenkung im Krieg: Kriegserfahrungen deutscher Soldaten und ihre Deutung, 1914–1918* (Göttingen: Vandenhoeck & Ruprecht, 2003), 132–139.

11. Jason Crouthamel, "Cross-Dressing for the Fatherland: Sexual Humour, Masculinity and German Soldiers in the First World War," *First World War Studies* 2, no. 2 (1 October 2011): 198. https://doi.org/10.1080/ 19475020.2011.613240.

12. Duffet, *The Stomach for Fighting*, 188.

13. Ibid.

14. „Fink war in der ausgelassensten Stimmung. Sein stählerner Körper ertrug die Strapazen mit Leichtigkeit. „Da trink, armer Teufel! Gott sei Dank, daß du wieder da bist, ich hab' schön Angst um dich gehabt." Und freudestrahlend hielt er mir einen ganzen Feldkessel voll verdünntem Rotwein hin. „Das tat gut, Fink, ich werde dir die Wohltat nicht vergessen", sagte ich und drückte ihm die Hand. Währenddessen kam der brave Jennrich mit zwei Bund Hafer unterm Arm zu unserer Gruppe." Wilhelm Spengler, *Wir waren drei Kameraden: Kriegserlebnisse* (Freiburg i.B.: Herder, 1917), 21. Translation mine.

15. „Meine beiden Freunde schüttelten mir freudig die Hand. Sie hatten mich auf der Höhe aus den Augen verloren, da ich durch das Verbinden der Verwundeten in einen andern Zug gekommen war. Hinter einem Gartenzaun knallte der erste Pfropfen. Schäumend quoll der Wein aus der Flasche, und Arm in Arm tranken wir auf Deutschlands Zukunft. Von neuem wurden die Becher gefüllt. Und wie aus einem Mund riefen wir: „Wir wollen Freunde sein fürs Leben!" Mit glänzenden Augen tranken wir aus, dann nahmen wir, wie in eine andere Welt versetzt, die Tornister auf, hängten das Gewehr um und traten zur Kompagnie." Ibid., 99. Translation mine.

16. "Die Nacht knistert elektrisch, die Front gewittert dumpf wie ein Trommelkonzert. Meine Glieder bewegen sich geschmeidig, ich fühle meine Gelenke stark, ich schnaufe und schnaube. Die Nacht lebt, ich

lebe. Ich spüre Hunger, einen größeren als nur vom Magen. Müller steht vor der Baracke und erwartet mich. Ich gebe ihm die Schuhe. Wir gehen hinein, und er probiert sie an. Sie passen genau. — Er kramt in seinen Vorräten und bietet mir ein schönes Stück Zervelatwurst an. Dazu gibt es heißen Tee mit Rum." Remarque, *Im Westen nichts Neues*, 39. English translation in Erich Maria Remarque, *All Quiet on the Western Front* (New Jersey: Everbind Anthologies, 2011), 39.
17. Crouthamel, "Cross-Dressing for the Fatherland," 3.
18. Michael Roper, *The Secret Battle: Emotional Survival in the Great War* (Manchester: Manchester University Press, 2009), 132–133.
19. In einem Hause hatte ein Mann zwei lange Weißbrote aufgetrieben und brachte sie jetzt zum Herrn Hauptmann. Wie ein Vater stand unser lieber Hauptmann unter uns, schnitt kleine Stückchen ab und teilte sie aus. „Nur wer sehr Hunger hat, soll kommen." Aber wer hatte nicht sehr Hunger? Einen Bissen reichte er jedem, und zum Schluß blieb ihm selbst nur das Messer in der Hand. Spengler, *Wir waren drei Kameraden*, 69. Translation mine.
20. Alice Weinreb, *Modern Hungers: Food and Power in Twentieth-Century Germany* (New York: Oxford University Press, 2017), 9. https://doi.org/10.1093/acprof:oso/9780190605094.001.0001.
21. Bernd Ulrich, *Die Augenzeugen: deutsche Feldpostbriefe in Kriegs- und Nachkriegszeit 1914–1933* (Essen: Klartext, 1997), 12–26, 38.
22. Brian K. Feltman, *The Stigma of Surrender: German Prisoners, British Captors, and Manhood in the Great War and Beyond* (Chapel Hill: The University of North Carolina Press, 2015), 9.
23. "Bei schlechter und unzureichender Verpflegung wird der Soldat dienstunwilliger und stärker zur Kritik geneigt. Das zeigte sich deutlich Ende des vorigen Jahres, als die Heeresverwaltung dazu überging, die Kartoffelration mit Rüben zu strecken. Eine geradezu unglaubliche Wirkung rief aber die vor einigen Monaten eingetretene Kürzung der Brotration hervor (März 1917). Die heftigsten Klagen und Vorwürfe gegen die Militärbehörden gaben hiervon beredtes Zeugnis. Die Wirkung hat heute noch nicht nachgelassen, im Gegenteil, in jedem Brief wird mehr oder weniger temperamentvoll die Verpflegungsfrage gestreift." In Ulrich and Ziemann, *Krieg im Frieden*, 92. Translation mine.
24. Ziemann, *War Experiences in Rural Germany*, 75–76.
25. "Hunger zum Erbrechen; es ist nicht mehr länger zum Aushalten"; one soldier speculates that he may die of hunger and asserts that he will soon eat his own excrement; still others make clear the causal link between hunger and loss of fighting spirit: "Ich habe eigentlich keine Lust mehr, den Heldentod zu sterben, oder soll man vielleicht den Hungertod sterben"; "Sie sehnen sich alle hier nach Frieden; denn es kann nicht mehr

lange mit dem Essen so weitergehen." Ulrich and Ziemann, *Krieg im Frieden*, 90. Translation mine.
26. Roper, *The Secret Battle*, 126.
27. „Nach dem Essen wurde die Post verteilt. Ich erhielt ein kleines Kistchen mit Schokolade, Zigarren, Zigaretten, Wurst, Taschentüchern usw. [...] Mit dem Seitengewehr wurde sie erbrochen und ihres Inhalts beraubt. Wer in der Nähe lag, teilte mit uns die kostbaren Sachen. Von den vielen Zigarren rettete ich selbst nur wenige, von den Würsten las ich nur in dem Begleitschreiben der lieben Schwester. Ehe ich mich versah, war alles verschwunden. Jeder rief: 'Deine Mutter ist auch unsere Mutter, also wird brüderlich geteilt.'" Spengler, *Wir waren drei Kameraden*, 110–111. Translation mine.
28. See Ulrich, *Die Augenzeugen*, 32.
29. „Bei uns im Feld ist es schon gans Bruch, den das Essen ist so knap das man nicht mehr ausreichen kann. Das Essen ist nicht als ein Saufutter aber Essen müssen wirs doch, weil man sonst nichts hat. [...] Alle 3. Tage bekommen wir 1 Brot da muß dan wieder 3. Tage reichen u. Hunger leiden müssen wir immer. Wenn die Herrn Offiziere das Essen wie wir dan wäre der Kreig schon längst gar" [sic]. In Ulrich and Ziemann, *Krieg im Frieden*, 92. Translation mine.
30. Ziemann, *War Experiences in Rural Germany*, 75.
31. Ibid., 76.
32. Roper, *The Secret Battle*, 128.
33. Ziemann, *War Experiences in Rural Germany*, 77.
34. "Im übrigen führen wir hier drei Kämpfe: gegen die lausigen Russen, die russischen Läuse [...] und – um das Dicke im Feldkessel. [...] [Es] gibt Speckerbsen, und so reißen sich die lieben Kameraden um die Ehre, das Essen für je acht Mann zu holen. Du glaubst wohl gar aus Nächstenliebe? Mit den Erbsen ist's wie im Leben: die Hohlköppe schwimmen oben, die "mit was in" gehen der Sache, hier dem Feldkessel, stets auf den Grund! Nun kommt mein Partner zurück und meldet mir traurig, daß er nichts als "Dünnes" bekommen, und läßt mich zum Verweise auch mal hineinsehen; aber ängstlich, nicht umrühren. Dann gießt er vorsichtig, jede "Erschütterung" vermeidend, die Suppe in meinen Napf, immer wieder klagend, daß kein "Dickes" darin. Doch, mit einem schnellen Griffe lange ich hinein und hole mir meinen Teil [...] heraus, unter wildem Gefluche seinerseits: "Vielfraß, Unkameradschaftlich" usw. – Dieser Kampf, umso schwerer, da wir bisher nur nachts Essen erhielten, spielt sich täglich ab, überall das gleiche Theater." In Philipp Witkop, ed., *Kriegsbriefe gefallener Studenten* (Munich: Albert Langen, 1928), 303–304. Translation mine.

35. „[...] mein bester Kamerad [ist] ein Maurer, ein anderer ein Eisengießer." Ibid., 125. Translation mine.
36. „[...] gerade das, was wir erhofft hatten, nämlich den völligen Ausgleich der Standesunterschiede vor der Majestät der Opfer und vor dem allen gleichen Tod, gerade diesen Ausgleich wird es nicht geben. Sie glauben es nicht, - hier ein Bild: Schützengraben, drei Leute zanken sich um ein Brot. Drinnen die Offiziere bei Wein im Überfluß. Das Herz blutet." Ibid., 125. Translation mine.
37. Barbara Duden, "Das schöne Eigentum: Zur Herausbildung des bürgerlichen Frauenbildes an der Wende vom 18. zum 19. Jahrhundert," *Kursbuch* 47 (1977): 125–142, here 135–136.
38. „Weihnachten im Felde! [...] Schön war es, wie die Leute zusammenstanden, die Namen aufgerufen wurden, und die Pakete dann über die Köpfe hingereicht wurden – alle waren Weihnachtskinder, die vor ihren Paketen knieten, und kramten, bei Kerzenlicht [...]. [...] Alles, was man sich wünschen mochte, war überreich da: Wollsachen, Tabak, Spekulatius, Schokolade, Würste – alles Liebesgaben. Was hat Deutschland für uns getan!" Witkop, *Kriegsbriefe gefallener Studenten*, 29–30. Translation mine.
39. „Meine Lieben zu Hause essen jetzt wohl zu Mittag. Uns knurrt der Magen. Wenn ich daran denke, daß wir vielleicht noch zwei Tage hier sind ohne Brot und Wasser! Das ist gräßlich." Spengler, *Wir waren drei Kameraden*, 122.
40. Ziemann, *War Experiences in Rural Germany*, 199.
41. Ibid.
42. Weinreb, *Modern Hungers*, 20.
43. Belinda J. Davis, *Home Fires Burning: Food, Politics, and Everyday Life in World War I Berlin* (Chapel Hill: The University of North Carolina Press, 2000).
44. Robert L. Nelson, *German Soldier Newspapers of the First World War* (Cambridge: Cambridge University Press, 2011), 14.
45. Roper, *The Secret Battle*, 94–95.
46. Ulrich and Ziemann, *Krieg im Frieden*, 43, 47, 50.
47. See for instance Ulrich and Ziemann, *Krieg im Frieden*, 44, 50.
48. Ibid., 50.
49. "Es paßt sich nicht, daß ich in so ernster Zeit, wo das Schwarzbrot großen Wert hat, solch schwelgerisches Leben führe. Vor meinen weniger beachten Kameraden wurmt mich das, selbst wenn ich ihnen abgebe." In Witkop, *Kriegsbriefe gefallener Studenten*, 116–117. Translation mine.
50. Ziemann, *War Experiences in Rural Germany*, 92.
51. Ibid.

52. "Mein lieber Julius, [...] Für uns fangen jetzt schlimme Zeiten an, es gibt keine Kartoffeln mehr. Dafür gibt es 1 Pf. Brot und 100 g. Mehl. Leider kann man aber beides nicht bekommen, so hatten sie im Konsum in der ganzen Woche kein Brot. Ich bin froh, dass ich mir einige Kartoffeln im Keller gespart habe. Wenn doch der Frost nur endlich vorbei wäre, dann könnte man wenigstens etwas teures Gemüse kaufen. Das ganze Denken ist jetzt nur daruaf gerichtet, was können wir essen." In Jens Ebert, ed., *Vom Augusterlebnis zur Novemberrevolution: Briefe aus dem Weltkrieg 1914–1918* (Bremen: Donat, 1999), 191. Translation mine.
53. "Wenn du mal hier wärest, dann wärest du es schon länger satt. [...] Es ist in der Menage eine Kriegsküche gemacht worden und ich muss mir darin das Essen holen: du kannst dir wohl denken, welcher Frass das ist: wenn du das mal sähst, dann bekämst du eine Ahnung, was wir Frauen mitzumachen haben. 3 Pfund Kartoffeln, da müssen wir die ganze Woche von kochen; 50 gramm Fett pro Kopf. Reis gibt es, da laufen die Käfer durch, das ist allerhand für uns." In Ulrich and Ziemann, *Krieg im Frieden*, 79. Translation mine.
54. Ibid., 80.
55. „Im Gegensatz zu dem Schrecklichen, das wir erleben, haben wir hier im Ruhequartier, außer d. täglichen Dienst ein Schlemmerleben geführt; mehrere Treibjagden lieferten uns Hasenbraten u. Rebhühner u. das mit Nudeln u. Tunke und ein Glas Portwein dazu schmeckt doch herrlich; man dürfte es Euch, im darbenden Inland gar nicht erzählen." In Ebert, *Vom Augusterlebnis zur Novemberrevolution*, 195. Translation mine.
56. Ziemann, *War Experiences in Rural Germany*, 91.
57. "Daß unsere Verpflegung sehr mangelhaft ist, brauche ich wohl kaum zu versichern. Ich bitte aber, meiner Frau von all dem nichts zu sagen, ich habe ihr nämlich alles in möglichst günstigem Licht geschildert, um sie zu beruhigen und damit sie mir nichts schicken soll. Sie hat zwar selber nichts, aber sie würde sich das letzte vom Munde absparen und das muß ich naheliegenden Gründen doch verhindern." In Ulrich and Ziemann, *Krieg im Frieden*, 93. Translation mine.
58. "Mit dem Essen bin ich zufrieden - - - Liebe Frau ich bitte dich mach dir um mich keine Sorgen. Wir hierauße bekommen immer noch mehr wie Ihr. Kann auch bis jetzt nicht klagen - - - Liebe Frau mache Dir auch weiterhin um mich keine Sorgen, bin ja noch gesund u. mit dem Essen ist es auch reichlich." In Ulrich and Ziemann, *Krieg im Frieden*, 93. Translation mine.
59. „Unter lustigen Marschliedern marschierten wir durch die gepflasterten Gassen. Die Leute rannten herbei, brachten Körbe voll Schinkenbrötchen, Obst, Schokolade, Brot, Zucker, Marmeladen usw. Wo die Taschen nicht mehr ausreichten, wurden die Helme gefüllt. Das ganze Bataillon war ein essender, singender, springender, lachender

Soldatenzug, umringt von Hunderten von Einwohnern." Spengler, *Wir waren drei Kameraden*, 156–157. Translation mine.
60. "Eine in der Nähe wohnende Elsässerin, die gut deutsch sprach, lud mich zweimal zum Mittagessen ein. In der sauberen Wohnstube saß ich dann noch ein Stündchen mit andern Kameraden und der alten Großmutter, die Deutsche war, zusammen. Bei Plaudern und Zigarren verlebte ich hier nette Stunden, für die ich der Dame heute noch dankbar bin." Ibid., 149–150. Translation mine.
61. Schouten, "Fighting a Kosher War".
62. See Eugen Tannenbaum, ed., *Kriegsbriefe deutscher und österreichischer Juden* (Berlin: Neuer Verlag, 1915). http://sammlungen.ub.uni-frankfurt.de/freimann/content/titleinfo/1921612.
63. "Ich war durstig und bat in einem Haus um ein Glas Wasser. Eine jüdische Witwe gab mir das Verlangte; wir kamen ins Gespräch, und als sie hörte, dass ich auch Jude sei, führte sie mich ins Zimmer, wo der jüdische Feiertagstisch mit den beiden Kerzen, mit Äpfeln und Brot gedeckt war. „Sie müssen hier mit uns essen," und da nutzte kein Sträuben. Ich sprach das Kiduschgebet, teilte mit der guten Frau und ihren beiden Kindern das wohlschmeckende Abendessen, und wenn auch (die Unterhaltung, halb jiddisch, halb deutsch, einige Schwierigkeiten bereitete, so wandelte sich meine Rührung bald in Behaglichkeit." In Tannenbaum, *Kriegsbriefe*, 47–48. Translation mine.
64. "Die arme Marktfrau, die mit Äpfeln handelt, ruft: 'Do is er, der Jid,' Gott lass ihn gesund,' und täglich muss ich Einladungen zum Tee, zum Mittag- und Abendessen Folge leisten." Ibid., 49. Translation mine.
65. „Mein Quartier war äußerst behaglich; selten ließen meine Wirte, das freundliche Juwelierehepaar Plancot-Bourlon, mich mittags essen, ohne mir irgend etwas Gutes heraufzuschicken. Abends saßen wir bei einer Tasse Tee zusammen, spielten und plauderten. Besonders oft wurde natürlich die schwer zu beantwortende Frage erörtert, warum die Menschen Krieg führen müßten." Ernst Jünger, *In Stahlgewittern. Aus dem Tagebuch eines Stoßtruppführers* (Berlin: E. S. Mittler & Sohn, 1922), 122. http://www.gutenberg.org/files/34099/34099-h/34099-h.htm. English translation in Ernst Jünger, *Storm of Steel* (London: Penguin, 2003), 157.
66. "Vor einer armseligen Hütte setzte ich mich auf die Hausbank nieder, um etwas auszuruhen. Plötzlich stand neben mir ein altes Großmütterchen mit einem Holznapf voll Milch und einem Butterbrot. Wortlos reichte sie mir beides hin. Gierig aß ich, während mich die Alte mitleidig betrachtete und immer sagte: „O der Krieg! O der Krieg!" Ich dankte der Frau mit einem Vergelt's Gott, wie ich es aufrichtiger und inniger noch nie gesagt habe, und neu gestärkt, ging ich weiter." Spengler, *Wir waren drei Kameraden*, 48. Translation mine.

67. „Vor den Häusern standen massenhaft Juden mit Frauen und Kindern und hielten Zigaretten und Schokolade feil. Wir kauften gerne, denn uns dauerten all diese armen Teufel, wie sie [...] in ihre langen Kaftane gehüllt [...] uns so traurig anblickten." In *Die Sappe: 1. Bataillon, 19. Reserve-Infanterie-Regiment* No 7 – 1. Januar 1916. http://wl.bnu.fr/journauxtranchees/DieSappe.aspx. Translation mine.
68. „[...] in München hatte ich sie vor dem Ausmarsch gekauft und mir fest vorgenommen, sie nur zu essen, wenn ich länger als 24 Stunden irgendwo verwundet liegen sollte." Spengler, *Wir waren drei Kameraden*, 107. Translation mine.
69. Ibid., 87.
70. "[...] die Frau merkte, daß sie sich ein falsches Bild von den erwarteten Barbaren gemacht hatte. Zum Zeichen ihrer Dankbarkeit ('weil wir ihr das Haus nicht anzünden und sie und das Kind, das doch gar nichts für den Krieg könne, nicht ermorden wollten') holte sie drei Flaschen Rotwein aus dem Keller." Ibid., 84–85. Translation mine.
71. Hamlin, "The Fruits of Occupation," 87.
72. Ibid.
73. „Auf der Treppe sagte der alte Bauer weinend: „O, monsieur, c'est la guerre, quel malheur!" In der Küche schenkte er mir Milch und Brot, und die eine Frau kochte Kaffee. Dann schleppten sie Betten und Decken herbei. Der Alte und die zwei Frauen gingen in eine kleine Rumpelkammer, darin der tägliche Bedarf an Holz, Kartoffeln, Körbe, Gartengeräte und sonstiges Zeug aufgestapelt waren, und hockten sich weinend auf den blanken Steinboden." Spengler, *Wir waren drei Kameraden*, 107. Translation mine.
74. Hamlin, "The Fruits of Occupation," 87.
75. „[...] lange keine Frau oder ein Mädchen in den Armen gehabt." In Ebert, *Vom Augusterlebnis zur Novemberrevolution*, 73. Translation mine.
76. „[I]n den Stuben waren ein paar herrliche Mädchen. Ich setzte mich und verlangte ein Glas Tee, welchen man in jedem Hause haben kann." Ibid., 73. Translation mine.
77. *Die Sappe: 1. Bataillon, 19. Reserve-Infanterie-Regiment* No. 19 – 20. Februar 1917, 15.

Bibliography

Barthes, Roland. "Toward a Psychosociology of Food Consumption." In *Food and Drink in History*, edited by Robert Forster and Orest Ranum, 166–173. Baltimore: Johns Hopkins University Press, 1979.

Crouthamel, Jason. "Cross-Dressing for the Fatherland: Sexual Humour, Masculinity and German Soldiers in the First World War." *First World War Studies* 2, no. 2 (1 October 2011): 195–215. https://doi.org/10.1080/19475020.2011.613240.

Cwiertka, Katarzyna J. "Sustaining and Comforting the Troops in the Pacific War." In *Food in Zones of Conflict: Cross-Disciplinary Perspectives*, edited by Paul Collinson and Helen Macbeth, 133–144. New York, NY, US: Berghahn Books, Incorporated, 2014. http://ebookcentral.proquest.com/lib/unimelb/detail.action?docID=1644362.

Davis, Belinda J. *Home Fires Burning: Food, Politics, and Everyday Life in World War I Berlin*. Chapel Hill: The University of North Carolina Press, 2000. Accessed November 28, 2018. ProQuest Ebook Central.

Die Sappe: 1. Bataillon, 19. Reserve-Infanterie-Regiment No 7 – 1. Januar 1916 (in Colmar gedruckt). http://w1.bnu.fr/journauxtranchees/DieSappe.aspx.

Die Sappe: No. 19 – 20. Februar 1917 [Rumänien, gedruckt in Brasov-Kronstadt].

Douglas, Mary. "Deciphering a Meal." In *Food and Culture: A Reader*, edited by Carole Counihan and Penny Van Esterik, 36–54. New York: Routledge, 1997.

Duden, Barbara. "Das schöne Eigentum: zur Herausbildung des bürgerlichen Frauenbildes an der Wende vom 18. Zum 19. Jahrhundert." *Kursbuch* 47 (1977): 125–142.

Duffett, Rachel. *The Stomach for Fighting*. Manchester: Manchester University Press, 2015.

Ebert, Jens, ed. *Vom Augusterlebnis zur Novemberrevolution: Briefe aus dem Weltkrieg 1914–1918*. Göttingen: Wallstein, 2014.

Feltman, Brian K. *The Stigma of Surrender: German Prisoners, British Captors, and Manhood in the Great War and Beyond*. Chapel Hill: The University of North Carolina Press, 2015.

Gibson, Craig. *Behind the Front: British Soldiers and French Civilians, 1914–1918*. Cambridge: Cambridge University Press, 2014.

Hamlin, David. "The Fruits of Occupation: Food and Germany's Occupation of Romania in the First World War." *First World War Studies* 4, no. 1 (1 March 2013): 81–95. https://doi.org/10.1080/19475020.2012.761389.

Healy, Maureen. *Vienna and the Fall of the Habsburg Empire: Total War and Everyday Life in World War I*. Cambridge: Cambridge University Press, 2004.

Jünger, Ernst. *In Stahlgewittern. Aus Dem Tagebuch Eines Stoßtruppführers*. Berlin: E. S. Mittler & Sohn, 1922. http://www.gutenberg.org/files/34099/34099-h/34099-h.htm.

———. *Storms of Steel*. Translated by Michael Hoffmann. London: Penguin Books, 2003.

Lévi-Strauss, Claude. 1966. "The Culinary Triangle." Translated by Peter Brooks. *The Partisan Review* 33: 586–596.
Lipp, Anne. *Meinungslenkung im Krieg: Kriegserfahrungen deutscher Soldaten und ihre Deutung, 1914–1918*. Göttingen: Vandenhoeck & Ruprecht, 2003.
Nelson, Robert L. *German Soldier Newspapers of the First World War*. Studies in the Social and Cultural History of Modern Warfare. Cambridge: Cambridge University Press, 2011.
Remarque, Erich Maria. *Im Westen Nichts Neues*. Berlin: Propylän Verlag, 1929. https://archive.org/details/in.ernet.dli.2015.168305.
———. *All Quiet on the Western Front*. Lodi, NJ: Everbind Anthologies, 2011.
Roper, Michael. *The Secret Battle: Emotional Survival in the Great War*. Manchester: Manchester University Press, 2009.
Scheddin, Ernst. „Die leere Konservenbuechse bei uns als Universum." In *Die Wacht im Westen/Somme-Wacht: Kriegszeitung d. 1. Armee — 1917 (Januar–Mai)*, Nr. 21. Heidelberg University Library. https://doi.org/10.11588/diglit.2832#0187.
Spengler, Wilhelm. *Wir Waren Drei Kameraden: Kriegserlebnisse*. Freiburg i.B.: Herder, 1917. http://digital.staatsbibliothek-berlin.de/werkansicht?PPN=PPN734553889&PHYSID=PHYS_0008&DMDID=DMDLOG_0001&view=fulltext-endless.
Tannenbaum, Eugen, ed. *Kriegsbriefe deutscher und österreichischer Juden*. Berlin: Neuer Verlag, 1915. http://sammlungen.ub.uni-frankfurt.de/freimann/content/titleinfo/1921612.
Teuteberg, Hans-Jürgen. "Food Provisioning on the German Home Front, 1914–1918." In *Food and War in Twentieth Century Europe*, edited by Rachel Dufet, Alain Drouard, and Ina Zweiniger-Bargielowska, 57–59. Farnham: Ashgate, 2011.
Ulrich, Bernd. *Die Augenzeugen: deutsche Feldpostbriefe in Kriegs- und Nachkriegszeit 1914–1933*. Essen: Klartext, 1997.
Ulrich, Bernd, and Benjamin Ziemann, eds. *Krieg im Frieden: Die umkämpfte Erinnerung: Quellen und Dokumente*. Frankfurt/Main: Fischer, 1997.
Vincent, C. Paul. *The Politics of Hunger: The Allied Blockade of Germany, 1915–1919*. Athens, OH: Ohio University Press, 1985.
Weinreb, Alice. *Modern Hungers: Food and Power in Twentieth-Century Germany*. New York: Oxford University Press, 2017. https://doi.org/10.1093/acprof:oso/9780190605094.001.0001.
Witkop, Philipp, ed. *Kriegsbriefe gefallener Studenten*. Munich: Albert Langen, 1928.
Ziemann, Benjamin. *War Experiences in Rural Germany: 1914–1923*. London, UK: Bloomsbury Publishing PLC, 2006. http://ebookcentral.proquest.com/lib/unimelb/detail.action?docID=487187.

CHAPTER 4

Public Feeding in the First World War: Berlin's First Public Kitchen System

Jenny Sprenger-Seyffarth

Germany's global century was only a few years old when one of its most severe events took place in 1914. The First World War had impacts on people's everyday life all around the globe. One unifying element of almost all belligerent states was the effects of war on food and nutrition. Because of the war economy and food supply problems, most of them were more or less faced with food shortages during the years of warfare. Large European cities with their extreme supply difficulties were hit particularly hard. Within the framework of introducing a number of rationing and price control measures, public feeding institutions were established in almost every big city which was not only seen as an important measure to feed large parts of the population, but also to simplify the women's and families' everyday wartime routine.

In their management of the food supply in their cities, many German municipalities cooperated with philanthropic and charitable associations

J. Sprenger-Seyffarth (✉)
Freie Universität Berlin, Berlin, Germany

© The Author(s) 2019
H. M. Benbow and H. R. Perry (eds.), *Food, Culture and Identity in Germany's Century of War*,
https://doi.org/10.1007/978-3-030-27138-1_4

and set up public kitchens during the first weeks of the war. One of these cities, which made early experiences in the field of public charitable dining in wartime, was Berlin. Supported by different private charities with comprehensive expertise in the public provision of meals, the administration of Berlin and the local women's organization *Nationaler Frauendienst* (NFD, National Women's Service) developed a large network of so-called *Notküchen* (emergency kitchens) in the first half of the war. This mainly improvised system of emergency kitchens provided meals for thousands of needy Berliners daily and ensured Berlin's ability to adequately cushion the hardship of its population until state authorities began to intervene in the local supply policy during the spring of 1916.[1] After nearly two years of continuing deterioration of Germany's supply situation, military and state officials were under great pressure and forced to find appropriate means for the stretching and saving of available foodstuffs. Therefore, they tried to gain a hold on the food situation not only by giving instructions on the local policy of rationing but also by requesting the extensive creation of municipal kitchens. Subsequently, Berlin was asked to reorganize its public kitchen network. Being concerned about future food shortages the city administration began to set up a new public feeding program for all Berliners, the so-called *Berliner Volksspeisung* which was planned to become the flagship of the state's ability to provide an equitable distribution of foodstuffs. Surprisingly, little attention was given to Berlin's pre-1916 public feeding network which was not only dropped by city authorities but also considered as expendable.[2]

The development of Berlin's emergency kitchen system until 1916 has hardly been examined by previous research so far. Numerous publications like the works of Avner Offer and Dieter Baudis deal with Germany's or Berlin's food supply problems during the First World War without going into detail about public feeding.[3] George Yaney's study on the city's food administration during the First World War delivers a detailed description of Berlin's food supply problems, too.[4] Yaney's work as well as other research studies on welfare measures and people's everyday life during wartime mention the subject of public feeding but often treat it as a rather marginal issue. There is Ute Daniel's prominent study about German working-class women in wartime society which focusses on the nationwide development of public kitchens.[5]

Another general overview on public feeding in Germany is provided by Anne Roerkohl's work on municipal food supply in Westphalia during the First World War.[6] There also are some publications on wartime Berlin which draw attention to the development of public feeding in the capital city like Belinda J. Davis' comprehensive study on the Berlin "homefront."[7] Another important contribution is Keith R. Allen's work on the emergence of Berlin's public dining facilities since the nineteenth century.[8] However, Davis' and Allen's contributions concentrate on the events since spring 1916. They give little insight into the pre-1916 processes and primarily describe the development and ensuing failure of the *Berliner Volksspeisung* during the second half of the war. Not only the history of Berlin's first public kitchen system of 1914–1916 is left out in previous studies. The question of possible alternatives to the newly established municipal kitchen program of 1916 was also not raised.

In consideration of several archival resources, this chapter examines the emergence, structure and development of Berlin's first war kitchens during the First World War. It argues that the metropolis of two million inhabitants already had a broad and generally well-functioning public feeding system in 1916. With an expansion based on customer's needs, Berlin's charity-run system was an expedient and perhaps a more worthwhile alternative to the new introduced public feeding program in July 1916. After the examination of the pre-1916 system, the chapter demonstrates that Berlin's first public kitchen system was not perfect but had the potential to meet the needs of Berliners during forthcoming severe food crises. Thereafter the chapter gives an overview on the already well examined *Volksspeisung* and the context of its emergence. Like no other German city, the capital experienced an intensive state intervention in the field of public feeding. Military, state and city officials insisted on presenting a pioneering supply system and failed to recognize the potential of the previous feeding network. Moreover, because German authorities chose Berlin for a communal dining experiment which should serve as a role model for other cities, the attention of city and state authorities focused more on the set up of a prestigious large-scale meal hall system than on the actual needs of Berliners. Finally, the chapter draws attention to the developments of public feeding in the German cities Dresden and Hamburg and stresses the connection of continuity of one public kitchen system and its acceptance by the people.

Berlin's First Network of War Kitchens

When the war broke out in August 1914, the Berliners were familiar with public feeding institutions. Since the late nineteenth century an increasing number of—particularly working-class—Berliners were reliant on meals offered outside their homes. "[T]he rise of the wage economy, the growing distance between residence and workplace, the adoption of modern time-work discipline (especially the implementation of shorter lunch breaks) and the perception that greater numbers of women were working outside the home," Allen summarized, "created a new, and distinctly urban, diet."[9] Away from traditional and ordinary private family meal at home, the intake of meals in factory canteens and the use of public feeding facilities prevailed in everyday life of many working-class Berliners. As an alternative to the partially unaffordable meals of the factory canteens, public meal halls were created which offered cheap and nutritious food and drinks to their customers. A prominent operator of these meal halls was the *Volks-Kaffee- und Speisehallen-Gesellschaft* (People's Coffee and Dining Hall Society) with seven locations in Berlin and its surrounding area and almost 12,000 attendees per day on the eve of the war.[10] In addition to these commercial meal halls, a number of *Volksküchen* (public kitchens) run by philanthropic and charitable societies were available to Berliners. One of the best-known charities in the capital city was the *Verein der Berliner Volksküchen von 1866* (Berlin's Society for Public Kitchens since 1866) founded by philanthropist Lina Morgenstern during the Austrian–Prussian War. The society maintained several kitchens in the Berlin area that almost every day offered a low-priced, warm meal and were at times frequented by more than 7000 Berliners daily.[11] During the last years before the war, Morgenstern's facilities lost popularity due to the monotony of their meals which resembled more and more the soups for the poor provided by Berlin's *Armen-Speisungs-Anstalt* (Food Relief Centre for the Poor), which was a municipal offer for the poorest. Another big player in the field of pre-war public feeding in Berlin was the Jewish merchant Herrmann Abraham. The philanthropist addressed his public feeding engagement primarily to the youngest city dwellers. In 1893, Abraham founded the *Verein für Kindervolksküchen und Volkskinderhorte* (Society for the Care and Feeding of Children) that provided midday meals for thousands of young Berliners and schoolchildren in its numerous branches.

During the first days of the First World War, these and similar associations with their public meal facilities moved into focus of Berlin's city administration. As part of Berlin's food support program, the cities' charity-run public dining locations should play a major role in supplying food for the needy during wartime. On behalf of the magistracy of Berlin, the NFD organized the cooperation between city and its public feeding operators. Started in September 1914, the women had researched and got in touch with associations in Berlin which already ran or catered for one or more kitchen facilities. Moreover, attempts were made to locate corresponding premises that were suited for feeding larger groups of people.[12] The NFD had also enquired with various associations without feeding facilities whether they were willing to establish emergency kitchens during the difficult times. In doing so, they were supposed to take city regions without available public kitchens into account. Where the set-up of a kitchen was not considered necessary, the NFD strived for the construction of supply stations to which finished meals would be delivered.[13] Finally, during the first year of war the NFD's collaboration with a variety of associations had resulted in the development of a network of kitchens, dining rooms and meal supply stations spread across large parts of the capital city.

With the help of several archival documents and publications of the association *Zentrale für private Fürsorge* (Center for Private Welfare), it is possible to collate almost all public feeding facilities in Berlin (excluding suburbs).[14] The evaluation shows that there were at least 175 dining facilities in operation until 1916. Compared to other German and European metropolitan cities, practically nowhere else that many feeding facilities were located in one area.[15] The detected kitchens and dining rooms were provided by private charities, church associations, enterprises, municipal institutions as well as individuals who offered meals at their homes.[16] The majority of public feeding facilities was located in the north and east of Berlin and thereby in particular in the capital's working-class districts (see Fig. 4.1). A great number of facilities were offered in the affluent west; these facilities were predominantly private lunch tables of wealthy people for smaller groups of needy Berliners. A small number of dining rooms were also located in the south of the city, where Berlin's biggest dining hall, the *Kaiserhallen* at *Moritzplatz* was hosted. According to the newspaper *Berliner Tageblatt*, on its opening day 6000 vouchers were sold.[17] The second-largest dining facility with capacities for around 4500 Berliners was located in the *Landesausstellungspark*

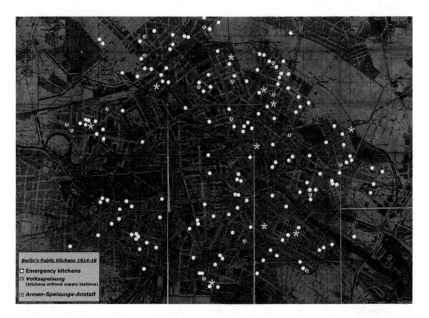

Fig. 4.1 Map of Berlin's public feeding network during the First World War

Moabit in the northwest.[18] Opened already on August 20, 1914, both of these citizen dining halls were two of four newly established facilities run by the Red Cross Society (see Fig. 4.2).

While the Red Cross Society held the largest dining halls, Abraham's *Verein für Kindervolksküchen* provided the greatest number of eateries. At the beginning of the war, the *Verein* was quick to take measures to meet the increased demand of children as well as adults. In early October 1914, Abraham's Verein explained to the magistracy:

> [...] We were obliged [...] to expand our institutions significantly and to enhance our service as well as to fulfill a fivefold increase of feeding. [...] At the suggestion of the Nationaler Frauendienst we created dining facilities for the unemployed wherever they were missed and agreed to establish new ones in all areas where they are considered necessary.[19]

For realization, Abraham's society made use of the entire assets of the *Verein* consisting of voluntary donations of citizens as well as dues of

Fig. 4.2 Outdoor view of Red Cross dining hall in Berlin, 1914

municipal authorities. Hence, in addition to the 18 existing eatery locations for children established until 1911 another 32 facilities were opened until early September 1914 (see Fig. 4.3).[20] Since the war broke out Abraham's *Verein* expanded and addressed a number of his eateries to adults. There were children kitchens with supply stations for adults as well as *Bürgerküchen* (citizen kitchens), *Mittelstandsküchen* (middle-class kitchens), kitchens for civil or public servants and eateries for artists. Side by side with the Red Cross and Abraham's kitchens, the *Verein der Berliner Volksküchen von 1866* and the *Volks-Kaffee- und Speisehallen-Gesellschaft* were largely responsible for the supply of poor Berliners. These two associations did not only run eight and six eateries, respectively, but also catered to a multitude of other facilities. Since spring 1916 the *Berliner Volksküchen* also provided their meals via traveling kitchens. These so-called *Goulaschkanonen* (stew cannons) were horse-drawn carriages which wheeled large kettles of soup through the streets of Berlin every day.[21] Another supplier was the *Verein zur Errichtung von Arbeiterinnenheimen* (Society for the Support of Female Workers Home).

Fig. 4.3 Feeding of army reservists' children by the *Verein für Kindervolksküchen und Volkskinderhorte* (Postcard, August 1914)

Its four institutions provided 1500 meals per day.[22] Not every kitchen and facility prepared meals at this scale. For the majority of the kitchens, there is often no more left than evidence of their—partly temporary— existence. It is difficult to assess how many meals were issued altogether by all emergency kitchens. Probably several thousand Berliners were supplied with lunch meals every day. And all of them had in common that they fulfilled the criterion of need.

As a measure for people who suffered hardship due to war, the participation of Berlin's emergency kitchens was exclusively reserved to needy Berliners. From the beginning, the magistracy instituted a procedure for the issue of meal tickets and distribution of meals. For the period of crisis caused by the war, the meal passes were given out in the first place to unemployed Berliners and needy relatives of soldiers who had continuous residence in Berlin since June 1, 1914.[23] Moreover, participation of people was accepted who did not belong to one of these groups and whose living conditions strongly deteriorated. Many of these were women who, despite the fact that they were active in the labor market, were not able to care for themselves. The Berliners concerned received their meal passes in the NFD's aid offices which worked closely with the municipal wartime welfare agency, in the institutions of the trade unions and the regional insurance institute. Following the magistracy's guidelines, two different passes were distributed. According to the degree of need, participants received white passes free of charge or gray passes with a deductible of ten pfennig.[24] The passes were issued for particular feeding facilities of contributing associations or enterprises and had validity only there. But they could be valid in other dining rooms and supply stations without own food preparation as well, because some public charities merely provided the premises and were supplied with meals by other associations or enterprises. For every pass, participants should receive half a liter "thick vegetables and potatoes as well as 50 to 70 [… grams of] meat in gross weight."[25] However, in practice both quantity and food ingredients varied from kitchen to kitchen.[26] Differences also existed regarding the pricing of portions in these various establishments. Initially, the magistracy calculated 25 Pfennig for each issued portion. Assuming that the majority of participants will bear two-fifths of the costs, the charities and the city shared expenses. In fact, in most cases the city bore the participant's costs as well. In this respect, the city was the main sponsor of the meals in Berlin's emergency kitchens.[27] The operators of emergency kitchens initially passed out the meals at their own expense. Redeemed meal passes in the kitchens had to be returned to the NFD's central office every week.[28] In the course of this, the advanced payment for food preparation was refunded by the NFD's budget for the food support program.[29]

The early efforts of the magistracy and the NFD to launch a large-scale and coordinated public meal service for large areas of the capital indicate that there was an increased need for public kitchens from the very beginning of the war. For example, in their opening days the spacious dining halls of the Red Cross experienced such a big rush that several customers were dismissed.[30] During the first days of their existence between 2000 and 6000 people went for lunch in these halls every day. Actually, in three of four Red Cross' facilities up to 12,000 portions were temporarily issued per day.[31] The daily numbers of issued meals decreased between 1500 and 2300 portions in November 1914. A month later they continued to decline (see Fig. 4.4). In March 1915, only about 2600 people visited the three facilities altogether. Thus, participation in the citizen dining halls had more than halved between November and March. This development started despite bread shortage and the commencing potato crisis. At the same time, it was the period

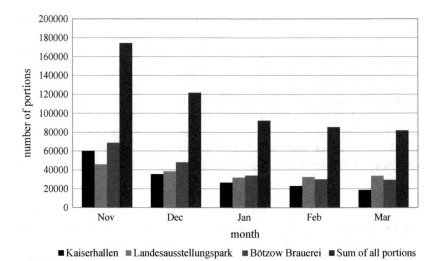

Fig. 4.4 Chart comparing number of meals served by Berlin Red Cross kitchens between November 1914 and March 1915

when unemployment had declined significantly and, therefore, a large part of participants disappeared.

Precise evidence for the use of all of the emergency kitchens is not provided by the available sources. There is no comprehensive overview of issued meals in Berlin's public kitchens during wartime. In addition to the early attendance figures for the citizen halls of the Red Cross, merely the NFD's weekly registrations for meal passes are available (see Fig. 4.5). As already mentioned, the NFD offices were not the only meal pass desks; hence, the registrations did not cover all of needy Berliners. A comparison of issued portions in the Red Cross facilities and the number of registered meal passes by NFD indicates that a considerable amount of meal tickets was approved outside NFD offices. Nevertheless, the data indicate a tendency of the development of the use of the war kitchens during the first half of the war. Similar to the development of participation in the Red Cross' dining halls, the weekly registrations for meal passes had already dropped by more than half between November and December 1914. The highest demand during the war—at least since the start of reports—was reported shortly before, in November, with more than 30,000 registrations per week. This was the same month when

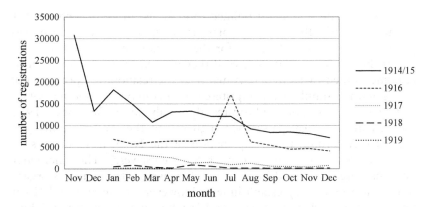

Fig. 4.5 Graph of weekly registration figures for meal passes from the NFD, 1914–1919

the offices recorded again a wave of new cases of people seeking help. Especially single unemployed women who lived on their savings until that time, now applied for unemployment benefit and, therefore, ranked among the participants of public kitchens.[32] Furthermore, since the end of November more members of soldiers' families were issued with meal passes on average than unemployed or other help-seeking people.[33] In January, the demand rose again to about 18,000 registrations per week. Even this figure was not reached again during the war. The registrations provide no evidence for an increased demand for public meals caused by the potato crisis in spring 1915. Even though the number of weekly registrations slightly rose again from March/April 1915, this seemed to be a consequence of the increased draft of new recruits. The NFD informed the magistracy that, as a result, not only the number of soldiers' families seeking help rose but also the headcounts of families. While during the beginning of war primarily young men were enlisted who often were "breadwinner of their mother or childless wife," now older men were recruited whose families counted "naturally much more children."[34] Since June, registrations declined month by month and even decreased under 10,000 per week in August 1915. This continued until June 1916. With regard to the other meal pass registration institutions, this trend of participation represents a small selection of the overall development in Berlin.

Needy Berliners were not obliged to make use of Berlin's emergency kitchen network. By choosing particular coupons in the NFD offices people concerned could decide for themselves if they wanted to make use of the charity-run kitchens or if they wanted to prepare their meals at home in their own kitchen. A glance at the relation of reported meal passes and the simultaneous registered food coupons (including potato and vegetable coupons) illustrates that only until December 1914 the demand for meal passes was higher than the food coupons (see Fig. 4.6). According to an explanation of the NFD, this can be seen as the desire of the women to cook for themselves.[35] The emergency kitchens were considered by city officials as well as the women's organization as a temporary establishment. However, at the end of 1914 it became obvious that the war would last longer than expected. Thus, the strengthened urge for domestic preparation of meals can also be understood as wish to return to halfway familiar conditions. Despite rarely available foodstuffs, the majority of Berliners preferred self-sufficiency. Regarding the everyday routine of war preservation of the private family meal (as paltry as it was) was an attempt to preserve old (pre-war) habits and through this one's own identity as well. Evidently, people equated the public kitchen attendance with social descent. Many

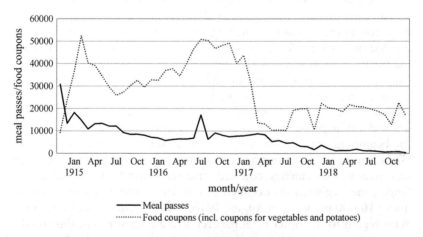

Fig. 4.6 Relation of weekly registered meal passes and food coupons, November 1914–December 1918

Berliners avoided the public meal because they were afraid that they would be spotted by acquaintances while visiting the kitchens.[36]

Nevertheless, in general the development of meal pass registrations emphasizes two things: On the one hand, it proves that several thousand inhabitants in need made use of the public kitchens every day, and on the other hand, the decreasing frequency can be considered as an indication for a halfway decent supply situation. However, the latter does not inevitably mean that needy Berliners were actually supplied sufficiently.

In early 1916, difficulties in the supply of food became pervasive in people's lives and as a consequence of people's insufficient nutrition health problems appeared increasingly. Besides the lack of foodstuffs and their high prices that caused supply problems, the increased growth of female employment in factories was another issue that hampered the self-supply of a large part of the population.[37] Women did no longer have the time to line up for hours in front of grocery stores. The overall situation called for action by military and state authorities. Having in mind prospective supply crises and the growing number of people in need, they were forced to find a long-term solution. The officials "came to the conclusion that the mass feeding institution could provide a comprehensive approach to tackling the changes wrought by the war economy as well as the food supply crisis."[38] In April 1916, Berlin and other Prussian cities received an order by the Prussian ministry of the interior to expand their public kitchen facilities. State officials regarded Berlin's activities during the first half of the war as a positive example of a functioning mass feeding initiative.[39] However, authorities on all levels were aware of the fact that an expansion of the public meal facilities would be necessary. As mentioned before, a further continuation of Berlin's first public feeding network was not considered.

Berlin's Public Kitchen System: Problems and Potential

Indeed, the emergency kitchen system had its pitfalls. First of all, the capacities to feed a larger part of the population were limited, though expandable. More problematic were organization and functioning regarding the control of an economical food consumption in the kitchens. Established as a temporary solution from the start, public kitchen operators enjoyed a relatively high level of autonomy in organizing their facilities. The procurement of food was managed with municipal assistance but mainly independent by the operating associations and enterprises. They received instructions for economical cooking as well but city officials had no certainty that the kitchens followed these cooking guidelines. Additionally, a degree of unwanted autonomy arose in terms of collecting the food coupons of rationed foodstuffs. Because not all public kitchens diligently collected food coupons, a legal increase of rations for single kitchen attendees was possible.[40] It must also be added that some kitchen operators and their cooks had not only a lot of experience but also were ingenious in combining non-rationed and unorthodox foodstuffs whereby the collection of food coupons was not always required and misconduct of kitchen operators was not in evidence.[41]

The magistracy, in principle, made efforts to avoid the misuse of emergency kitchens but was also permissive when its rules were neglected. For example, to stem the misuse of meal passes the NFD's aid offices got clear instructions from municipal authorities. The passes had to be stamped with the name of the participant and be "issued only in exchange for a receipt."[42] In addition to this, the magistracy requested that all meal pass permissions had to be compiled in a list which had to be submitted to the heads of district every week. After a number of aid offices considered the drawing up of the lists "completely impracticable" and criticized them as "unnecessary paperwork" the latter regulation was rejected by the NFD.[43] One of the aid offices also questioned that the personalization of meal passes would be of use:

> [... We would] undertake this extensive additional work if we were convinced about its appropriateness and were able to notice that a misuse of meal passes would be prevented by this. It is obvious that someone who wants to buy meal passes will not be stopped by personalization; eventually, the person who illegally buys the pass can easily take over the noted name on the pass.[44]

The majority of NFD offices, of course, followed the request of the magistracy and issued personalized meal passes but there were a couple of offices having not implemented this rule because of its additional workload.[45] A potential misuse of meal passes and food coupons enabled by the aid offices and kitchen operators was tolerated by city officials.

The structure of the kitchen network had two other characteristics that had a negative impact on the use of the kitchens by potential participants: its complexity and the verification of indigence. As a decentral organized system with more or less autonomously operating kitchen providers uniformity of the kitchen facilities was not given. On the contrary, complexity was created not only by the variety of public kitchens with different names like *Volksküche*, *Volksspeisehalle* (public dining hall), *Bürgerküche* or *Bürgerspeisehalle* (citizen dining hall) but also by the existence of some semi-public kitchens that were addressed to a particular group of the needy, including children's kitchens, canteens and middle-class kitchens. Little efforts were made to promote or explain the emergency kitchen network and its aim to Berliners.[46] The probably most difficult regulation was the verification of indigence. The disclosure of need was an obstacle for interested indigent Berliners and gave the kitchens a negative image. Furthermore, in some ways the limitation to the needy was contrary to the city officials' efforts to differentiate the war kitchens from the facilities of the separately operating municipal *Armen-Speisungs-Anstalt* which was already founded in 1800 and, since 1914, provided soups for poor Berliners whose plight was not caused by war.[47] From the point of view of many Berliners, there was no obvious difference between emergency kitchens and soup kitchens for the poor. Especially indigent lower middle-class women who feared losing their social status refused to use the public kitchens and stressed their preference for the private family meal.[48] Nonetheless, early newspaper articles provide some evidence that there were middle-class Berliners who used to participate in public feeding. The *Lokal-Anzeiger* reported on the public dining halls of the Red Cross that they united attendees from different social classes:

> Workers, business women, teachers, young men from the offices, haggard women in poor clothing holding their small ones or having them close, and so you sit here together, here in Berlin where otherwise every class, every small group likes to be separated from each other.[49]

It can be assumed that this described social diversity neither was continuously present until 1916 nor did it exist in all public kitchens. In general, middle-class Berliners avoided the public eateries but did not entirely reject the public meal at all. Abraham's semi-public middle-class kitchens which were addressed to skilled laborers as well enjoyed popularity to some extent and proved that an individual offer of public meals was worthwhile.[50] Among their peers, middle-class Berliners were willing to eat in a public kitchen. Between September 1914 and June 1916, Abraham's *Verein* issued about 7.4 million portions in the middle-class eateries and kitchens for civil servants. In May 1916, these kitchens' daily amount of issued portions was 27,380.[51] Abraham's facilities obviously met the needs of (middle-class) Berliners and are an excellent example of the public kitchen system's feasibility of an extensive public meal supply in Berlin. With the set-up of further (semi-)public facilities, Berlin's kitchen network not only was potentially able to supply even more people but also met the demands of the Prussian ministry of the interior.[52] With regard to the needs of the city's population, the city officials needed to abolish the verification of indigence and to promote the structure and aim of the public kitchen network in full transparency. And as shown, a further continuation of the emergency kitchen system necessarily needed a consequent implementation of control options that prevented a double coverage of participants and ensured economical food consumption in the kitchens.

BERLIN'S NEEDS IGNORED: THE FAILURE OF THE *VOLKSSPEISUNG*

Instead of using the potential of Berlin's charity-run kitchen network and in expanding the system in accordance with changing conditions, officials at all levels decided to initiate a completely new, large-scale and costly meal hall program. As Berlin's mayor Adolf Wermuth pointed out, from the point of view of the state authorities, public kitchens were kind of an "universal remedy," a solution for any food supply problem.[53] In addition to the order of the Prussian minister of the interior, the overall skeptical municipal leader received another instruction from the German chancellor Theobald von Bethmann-Hollweg to set up municipal meal halls that would serve "as a role model for other German cities."[54] Although Wermuth and other city officials were not convinced that a public meal program would solve the cities' supply problems in the long run, they yielded to the pressure of government and military authorities. George Yaney's assertion that "the directors of Berlin's food [administration] did not follow the army's commands or the commands that came down to them from civilian statesmen"[55] is not quite tenable given the city's course of action in the field of public feeding. Nonetheless, there was a kind of opposition among Berlin's food administrators to the governmental suggestions on how to reorganize the city's public meal distribution system. The state authorities' proposal to feed the capital by means of *Goulaschkanonen* was completely rejected by the city administration.[56] Wermuth and his subordinates preferred to think big and set up a system of ten main kitchens and a network of more than 70 supply stations. As Davis demonstrated:

> The kitchens and outlets would have a far greater capacity for production and distribution than stew cannons and would provide the opportunity for clients to eat on-site as well as to purchase food to take home. Wermuth also proposed that to improve equitable distribution, sites should be chosen by determining where the greatest need and demand for these kitchens existed.[57]

In the summer of 1916, the largest experiment of municipally sponsored restaurants called *Volksspeisung* was introduced in the capital. As Keith R. Allen pointed out "[w]ithin ten weeks, the city had assembled the kettles, cooks and storage space to create a quarter million quarts of soup per day."[58] It was the broadest and most promising meal distribution system throughout the German Empire.[59] Berlin's prestigious *Volksspeisung* was to demonstrate that the state had assumed control of the challenging food supply issue. State and city administrations hoped for great success of the public dining system that was financed by extensive state and imperial subsidies.[60] "Regardless of social classes and income differences," the Berlin archivist Ernst Käber pointed out, "the meal halls aimed to offer a midday meal for everyone that was enough for modest requirements [...] and tasteful, hearty and affordable."[61]

In fact, the *Volksspeisung* failed in practice because Berlin's food supply situation was not capable to meet the requirements of the large-scale communal feeding program.[62] Long before its establishment, the city was recurrently faced with supply shortages. To guarantee cheap, tasty and enough dishes, the *Volksspeisung* was reliant on constant and sufficient supply. This was the reason for widespread skepticism in Berlin's city administration. The supply situation itself was challenging and the new public kitchens that should be supplied by preference with foodstuffs made it even more difficult. Moreover, the *Volksspeisung* did not meet the needs of Berliners. It was capable of feeding 20% of the capital's population.[63] In fact, not even half of them made use of the kitchens in the darkest days of the war. During times of crisis, February and July 1917 in particular, the daily participation rate was 9–10%. In general, the facilities were frequented by 3–5% of Berliners on average. The Berlin officials believed that it would be enough to operate a public meal hall system that organized an equal distribution and meals to everyone without verification of indigence. The *Volksspeisung* convinced neither the middle-class nor the working-class Berliners.[64] The latter demanded a "kitchen for everyone" in the spring of 1916,[65] but with its main concentration on Berlin's working-class districts the *Volksspeisung* was neither designed for all Berliners—nor did its operation comply with the working day timetable of Berliners. An early targeted support for an extension of factory canteens expedited by military leaders in 1917 could have been more rewarding. Lower middle-class Berliners should have been addressed specifically as well. It was a fallacy to think that hardship would drive starving Berliners into the public eateries. As Davis pointed out, "hungry women remained resigned to running helplessly in the bitter cold from municipal sales outlet to retail shop and to protesting violently in the streets, still finding this more respectable than mass dining."[66]

Continuity and Acceptance: Positive Examples of Public Feeding in Germany

People's rejection of the public meal hall was not limited to the capital city. Even though the refusal was very strong in Berlin, it was also observed in other German cities.[67] The extent of reluctance was usually proportional to the public feeding system's design. This also included the time of the introduction of the particular kitchen system and its continued existence during wartime. A look at the public feeding developments in the cities Dresden and Hamburg illustrates that the continuity of one kitchen system can be seen as a relevant factor that had an effect on its acceptance.

In the early days of the war, Dresden established a public kitchen system which was similar to Berlin's pre-1916 system. The city administration cooperated with different private charities and philanthropic associations. All of them were united in the *Kriegsorganisation Dresdner Vereine* (Wartime organization of associations in Dresden) that formed a committee for public kitchens. This organized a decentral kitchen system that from the start was addressed to different groups of the needy. There were kitchens for the poor and unemployed as well as kitchens for soldiers' families. Since 1916 the kitchen system was opened to all Dresdners but its supplemented facilities were still aimed at different groups. Among others mobile kitchens, public kitchens and central kitchens with supply stations for civil servants and skilled laborers were set up. The number of facilities whose organization was controlled by the committee increased from 74 in September 1914 to 272 in early 1918.[68] During times of crisis, approximately 19% of the population made use of the public kitchens.[69] Even until the last days of the war, the rate of participants was 12%.[70] Partly due to tremendous propagandistic efforts, Dresden's city administration obviously managed to promote its public feeding system better than Berlin's did.

The public kitchens in Hamburg experienced an even broader participation. The second-largest German city in turn established a central kitchen system at the beginning of the war that was comparable to the *Volksspeisung* in Berlin. The city administration of Hamburg counted on public kitchens that were open to every Hamburger without verification of indigence. In August 1914, the system started with 54 kitchens which were set up in gyms, welfare institutions, factories and vacant offices. All of them were subordinated to and controlled by the *Speiseausschuss der Hamburgischen Kriegshilfe* (Public feeding committee of Hamburg's wartime welfare). Until June 1916, not only the number of kitchens rose to 80 but also 20% of the Hanseatic city population was supplied with a daily midday meal.[71] The early and swift expansion of Hamburg's war kitchens is an evidence that the people's demand for these facilities existed from the beginning and increased gradually. With up to 300,000 portions per day, the highest number of issued war kitchen meals was recorded in April 1917. According to Volker Ullrich, almost a third of Hamburg's inhabitants visited the public dining facilities at that time.[72] And the public kitchen's attendance rate remained at a relatively high level. By the end of the war, about 18% of Hamburgers made use of the kitchens every day. The city was not half as large as Berlin and its kitchens issued almost as many portions as the *Volksspeisung* in Berlin did.[73]

Previous research consistently concludes that the actions on public feeding in Germany in general were not a story of success.[74] In fact, it is undeniable that most Germans refused to make use of public kitchens as the cases Berlin, Dresden and Hamburg illustrate. Nonetheless, it must be recognized that the wartime dining halls met the needs of hundreds of thousand city dwellers. The demand for public meals which was mainly a reflection of the severity of the food supply crisis varied from place to place. It was also related to the developments of public feeding in the cities. The early established long-term kitchen systems of Hamburg and Dresden allow the assumption that the earlier a system was introduced the better it worked. On the one hand, early introduced public meal systems were already tested during the first food crises of the war. Due to these early experiences, the city administrations were able to optimize their systems regarding respective crises and increased hardship. On the other hand, the kitchens represented a kind of continuity. The kitchens' audience was clearly defined from the start and the people had time to accept the new institution as necessary relief effort. Considering the degree of acceptance as a benchmark, the cities Dresden and Hamburg represent successful examples.

Conclusion

Contrary to the hopes of German authorities the public kitchen turned out to be no "universal remedy." Even in Hamburg and Dresden public feeding did not help to solve local food supply problems. Of course, a further perpetuation of Berlin's first public feeding system would not have resolved the capital's problems of supply. The procurement of sufficient foodstuffs was the main concern of Berlin's administration which had to ensure the food supply autonomously from the beginning of the war and complained about the lack of state support.[75] Governmental aid in the form of securing a regular food supply would have been a greater benefit for Berlin's administration than a public meal hall program that was much too large and inoperative without sufficient foodstuffs.

Without doubt, a further perpetuation of Berlin's charity-run feeding system would not have won over the majority of Berliners for public dining. War changed the living conditions of families as well as their life together. The ritual of the private family meal was one of a few things in people's everyday life that provided a sense of "normality." Furthermore, the domestic table fellowship represented a social status which many Berliners were afraid to lose. Not only middle-class people but also many working-class Berliners refused to reveal their indigence and to make use of the public kitchens. As Allen pointed out, "in the realm of social reproduction the wartime state is believed to have aggressively intervened in the home lives of German men, women and children."[76] But wartime innovations that "brought entire industries under state control and reconfigured the labour force," Allen explained further, "did not [...] challenge the balance of power at the dinner table."[77] In the end, especially those made use of the municipal public meals who had no other choice due to their hardship. Because Berlin made the mistake to offer public kitchens only to needy people who had to verify their indigence, in the spring of 1916 the city administration and governmental advisors had to draw conclusions from the people's reluctance. According to Davis, the limits of unity of Berlin consumers were reflected by the public kitchens.[78] Besides a further perpetuation of Berlin's first public kitchen network, the promotion of an expansion of middle-class kitchens and factory canteens would have been a more appealing response to popular bias. Moreover, instead of ignoring the offers of assistance from experienced philanthropic meal providers and to compete with early public kitchen operators,[79] a further cooperation of all involved would have been more worthwhile. The continued existence of many kitchens of Berlin's pre-1916 system and their high level of participation confirm that Berliners who had the choice preferred to preserve a sense of personal identity. Finally, the examples of Dresden and Hamburg demonstrate as well, that more than the "mass feeding" of the *Volksspeisung*—which in the view of Abraham had been set up "to conform to an abstract ideal of equitable distribution, not to fulfill the actual needs of real people"[80]—an already established public kitchen system would have more readily earned the confidence of Berliners beyond the moments of crisis in 1917.

Notes

1. See Keith R. Allen, *Hungrige Metropole. Essen, Wohlfahrt und Kommerz in Berlin, 1870–1950* (Hamburg: Ergebnisse Verlag, 2002), 68.
2. This derives not only from the review of Berlin's wartime activities by the capital's mayor Adolf Wermuth but also from the interaction of Berlin's administration with its philanthropic public feeding operators in the summer of 1916 and afterward. During the construction phase of the new public feeding program, the city's food administration rejected philanthropic offers of support. See Adolf Wermuth, *Ein Beamtenleben: Erinnerungen* (Berlin: Scherl, 1922), 380. See also "Speisegemeinschaften," *Vorwärts*, 14 May 1916; Allen, *Hungrige Metropole*, 77. The Volksspeisung was intended to supply all Berliners including those who were formerly customers of the philanthropic emergency kitchens and should basically replace previous facilities for the needy.
3. See for example Avner Offer, *The First World War: An Agrarian Interpretation* (Oxford: Clarendon Press, 1989), 22–78; Dieter Baudis, "'Vom Schweinemord zum Kohlrübenwinter'. Streiflichter zur Entwicklung der Lebensverhältnisse in Berlin im Ersten Weltkrieg, August 1914 bis Frühjahr 1917," *Jahrbuch für Wirtschaftsgeschichte* (1986): 128–157.

4. George Yaney, *The World of the Manager: Food Administration in Berlin During World War I* (New York: Peter Lang, 1994).
5. Ute Daniel, *Arbeiterfrauen in der Kriegsgesellschaft* (Göttingen: Vandenhoeck & Ruprecht, 1989).
6. Anne Roerkohl, *Hungerblockade und Heimatfront. Die kommunale Lebensmittelversorgung in Westfalen während des Ersten Weltkrieges* (Stuttgart: Franz Steiner, 1991), 230–260.
7. Belinda J. Davis, *Home Fires Burning: Food, Politics, and Everyday Life in World War I Berlin* (Chapel Hill: University of North Carolina Press, 2000), 137–158.
8. Allen, *Hungrige Metropole*, 59–82.
9. Keith R. Allen, "Food and the German Home Front: Evidence from Berlin," in *Evidence, History and the Great War*, edited by Gail Braybon (New York: Berghahn Books, 2002), 174.
10. See "Geschäftsbericht der *Volks-Kaffee- und Speisehallen-Gesellschaft*," 25. Betriebsjahr (1913), 20. LAB, Rep. 001–02, Nr. 1931.
11. For further details on the society see Allen, *Hungrige Metropole*, 41–50; Harald Dehne, "'Das Essen wird also auch 'ambulando' eingenommen.' Das 'belegte Brot' und andere schnelle Kostformen für Berliner Arbeiterinnen und ihre Kinder im Kaiserreich," in *Brot, Brei und was dazugehört. Über sozialen Sinn und physiologischen Wert der Nahrung*, edited by Martin Schaffner (Zürich: Chronos, 1992), 116–117.
12. This emerges from several letters of the NFD's co-founder, Hedwig Heyl, to Berlin's second mayor, Georg Reicke, in September 1914. LAB, A Rep. 001–02, 1931.
13. Nationaler Frauendienst, Abteilung Berlin, Kriegsjahr 1914–1915 (Berlin: W. Moeser Buchdruckerei, 1915), 20.
14. For the near-complete list see Jenny Seyffarth, "'Wenn Hunger und Not in den Krieg ziehen...' Zur Rolle großstädtischer Massenspeisungsanstalten während des Ersten Weltkrieges am Beispiel Berlins" (Master thesis, Freie Universität Berlin, 2009), 105–108. Among others profitable sources were "Vervollständigtes Verzeichnis der Speiseanstalten in Berlin nach dem Bericht des Polizeipräsidenten." LAB, A Rep. 001–02, 1932. And Siddy Wronsky and Edmund Friedeberg, *Handbuch der Kriegsfürsorge im Deutschen Reich*, edited by Zentrale für private Fürsorge (Berlin: Franz Vahlen, 1917), 266–270.
15. Another city with a large number of public kitchens was Vienna. In 1916/17, the capital of the Habsburg Empire had about 300 facilities. But in comparison with Vienna which, too, had a population of two million, the Berlin area was more than four times smaller (5.9–27.3 hectare).
16. This is the result of evaluation of available sources. It can be assumed that there were more (especially private) eateries, which have not been

mentioned. Furthermore, beside temporary closures not every kitchen survived the first two years of war. According to Käber, the number of all kitchens in the Greater Berlin area was 220. See Ernst Käber, *Berlin im Weltkriege: Fünf Jahre städtischer Kriegsarbeit* (Berlin: Trowitzsch, 1921), 563.

17. See "Die Massenspeisung," *Berliner Tageblatt*, 20 August 1914.
18. See "Beim Mittagessen für 10. Pf.," *Lokal-Anzeiger*, 1 September 1914.
19. *Verein für Kindervolksküchen* to the magistracy, 3 October 1914. LAB, A Rep. 001–02, 1931. Transl. mine.
20. See overview of kitchens for children of the *Verein für Kindervolksküchen*, ibid.
21. See Allen, *Hungrige Metropole*, 59.
22. See *Verein zur Errichtung von Arbeiterinnenheimen* to the magistracy, 8 September 1914. LAB, A Rep. 001–02, 1931.
23. These persons usually were recipients of financial support by city and state, hence their indigence was validated by the welfare and NFD offices. See "Regelung der Speisemarken in 12 Punkten," in Hilfefonds- und Zuwendungen für Volksküchen und Speiseanstalten, 33–34; "Beschlussfassungsvorlagen für die Stadtverordnetenversammlung zu Berlin," 7 November 1914, 872; Gertrud Bäumer (NFD) to the magistracy, 27 November 1914. LAB, A Rep. 001–02, 1932.
24. The decision of additional payment was made by the NFD office members. Generally, single persons "who had to be regarded by preference," payed extra. See "Regelung des Speisemarkenverkehrs für den Nationalen Frauendienst," in Hilfefonds- und Zuwendungen für Volksküchen und Speiseanstalten, 30, ibid.
25. Nationaler Frauendienst, 1914–1915, 20; Catherine Elaine Boyd, "Nationaler Frauendienst. German Middle-Class Women in Service to the Fatherland, 1914–1918" (PhD diss., University of Georgia, 1979), 99.
26. See "Berichte des Städtischen Untersuchungsamtes für hygienische und gewerbliche Zwecke über die Untersuchung der verabreichten Speisen in den Berliner Notstandsküchen und anderen gemeinnützigen Speiseanstalten," 26 October 1914, 6 November 1914, and 16 December 1914. LAB, A Rep. 001–02, 1932. See *Verein für Kindervolksküchen* to the magistracy, 3 October 1914. LAB, A Rep. 001–02, 1931. NFD to councilor Karl Doflein, 7 March 1916. LAB, A Rep. 001–02, 1934.
27. See "Stenographischer Bericht über die Sitzung der Stadtverordnetenversammlung," 12 November 1914. LAB, A Rep. 001–02, 1932. The regulations can be retraced in the correspondence between the Red Cross Society and the magistracy. See letter of the Red Cross to mayor Wermuth, 18 August 1914 and 31 October 1914. LAB, A Rep. 001–02, 1931/1932.

28. See NFD to the magistracy, 7 September 1914. LAB, A Rep. 001–02, 1931.
29. Every week the NFD received municipal funds amounting between 15,000 and 20,000 Marks per week. See "Stenographischer Bericht." Furthermore, see the letter of the NFD to Berlin's lord mayor Adolf Wermuth, 4 December 1914 (ibid.). See also various written weekly demands of the NFD to the magistracy. LAB, Rep. 001–02, 1931–1935. See also Boyd, "Nationaler Frauendienst," 64.
30. See "Massenbesuch in den Bürgerspeisehallen," *Berliner Morgenpost*, 21 August 1914. See also "Beim Mittagessen für 10. Pf." and "Die Massenspeisung."
31. See "Beschlussfassungsvorlagen." In comparison with other information, the number of issued portions was relatively high. Even though a verification is not possible, it should be queried.
32. See NFD aid office (*Hilfskommission*) no. IVA to the NFD head office, 19 November 1914. LAB, A Rep. 001–02, 1932.
33. See NFD to the magistracy, 27 November 1914, ibid. Letter of the NFD to the magistracy, 22 April 1915. LAB, A Rep. 001–02, 1933.
34. NFD to the magistracy, 13 and 22 April 1915, ibid.
35. See Nationaler Frauendienst, 1914–1915, 24.
36. See Agnes von Harnack, *Der Krieg und die Frauen* (Berlin: Springer, 1915), 8–9.
37. Hugo Lindemann, *Die deutsche Stadtgemeinde im Kriege* (Tübingen: Mohr, 1917), 91.
38. Jenny Sprenger-Seyffarth, "Public Kitchens (Germany)," in *1914–1918-Online. International Encyclopedia of the First World War*, edited by Ute Daniel, Peter Gatrell, Oliver Janz, Heather Jones, Jennifer Keene, Alan Kramer, and Bill Nasson, issued by Freie Universität Berlin, Berlin, 16 January 2017, https://doi.org/10.15463/ie1418.11033.
39. See Allen, "Food," 176.
40. See Daniel, *Arbeiterfrauen*, 202.
41. See for example Yaney's presentation on the extraordinary performance of Herrmann Abraham's kitchens. Yaney, *The World*, 207.
42. See "Regelung des Speisemarkenverkehrs," 30.
43. See NFD to the magistracy, 27 November 1914. See also letters of the NFD aid offices no. IVA and no. VIIIB to the NFD head office, 19 and 21 November 1914. LAB, A Rep. 001–02, 1932.
44. NFD aid office no. IVA to the NFD head office, 19 November 1914, ibid. Transl. mine.
45. See NFD aid office no. XIIB to the NFD head office, 20 November 1914, ibid.

46. Besides some newspaper articles about single facilities, information on the whole kitchen network was rarely available. The *Zentrale für private Fürsorge* published some handbooks on Berlin's welfare institutions that included a list of the city's public kitchens but it is unclear how many Berliners were able to access the publications.
47. There was a difference between "new" needy people who suffered hardship due to war and were supported by wartime public relief and the "old" needy who were—like in pre-war years—recipients of poor relief and often participants of the associated *Armen-Speisungs-Anstalt*. City authorities dismissed the involvement of the *Armen-Speisungs-Anstalt* in the public kitchen network. Similar to the wartime public relief support they emphasized that the emergency kitchens do not give the impression of the disdained soup kitchens for the poor. Recipients of poor relief have not received meal passes for the cities' emergency kitchens and were supposed to continue visiting the kitchens of the *Armen-Speisungs-Anstalt*. See Seyffarth, "Hunger und Not," 52.
48. See Daniel, *Arbeiterfrauen*, 203–204. See also "Die billige Küche des Berliners," *Der Morgen*, 24 January 1916; August Skalweit, *Die deutsche Kriegsernährungswirtschaft* (Stuttgart: Deutsche Verlags-Anstalt, 1927), 47.
49. "Beim Mittagessen für 10. Pf." Transl. mine.
50. See Allen, "Food," 175; Allen, *Hungrige Metropole*, 67; Yaney, *The World*, 221–224.
51. Figures without additional portions. See Herrmann Abraham, *Drei Kriegsjahre. Erlebtes und Geschaffenes* (Berlin: Kießling & Krüger, 1917), 18.
52. See order of the Prussian ministry of the interior on public feeding in Prussian cities, 14 April 1916. GStAPK, I. HA 197A, Nr. 164, 2–3.
53. See Wermuth, *Beamtenleben*, 380; Roerkohl, *Hungerblockade*, 234. On the development of the *Volksspeisung* see Allen, *Hungrige Metropole*, 70–77; Davis, *Home Fires*, 137–158; Jenny Sprenger-Seyffarth, "'Es ist doch geradezu ein Skandal...!' - Die Berliner Volksspeisung im Ersten Weltkrieg zwischen Qualität und sozialem Stigma," in *Semmeln aus Sägemehl. Lebensmittelskandale des 19. und 20. Jahrhunderts als Orte des Wissens*, edited by Swen Steinberg and Frank Jacob (Baden-Baden: Nomos, forthcoming).
54. Wermuth, *Beamtenleben*, 380.
55. Yaney, *The World*, 5.
56. See Wermuth, *Beamtenleben*, 380; Theodor Wolff, *Tagebücher 1914–1919*, vol. 1 (Boppard am Rhein: Harald Boldt Verlag, 1984), 377.
57. Davis, *Home Fires*, 140.
58. Allen, "Food," 176.

59. See Allen, *Hungrige Metropole*, 70.
60. See Allen, "Food," 178.
61. Käber, *Berlin*, 146. Transl. mine.
62. See Allen, *Hungrige Metropole*, 74.
63. See Seyffarth, "Hunger und Not," 79.
64. See Davis, *Home Fires*, 145.
65. See "Der 'Lebensmittel-Diktator' und die Massenspeisung," *Vorwärts*, 18 May 1916.
66. Davis, *Home Fires*, 152.
67. Seyffarth, "Hunger und Not," 85–86.
68. See *Schlußbericht über die Tätigkeit der Kriegsorganisation Dresdner Vereine* (Dresden, 1920), 37.
69. According to the census of December 1910 indicating a population of 548,308. See Friedrich Döhling, *Das Problem der Massenspeisung und die Massenspeisungsbewegung in Deutschland, im Speziellen in München* (München: Max Steinebach, 1918), 65–66. See also *Schlußbericht*, 19. A much higher result is presented in Carsten Schmidt, "Zwischen Burgfrieden und Klassenkampf. Sozialpolitik und Kriegsgesellschaft in Dresden 1914–1918" (PhD diss., Technische Universität Dresden, 2007), 255.
70. See Skalweit, *Kriegsernährungswirtschaft*, 51.
71. See Dieter Riesenberger, *Das Deutsche Rote Kreuz. Eine Geschichte 1964–1990* (Paderborn: Schöningh, 2002), 170.
72. See Volker Ullrich, *Kriegsalltag. Hamburg im ersten Weltkrieg* (Köln: Prometh, 1987), 64.
73. See Seyffarth, "Hunger und Not," 85; Skalweit, *Kriegsernährungswirtschaft*, 50–51.
74. See for example Roerkohl, *Hungerblockade*, 243.
75. Anne Roerkohl, "Die Lebensmittelversorgung während des Ersten Weltkrieges im Spannungsfeld kommunaler und staatlicher Maßnahmen," in *Durchbruch zum modernen Massenkonsum. Lebensmittelmärkte und Lebensmittelqualität im Städtewachstum des Industriezeitalters*, edited by Hans-Jürgen Teuteberg (Münster: Franz Steiner 1987), 312; Wermuth, *Beamtenleben*, 374–375.
76. Allen, "Food," 179.
77. Ibid.
78. See Davis, *Home Fires*, 141.
79. See Allen, *Hungrige Metropole*, 77.
80. Yaney, *The World*, 224.

Bibliography

Abraham, Herrmann. *Drei Kriegsjahre. Erlebtes und Geschaffenes.* Berlin: Kießling & Krüger, 1917.
Allen, Keith R. "Food and the German Home Front: Evidence from Berlin." In *Evidence, History and the Great War*, edited by Gail Braybon, 172–197. New York: Berghahn Books, 2002.
Allen, Keith R. *Hungrige Metropole. Essen, Wohlfahrt und Kommerz in Berlin, 1870–1950.* Hamburg: Ergebnisse Verlag, 2002.
Baudis, Dieter. "'Vom Schweinemord zum Kohlrübenwinter.' Streiflichter zur Entwicklung der Lebensverhältnisse in Berlin im Ersten Weltkrieg, August 1914 bis Frühjahr 1917." *Jahrbuch für Wirtschaftsgeschichte* (1986): 128–157 (Special Issue).
Boyd, Catherine Elaine. "Nationaler Frauendienst. German Middle-Class Women in Service to the Fatherland, 1914–1918." PhD diss., University of Georgia, 1979.
Daniel, Ute. *Arbeiterfrauen in der Kriegsgesellschaft.* Göttingen: Vandenhoeck & Rupprecht, 1989.
Davis, Belinda J. *Home Fires Burning: Food, Politics, and Everyday Life in World War I Berlin.* Chapell Hill: University of North Carolina Press, 2000.
Dehne, Harald. "'Das Essen wird also auch 'ambulando' eingenommen.' Das 'belegte Brot' und andere schnelle Kostformen für Berliner Arbeiterinnen und ihre Kinder im Kaiserreich." In *Brot, Brei und was dazugehört. Über sozialen Sinn und physiologischen Wert der Nahrung*, edited by Martin Schaffner, 105–123. Zürich: Chronos, 1992.
Döhling, Friedrich. *Das Problem der Massenspeisung und die Massenspeisungsbewegung in Deutschland, im Speziellen in München.* München: Max Steinebach, 1918.
Harnack, Agnes von. *Der Krieg und die Frauen.* Berlin: Springer, 1915.
Käber, Ernst. *Berlin im Weltkriege: Fünf Jahre städtischer Kriegsarbeit.* Berlin: Trowitzsch, 1921.
Lindemann, Hugo. *Die deutsche Stadtgemeinde im Kriege.* Tübingen: Mohr, 1917.
Nationaler Frauendienst, Abteilung Berlin, Kriegsjahr 1914–1915. Berlin: W. Moeser Buchdruckerei, 1915.
Offer, Avner. *The First World War. An Agrarian Interpretation.* Oxford: Clarendon Press, 1989.
Riesenberger, Dieter. *Das Deutsche Rote Kreuz. Eine Geschichte 1964–1990.* Paderborn: Schöningh, 2002.
Roerkohl, Anne. "Die Lebensmittelversorgung während des Ersten Weltkrieges im Spannungsfeld kommunaler und staatlicher Maßnahmen." In *Durchbruch zum modernen Massenkonsum. Lebensmittelmärkte und Lebensmittelqualität*

im Städtewachstum des Industriezeitalters, edited by Hans-Jürgen Teuteberg, 309–370. Münster: Franz Steiner, 1987.

Roerkohl, Anne. *Hungerblockade und Heimatfront. Die kommunale Lebensmittelversorgung in Westfalen während des Ersten Weltkrieges.* Stuttgart: Franz Steiner, 1991.

Schlußbericht über die Tätigkeit der Kriegsorganisation Dresdner Vereine. Dresden, 1920.

Schmidt, Carsten. "Zwischen Burgfrieden und Klassenkampf. Sozialpolitik und Kriegsgesellschaft in Dresden 1914–1918." PhD diss., Technische Universität Dresden, 2007.

Seyffarth, Jenny. "'Wenn Hunger und Not in den Krieg ziehen… ' Zur Rolle großstädtischer Massenspeisungsanstalten während des Ersten Weltkrieges am Beispiel Berlins." Master thesis, Freie Universität Berlin, 2009.

Skalweit, August. *Die deutsche Kriegsernährungswirtschaft*. Stuttgart: Deutsche Verlags-Anstalt, 1927.

Sprenger-Seyffarth, Jenny. "'Es ist doch geradezu ein Skandal…!' - Die Berliner Volksspeisung im Ersten Weltkrieg zwischen Qualität und sozialem Stigma." In *Semmeln aus Sägemehl. Lebensmittelskandale des 19. und 20. Jahrhunderts als Orte des Wissens*, edited by Swen Steinberg and Frank Jacob. Baden-Baden: Nomos, forthcoming.

Sprenger-Seyffarth, Jenny. "Public Kitchens (Germany)." In *1914–1918-Online. International Encyclopedia of the First World War*, edited by Ute Daniel, Peter Gatrell, Oliver Janz, Heather Jones, Jennifer Keene, Alan Kramer, and Bill Nasson. Issued by Freie Universität Berlin, Berlin, 16 January 2017. https://doi.org/10.15463/ie1418.11033.

Ullrich, Volker. *Kriegsalltag. Hamburg im ersten Weltkrieg*. Köln: Prometh, 1987.

Wermuth, Adolf. *Ein Beamtenleben: Erinnerungen*. Berlin: Scherl, 1922.

Wolff, Theodor. *Tagebücher 1914–1919*, vol. 1. Boppard am Rhein: Harald Boldt Verlag, 1984.

Wronsky, Siddy, and Edmund Friedeberg. *Handbuch der Kriegsfürsorge im Deutschen Reich*, edited by Zentrale für private Fürsorge. Berlin: Franz Vahlen, 1917.

Yaney, George. *The World of the Manager: Food Administration in Berlin During World War I*. New York: Peter Lang, 1994.

CHAPTER 5

Coping with Hunger in the Ghettos: The Impact of Nazi Racialized Food Policy

Helene J. Sinnreich

The Nazi regime, traumatized by the impact of food shortages during World War I, ruthlessly guarded food access for Germans which the Nazis deemed racially superior.[1] By extension, those deemed by the regime as racially inferior were not allocated resources and in fact resources could be extracted from those deemed racially inferior to benefit those categorized as racially superior.[2] Thus, Nazi racial policy enabled some groups, including Jews, to be stripped of their valuables based on race while others by virtue of their birth were entitled to goods and valuables. In addition, Germans were paid more for labor than those deemed racially inferior and were exclusively permitted to engage in certain types of labor while those deemed racially inferior or not politically aligned to the regime were excluded from certain occupations, earning less or not compensated at all for the same labor. This meant that individuals' resources in the form of labor and valuables were impacted by the regime's racial categories. Not only did race influence the value of resources available to different individuals, but the price

H. J. Sinnreich (✉)
University of Tennessee, Knoxville, TN, USA

© The Author(s) 2019
H. M. Benbow and H. R. Perry (eds.), *Food, Culture and Identity in Germany's Century of War*,
https://doi.org/10.1007/978-3-030-27138-1_5

of food and rations available were different for various racially defined groups within Nazi-occupied Europe, resulting in different prices for the same food. Germans received higher rations while those of lower racial status within the Nazi hierarchy were eligible for fewer rations. In addition to rationing in the licit markets, the actual price at which individuals could permissibly purchase food was sometimes different than those from lower racial categories. For the Jews of Nazi-occupied Europe who inhabited such a lowly status within the Nazi hierarchy, food deprivation was widespread. Jews were doubly impacted in that (1) their ability to put together a mass of valuables and labor sufficient to survival was hampered by Nazi policy and (2) the prices they paid for food on both the legal and illegal markets were often higher than for non-Jews. As a result, Jews suffered impoverishment and starvation at high rates, which resulted in rapid decimation of the population.[3] Such dispossession occurred is in the Jewish ghettos of the Nazi period.

Ghettos were created in occupied territories outside pre-war Germany and Jewish entry into ghettos often preceded Jewish entry into concentration camps. As scholarship on ghettos in Nazi-occupied Europe has expanded, it has become apparent that one cannot speak of a monolithic ghetto experience.[4] A wide variety of ghetto configurations under Nazi occupation adopted different food policies in different ghettos and at various points in individual ghettos' existence.[5] Despite the variety of ghettos, overall ghetto conditions in Nazi-occupied Europe were sites of great food insecurity and a site where Jews make active of many of their resources. Although concentration camps often had even worse conditions, a great deal of documentation from within ghettos and about ghettos survived the war, including diaries and Jewish ghetto administration records, as well as Nazi records.

This chapter seeks to examine access to food as an aspect of wartime survival for Jewish ghetto populations during World War II. While seeking to demonstrate common experiences in the Jewish ghetto experience vis-à-vis food, it also strives to document different experiences of wartime hunger based on socioeconomic status, geographic location, and coping methods.

Setting the Stage: Food Security and Insecurity Before Ghettoization

Pre-war socioeconomic status greatly impacted the level of resources available to individuals, families and even communities to resist hunger. Food insecurity began for some Eastern European Jews well before Nazi occupation. In many places, wide sections of the Jewish population were reliant on food assistance from local and international charities. In fact, even after German Jews were under Nazi authority and denied state, aid, the Joint Distribution Committee which provided relief funds to European Jewry continued to focus on providing the largest share of their funds in assistance of Eastern European Jews living in poverty.[6] The Nazi offensive coupled with the exclusion of Jews from emergency food relief created a strain on Jewish access to food. For those who were already food insecure before the German invasion, this became a deadly situation. For those Jews who were not food insecure before the Nazi conquest, the German invasion and subsequent occupation etched away at Jews' ability to insulate themselves from food insecurity and impoverishment. For those with modest means, the selling of possessions served as an important coping strategy to keep food on the table but often eventually led a family into impoverishment. Looting of Jewish homes and places of business, the seizing of bank accounts, the confiscation of businesses and the exclusion from practicing many professions impacted Jews from all socioeconomic strata. The affluent, however, if they were able to protect valuables from theft and seizure, often had a better situation and could sell off valuables for food for a longer period of time. For example, after the German occupation of Lvov, Leszek Allerhand's "affluent family still had resources to purchase white bread from the Germans for his parents and grandparents, as it struggled to adapt to a diet consisting of black bread and marmalade."[7]

Pre-war socioeconomic status of individuals was not the sole metric in determining food accessibility. The pre-ghetto experience of Jews, including how much of their valuables they were able to retain as they entered the ghetto, often played a significant role in food access during the ghetto period. One important factor was location at the time of ghettoization. A person's country of residence and when it came under occupation could be significant. For example, Jews in Hungary were ghettoized for a much shorter period than Jews in many Polish cities. This meant that the resources an individual had in a protracted ghetto would have to last longer. The type of community could be impactful on food access. In some cases, rural Jews were not ghettoized until later and could benefit from the ability to live off the land. Other times, provincial or smaller town ghettos were liquidated early and the survivors of the liquidation would be deported with few belongings to a ghetto in a larger city. The individual path to ghetto residence was an important factor in the person's economic situation. For those who lived in a home that was included in the ghetto area, they were often spared the trauma of having to carry their possessions with them and being limited in what they could bring. However, this did not guarantee the safety of their belongings because even after the closing of the ghettos, there were often thefts and raids. "In the Kassa ghetto, for example, according to a survivor's report she was to bring with her two pieces of clothing, a pair of shoes, two weeks' worth of groceries, two blankets, and two pillows. Most of these items, however, were taken by gendarmes in the course of 'house searches,' after which only a few articles of clothing were left for the ghetto inhabitants."[8] In addition to official property seizures, there were also official and unofficial raids of Jewish homes by various German and local authorities. These lootings often targeted small valuables as well as commodities such as food. Eva Heyman from the Nagyvarad Ghetto noted in her diary when they were moving into the ghetto that the gendarmes seized all the food they had intended to take from their pantry to the ghetto.[9]

Those deported to ghettos often had varying amounts of notice, ranging from a few hours to a few months, to make preparations and select belongings to take with them. For those with little notice, this could heavily impact their selection of personal items. Due to religious restrictions on maintaining stores of leavened products during the Passover holiday, the Jews from the Transcarpathian region who were deported to ghettos in April of 1944, during Passover, were deported without adequate food resources.[10] Many Jews who ended up in ghettos had also had a period preceding ghettoization where they were in transit which might have led to further lack of possessions with them at moment of internment. They might either be ghettoized in a city they were not from as a result of their voluntary or involuntary migration during the war which might also impact their access to social networks after ghettoization or they might return to their hometown to find their possessions looted.

Food Distribution in the Ghetto: A Varied and Evolving Phenomenon

How individuals obtained food within the ghettos—licitly and illicitly—was based on factors as diverse as German administration, date of establishment, the porousness of the ghetto and region. There were "closed" ghettos where the German authorities dictated what food was allowed into the ghetto and the Jewish ghetto administration would distribute that food, "open" ghettos where Jews could leave and re-enter the ghettos, in some cases allowing them to obtain food from outside the ghetto, as well as variants of these two models.

When German authorities dictated the food entering the ghettos, they allowed far less food than was necessary to sustain the projected population. While the Germans deemed 1800 calories a minimum for someone not doing work, individuals in the ghetto were only allocated 800–1200 calories per day.[11] Low food quality, spoilage and theft all along the food supply chain played a significant role in reducing calories to starvation levels. Food access in ghettos varied. In some ghettos, the Germans restricted what entered and exited the ghetto and the respective community's methods of distributing limited food resources was important to individual food access. Not all ghettos were exclusively provisioned by the German authorities. In some places, the Jews were allowed to enter and exit the ghetto area. Jews in "open" ghettos were nevertheless subjected to strict control of their movement. This meant that in some cases, Jews were only allowed to purchase food during certain time frames. For example, the third largest ghetto under Nazi occupation, the Lvov Ghetto, was relatively open for most of its existence. Jews could buy their own food in the markets, but their shopping was constrained to restricted hours—between noon and 2 p.m.[12] In Budapest, the ghetto consisted of geographically unconnected designated ghetto buildings. Each of the 10 district leaders was responsible for food distribution to their district.[13] In the Starachowice Ghetto, according to Howard C, although the Jews were confined to certain streets, there was no wall or barbed wire around the ghetto and the Polish population was not required to leave the area, so Jews had the opportunity to purchase food from their non-Jewish neighbors who were not subject to the same restrictions.[14]

Open ghettos were not necessarily better, in terms of food access, than closed ghettos. Ghettos with restricted hours to purchase food could suffer from local inhabitants' price gouging food or there might be limited food available. Jan Wiktor, a non-Jewish Polish diarist, described the poor food situation in his area as well as the Jews in Radomyśl nad Sanem, a village in southeastern Poland. The poor food situation for the Jews led to them begging. Wiktor describes the Jews (or as he refers to them "dirty skeletons") who dragged themselves from house to house to beg for food. He noted that sometimes they found a Jewish corpse in the ditch covered in frost.[15] In this way, the open ghetto allowed not only for more free exchange of food between Jews and their non-Jewish neighbors, it also exposed the plight of the Jews to their neighbors.

In addition to open ghettos and so-called closed ghettos, there were also ghettos, often located in Reichskommissariat Ukraine, with a short lifespan which have been called "destruction" ghettos due to the almost total mortality of their inhabitants. These ghettos often allowed no one in or out, and the victims were trapped inside with only the food they brought with them. According to survivor Harry S., the Chust Ghetto, which was a short-lived four- to five-week ghetto, the Jews were not allowed to obtain food from outside and had to share food that was brought in already.[16] Unsurprisingly, there are few survivors of these ghettos.

Jewish ghetto administrations experimented with food distribution methods ranging from distributing food to shops and restaurants where it was sold, ration systems where food was distributed using a ration card, soup kitchens, and feeding individuals at work sites.

In numerous ghettos where the administration dabbled in the free market such as Łódź, Warsaw, and others, the free market shops were quickly replaced with a ration card system. However, in many places even those distributing rations sold the choicest food under the counter.[17] The poorest of the ghetto were left with the remnants or in worse cases, faced empty food depots. The communal kitchen or soup kitchen became a popular method of feeding the ghetto population because it eliminated the need for obtaining cooking fuel food and provided prepared meals for those who worked all day and could not make food for themselves. Despite these various strategies, the Jewish ghetto administrations could not provide enough food to sustain their populations. Instead, individuals exploited whatever means they had to obtain adequate food.

Beggars and Elites: Socioeconomic Status and Food Access in the Ghetto

For those inhabitants who had exhausted their resources, many ghettos offered some sort of social welfare. In Warsaw, soup kitchens were organized by pre-war political organizations while in Łódź, they were organized by the official Jewish community. Some ghettos like Warsaw and Krakow had private organizations which took collections from their more affluent members. Other ghettos, for instance, in Rymanow and Łódź, offered welfare but required its recipients to volunteer for hard labor.[18] Some smaller ghettos had informal relief networks like in Murafa where families left food out for those in need.[19] Collecting welfare in many ghettos ultimately proved dangerous because when deportations to the death camps began, it was those on welfare who were the first to be deported from the Lvov and Łódź Ghettos.[20]

Many families who were destitute in the ghetto and reliant on aid did not start out poor but were impoverished by ghetto conditions. For example, Erica R. reported that by the end of the first year in the Warsaw Ghetto, her mother had sold everything in their home including the bed.[21]

This impoverishment using food was intentional. During the summer of 1940, the Germans sought to "draw out" the wealth of the Jews interned in the Łódź Ghetto by forcing them to exchange their valuables for food. By August of 1940, only 52.2% of the ghetto inhabitants had resources to purchase rations.[22] Those with the fewest resources quickly exhausted them, and hunger became an early experience in the ghetto. There were others, however, who due to pre-war reserves of valuables slid gradually toward hunger as the Nazi restrictions led to their impoverishment. Despite social welfare and individual charity in many ghettos, virtually all ghettos had beggars.[23] As one woman wrote of her experiences in the Warsaw Ghetto, "I did not have the wherewithall to live, so I began to beg; the best area – that was Leszno. I was often ashamed, but hunger nagged."[24] Particularly difficult for many was seeing the child beggars in the street.[25]

The elites in the ghetto suffered fewer privations. The social elite had special access to food stores which sold goods unavailable to the rest of the population. Within their circles, the elites' networking involved a gift economy which included food gifts. In the Łódź Ghetto, Mordechai Chaim Rumkowski's secretary, Dora Fuchs, who supervised the main offices of the ghetto had eggs delivered each morning for breakfast. This was at the end of the ghetto period when food was in short supply in the ghetto, and eggs had not been seen by the rest of the ghetto population in years. Elites not only had enough to eat but could trade food and valuables for things beyond their basic survival. Sex was a commodity in the ghetto with women who worked as prostitutes and those who indirectly sold their bodies forming relationships—temporary or permanent—with members of the elites as a matter of survival.[26]

Other elite members of the ghetto rose to their position due to their abilities in obtaining food by illicit means. Smuggling and food theft, discussed in depth later in this chapter, were among the most important means of obtaining food in the ghetto. Those who were sufficiently adept at these activities were able to ensure their own food security and become consumers and suppliers to the elite sections of the ghetto economy. There were restaurants, cafés and private parties in various ghettos that were both stocked by the spoils of smuggling and which catered to entertaining the elites including smugglers. The overlap between the underground world and the ghetto administration was not limited to patronizing the same cafés. Some high-ranking members of the ghetto administration were able to get passes unavailable to others to pass in and out of the ghetto to obtain food without fear of search and seizure. They thus embodied at once the ghetto official elite and smuggler elite. In this way, elites in the ghetto often lived by a different set of rules vis-a-vis entry and return to the ghetto which significantly impacted their food security.

LABOR AND PRIVILEGED POSITIONS AND THEIR RELATIONSHIP TO FOOD ACCESS IN THE GHETTO

When resources that could be bartered for food were depleted, most ghetto inhabitants relied on their labor to secure food. The type of occupation in the ghetto often had a direct impact on food supply. Some ghettos adjusted their food distribution policies to favor workers as food acquisition from the Germans was often connected to ghetto production. By November of 1942, Jews in the Lvov Ghetto began receiving their food at their place of work.[27] This ensured that the worker and not his or her family benefited from the additional food. Other ghettos instituted food benefits for those engaged in labor for the Germans such as in Kaunaus where the food ration for workers was double in comparison with those without work.[28] At the Starachowice Ghetto, Howard C.'s father obtained extra food rations while at his factory job.[29]

Most individuals in the ghetto sought to improve their circumstances by acquiring jobs with greater food opportunities or which expended fewer calories. Survivor Sidney F.'s job in the Mateszalka Ghetto allowed him to scavenge food from homes he was emptying as part of his forced labor assignment.[30] There were also those in the ghettos who worked as domestic helpers of their fellow Jews: cooking, cleaning and tending children. Erica R.'s mother in the Warsaw Ghetto tried to feed her children through washing clothes in exchange for soup. While Erica R.'s family was already destitute before the war, there were others in the ghetto with surplus provisions to pay for domestic labor. Erica's mother would drink some of the soup and then pass the bowl to each of her children.[31] Some jobs were heavy in labor, requiring more calories to do but had the advantage of supplemental rations to compensate. In the Łódź Ghetto, individuals who were hungry would pull the feces cart or perform other hard labor in exchange for food.[32] The intensity of such labor meant that only those who were in a desperate situation would take these positions for a short period and then return to labor less energy-consuming.

Some jobs were advantageous because one could steal extra food. In the Theresienstadt Ghetto, bakers received extra food portions through their positions while agricultural workers were able to steal extra food. In the Kovno Ghetto, Berel Z.'s father had a privileged position as a bakery overseer of bread produced for special stores in the ghetto. Berel's father was able to make extra bread.[33] Abraham P. noted that his mother worked in the communal kitchen in the Łódź Ghetto. Not only was she able to eat at her job but was also able to steal food and bring it back to her children.[34] In these cases, the extra food was sufficient to support themselves and others. The deportations to death camps and concentration camps complicated survival strategies in the ghetto, because some types of work protected against deportation but did not necessarily provide enough compensation to prevent hunger. In other instances, a job which provided adequate food might offer little or no protection from deportation. Eddie Klein's father worked in the Łódź Ghetto in the leather shop. This work provided protection from deportations to forced labor or, later, an extermination camp, but it very often did not provide enough money to feed a family. The constant cycling between jobs which paid enough to survive, protected one from deportation, or were not so dangerous as to be untenable for any lengthy period meant that many ghetto dwellers cycled through different jobs as part of their survival strategy, one in which obtaining sufficient food could only be part of the consideration.

ILLICIT FOOD ACQUISITION: SMUGGLING, THEFT AND THE BLACK MARKET

Persons who could not find adequate work turned to selling their family's movable goods or whatever else could be sold or traded. Furniture was traded for use by other families, as well as for firewood. Clothes, shoes, and items which protected against the cold were especially sought after and could be traded for food both inside and outside the ghetto. In addition to movable goods, some people engaged in trading more valuable portions of their food ration allowance, such as meats and fats, for a larger quantity of less valuable items, such as vegetables. There was also a black market in processed foods, including meatballs, candy and cooked food served in restaurants, cafés, or private catering for elites. Coveted goods were purchased by ghetto elites, and once a person or family sold off all of their valuables, they found themselves without means to protect themselves from hunger. Krystyna Chiger's upper-middle-class family sold off their belongings in the Lvov Ghetto to purchase food on the ghetto black market. Being forced to move as the ghetto shrank in size also resulted in the family being able to retain less and less of their material goods, resulting in less available to exchange for food.[35]

One major factor of food access was how isolated the ghetto inhabitants were from the outside world. Nazi-era ghettos are perceived as having been hermeneutically sealed off from those outside. In reality, ghettos varied in porousness depending on location and their status changed over time. For example, the Łódź Ghetto, the second largest ghetto in Nazi-occupied Europe, was also one of the most closed ghettoes of Nazi-occupied Europe. It was surrounded by barbed wire and had only one main entrance, making smuggling or escape nearly impossible. However, even this ghetto—during the first few months—allowed its inhabitants to travel and in and out with special passes. It was also more possible to smuggle in that period. Helen C. smuggled in and out of the Łódź Ghetto by digging a tunnel under the wall of the cemetery.[36] Other ghettos allowed individuals to leave and return throughout the existence of the ghetto. For example, some ghettos had no walls and allowed Jews to trade with the local population for food. The Krakow Ghetto went through multiple phases. In the initial period, the Germans allowed more relaxed entry and return regulations, and then after each successive major deportation, Jewish entry and exit from the ghetto became more restrictive, until finally almost all movement between the ghetto and the outside world was banned. During times of relaxed regulations, this ability to leave for food had a propitious impact on food security. Helena Tichauer, who was interned in the Krakow Ghetto would regularly leave to procure food.[37]

Due to the difficulties of smuggling food across ghetto borders including risks of incarceration and death as well as food loss during attempted crossings, illicit food in the ghetto was generally higher in cost than black market food just outside the ghetto, in some cases, double the price. Smuggling food between the ghetto and the outside world involved various types of unique relationships. Some Jews relied on pre-war connections outside the ghetto to obtain supplies. Sometimes these were fellow Jews on the outside of the ghetto or non-Jews. For example, Nelly C. had a relative who was a member of the Polish underground who would smuggle himself into the ghetto through the sewers and bring her food.[38] In one Hungarian Ghetto, the Mateszalka Ghetto, the Jewish forced labor brigades which were comprised of conscripted Jewish men helped provide food for the Jews trapped in the ghetto.[39] Sometimes the relations between smuggler and his supplier were not all positive. Jews in the Lvov Ghetto were forbidden to participate in the black market of the general population. Various individuals did engage in the black market but were at risk of blackmail or arrest.[40]

Sometimes people engaged in theft to feed themselves. There were large scale thefts organized by multiple individuals. There were also very small scale thefts made out of desperation. For example, one day someone stole food from Erica R.'s 4-year-old brother. People attacked and beat the thief.[41] Alice H. who was also in the Warsaw Ghetto recounted someone grabbing their bread rations as well as witnessing little children running up to people and stealing their bread and eating it up as they ran away—before they were caught.[42] However, theft was extremely risky because being caught stealing food could get one deported to a concentration camp or cut off from food rations.[43]

Living with Hunger

Ultimately, many people in ghettos had to constantly cope with food scarcity. Individuals resorted to eating items which were inedible, such as motor oil, wall plaster and grass. They ate items which were not traditionally consumed including potato peels, and leaves of vegetables. Erica R. recalled that she would search garbage bins for potato peels, which her mother would then wash and cook. The result tasted terrible.[44] They added saccharine to spoiled meat to hide the spoiled taste. As one female diarist wrote in the Minsk Ghetto, "We ate pieces of paper, scratched away the chalk from the stoves."[45] They also stretched food items by boiling leaves and drinking the soup and then grinding the tasteless boiled leaves into other foods to increase the volume. A great deal of the food-stretching and processing fell to the women of the household. Many had experience from times of deprivation before the war. However, for a number of women from more privileged backgrounds who had found themselves in want for the first time, it was a struggle to find ways to meet their family's needs. For those who had grown up with servants and did not even know how to cook, the situation was even more of a challenge.

Hunger in the ghetto had a significant impact on various aspects of life. For example, it impacted the very act of eating. Hungry people wolfed down food or slowly savored it depending on their condition and psyche. Survivor Ray Kaner describes her brother eating with his hand underneath his mouth so that if a bit of food were to fall, he would be able to save it.[46] Individuals deprived of food also indulged in extensive food fantasy. Food entered the imagination and found expression in the cultural output of the ghetto. Food was a rather popular topic of ghetto songs.[47] There was copious artwork related to food created in the ghettos. Not only photographs, drawings and other traditional artistic items but also even food-related jewelry. Chaim Klieger, a craftsman in the Łódź Ghetto, made a brooch in the shape of a bread ration card issued to his younger sister Sara Klieger.[48] Some people fantasized about recipes and food from before the war or food they would consume after the war. Some writers have depicted this food fantasy as a type of resistance, but in hunger situations, this type of food fantasy is typical as a symptom of extreme hunger.[49]

In the ghetto, individuals came together over meals—even when they were paltry. There were birthday celebrations in the ghetto where a cake was baked from potato peels or using ersatz coffee in lieu of flour. Among the elite, there were even birthday celebrations with chocolate. Similarly, there were weddings where a meal was shared. In more, elite circles that meal might include champagne or other luxuries. There were Passover seders and fulfillments of the requirement to eat in a sukkah. Food brought people together whether into a relationship or to bargain over its price. Helen C. claimed that she was partially motivated to marry her husband in the ghetto to obtain the extra food ration gifted to newly married couples by the head of the ghetto.[50]

Although most sought to augment their food resources through acquiring additional food in various licit and illicit ways, there were some ways of coping with food deprivation that was taboo to a portion of the ghetto population. One of the major struggles with food deprivation involved abandoning Jewish dietary restrictions or, in rare cases, at great personal sacrifice, trying to maintain a kosher diet despite the lack of food. Jewish law emphasizes that virtually, all Jewish observances, including dietary laws, can be dispensed with to save the life of a person. Despite this and numerous rabbinical statements issued in the ghettos allowing individuals to dispense with kosher food requirements to ensure their own survival, there were those whose identity was tied to their dietary restrictions and continued to observe kosher law.[51] "A Debrecen ghetto survivor recalled how the ultra-Orthodox families would not cook in the communal kitchens because they were not kosher."[52] This resulted in separate kitchens for the ultra-Orthodox. For those who maintained an adherence to kosher dietary law, this meant depriving themselves of available non-kosher meat, such as horsemeat and pork.[53] One ghetto singer in the Łódź Ghetto recalled that not only did some Orthodox Jews reject eating non-kosher food but they would spit when he mentioned eating horsemeat.[54] Some went to great lengths to obtain live animals for kosher slaughter. However, those who were obtaining the live animals were usually members of the elite such as the head of the Jewish police in Krakow Ghetto who procured live chickens in the ghetto.[55] Matzah was baked in numerous ghettos including the Łódź, Kovno and Krakow Ghettos. Individuals would use their bread rations to obtain matzah despite its less nourishing capacity.[56]

Although there were those who sacrificed to maintain their dietary restrictions, there were many who compromised for the sake of survival. Among those compromises included not only dispensing with strict adherence to kosher food but also engaging in theft and other illicit means. Theft of food in ghettos was widespread. Individuals in food production and distribution jobs stole food from work or distributed food disproportionately to their friends and relatives. People engaged in theft from food distribution carts and stores. People also stole from each other. Not only did hungry people grab food from the hands of strangers eating on the street but individuals stole from their own neighbors, friends and family.[57] Numerous ghetto diarists have written of guilt and shame over food theft.[58]

People also resorted to hiding the dead and continuing to use their ration cards. Family members' corpses would be hidden in the home so that rations could continue to be collected. Alternatively, people would continue to try to collect the food rations of those who had already been deported. This issue of eating the food of the dead was so widespread that numerous ghettos grappled openly with the issue. It was not only the food of the dead that was eaten. In several cases in the Warsaw Ghetto, women were reported for cannibalizing their dead children.[59] Despite the high levels of starvation, reports of cannibalism in the ghettos do not appear to be widespread.

Not every type of coping with extreme hunger in the ghettos was a form of food fantasy or geared toward increasing one's chance of survival. In the Warsaw Ghetto, the doctors faced with the impossible challenge of keeping people alive given the paltry number of calories available experimented with various treatments and ultimately created a record of the stages of hunger.[60] This study is the only one which follows the path of starvation all the way to the death stage. The deadly lack of food in the ghetto and the numerous diseases which afflicted the population as a result of the paltry food situation tend to be obscured as a result of the overwhelming destruction which would follow in the death camps of the Nazi regime. When contemplating hunger experienced during the Holocaust, many survivors of the ghettos also tend to focus on the more horrific food situation which followed in concentration camps and labor camps. Also, a disproportionate number of the survivors were likely part of the elite and experienced hunger stress than their fellow ghetto inhabitants. It makes obtaining testimonies of ghetto hunger complicated. Nevertheless, a plethora of diaries, immediate postwar writings and more contemporary oral testimonies and writings testify to the hunger experienced by the Jews of the ghetto. Numerous ghetto dwellers lost relatives to starvation and hunger-related diseases.

The Coercive Power of Food

Most ghetto Jews not killed by starvation, or ghetto-related diseases were deported from the ghetto to concentration camps, forced labor or killing sites. Ultimately, when it came time for Jews to be deported from ghettos to concentration camps or forced labor, the Nazis capitalized on the rampant hunger among most ghetto inhabitants to use food to entice them to show up on for the deportation trains. Very frequently, Jews were either told they were being deported to a place with ample food or lured with food to get on a deportation train. When survivor Howard C. was deported from the Starachowice Ghetto, he was told he was being sent to work on a Ukrainian farm.[61] Martin G. reported that in the Tacova Ghetto, they were promised that they would be given work and plenty of food to eat if they got on the deportation train.[62] The lack of food had similarly been exploited to compel people to work on behalf of the Germans. By dispensing food at factories and worksites, individuals in food-deprived states were compelled to show up for work to eat. There was a continual tension between the Nazi creation of deadly conditions and Jewish agency in employing coping methods in an attempt to survive. This remained true even as the Germans tried to compel Jews to board deportation trains using food as a lure. As the Lvov Ghetto shrank and Jews in the ghetto realized that they could soon be deported, people stopped registering for food rations with the Jewish ghetto authorities to facilitate going into hiding and evading deportation.[63] Sometimes food could be used to delay deportation rather than entice Jews onto deportation trains. In the Aknaszlatina Ghetto, they were able to delay their deportation through trying to trigger a typhus epidemic. "We wanted to trigger a typhus epidemic so they wouldn't be able to take us away. We did this by drinking black coffee with salt, which made us feverish. This is how we managed to defer our deportation for two weeks."[64] Ultimately, most Jews interned in ghettos were murdered at killing sites or through the even more extreme conditions of labor and concentration camps, but various ghetto strategies of food acquisition before deportation may have been an important factor in survival of the war period.

Conclusion

Throughout German-occupied Europe, German control of food resources during World War II barred most Jewish communities under their jurisdiction from licit access to adequate food for survival. The food deprivations of the Jews in the ghetto resulted in genocidal conditions. However, for the Jews of Europe incarcerated in ghettos, the experience of food deprivation varied dramatically based on their location. Even within the different communities which were ghettoized during the Nazi period, there was a great deal of variance in individual experiences of food security which ranged from those who were well fed to those who literally starved to death in the streets of the ghetto. Many factors contributed to these individual experiences within the ghetto, but notably, social networks and pre-war socioeconomic status were among the most significant factors in the variety of experiences. Pre-war social networks were significant in obtaining jobs in the ghetto which provided sufficient resources or access to food resources to survive. Very significant, too, was pre-war socioeconomic status. Being food secure before the war, owning movable valuable assets which could be transported in the ghetto and exchanged for food inside or outside the ghetto, and having an existing stockpile of food were all contributing factors to a sufficient food supply. However, none of these factors alone ensured survival. Internal food distribution systems in the ghettos privileged different types of individuals at different times and different places. This meant that most ghetto inhabitants except the most elite, had to adopt coping methods or adapt their food acquisition strategies. In their struggle for survival, many ghetto dwellers cycled between jobs and experimented with illicit food acquisition activities in an attempt to survive while minimizing their risks for deportation. Sometimes family members sacrificed themselves to save loved ones whether it was using their limited resources to purchase medicine instead of food or sacrificing their food portion to a child or spouse. Ultimately, for the Jews of the ghetto, survival required gaining access to food adequate to sustain life and there was not enough food in many of the restricted ghettos for everyone to survive. Those unable to adapt to the brutal surroundings were often killed by ghetto conditions. Those able through various methods to find a path to survival in the ghetto often were ultimately killed when the Germans used food to compel Jews to board the deportation trains to the death camps.

NOTES

1. See, for example, Lizzie Collingham, *The Taste of War: World War II and the Battle for Food* (London: Penguin Books, 2012).
2. See, for example, Aly Gotz, *Hitler's Beneficiaries: Plunder, Racial War, and the Nazi Welfare State* (New York: Picador, 2008); Christian Gerlach, *Krieg, Ernährung, Völkermord: Forschungen zur deutschen Vernichtungspolitk im Zweiten Weltkrieg* (Hamburg: HIS Verlag, 1998); Gerlach, *Kalkulierte Morde. Die deutsche Wirtschafts- und Vernichtungspolitik in Weißrußland 1941 bis 1944* (Hamburg: HIS Verlag, 1999); E. Collingham, *The Taste of War: World War II and the Battle for Food*, 1st American ed. (New York: Penguin Press, 2012); and Gesine Gerhard, *Nazi Hunger Politics: A History of Food in the Third Reich* (Lanham, MD: Rowman & Littlefield, 2015).
3. For more on the overlap between starvation and genocide, see Gerlach, *Extremely Violent Societies* (Cambridge: Cambridge University Press, 2010); Jenny Edkins, "Mass Starvation and the Limitations of Famine Theorising," *IDS Bulletin* 33 (2009): 12–18; A. De Waal, *Famine Crimes: Politics and the Disaster Relief Industry in Africa* (1997; repr., Oxford: African Rights and the International African Institute, in association with James Currey and E. Howard-Hassmann, Rhoda, 2005); and Rhoda E. Howard-Hassmann, "Genocide and State-Induced Famine: Global Ethics and Western Responsibility for Mass Atrocities in Africa," *Perspectives on Global Development and Technology* 4 (2005): 487–516.
4. See Helene J. Sinnreich, "Victim and Perpetrators Perspectives of World War II Era Ghettos," in *The Routledge History of the Holocaust*, edited by Jonathan C. Friedman (London: Routledge, 2011).
5. Expansion of our understanding of ghettos has been particularly pushed forward by recent documentation efforts of ghettos by the United States Holocaust Memorial Museum in Washington, DC and Yad Vashem in Jerusalem. Scholars examining ghettos in Nazi-occupied Europe have often looked at Nazi administrative oversight of ghettos and the role of Jewish leadership in ghettos with the aim of determining its purpose within Nazi policy and extermination plans including some examinations of how and why the Nazis implemented food policy in ghettos. However, few until recently looked at Jewish agency in food policy or hunger as it impacted ghetto society. On Jewish leadership, see: Isaiah Trunk, *Judenrat: The Jewish Councils in Eastern Europe Under Nazi Occupation* (Lincoln: University of Nebraska Press, 1996); Christopher R. Browning, *Ghettos 1939–1945: New Research and Perspectives on Definition, Daily Life, and Survival: Symposium Presentations* (Washington, DC: Center for Advanced Holocaust Studies, United States Holocaust Memorial

Museum, 2005); and Dan Michman, *The Emergence of Jewish Ghettos During the Holocaust* (2014). On food policy, see C. Browning, "Nazi Ghettoization Policy in Poland: 1939–41," *Central European History* 19, no. 4 (1986): 343–368; Sinnreich (2011).
6. Aid to Jews Overseas: Report on the Activities of the American Jewish Joint Distribution Committee for the Year 1936.
7. Natalia Aleksiun, "Food, Money and Barter in the Lvov Ghetto, Eastern Galicia," in *Coping with Hunger and Shortage Under German Occupation in World War II*, edited by Tatjana Toensmeyer et al. (Basingstoke: Palgrave Macmillan, 2018), 226.
8. Regina Fritz, "Inside the Ghetto: Everyday Life in Hungarian Ghettos," *Hungarian Historical Review* 4, no. 3 (2015): 606–640.
9. Eva Heyman, "On the Hardships of the Ghetto," accessed August 16, 2018, http://www.yadvashem.org/odot_pdf/Microsoft%20Word%20-%203697.pdf.
10. Fritz, 606–640.
11. William Moskoff, *The Bread of Affliction: The Food Supply in the USSR During World War II* (Cambridge: Cambridge University Press, 1990), 53.
12. Aleksiun, 226.
13. Fritz, 606–640.
14. Howard C. (53598), *USC Shoah Foundation Visual History Archive* (November 26, 1981), Segment #17–19.
15. Michał Maksymilian Borwicz, Nella Rost, and Joseph Wulf, *W trzecia rocznice zaglady getta w Krakowie* (Krakow: Zydowska Komisja Historyczna, 1946), 19.
16. Harry S. (20434), *USC Shoah Foundation Visual History Archive* (October 2, 1996), Segment #6.
17. Marcus L. (54896), *USC Shoah Foundation Visual History Archive* (February 28, 1997), Segment #154.
18. *Gazeta Żydowska*, July 8, 1942; *Lodz Ghetto Chronicle*, July 5–12, 1941.
19. Rosen, "Surviving in the Murafa Ghetto," 171.
20. Eliyahu Yones, *Smoke in the Sand: The Jews of Lvov in the War Years 1939–1944* (New York: Geffen Publishing House, 2004), 164 and USHMM RG 02 *127; Josef Zelkowicz, *In Those Terrible Days*, 199–201; *Chronicle*, January 1–5, 1942; YIVO RG 241, doc. 927.
21. Erica R. (31559), *USC Shoah Foundation Visual History Archive* (July 20, 1997), Segment #8.
22. YIVO RG 241, doc. 883.
23. For the Krakow Ghetto, see, for example: Marcus L. (54896).
24. Zoe Waxman, *Women and the Holocaust: A Feminist History* (Oxford: Oxford University Press, 2017), 38.

25. Chuna T. (54502), *USC Shoah Foundation Visual History Archive* (August 21, 2001); Erica R. (31559), *USC Shoah Foundation Visual History Archive* (July 20, 1997), Segment #10.
26. Katarzyna Person, "Sexual Violence During the Holocaust—The Case of Forced Prostitution in the Warsaw Ghetto," *Shofar* 33, no. 2 (2015): 103–121; and Anna Hajkova, "Sexual Barter in Times of Genocide: Narrating the Sexual Economy of the Theresienstadt Ghetto," *Signs: Journal of Women in Culture and Society* 38, no. 3 (Spring, 2013): 503–533.
27. Aleksiun, 235.
28. Tauber.
29. Howard C. (53598), *USC Shoah Foundation Visual History Archive* (November 26, 1981), Segment #17–19.
30. Sidney F. (6119), *USC Shoah Foundation Visual History Archive* (August 30, 1995).
31. Erica R. (31559), Segment #9.
32. Zelkowicz, 131.
33. Berel Z. (39286), *USC Shoah Foundation Visual History Archive* (February 15, 1998), Segment #17.
34. Abraham P. (37735), *USC Shoah Foundation Visual History Archive* (December 29, 1997), Segment #106.
35. Aleksiun, 233.
36. Helen C. (55089), *USC Shoah Foundation Visual History Archive* (February 24, 1991), Segment #20.
37. Helana Tichauer. (11310), *USC Shoah Foundation Visual History Archive* (January 22, 1996).
38. Nelly C. (52994), *USC Shoah Foundation Visual History Archive* (February 28, 1991).
39. Sidney F. (6119), *USC Shoah Foundation Visual History Archive* (August 30, 1995).
40. Aleksiun, 226–227.
41. Erica R. (31559), Segment #10.
42. Alice H. (17), *USC Shoah Foundation Visual History Archive* (July 20, 1994), Segment #12 and 13.
43. Abraham P. (37735), Segment #104.
44. Erica R. (31559), Segment #9.
45. Zoe Waxman, *Women and the Holocaust: A Feminist History* (Oxford: Oxford University Press, 2017), 38.
46. Testimony of Ray Kaner, "The Effects of Hunger on a Łódź Ghetto Resident," https://www.youtube.com/watch?v=OtshagboZ-g.
47. See, for example, G. Flam, *Singing for Survival: Songs of the Lodz Ghetto, 1940–45*, 102.

48. Accessed July 12, 2018, http://www.yadvashem.org/artifacts/museum/mementos-lodz.html.
49. For an example of the elevation of food fantasy to act of resistance, see Cara DeSilva, *In Memory's Kitchen: A Legacy from the Women of Terezin* (Northvale: Jason Aronson, 2006).
50. Helen C. (55089), Segment #69.
51. Flam, 70.
52. Fritz, 606–640.
53. Flam, 70.
54. Ibid., 45.
55. Joanna Sliwa, "A Link Between the Inside and the Outside Worlds: Jewish Child Smugglers in the Kraków Ghetto," in *Zeitschrift für Genozidforschung: Alltag im Ghetto. Strukturen, Ordnungen, Lebenswelt(en) im Blick neuer Forschung*, edited by Stephan Lehnstaedt and Kristin Platt (13 Jahrgang 2012), Heft 1–2, 74.
56. Flam, 111.
57. Nechama Tec, *Resilience and Courage: Women, Men, and the Holocaust* (New Haven: Yale University Press, 2004).
58. See, for example, Dawid Sierakowiak, *The Dairy of Dawid Sierakowiak: Five Notebooks from the Lodz Ghetto*, translated by Kamil Turowski, edited by Alan Adelson (London: Bloomsbury, 1997).
59. M. Winick, *Hunger Disease: Studies, Current Concepts in Nutrition 7* (New York: Wiley, 1979).
60. Ibid.
61. Howard C. (53598), Segment #17–19.
62. Martin G. (42255), *USC Shoah Foundation Visual History Archive* (May 18, 1998), Segment #9.
63. Aleksiun, 234.
64. Fritz, 606–640.

Bibliography

Aleksiun, Natalia. "Food, Money and Barter in the Lvov Ghetto, Eastern Galicia." In *Coping with Hunger and Shortage Under German Occupation in World War II*, edited by Tatjana Toensmeyer et al. Basingstoke: Palgrave Macmillan, 2018.

Aly, Gotz. *Hitler's Beneficiaries: Plunder, Racial War, and the Nazi Welfare State*. New York: Picador, 2008.

Borwicz, Michał Maksymilian, Nella Rost, and Joseph Wulf. *W trzecia rocznice zaglady getta w Krakowie*. Krakow: Zydowska Komisja Historyczna, 1946.

Browning, C. "Nazi Ghettoization Policy in Poland: 1939–41." *Central European History* 19, no. 4 (1986): 343–368.

———. *Ghettos 1939–1945: New Research and Perspectives on Definition, Daily Life, and Survival: Symposium Presentations*. Washington, DC: Center for Advanced Holocaust Studies, United States Holocaust Memorial Museum, 2005.

Collingham, E. *The Taste of War: World War II and the Battle for Food*. 1st American ed. New York: Penguin Press, 2012.

DeSilva, Cara. *In Memory's Kitchen: A Legacy from the Women of Terezin*. Northvale: Jason Aronson, 2006.

De Waal, A. *Famine Crimes: Politics and the Disaster Relief Industry in Africa*. 1997. Reprint, Oxford: African Rights and the International African Institute, in association with James Currey and E. Howard-Hassmann, Rhoda, 2005.

Edkins, Jenny. "Mass Starvation and the Limitations of Famine Theorising." *IDS Bulletin* 33 (2009): 12–18.

Flam, Gila. *Singing for Survival: Songs of the Lodz Ghetto, 1940–45*.

Fritz, Regina. "Inside the Ghetto: Everyday Life in Hungarian Ghettos." *Hungarian Historical Review* 4, no. 3 (2015): 606–640.

Gerhard, Gesine. *Nazi Hunger Politics: A History of Food in the Third Reich*. Lanham, MD: Rowman & Littlefield, 2015.

Gerlach, Christian. *Krieg, Ernährung, Völkermord: Forschungen zur deutschen Vernichtungspolitik im Zweiten Weltkrieg*. Hamburg: HIS Verlag, 1998.

———. *Kalkulierte Morde. Die deutsche Wirtschafts- und Vernichtungspolitik in Weißrußland 1941 bis 1944*. Hamburg: HIS Verlag, 1999.

———. *Extremely Violent Societies*. Cambridge: Cambridge University Press, 2010.

Hajkova, Anna. "Sexual Barter in Times of Genocide: Narrating the Sexual Economy of the Theresienstadt Ghetto." *Signs: Journal of Women in Culture and Society* 38, no. 3 (Spring, 2013): 503–533.

Howard-Hassmann, Rhoda E. "Genocide and State-Induced Famine: Global Ethics and Western Responsibility for Mass Atrocities in Africa." *Perspectives on Global Development and Technology* 4 (2005): 487–516.

Michman, Dan. *The Emergence of Jewish Ghettos During the Holocaust*, 2014.

Moskoff, William. *The Bread of Affliction: The Food Supply in the USSR During World War II*. Cambridge: Cambridge University Press, 1990.

Person, Katarzyna. "Sexual Violence During the Holocaust—The Case of Forced Prostitution in the Warsaw Ghetto." *Shofar* 33, no. 2 (2015): 103–121.

Schneider, Gertrude, ed. *Mordechai Gebirtig Hist Poetic and Musical Legacy*, 173. London: Praeger, 2000.

Sen, Amartya. *Poverty and Famines: An Essay on Entitlement and Deprivation*. Oxford and New York: Clarendon Press and Oxford University Press, 1982.

Sierakowiak, Dawid. *The Dairy of Dawid Sierakowiak: Five Notebooks from the Lodz Ghetto*. Translated by Kamil Turowski, edited by Alan Adelson. London: Bloomsbury, 1997.

Sinnreich, Helene J. "Victim and Perpetrators Perspectives of World War II Era Ghettos." In *The Routledge History of the Holocaust*, edited by Jonathan C. Friedman. London: Routledge, 2011.

———. "Introduction." In *Inside the Walls*, edited by Eddie Klein. Toronto: Azrieli Foundation, 2016.

Sliwa, Joanna. "A Link Between the Inside and the Outside Worlds: Jewish Child Smugglers in the Kraków Ghetto." In *Zeitschrift für Genozidforschung: Alltag im Ghetto. Strukturen, Ordnungen, Lebenswelt(en) im Blick neuer Forschung*, edited by Stephan Lehnstaedt and Kristin Platt, Heft 1–2, 13 Jahrgang 2012.

Tauber, Joachim. "'Purchasing and Bringing Food into the Ghetto Is Forbidden': Ways of Survival as Revealed in the Files of the Ghetto Courts and Police in Lithuania, 1941–44." *Remembrance and Solidarity Studies* (2017).

Tec, Nechama. *Resilience and Courage: Women, Men, and the Holocaust*. New Haven: Yale University Press, 2004.

Trunk, Isaiah. *Judenrat: The Jewish Councils in Eastern Europe Under Nazi Occupation*. Lincoln: University of Nebraska Press, 1996.

Waxman, Zoe. *Women and the Holocaust: A Feminist History*. Oxford: Oxford University Press, 2017.

Yones, Eliyahu. *Smoke in the Sand: The Jews of Lvov in the War Years 1939–1944*. New York: Geffen Publishing House, 2004.

Zelkowicz, Josef. *In Those Terrible Days: Notes from the Lodz Ghetto*. Jerusalem: Yad Vashem, 2002.

CHAPTER 6

Bee Stings and Beer: The Significance of Food in Alabamian POW Newspapers

Christine Rinne

The Allies captured over 370,000 German soldiers during the Second World War and brought them to the USA as prisoners of war (POWs), because there was no place to hold them in northern Africa or Europe. Aliceville, in rural west-central Alabama, was one of the largest camps built that was not near an existing military base and had two influxes of prisoners: soldiers captured in North Africa in June 1943, and soldiers taken captive at Normandy in June 1944.[1] By 1945, approximately 6000 POWs were housed at Camp Aliceville, providing an economic boom to the area. Fort McClellan, in northeastern Alabama, began as Camp Shipp during the Spanish-American War and rapidly expanded at the end of the First World War.[2] In July 1943, the first POWs arrived at Fort McClellan, and by the end of 1944, it housed over 3000.[3] German prisoners were initially separated by perceived political leanings as well as rank, as required by the 1929 Geneva Convention.[4] By July 1944, non-commissioned officers (NCOs) were also housed together, and

---

C. Rinne (✉)
University of South Alabama, Mobile, AL, USA

© The Author(s) 2019
H. M. Benbow and H. R. Perry (eds.), *Food, Culture and Identity in Germany's Century of War*,
https://doi.org/10.1007/978-3-030-27138-1_6

125

those in the first through fourth commands who refused to work were sent to Aliceville.[5] Fort McClellan held a mixture of NCOs and enlisted prisoners, and while exact numbers are not available, it appears that many of the NCOs worked in supervisory positions. These POWs helped fill a labor shortage both on and off base as American men were called to fight.[6] The War Department encouraged POWs to produce their own newspapers, both as a method to transmit information and as a means to gauge the soldiers' attitudes.[7] Articles could not be political in nature, but they could include current events and information about camp life, as well as fiction, cartoons and games. The two newspapers discussed here, Camp Aliceville's *Der Zaungast* and Fort McClellan's *POW-Oase*, have similar content and format.[8] The first few pages contain updates about recent events and/or original fiction, often followed by details about sporting events, and the newspapers conclude with humorous anecdotes or cartoons and brainteasers.[9] The content was meant to document, inform and entertain. While there was formal censorship, much of the elision likely occurred in the form of self-censorship, as the editors knew some subjects were not permissible, while others might spark conflict, either among the POWS or with their American overseers.[10]

Der Zaungast and *POW-Oase* form collected memories, intended to chronicle the POWs experiences in combat, and primarily, their lives in American captivity. Samuel Hynes writes that war narratives record "the things men do in war" and "the things war does to them"; both aspects are seen in these reflections.[11] For example, some articles describe a combat experience, while others speculate about the consequences of time and distance away from family. The scope is narrow, because as POWs they had restricted access to outside news and they were "not concerned with *why*," as Hynes argues.[12] He continues: "the stories that soldiers tell are small-scale, detailed, and confined… and necessarily so, for that is the way they see war."[13] These soldiers are not providing a broad analysis or rationalization; rather through these articles, they are cobbling together a sampling of their experiences and collectively preparing for an uncertain future. The POWs knew that no one else could or would tell their stories. Marius Kwint writes that objects spur memories in three ways: they furnish recollections, stimulate remembering and form records.[14] The stories told and events documented validate their memories and aid them in their own evocation, as their nation could or would not.[15] One central element in the lives of soldiers is food. As Katarzyna Cwiertka points out: "The potential meaning of food at the front sharpens [during military conflicts] – it can become a weapon, an embodiment of the enemy, but also a token of hope, a soothing relief."[16] The multifaceted significance of food continues in captivity and is reflected in fiction, commentary and extant documentation about camp life in *Der Zaungast* and *POW-Oase*. Here, I will demonstrate that food functions as a means to unify a diverse group of soldiers, maintain ties to an increasingly distant homeland, redefine a defeated nation, find hope and humor in moments of doubt and frustration, but also as a means to punish.

While historians have explored the lives of German POWs in a variety of camps during both world wars, and scholars have begun to explore newspapers produced at German internment camps during the First World War, there has been little analysis of the contents of the newspapers from the Second World War, which provide a tremendous resource of how the soldiers saw themselves and their time in captivity.[17] A large body of research does exist, however, on *Der Ruf* (The Call), which was created as a national POW newspaper in March 1945 under American auspices and intended to reeducate German POWs held throughout the USA. Paul Metzner, one of the editors of *POW-Oase*, left Fort McClellan in July 1945 to be part of these efforts. *Der Ruf* has received extensive scholarly attention, not only because of its political intentions and intellectual content, but because some of its writers went on to form Group 47, an influential West German literary institution.[18] This article is a contribution to a broader understanding of how the German POWs held in the US understood their role in the war, documented their time in captivity and prepared for a return, through the signifier of food.

OASES AS SITES OF TEMPORARY REFUGE

The first German troops brought to the US were captured in northern Africa, and impressions of the desert landscape and its inhabitants crossed the Atlantic with them.[19] In both newspapers, there are pieces of original fiction set in Tunisia, Libya and Egypt, countries where the soldiers had recently fought. The setting is frequently an oasis, a location abundant with food and drink, and a place to rest in the unforgiving desert known for its scarcity. Intercultural encounters in Africa between German soldiers and the local population also provided a way for the POWs to later understand their time in captivity. As POWs, the men were well provided for in the US, the only country which produced a food surplus during the Second World War.[20] Especially when compared to their counterparts held in other countries who experienced severe rations and shortages, these POWs did not suffer, yet the US was foreign and a temporary residence. While interned they were able to pause and reflect, before embarking on an uncertain journey of rebuilding a devastated nation.

The title of the newspaper at Fort McClellan, *POW-Oase*, is a nod to the soldiers' shared time in battle. In the opening article of the first edition, the editorial staff writes that the name was chosen as an embodiment of their shared past. *The Oasis* was the title of the *Feldzeitung* (field newspaper) they read in northern Africa, and the editors state that "it was like a little piece of home for us."[21] For the *POW-Oase*, they are borrowing the familiar format and providing the POWs some of the same comforts as they again face during a daunting time together in a foreign land. The article continues: "We stand in the foreign country like an oasis, which separates itself from the world around it."[22] War brings these men together at Fort McClellan, surrounded by people and a culture that is unfamiliar to them, and together they build a kind of oasis through their commonalities. As pieces of original fiction will demonstrate, food becomes central in creating camaraderie among a diverse group of men, as it was an available means to reassert and define national identity. Food allowed the POWs to differentiate themselves from others.

Both *Der Zaungast* and *POW-Oase* contain a variety of original fiction, which the editors solicited from the men as a creative outlet and a means to fill the pages. The frequent occurrence of the oasis topos is noteworthy.[23] In the first edition of *POW-Oase*, there is a short story entitled "As a Guest of Arabs. In a tent village in the Libyan desert," which the editors preface as a soldier's *Erlebnisbericht* (personal experience).[24] The narrative takes place during the war. Most residents have fled as supplies became scarce, but several Bedouin remain, as they are better equipped to manage the sparse resources. A nomad takes the soldiers to the sheik's tent, where they are given food, drink and a bed, even though they did not ask for this hospitality. The narrator emphasizes that they do not belong there and do not understand the customs. For example, the soldiers must see the garden with their own eyes before they are prepared to believe that it does in fact produce the delicious melons they enjoy. The men are impressed with the lavish conditions and the generosity of their Muslim hosts, who are fasting for Bayram. Because of this aid, the foreign soldiers are able to get to their destination in this unfamiliar territory with full stomachs. They leave the desert and "its secrets" behind them, the story concludes.[25] Another story, "Abdallah's Letter of Recommendation" was published in *Der Zaungast* and tells of an unnamed narrator and his Algerian friend, who is concerned that the foreigner is too "idiotic" and "childish" to overcome the many hurdles involved in a trip through the Sahara.[26] In an attempt to lessen the narrator's burdens, Abdallah gives the traveler a letter of introduction. Once in Laghouat, which means "the oases," the letter secures him generous food and lodging. When the narrator prepares to leave, he discovers that his host and friend do not know each other, which Abdallah later explains away as "oriental customs" that the narrator would not understand.[27] Again, the deep cultural divide between these men is noted: While they can conceivably sip Turkish coffee together, ultimately this is not a place for the Germans to stay, "in a foreign city, in which Orient and Occident extend a hand to each other and show their teeth."[28] Both stories praise the ability of the locals to extract supplies from the sparse desert resources and their tremendous hospitality, but also highlight the material dependence of Germans on the local people. Their visits are fleeting; these are not places where Germans can feel at home.

The *POW-Oase* logo is reminiscent of an image in the middle of a story that appeared in the Christmas 1944 edition of *Zaungast*.[29] The sketch has four small buildings, likely a mosque with two minarets in the background, accompanied by two palms, two cacti and several stones in the foreground. The story, "Dream on the Edge of Gafsa," is about a soldier in the Tunisian city and an extraordinary encounter. He feels he has entered a fairytale, explicitly mentioning *One Thousand and One Nights*, and is drawn to a set of double doors, which are engraved with the cautionary hand of Fatimah, Muhammad's daughter and guardian of good morals.[30] It is unclear what compels the narrator to knock, though he seems driven by an internal force. A wealthy young woman, barely 18 he states, greets him. She recognizes him as German and brings him fresh fruit, another instance of the unrequested hospitality that is frequently described. As he tries to find a way to express his gratitude, she kisses his forehead and hand, before softly pushing him back out of the entryway, where he again sees the warning Fatimah. The story concludes: "I left. I left very quickly and didn't know where I was going."[31] The soldier knows that he is testing cultural boundaries and cannot remain at her home. Earlier in the story, he comments that Germans, as well as other Europeans in Tunisia, are foreign, and though

Germans and Arabs are kindly disposed toward each other, their social and religious practices are distinct.[32] While the young woman willingly gives him food, she cannot offer him more.

The story about Gafsa is preceded and followed by stories about Christmas in Germany, reflecting on the approaching holiday. The story immediately following, "At Home…," tells of a Christmas during the air raids. The story concludes with the snow stopping, causing the narrator's companion to remove her hood, revealing a "German" woman, and the narrator feels that it is now palpably a "German" Christmas.[33] The next piece is presented as a series of diary entries from 1918, 1936 and 1941.[34] The middle entry, made between the wars, depicts the kind of peacetime holiday that the soldiers fondly remember; while his mother cooks, his sister is decorating the tree, and his father brings home the presents.[35] In the last entry, the narrator is in a desert, likely the Sahara. The soldiers receive a shipment of cognac, which they immediately drink, and observe the stars above them. The story concludes with one soldier reflecting that they can find comfort knowing that these are the same stars that shine above their home.[36] In these stories, the German mothers cook the food they so fondly remember, and the German women make the men feel at home, a stark contrast to the allure of a young Tunisian woman and warning Fatimah, whom the narrator of "Dream on the Edge of Gafsa" must flee.

In each of these stories, food and drink offer hospitality and comfort to both family and guests. The remote surroundings remind the men that they are in a foreign land, and the image of the oasis helps them frame their time in the US. They are no longer potential conquerors as they were in Africa, but still must live surrounded by a foreign culture and heed the warnings. Brian Feltman, in his analysis of German prisoners held by the British during the First World War, argues that: "after overcoming the initial shock of capture and confinement, German prisoners dedicated themselves to finding a new sense of purpose that involved rebuilding the psychological links to the homeland that had been severed when they fell into British hands."[37] Something similar is happening here as well. The stories about their time in war allow the POWs to acknowledge their past experiences, and when those stories are sandwiched between other instantly relatable "German" memories, they articulate and reproduce a common past, and as detailed below, reflect on the values necessary when returning to a militarily and morally defeated nation.

German POWs as Cautious Consumers of American Culture

Due to camp regulations, POW mobility was severely restricted. Nevertheless the men were exposed to American culture through what they ate, what they could purchase in the canteen and, especially for those held at Fort McClellan who regularly travelled to their work details, what they saw. Advertisements for products influenced their perceptions of the US, perhaps also their own consumption, and how they came to define themselves as Germans. At the same time, they were able to find temporary comfort and relief from the hot Alabama summers in typical American products available at the canteens.

In November 1943, the chief editor of *POW-Oase* accompanied ten POWs on their farm detail.[38] The report's first page reveals very little about the men or their work, rather describes the city of Anniston just outside of the Fort and the surrounding countryside, which they drive through on their way to the farm. Paul Metzner comments on the noticeable lack of advertising that the POWs otherwise find pervasive: "Signs on the side of the street, which for once did not entice with a woman's head and praise Coca-Cola as an essential beverage, show the way to the lake."[39] These signs are merely directional, not the usual sexualized, gaudy signage for the sugary soda they have become accustomed to. Work affords the men some freedoms and permits them to momentarily forget where they are and why. The report continues: "The workday is concluded and turns into quitting time, during which the farm workers again transform into that which they ultimately also were outside of the work detail: German-thinking people in a POW's uniform."[40] Working on a farm, cultivating, as well as spending their hard-earned money at the canteen, allowed the men to feel free. Their first identity is a human, then as German, then as a POW. Exactly what it might mean to be German-thinking is up to interpretation, though here it certainly means a particular notion of home, one that they longed for and whose current state was uncertain. Their loss of homeland and familiar connections causes them to cling to traditions.

A similar experience is documented in July 1944, when a small POW orchestra from Fort McClellan performs at satellite camps. Baumann describes what they see along the way: "Although the streets are first-class just like in our fatherland, the quaint, clean little towns are missing."[41] He continues: "Instead of a dreamy little church tower, which impudently greets us in our hometown, above the fruit trees, here the most garish billboards cry out to us 'Pepsicola is the drink for you.'"[42] Unlike the Sahara, the rolling, farm-dotted landscape of northern Alabama is familiar, but the advertisement strikes him as artificial and foreign. The American roads are not lined with fruit trees, providing shade and fruit; instead, they are lined with fabricated, glaring signs. The author thinks that his and the orchestra members' experience applies to emigrants in general. "Today I can understand when European, and there again primarily German emigrants, who have gained reputation and fortune in the new world, are consumed by quiet homesickness."[43] All Germans in the US are thought to have a similar experience of homesickness, regardless of reasons for migration and intended length of stay. While some similarities exist between captor and captive cultures, many more than with the Arabs encountered earlier in the war, the underlying values remain distant and cannot be fully bridged.

The *POW-Oase* published several articles written by an editor that depict "a day in the life of" various jobs, as part of the attempt to document and reflect on a rather unique daily routine. "In Troy and Luverne" summarizes a conversation that Paul Metzner has with POWs who have returned from the peanut harvest in southern Alabama.[44] Much of the initial description is not of the trip or work, rather describes their impressions of Luverne, which a road sign declares the most beautiful city in the South. The POWs agree that the sparse home décor (*Wohnkultur*) leaves plenty to be desired. "Plus the empty tin cans of course, Coca-Cola bottles and... a more or less luxurious Ford in the farm shed."[45] The men are perplexed by these consumption practices, by the trash and visible signs of poverty, juxtaposed with an expensive vehicle. While fruit trees were absent in the article above, here the landscape is too cluttered with the artifical, obscuring what is otherwise familiar.

American advertisements are a frequent theme for more explicit commentary. An article from Camp Aliceville suggests that American newspapers, magazines and radio are flooded with advertisements, which are generally far more prevalent and elaborate than in Germany.[46] Exact sources for the information are not provided, though the author, only identified as Gross, describes radio advertisements, as well as those printed in magazines and newspapers, which would have been available for purchase in the canteen. Twice he points out the role of women, both as objects of male consumption and as consumers. He argues that

American advertisements try to fulfill all of the wishes of American women, "for example to decrease housework through electric kitchens, ease and simplify cooking with prepared, canned foodstuffs, increase cosmetics according to Hollywood's example, etc."[47] The "free, uninhibited" market is reducing women's domestic duties, giving them too much time to focus on their appearance and be overly concerned with vanity. This theme is depicted in a cartoon several months later with the caption: "Why not? You constantly come to breakfast in this getup too, dear!" (see Fig. 6.1).[48] By German standards, American advertisements are too exaggerated, too colorful, and the caricatures too ludicrous

Fig. 6.1 "Why not? You constantly come to breakfast in this getup too, dear!" cartoon from *Der Zaungast*, June 10, 1945 (*Source* Reproduced by permission of the Aliceville Museum)

(*grotesk*).[49] The only positive aspect of advertisements noted is the use of radio for public service announcements, which discuss "the importance of vitamins in nutrition, the tasks of the postwar period, the current concerns of war and much more."[50] Gross concludes that one finds insight into the nation through this analysis: "Advertising is a reflection of the economy and the nature of a people."[51] This article is followed by one entitled "German Beer," which focuses on the central role of the German purity laws in beer brewing. Author Hans Leupelt emphasizes the national pride that beer provides, as well as the economic opportunities for the nation.[52] This juxtaposition of American superficiality and new inventions with German authenticity and time-honored traditions offers a chance for the POWs to value their own culture, while criticizing the culture of their captors and which they struggle to understand: Instead of taking pride in long history of brewing beer with local, natural ingredients, Americans, the POWs seem to think, market artificial drinks as the ideal beverage with an image of a vain woman. Americans respond to gaudy marketing and do not value natural resources.

In canteens, the POWs found an opportunity to purchase toiletries, snacks, luxury items such as beer and cigarettes, as well as clothing and hobby supplies, even seasonal peaches.[53] The POWs were paid in coupons, which they were free to spend or save and receive after repatriation. Walker states that the profit margins at the Camp Aliceville canteen were around 15%, and allowed the POWs to purchase the printing press that was used for *Der Zaungast* as well as a variety of other items for the POWs.[54] An article titled "...and at quitting time: to the canteen!" specifically addresses the value of the canteen for the men at Fort McClellan, which likely had an additional function when compared to Camp Aliceville, as these POWs worked for their earnings.[55] Canteens allowed the captured men to briefly feel like civilians, also turning the men into consumers, as they spend their earnings. These experiences differ profoundly from their life during peacetime; nevertheless, the canteens serve as the site of "pleasure after closing time" (*Freude des Feierabends*), again emphasizing that this is a pastime available after they have put in a day's work.[56] The men also came to take pleasure in partaking in some American products. To demonstrate the value of the canteens, the article lists the following monthly average sold for *Kantine II*, which supplied 1000 POWs: 4560 bottles of milk, 31,050 bottles of beer, 21,600 bottles of soda (Coca-Cola and Nehi are named elsewhere), 3220 ice cream bars, 381,090 cigarettes, 8900 cigars and 389,060 matches.[57] The article requests that customers return the empty bottles, as they are only able to receive as many full bottles as they have empties, suggesting that supply did not always meet demand. In an article about a camp concert, co-editor Klemm describes his joy at eating a Lily-Pure ice cream and drinking a Coca-Cola on a typical hot Alabama afternoon, items that he would have purchased in the canteen.[58] Ice cream and soda were not foreign to these soldiers before arriving in the USA, but now that they have some disposable income, few immediate needs and little motivation to save, they increase their consumption. In these cases, the American products have been incorporated into their everyday lives, allowing them some brief pleasure. The POWs staffed the canteens as well, and the article details their typical day and praises their efforts, suggesting that all the men toast them this evening.[59] If the numbers above were typical, each POW purchased a bottle of beer a day, so they could in fact all toast that evening. Once the war ended, beer and soda were among the luxury items no longer available in the canteens; their removal served as a form of punishment.[60]

The canteens at Camp Aliceville also served as a place to congregate and relax. While *Der Zaungast* does not describe how the canteens there function, a piece of original fiction takes place in a canteen and demonstrates its role in providing community. "Germanin" is about a soldier who goes to drink a Coca-Cola at the canteen of another compound, because he does not want to appear as a big spender.[61] He stands at the counter and daydreams of being at a bar. Similar to the experiences described at Fort McClellan, he is able to feel like he is home, as though he were not a prisoner. While the narrator claims that he is trying to mind his own business, he is aghast at an overheard discussion.[62] Two soldiers are debating the meaning of "Germanin," which they recently heard in a marionette show.[63] Hans believes the term to mean a Nordic woman, while Erich suggests it is a skin care product. Since they cannot come to a consensus, they each bet a case of beer. Erich asks the narrator which of them is right, and since the narrator claims to know the correct meaning, they drink the beer together. The second half of the story is taken from Hellmuth Unger's 1938 novel *Germanin* and tells how German scientists discovered a cure to the "sleeping disease" (*African Trypanosomiases*).[64] The story does not return to the canteen, rather ends by emphasizing the benefit the world received from I.G. Farben's drug. While the story was likely intended to educate the POWs about this invention and give the men something German to be proud of, it also speaks to the canteen's social function in the camp.

Lizzie Collingham argues that during the Second World War, "most Americans felt that they were fighting to preserve the American way of life and one of the most powerful symbols of this lifestyle came to be the abundance of American food."[65] While the German POWs waistlines benefitted from this abundance, it also provided a point of critique and ways to differentiate themselves from their captor. Perhaps also out of resentment, they chose to critique new products that did not have an obvious positive social impact, unlike a new medicine. The canteens, ironically, provided the men with the luxurious Americans goods, giving them temporary physical comfort, yet also served as a place to gather and find camaraderie, to feel less alone in their oasis.

HOLIDAY TRADITIONS HELP DEFINE NATIONAL IDENTITY

As discussed briefly above, holiday traditions were a way for POWs to both remember their loved ones at home and to create enjoyable moments at the camps. They draw on common customs and practices, which are often tied to traditional foods. While POWs organized holiday festivities for themselves and publically reminisced, they also received packages from abroad to help them celebrate. The *POW-Oase* features numerous articles that document the packages prisoners received through Red Cross organizations.[66] For Christmas 1943, the POWs received a shipment from "the German Chancellor and Commander in Chief as a Christmas present to all prisoners of war" through the International Committee of the Red Cross.[67] The large shipment, weighing over 7500 kg, contained primarily foodstuffs, as well as cigarettes. Some of the food was also traditional for the holidays, including nuts and stollen. The article's title, "Our Homeland Remembers Us," acknowledges the tie that this donation helps maintain between the soldiers and their nation. Those at home are the ones who actively remember, who have not forgotten the soldiers. There is a sense of indebtedness on the part of the soldiers, or should be, as is made clear by the final paragraph: "Through the donations we all see empathic proof of our ties to home and will know to repay our thanks through appropriate conduct."[68] The men remain loyal to their nation and are reminded of their obligations as soldiers held captive in a foreign land through these gifts. In September 1944, the POWs at Fort McClellan received packages from a group of German women active in the Argentinian Red Cross. "Our whole-hearted thanks goes out to our fellow Germans in this South American state, who, out there in the wide world, have not forgotten their homeland."[69] This is a public acknowledgment of their generosity, but not intended for the givers, rather for the recipients, as a reminder that they are supported by Germans everywhere. Oliver Wilkinson, in his analysis of magazines published by British soldiers held in Germany during the First World War, argues that "the magazines exercised their own form of authority. Their pages constructed a moral universe, intended to reassure and direct POW behaviour."[70] A "moral universe" is being crafted in these newspapers as well. The editors determine what is acceptable and appropriate behavior in this foreign environment, drawing on a sense of national loyalty. Their common beliefs and traditions have not been destroyed by war and help unite them.

For Christmas 1944, the POWs again received packages from the German Red Cross.[71] After an introductory article about the ways they are celebrating this year, there are articles about previous wartime Christmases. One soldier writes about Christmas in 1942, while he was still in the barracks in Germany, yet many were able to spend their leave with family.[72] Next, another soldier writes about Christmas 1943 in northern Africa, where they did not have much to enjoy: "No Christmas tree, no nuts and fruitcake – we just had a hot gulp of coffee and some chocolate as our little Christmas present."[73] While the soldiers had few consumable luxuries, they celebrated their military victories and saw those as rewards for their efforts. A similar sentiment is seen a few months later, in an article reflecting on Easter 1945. Heinz Fischer recalls how the men experienced Easter as children, hunting for eggs, then as adults, playing the Easter Bunny for their children, and most recently as soldiers, finding time for reflection during a brief break from the fighting.[74] The experiences they had in war now provide "the authority, the confidence, to carry the hope in us, which is stronger than that experienced in the past, that lets us remain strong in our belief in our homeland, in our belief in the future."[75] A similar Easter article appears in *Der Zaungast*, written by a POW as a letter to his wife. It is a series of memories, from their younger years, through being separated by war, and now as parents of a child whom he has not seen.[76] His wife's letters about their daughter's Easter egg hunt provide him strength during this uncertain time. These personal reflections on the privations endured during recent wartime, together with those about fond holidays spent with family, help forge collective memories of the past. These collective memories in turn allow them to get through the current unfamiliarity. Just as they do not forget those at home, the packages prove that the nation has not forgotten the POWs and that they owe their nation gratitude in the form of good conduct.

POWs as Cultivators and Cooks

The POWs at both Fort McClellan and Camp Aliceville cooked their own meals, baked their own bread, and at Fort McClellan, they also prepared food for American soldiers and civilians. This arrangement both allowed the prisoners to provide some of their own care, and gave the prisoners more control over what they ate, improving their disposition.[77] In the prisoners' own descriptions of themselves as food growers and preparers, we see their fears reflected about what Germany will be like when they return, what impact their time in captivity will have on their homecoming and their starting over, as well as some attempts at humor, in a situation that otherwise offered few reasons for levity.

The work details involving food preparation at Fort McClellan were among the many documented, including one at the local hospital kitchen. The report begins with the married author and co-editor, Paul Metzner, expressing his concern that his wife might later read his report and then want to "summon him 'to the test'… at home."[78] To reassure the reader that their work as POWs will not mean more housework once they return home, he says he was only an assistant, and he need not worry about her future demands. In the last paragraph, the POWs clean the kitchen and prepare to return to the camp. Again, fear that the men may be acquiring useful domestic skills surfaces, as they all must clean and "as a soldier everyone knows this side of a soldier's life. I am just afraid that some have become so experienced through years of practice, that in their own households later they will… or maybe they won't?"[79] The paragraph and report conclude with the POWs returning to their compound and reentering their existence as prisoners. "From the guard towers the spotlight's beam traces along the barbed wire fences and for five bakers, who have again turned into POWs, the gate opens to enter the everyday life of a POW."[80] The end of the report returns the men to their present condition of captivity. There is not an immediate need to worry about what may come when they are home, whether their wives will expect them to apply their acquired domestic skills in the kitchen. The middle of the article about the hospital kitchen focuses on the challenges of baking. American soldiers supervise them and create the menu, which causes some confusion, both because of the language barrier and because of the unfamiliar cuisine. One morning, the instructions simply state: "upside peaches, cake down."[81] Once the baker reflects on the previous day's conversation, he is able to decipher the vague instructions, though this is not his only frustration. It took some time to realize that biscuits are a type of roll and that marble cake does not refer to its density or weight; the POWs are still uncertain what is appetizing about Waldorf salad. The bakers struggle with supply shortages as well. On this day, they did not have much shortening, likely due to rationing, and are told to grease the pan very sparsely, though they do not follow these instructions.[82] An article a few months later about the Fort bakery, which was staffed by POWs, describes how each worker is responsible for one step of the bread baking, which he labels the "American system."[83] Their jobs provide an opportunity to interact with a different set of people, a chance to be productive, and to get away from the confines of their camp, but once behind barbed wire, the bakers are just POWs.

The POWs in Aliceville cultivated plants, it seems, primarily for decorative purposes.[84] At Fort McClellan, however, in addition to helping local farmers harvest cotton, peanuts and other foodstuffs, POWs grew some of their own food, initially in a greenhouse and on garden plots and later on a leased farm. One article puts the wide variety of new occupations in a military context: "One gets to know some things as a soldier that used to be far outside of one's area of interest: one becomes a cotton picker, the other a peanut harvester (a wonderful word, right?), farmer, baker's assistant… gardener, grass cutter, street builder, mosquito hunter and I don't know what all else."[85] The men knew that they would gain new skill sets in the military, but being held in Alabama provides some very unique and memorable ones. The new skills do not seem very applicable in the future, however, or in the case of the housekeeping, they hope they are not.

In April 1944, the POWs at Fort McClellan received a variety of vegetable and herb seed packets from the German Red Cross. Though the suggested planting time had passed, and they had little experience and poor soil, four men in the eighth company decided to plant them.[86] A few months later their efforts were rewarded when they could supply cucumber salad and maturing plants to transplant.[87] An article on beekeeping describes an apiary on the grounds, constructed and maintained by a POW.[88] The twelfth company had a greenhouse, which was functional by September 1944; it produced 70,000 cabbage plants and 10,000 tomato plants for the farm, in addition to a variety of flowers.[89] Around this time, the American military leased a nearby 150-acre farm.[90] Initially, POWs helped prepare the land, which had lain fallow in recent years, likely because the farmer was called to active military duty. The first harvest was not very successful, largely due to dry conditions. In the December 1944 article plans are already made for the next year, and while Alabamian soil and climate are inherently challenging, the work is rewarding: "I gladly believe all the comrades who have worked outside that the voice of our homeland sounded through their work on the farm. They were farmers on American soil – they will likely again one day break German soil with twice the respect and then laughing, remember the days that they experienced as farmhands on a POW farm."[91] Manual labor, and in this case working the land, allows the men to feel closer to home, as well as gain fond memories. This kind of work is familiar, unlike baking and cleaning in the kitchen, something many likely did before the war and will again do when they return home.

Medical articles frequently appear in the Camp Aliceville materials, as several POWs were trained medical professionals. One article on vitamins begins with the differences between packaging in the US and Germany, suggesting that the POWs may not understand the importance of vitamins and misunderstand the information on packaging and in advertisements as hype, similar to common perceptions discussed above regarding American marketing practices.[92] The article concludes with commentary on camp life, assuring readers that they are given sufficiently varied diet and need not fear avitaminosis.[93] Ten months later, after the war is over, an article by the Camp pharmacist on calories addresses the amount and kinds of food that the body needs to thrive.[94] This was likely published in response to reduced access to some food and luxury items, as well as a general reduction in the size and quality of the meals.[95] While there are no direct mentions of the Camp or what the men eat, the final paragraph discusses daily calorie requirements, depending on exertion levels. Immediately following it is an article titled "'From nothing comes nothing'... says Walter Fessel to the urgent calorie question."[96] This provocative title indicates that the POWs are frustrated with their reduced food intake, and Fessel argues that they cannot function on 2500 calories a day, explicitly contradicting the preceding article. He suggests that they can no longer perform simple duties such as kitchen patrol, much less strenuous ones, given their reduced intake. The POWs did receive sufficient nourishment, but this sudden scarcity resulted in some rebellion and fear that more restrictions are in their immediate future.

A more humorous take on this situation comes several weeks later in anecdotal form. Camp Aliceville also has apiaries and occasionally problems with swarming bees according to "Two Bee Stings."[97] The narrator complains of swollen cheeks after being stung, but spiteful POWs think he has gained weight and ask if he knows of an additional food source, likely in response to recent cutbacks in their diet. On Sunday, he is initially not given his piece of *Bienenstich* (bee sting), a cream-filled cake, because it is thought he has already eaten. After some convincing, he gets his cake, but the actual bee sting still plagues him.[98] This article evinces some humor in what was otherwise an uncertain time. As is true here, sometimes the humor becomes oblique because the contemporary reader lacks context, but the POWs seem to have also realized that their situation was not so dire. Humor is similarly reflected in "The 'Colorful Page'" of a November 1944 edition of *POW-Oase*, a page reserved for jokes, anecdotes and wordplay.[99] The four jokes all revolve around food, and two of them are about gluttony. In "Appetite again," Maier goes to a doctor and complains about his irregular appetite. The doctor suggests that when one eats pig knuckle and potato dumplings, two German favorites, one should not be surprised if one is no longer hungry. Maier replies: "That isn't the problem, Staff Surgeon! I didn't have an appetite before I ate."[100] In the second column, titled "Incoming Joke," the narrator states that the entrance to the canteen is rather narrow, causing difficulties when someone tries to enter while another is leaving. "One mumbles: 'I don't get out of the way for every ox!' – 'But I do!' said the other and went to the side."[101] These POWs knew that they did not face the food shortages, severe rations and scavenging that so many of their counterparts did. Their expanding waistlines provided something to laugh about, when little else did.

The two WWII Alabamian POW newspapers discussed here, *Der Zaungast* and *POW-Oase*, give us insight into how the German captives viewed themselves, their captors and both nations. Food is a prominent theme in the numerous editions of POW newspapers. It provides a rich source for scholarship on POWs because food, as Roland Barthes suggests, represents "a system of communication, a body of images, a protocol of usages, situations, and behavior."[102]

The images of oases and coke bottles, descriptions of growing and preparing food, moral reprimands, concerns about domestic chores once home—read together these descriptions of food cultivation, preparation and consumption help us identify and explore the many roles food played during internment. While these soldiers were in a rather unique situation of food abundance because they were in the US, food became no less important, and perhaps because of their relative wealth, they were able to see food through many lenses—the men created psychological links to their homeland through shared imagery and traditions; they established distinctions between themselves and their captors based on character perceptions of artificiality and superficiality; they expressed their fears about uncertain cultural changes during their absence; and they forged a moral universe to guide them on their way home. For a brief time, the soldiers were able to create their own oases at the POW camps, to be sheltered from the war waging at home and to mentally, physically and emotionally prepare for their return and next task, to rebuild a defeated nation.

Notes

1. See Chapters 2 and 11 in Ruth Beaumont Cook, *Guests Behind the Barbed Wire. German POWs in America: A True Story of Hope and Friendship* (Birmingham: Crane Hill Publishers, 2007).
2. Jack Shay, *The Fort McClellan POW Camp* (Jefferson, NC: McFarland, 2016), 15–16.
3. Shay, *Fort McClellan*, 35. Walker lists 11 temporary and 15 permanent camps in Alabama. Aliceville was by far the largest, with a capacity of 6150. Fort McClellan, Camp Rucker, and Opelika all had capacities of about 3000. E.B. Walker, *Prisoner of War Camp Aliceville* (Birmingham, AL: Published by Braxton Walker, 1993), 3.
4. Arnold Krammer, *Nazi Prisoners of War in America* (New York: Stein & Day, 1996), 175.
5. Walker, *Aliceville*, 19.
6. Krammer, *Nazi*, 81.
7. Ibid., 54, 61.
8. *Zaungast* is difficult to translate. As a noun compound, it is made of fence or gate and guest. However, the word can also mean uninvited spectator, which applies to these men. They were also fenced in guests.
9. Camp Rucker and Camp Opelika had newspapers as well, but I have not been able to obtain many editions, and they do not appear to have been

published as frequently or as long. For example, the June 1945 edition of *Der Querschnitt* (Fort Opelika) was intended to democratize and reeducate prisoners, as large portions of the newspaper are about the American constitution, the US's role in the world and various aspect of American history; it is likely they are comprised of summaries of other sources. See Krammer and Gansberg for details on the Reeducation Program.

10. Unsurprisingly, there is very little mention of censorship in the newspapers. See Chapter 6 in Krammer as well as Chapter 4 in Gansberg for more details: Judith M. Gansberg, *Stalag: USA. The Remarkable Story of German POWs in America* (New York: Crowell Company, 1977), 65–88.
11. Samuel Hynes, *Soldiers' Tale: Bearing Witness to a Modern War* (New York: Penguin Press, 1998), 3.
12. Ibid., 11.
13. Ibid., 12.
14. Marius Kwint, "Introduction: The Physical Past," in *Materializing Culture: Design and Evocation*, edited by M. Kwint, C. Breward, and J. Aynsley (Oxford: Berg, 1999), 2.
15. For a discussion of this paradox, see Mark Hewitson, "'I Witnesses': Soldiers, Selfhood and Testimony in Modern Wars," *German History* 28, no. 3 (2010): 313.
16. Katarzyna J. Cwiertka, "Sustaining and Comforting the Troops in the Pacific War," in *Food in Zones of Conflict: Cross-Disciplinary Perspectives*, edited by Paul Collinson and Helen Macbeth (New York: Berghahn, 2014), 133.
17. For studies on a First World War newspaper, see for example: Jeanne Glaubitz Cross and Ann K.D. Meyers, "*Orgelsdorfer Eulenspiegel* and the German Internee Experience at Fort Oglethorpe, 1917–1919," *The Georgia Historical Quarterly* 96, no. 2 (2012): 233–259. An important collection containing analysis of various forms of creative work by prisoners and captives during both world wars is found in: Gilly Carr and Harold Mytum, eds., *Cultural Heritage and Prisoners of War: Creativity Behind Barbed Wire* (New York: Routledge, 2012).
18. See, for example, Aaron Horton, *German POWs, Der Ruf, and the Genesis of Group 47: The Political Journey of Alfred Andersch and Hans Werner Richter* (Madison, NJ: Fairleigh Dickinson University Press, 2014); and Ron Robin, "*Der Ruf*: Inner Emigration, Collective Guilt and the POW," in *Barbed-Wire College: Reeducating German POWs in the United States During World War II* (Princeton: Princeton University Press, 1995), 75–90.
19. There is disagreement in the scholarship about whether or not those who initially came to Camp Aliceville and Fort McClellan were part of

Rommel's *Afrika Korps*. Some scholars suggest that those in Aliceville were primarily from the *Heeresgruppe Afrika*; see Walker, *Aliceville*, 13. It is not my goal here to determine exactly who was held at either camp and that will likely never be possible as the military records are no longer accessible (Shay, *Fort McClellan*, 62).

20. Donald Filtzer and Wendy Z. Goldman, "Introduction: The Politics of Food and War," in *Hunger and War: Food Provisioning in the Soviet Union During World War II*, edited by Donald Filtzer and Wendy Z. Goldman (Bloomington: Indiana University Press, 2015), 27.
21. All translations are my own. The original reads: "...es war um uns her wie ein Stueckchen Heimat." "Zum Geleit," *POW-Oase*, October 10, 1943, 1.
22. "Wir stehen in dem fremden Land wie eine Oase, die sich abhebt von der sie umgebenden Welt." "Zum Geleit," 1.
23. In Aliceville, for example, there were creative writing competitions sponsored by the YMCA's War Prisoners Aid Program. The winners are acknowledged in several editions of *Der Zaungast* when the pieces are published. For details on the YMCA's involvement, see Cook, *Guests*, 216–217.
24. "Bei den Arabern zu Gast. In einem Zeltdorf der libyschen Wueste," *POW-Oase*, October 10, 1943, 3–4.
25. Ibid., 4.
26. "Abdallahs Empfehlungsbrief," *Der Zaungast*, April 8, 1945, 1–2.
27. Ibid., 2.
28. Ibid., 1.
29. This story is cited as having won the first prize in the literary competition's (*Dichterwettbewerb*) short story category. Tonny Rosini, "Traum am Rande Gafsas. Afrikanische Skizze von Tonny Rosini," *Der Zaungast*, December 25, 1944, 5.
30. Ibid.
31. "Ich ging. Ich ging sehr schnell und wusste nicht wohin." Rosini, "Traum," 5.
32. Ibid.
33. I discuss the importance of holidays later in this article. Walter Muench, "In der Heimat...," *Der Zaungast*, December 25, 1944, 6.
34. Heinz Wagner-Richelmann, "Tagebuchskizzen," *Der Zaungast*, December 25, 1944, 6–7.
35. Ibid., 7.
36. Ibid.
37. Brian K. Feltman, *The Stigma of Surrender: German Prisoners, British Captors, and Manhood in the Great War and Beyond* (Chapel Hill: University of North Carolina Press, 2015), 195.

38. Paul Metzner, "Aus meinem Tagebuch," *POW-Oase*, November 9, 1943, 3–4. This article title speaks to another theme present, namely that the newspaper serves as a kind of diary that they can all take home to document their experience.
39. "Schilder an der Strassenseite, die ausnahmsweise einmal nicht mit Frauenkoepfen locken und Coca-Cola als lebenswichtiges Getraenk preisen, weisen den Weg zu einem See." Metzner, "Tagebuch," 3.
40. "Der Arbeitstag ist vollbracht und gleitet hinueber in den Feierabend, in dem sich die Farmarbeiter wieder zu dem wandeln, was sie schliesslich auch dort draussen im Arbeitseinsatz waren: deutsch denkende Menschen im uniformierenden Anzug eines POWs." Metzner, "Tagebuch," 4.
41. "Obwohl die Autostrassen genau wie in unserem Vaterland erstklassig sind, fehlen doch die idyllischen sauberen Doerfchen." H. Baumann, "Vom Podium aus. Mit der Kapelle auf grosser Fahrt," *POW-Oase*, July 27, 1944, 3–4.
42. "Statt eines vertraeumten Kirchetuermchens, das uns vorwitzig in unserer Heimat ueber die Obstbaeume hinweg gruesst, rufen uns hier die schreiendsten Reklameschilder 'Pepsicola is the drink for you' zu." Baumann, "Podium," 3.
43. "Heute kann ich es verstehen wenn europaeische und da wieder vorwiegend deutsche Auswanderer, die es in der neuen Welt Amerika zu Ansehen und Vermoegen gebracht haben, sich gar oft in stillem Heimweh verzehren." Baumann, "Podium," 3.
44. Paul Metzner, "In Troy und Luverne. Ueber ein Gespraech mit den rueckgekehrten Kameraden," *POW-Oase*, October 25, 1944, 5–6.
45. "Dazu natuerlich leere Konservenbuechsen, Coca-Cola-Flaschen und… ein mehr oder weniger luxurioeser Ford in einem Schuppen des Hofes." Metzner, "Troy," 5.
46. Friedrich Gross, "Von der amerikanischen Werbung," *Fortbildungsunterlagen fuer das Kriegsgefangenenlager Aliceville*, February 4, 1945, 3–4.
47. "…z.B. Verminderung der Hausarbeit durch elektrische Kuechen, Erleichterung und Vereinfachung des Kochens durch fertige Nahrungsmittel in Dosen, Steigerung der Schoenheitspflege nach Hollywood-Muster usw." Gross, "Werbung," 4.
48. Gross, "Werbung," 3. Not surprisingly, the POWs were concerned about what their wives would be like once they returned. For example, other cartoons in *Der Zaungast* depict fears about the women having affairs and meddling in their husband's careers.

49. Gross, "Werbung," 4. Ironically, this typical American cartoon style is used on the last page of later editions of *Der Zaungast*, frequently depicting highly sexualized women.
50. "Ueber die Wichtigkeit der Vitamine in der Ernaehrung, die Aufgaben der Nachkriegszeit, die derzeitigen Kriegssorgen und vieles andere mehr." Gross, "Werbung," 4.
51. "Die Werbung ist ein Spiegelbild der Wirtschaft und des Wesens eines Volkes." Gross, "Werbung," 4.
52. Hans Leupelt, "Deutsches Bier," *Fortbildungsunterlagen*, February 4, 1945, 4–6. *POW-Oase* has a similar article on the history of German beer, published in two consecutive editions: F. Blank, "Der Fachmann spricht. Das Deutsche Bier und seine Herstellung," *POW-Oase*, September 1, 1944, 3–4; F. Blank, "Das Deutsche Bier und seine Herstellung," *POW-Oase*, September 7, 1944, 5.
53. There are a few times in the *POW-Oase* where a list of available items is printed. A POW wrote in asking if one could grow a peach tree from a seed of a recently purchased peach. "Du fragst – wir antworten," *POW-Oase*, July 27, 1944, 8.
54. Walker, *Aliceville*, 3. Cook details the story of the printer purchase; see Cook, *Guests*, 340–341. The printing press explains why the materials from Camp Aliceville, which also include calendars and concert programs, look professional and neater. Materials at Fort McClellan were typed and then reproduced, as was generally true at POW camps.
55. Heinz Fischer, "…und zum Feierabend: in die Kantine!" *POW-Oase*, November 29, 1944, 3–4. In accordance with the Geneva Convention, the NCOs at Aliceville were paid 80 cents a day. Cook, *Guests*, 320.
56. Fischer, "…und zum Feierabend," 3.
57. Ibid.
58. Helmut Klemm, "Die Woche: Festliche Abende an der Lagerbuehne," *POW-Oase*, July 20, 1944, 1. Interestingly, he refers to the warm summer winds as *Schirokko* (sirocco), a wind that blows from North Africa to southern Europe, which is another example of the POWs bringing desert imagery with them.
59. Fischer, "…und zum Feierabend," 4. The changes made after the war ends are addressed in: Paul Metzner, "Einstmals Post Exchange," *POW-Oase*, May 15, 1945, 4–6.
60. Paul Metzner, "Einstmals Post Exchange," 4. The significant reductions, also affecting cigarettes, are mentioned again in: Paul Metzner, "Nach der Zählung. Wie ein Abend im PW-Camp McClellan aussieht," *POW-Oase*, May 30, 1945, 4.
61. "Germanin," *Fortbildungsunterlagen fuer das Kriegsgefangenenlager Aliceville*, January 21, 1945, 4–5.

62. "Germanin," 4.
63. It is unclear what the marionette show was about, but there was a well-known puppeteer at Camp Aliceville, Walter Büttner; therefore, this seems plausible. He crafted the marionettes and wrote some of his own material.
64. At the end of the story, the source is listed as "Quelle: Unger, Germanin," though it is unclear if someone had read the book before arriving at the camp or if it was available in the camp library or had been received in a shipment. "Germanin," 5.
65. Lizzie Cunningham, *The Taste of War: WWII and the Battle for Food* (New York: Penguin, 2012), 416.
66. Camp Aliceville received shipments as well, though they are not documented the same way in *Der Zaungast*; some are noted in the 1945 *Taschen Kalender* that they printed for themselves, as noteworthy events from 1944.
67. "Die Heimat gedachte unser," *POW-Oase*, January 10, 1944, 6.
68. "Wir alle sehen in der Spende einen eindringlichen Beweis der Verbundenheit der Heimat mit uns und werden unseren Dank durch eine entsprechende Haltung abzustatten wissen." "Die Heimat," 6.
69. "Unser herzlichster Dank gilt unseren Volksgenossen in diesem suedamerikanischen Staat, die draussen in der weiten Welt ihre Heimat nicht vergessen haben." "Ein Geschenk der Deutschen in Argentinen," *POW-Oase*, September 22, 1944, 3.
70. Oliver Wilkinson, "Captivity in Print: The Form and Function of POW Camp Magazines," in *Cultural Heritage and Prisoners of War*, edited by Gilly Carr and Harold Mytum (New York: Routledge, 2012), 227–243.
71. Helmut Klemm, "Weihnachten 1944," *POW-Oase*, December 25, 1944, 1–2.
72. Paul Metzner, "Weihnachten in der Kaserne," *POW-Oase*, December 25, 1944, 3–4.
73. "Kein Tannenbaum, keine Nuesse und Christfeststollen – nur ein heisser Schluck Kaffee und etwas Schokolade hatten wir als weihnachtliche Beigabe." "Weihnachten in Afrika," *POW-Oase*, December 25, 1944, 5.
74. Heinz Fischer, "Ostern 1945", *POW-Oase*, April 1, 1945. This edition is missing some pages and the pages are not numbered.
75. "...die Berechtigung, die Zuversicht, die Hoffnung in uns zu tragen, die staerker ist als das Erleben der Gegenwart, die uns stark bleiben laesst im Glauben an unsere Heimat, im Glauben an die Zukunft." Fischer, "Ostern 1945."
76. Werner Stein, "Ostererinnerungen," *POW-Oase*, April 1, 1945, 1–2.
77. The negotiation process and details are not clear, but the camps were willing to adjust the ingredients that they provided to the German POWs to prepare. Cook, *Guests*, 190.

78. "...mich dann 'zur Probe aufs Exempel' an dein heimischen Backtrog beordert." Paul Metzner, "Ich bin Baecker geworden," *POW-Oase*, September 7, 1944, 3.
79. "...jeder kennt als Soldat diese Seite des Soldatenlebens. Ich fuerchte bloss, dass einige in jahrelanger Uebung darin so firm geworden sind, dass sie spaeter im eignen Haushalt...oder etwas doch nicht?" Metzner, "Baecker," 4.
80. "Von den Postentuermen aus greifen die Lichtkegel der Scheinwerfer an den Stacheldrahtzaeunen entlang, und fuer fuenf wieder in Kriegsgefangene verwandelte Baecker oeffnet sich das Tor zum Eintritt in den PW-Alltag." Metzner, "Baecker," 4.
81. Metzner, "Baecker," 3.
82. Ibid., 4.
83. "Kommandos erzählen. Stimmungsbilder aus dem Arbeitseinsatz," *POW-Oase*, June 16, 1945, 3.
84. The Alabama Department of Archives and Records has several pictures of Camp Aliceville, which was almost entirely dismantled after the end of the war, including decorative gardens and a greenhouse. See, for example, "Elaborate Landscaping in a Garden Between Barracks at the German POW Camp in Aliceville, Alabama," Alabama Department of Archives and Records, accessed May 11, 2018, http://digital.archives.alabama.gov/cdm/singleitem/collection/photo/id/3059/rec/15.
85. "Man lernt eben als Soldat so manches kennen, das frueher weit ausserhalb der Interessenspaere lag; der eine wird Baumwollpfluecker, der andere Erdnuss-Ernter (ein wunderbares Wort, nicht wahr?) Farmer, Baeckergehilfe..., Gaertner, Grasschneider, Strassenbauer, Mosiktojaeger und was weiss ich sonst noch." Paul Metzner, "Auf Waldkommando," *POW-Oase*, August 17, 1944, 3–4.
86. "Wie unser Schrebergarten entstand," *POW-Oase*, July 8, 1944, 3–4.
87. In both POW newspapers, there are very few references to problems or conflicts that arose at the camps, likely so as not to arouse suspicion of any unruliness by the censors; however, here there is a plea that soldiers stop stealing vegetables at night, as they are for everyone's enjoyment. "Schrebergarten," 4.
88. "Ueber Bienenzucht," July 10, 1944, 3–4.
89. Paul Metzner, "'Lasst Blumen Sprechen.' Ein Besuch im Gewaechshaus unseres Camps," *POW-Oase*, November 11, 1944, 3–4.
90. Paul Metzner, "Unsere POW-Farm," *POW-Oase*, December 25, 1944, 6–7.
91. "Ich glaube all den Kameraden, die dort draussen gearbeitet haben, gern, dass durch ihre Farmarbeit hindurch die Stimme der Heimat klang. Sie waren Farmer auf amerikanischer Erde – sie werden vielleicht

dereinst wieder mit doppelter Ehrfurcht die deutsche Scholle brechen und sich dann laechelnd der Tage erinnern, die sie als Farmarbeiter einer POW Farm erlebten." Metzner, "POW-Farm," 7.
92. Kalkoff, "Vitamine," *Fortbildungsunterlagen fuer das Kriegsgefangenenlager Aliceville*, August 11, 1944, 5–6.
93. Kalkoff, "Vitamine," 6.
94. Lepel, "Kalorien – gewonnene Energie aus der Nahrung," *Der Zaungast*, June 3, 1945, 2.
95. Cook, *Guests*, 452.
96. Walter Fessel, "'Von nichts…kommt nichts…' meint Walter Fessel zur brennenden Kalorienfrage," *Der Zaungast*, June 3, 1945, 2–3.
97. Kurt Rahnenfuehrer, "Zweimal Bienenstich," *Der Zaungast*, July 17, 1945, 6–7.
98. Rahnenfuehrer, "Zweimal," 7.
99. "Die 'Bunte Seite'," *POW-Oase*, November 9, 1944, 7.
100. "Maier: 'Dos ist net schuld, Herr Stabsarzt! I hob schon vorher kan Appetit g'habt!'" "Nochmal Appetit," "Die 'Bunte Seite,'" *POW-Oase*, November 9, 1944, 7.
101. "Murmelt einer: 'Ich weiche doch nicht jedem Ochsen aus!' – 'Aber ich!' sagte der andere und ging zur Seite." "Witz zwischen Tuer und Angel," "Die 'Bunte Seite'," *POW-Oase*, November 9, 1944, 7.
102. Roland Barthes, "Toward a Psychosociology of Contemporary Food Consumption," in *European Diet from Pre-Industrial to Modern Times*, edited by Elborg Forster and Robert Forster (New York: Harper Torchbooks, 1975), 50.

Bibliography

"Abdallahs Empfehlungsbrief." *Der Zaungast*, April 8, 1945.
Barthes, Roland. "Toward a Psychosociology of Contemporary Food Consumption." In *European Diet from Pre-Industrial to Modern Times*, edited by Elborg and Robert Forster, 47–60. New York: Harper Torchbooks, 1975.
Baumann, H. "Vom Podium aus. Mit der Kapelle auf grosser Fahrt." *POW-Oase*, July 27, 1944.
"Bei den Arabern zu Gast. In einem Zeltdorf der libyschen Wueste." *POW-Oase*, October 10, 1943.
Blank, F. "Das Deutsche Bier und seine Herstellung." *POW-Oase*, September 7, 1944.
———. "Der Fachmann spricht. Das Deutsche Bier und seine Herstellung." *POW-Oase*, September 1, 1944.
Carr, Gilly, and Harold Mytum, eds. *Cultural Heritage and Prisoners of War: Creativity Behind Barbed Wire*. New York: Routledge, 2012.

Cook, Ruth Beaumont. *Guests Behind the Barbed Wire. German POWs in America: A True Story of Hope and Friendship*. Birmingham: Crane Hill Publishers, 2007.

Cross, Jeanne Glaubitz, and Ann K.D. Meyers, "*Orgelsdorfer Eulenspiegel* and the German Internee Experience at Fort Oglethorpe, 1917–1919." *The Georgia Historical Quarterly* 96, no. 2 (2012): 233–259.

Cunningham, Lizzie. *The Taste of War: WWII and the Battle for Food*. New York: Penguin, 2012.

Cwiertka, Katarzyna J. "Sustaining and Comforting the Troops in the Pacific War." In *Food in Zones of Conflict: Cross-Disciplinary Perspectives*, edited by Paul Collinson and Helen Macbeth, 133–144. New York: Berghahn, 2014.

"Die 'Bunte Seite.'" *POW-Oase*, November 9, 1944.

"Die Heimat gedachte unser." *POW-Oase*, January 10, 1944.

"Du fragst – wir antworten." *POW-Oase*, July 27, 1944.

"Ein Geschenk der Deutschen in Argentinen." *POW-Oase*, September 22, 1944, 3.

Feltman, Brian K. *The Stigma of Surrender: German Prisoners, British Captors, and Manhood in the Great War and Beyond*. Chapel Hill: University of North Carolina Press, 2015.

Fessel, Walter. "'Von nichts...kommt nichts...' meint Walter Fessel zur brennenden Kalorienfrage." *Der Zaungast*, June 3, 1945.

Filtzer, Donald, and Wendy Z. Goldman. "Introduction: The Politics of Food and War." In *Hunger and War: Food Provisioning in the Soviet Union During World War II*, edited by Donald Filtzer and Wendy Z. Goldman, 1–43. Bloomington: Indiana University Press, 2015.

Fischer, Heinz. "Ostern 1945." *POW-Oase*, April 1, 1945.

———. "...und zum Feierabend: in die Kantine!" *POW-Oase*, November 29, 1944.

Gansberg, Judith M. *Stalag: USA. The Remarkable Story of German POWs in America*. New York: Crowell Company, 1977.

"Germanin." *Fortbildungsunterlagen fuer das Kriegsgefangenenlager Aliceville*, January 21, 1945.

Gross, Friedrich. "Von der amerikanischen Werbung." *Fortbildungsunterlagen fuer das Kriegsgefangenenlager Aliceville*, February 4, 1945.

Hewitson, Mark. "'I Witnesses': Soldiers, Selfhood and Testimony in Modern Wars." *German History* 28, no. 3 (2010): 310–325.

Horton, Aaron. *German POWs, Der Ruf, and the Genesis of Group 47: The Political Journey of Alfred Andersch and Hans Werner Richter*. Madison, NJ: Fairleigh Dickinson University Press, 2014.

Hynes, Samuel. *Soldiers' Tale: Bearing Witness to a Modern War*. New York: Penguin Press, 1998.

Kalkoff. "Vitamine." *Fortbildungsunterlagen fuer das Kriegsgefangenenlager Aliceville*, August 11, 1944.

Klemm, Helmut. "Die Woche: Festliche Abende an der Lagerbuehne." *POW-Oase*, July 20, 1944.

———. "Weihnachten 1944." *POW-Oase*, December 25, 1944.

"Kommandos erzählen. Stimmungsbilder aus dem Arbeitseinsatz." *POW-Oase*, June 16, 1945.

Krammer, Arnold. *Nazi Prisoners of War in America.* New York: Stein & Day, 1996.

Kwint, Marius. "Introduction: The Physical Past." In *Material Memories: Design and Evocation*, edited by Marius Kwint, Christopher Breward, and Jeremy Aynsley, 1–16. Oxford: Berg, 1999.

Lepel. "Kalorien – gewonnene Energie aus der Nahrung." *Der Zaungast*, June 3, 1945.

Leupelt, Hans. "Deutsches Bier." *Fortbildungsunterlagen*, February 4, 1945.

Metzner, Paul. "Auf Waldkommando." *POW-Oase*, August 17, 1944.

———. "Aus meinem Tagebuch." *POW-Oase*, November 9, 1943.

———. "Einstmals Post Exchange." *POW-Oase*, May 15, 1945.

———. "Ich bin Baecker geworden." *POW-Oase*, September 7, 1944.

———. "In Troy und Luverne. Ueber ein Gespraech mit den rueckgekehrten Kameraden." *POW-Oase*, October 25, 1944.

———. "'Lasst Blumen Sprechen.' Ein Besuch im Gewaechshaus unseres Camps." *POW-Oase*, November 11, 1944.

———. "Nach der Zählung. Wie ein Abend im PW-Camp McClellan aussieht." *POW-Oase*, May 30, 1945.

———. "Unsere POW-Farm." *POW-Oase*, December 25, 1944.

———. "Weihnachten in der Kaserne." *POW-Oase*, December 25, 1944.

Muench, Walter. "In der Heimat...." *Der Zaungast*, December 25, 1944.

Rahnenfuehrer, Kurt. "Zweimal Bienenstich." *Der Zaungast*, July 17, 1945.

Robin, Ron. "*Der Ruf*: Inner Emigration, Collective Guilt and the POW." In *Barbed-Wire College: Reeducating German POWs in the United States During World War II*, 75–90. Princeton: Princeton University Press, 1995.

Rosini, Tonny. "Traum am Rande Gafsas. Afrikanische Skizze von Tonny Rosini." *Der Zaungast*, December 25, 1944.

Shay, Jack. *The Fort McClellan POW Camp.* Jefferson, NC: McFarland, 2016.

Stein, Werner. "Ostererinnerungen." *POW-Oase*, April 1, 1945.

Taschen Kalender 1945. Kriegsgefangenenlager Aliceville, AL, 1944.

"Ueber Bienenzucht." July 10, 1944.

Wagner-Richelmann, Heinz. "Tagebuchskizzen." *Der Zaungast*, December 25, 1944.

Walker, E.B. *Prisoner of War Camp Aliceville.* Birmingham, AL: Published by Braxton Walker, 1993.

"Wie unser Schrebergarten entstand." *POW-Oase*, July 8, 1944.

Wilkinson, Oliver. "Captivity in Print: The Form and Function of POW Camp Magazines." In *Cultural Heritage and Prisoners of War*, edited by Gilly Carr and Harold Mytum, 227–243. New York: Routledge, 2012.

"Zum Geleit." *POW-Oase*, October 10, 1943.

CHAPTER 7

The Productive *Heimat*: Territorial Loss and Rurality in German Identity at the *Stunde Null*

Christine Fojtik

Einstweilen, bis den Bau der Welt
Philosophie zusammenhält,
Erhält sie das Getriebe
Durch Hunger und durch Liebe.[1]
—Friedrich Schiller (1795), as quoted by a communist party food official in an internal memo about the dire nutritional situation in 1946 in Germany's Soviet Zone of Occupation

In 1948, three years after the end of the war and the subsequent division of Germany into zones of occupation administered respectively by the victorious Allies, a report circulated at the Administration for Food, Agriculture and Forests in the United Economic Zone [VELF—the Verwaltung der Ernährung, Landwirtschaft und Forsten des Vereinigten Wirtschaftsgebietes] about the continued difficulties of food production

C. Fojtik (✉)
Department of History and Political Science,
Saint Xavier University, Chicago, IL, USA

© The Author(s) 2019
H. M. Benbow and H. R. Perry (eds.), *Food, Culture and Identity in Germany's Century of War*,
https://doi.org/10.1007/978-3-030-27138-1_7

and distribution in the American- and British-controlled lands that made up the "United Economic Zone." The official report, written by a member of the food ministry and presented to agency head Dr. Schlange-Schöningen, struck a grave tone: "The East, with its surplus of food, was cut off, and its population forced out. The consequences were hopelessness, personal insecurity, unwillingness to work, unemployment misery, refugee chaos, a paralysis of economic life, the disruption of economic growth, and the unjust and inadequate distribution of needed goods."[2] In similar terms, the SED [*Sozialistische Einheitspartei Deutschlands*, Socialist Unity Party of Germany] noted in a 1946 report on conditions in the eastern zone that "Hunger, or the fear of hunger, defines the mental state of the modern German."[3] The missing "East" comprised the rich farmlands of eastern Prussia, which the Allied leadership awarded to Poland to compensate for the loss of eastern Polish lands to the Soviet Union. Ethnic Germans, some of whom had lived and farmed in the eastern lands for countless generations, made their way back to the truncated Reich in waves of expellees [*Volksvertriebene*], crowding the cities and straining already limited supplies of food. These "surplus lands" had ensured Germany's nutritional self-sufficiency—and now they were gone.

The "missing East," like a phantom limb, haunted postwar Germans; they hearkened to it again and again in their conversations with one another and their pleading letters to the food authorities, not to mention their official reports on food availability. They reminded the Allied occupiers that Germany's dire nutritional straits stemmed from the loss of territory that represented the disappearance of "48.5% of agricultural lands and 55% of the West's arable lands" overall.[4] The suffering of the expellees, who lost their homes to the redrawing of the map, emerged as synecdoche for the pain of the German people: from defeat, from humiliation, from hunger. The loss of the eastern lands was a loss of home, of material resources, and, symbolically, a loss of an entire way-of-life, of a particular understanding of homeland [*Heimat*] predicated on the maintenance of self-sustenance.

Other scholars have written about Germany's loss of land in the East and the role of food and hunger in representing loss of many kinds. Andrew Demshuk has written about the expellees' experience of integration in the West, challenging notions of their political radicalism while arguing that they held on to idealized notions of their lost *Heimat*.[5] Alice Weinreb explores how feeding refugees posed a central problem for German and occupation officials after the war, as well as how food and cooking accessed lost *Heimat* for expellees in the 1950s and 1960s.[6] Atina Grossmann has examined the ways that postwar hunger contributed to an emerging vocabulary of human rights in the postwar years, when the world grappled with a European refugee crisis of an unprecedented scale.[7] Here, I apply a broader lens to the experience of hunger and link it to past illusions about German self-sustenance. Just as food served as a link to past ways-of-life, hunger represented a negative link— to remembered hunger after the First World War and to remembered satiety in a better, more self-sufficient and agriculturally robust Germany.

Regional strife over access to food supplies reveals a key tension in postwar Germany: Would the new Germany conceive of itself as a nation of farmers, or one of large industrial cities? Conditions of scarcity brought out tensions between urban consumers and rural producers that the latter found especially galling given the apparently changing nature of the economic future. In letters to newspapers and the food ministry and in agricultural trade journals, farmers wondered aloud why they were being called on to work ever-harder for a German future with less and less room for them. If, in fact, future Germany would no longer define itself as an agricultural nation, why should the farmers be obligated to feed the countrymen working toward the extinction of the farming lifestyle? Conflict between town and country over food exposes questions about agriculture and industry that postwar Germans would have to answer in order to define their nation. It reinvigorated, too, the paradox the Nazis had sought to minimize by their valorization of the pre-industrial peasant-farmer: how to reconcile the progressive development of a highly industrialized economy with an agricultural historical identity.

The notion of *Heimat*, an idealized version of the local, embodied the duality and blurriness of this balance: The *Heimat* was self-sufficient, a town and its surrounding countryside, a perfect, closed ecosystem in which (semi)rural and (semi)urban lived in symbiotic harmony; it was both specific enough to appeal to the individual German and vague enough to resound with *all* Germans.[8] After 1945, Germans lost what some scholars have termed "alimentary sovereignty," that is, the ability to feed one's own population using the products of one's own land.[9] While this sovereignty was largely illusory in the first place—Nazi exploitation of the East, not prudent cultivation of pre-1939 German lands, had enabled seeming autarky—the physical loss of land in the East created a psychic sense of bodily vulnerability. Hunger and the need for food aid exacerbated this sense of vulnerability by providing daily reminders of the apparent consequences of this loss. A loss of *Heimat* in the East, really applicable only to the expellees who had been removed from lands awarded to Poland and other nations by the peace settlement, became a psychic loss of self-sufficiency for all Germans. All Germans lost their "*Heimat*" because they lost their ability to depend on rural identity as the underpinning of an imagined national self-concept.

Germans suffered materially from the loss of the lands beyond the Oder-Neisse and felt the pain of losing a critical component of their erstwhile national identity. The Oder-Neisse line marked off the historically Prussian, heavily agricultural lands awarded to Poland at Yalta. Germans' senses of anguish—and, sometimes, victimization—over the loss of lands in the East have often been framed in terms of a longing for *Heimat*, that ineffable connection between local and national identity that has defined and complicated Germanness since unification.[10] Eastern expellees presented such a compelling image of German victimhood because of their literal loss of home. *Heimat* is not just a spatial concept, however, but a psychological ideal, one associated with turn-of-the-century village life that retained a crucial bucolic component. The idealized *Heimat*, Alon Confino has suggested, is neither urban nor rural as such, but a culturally rich, locally cohesive hybrid.[11] In the wake of postwar food shortage, the connection of the idealized village to the rural breadbasket became increasingly salient and increasingly out-of-reach. Longing for *Heimat* entailed a nostalgic yearning for a time of alimentary plenty, characterized by a spiritual connection to the land and food self-sufficiency.

If Germany could no longer claim a strong connection to its rural past, what, exactly, made it *German*? How would the tension between the rural/agricultural and the urban/industrial be resolved, and what would be the consequences for a post-Nazi, postwar identity? To answer these questions, we must first revisit the importance of rurality to German identity; German connection with the land was not merely psychic or rhetorical, but was practically reinforced by the full bellies most Germans enjoyed throughout the Second World War. Second, loss of the expellees' literal *Heimat* in the East became a loss for all Germans: practically, because the mitigation of farmland cut into the ability to self-feed, and psychologically, because the very notion of *Heimat* was predicated on a productive semi-rurality.

A Brief History of German Industrialization

Germany's loss of agricultural identity was part of a larger, longer process of industrialization that had been going on since the rise of the first smokestacks in Central Europe in the nineteenth century. While France, Britain and other earlier-developing industrial powers struggled with the consequences of growing urban populations, loss of rural regional identities, galloping capitalism, and the social and spiritual fallout of mechanization throughout the nineteenth century, these changes came faster and, arguably, more violently for Germany, which developed into a formidable commercial and industrial opponent for Britain in the late nineteenth century.[12] Germany's debut as an international industrial powerhouse accompanied political unification and strident internal debate about the relative role of agriculture and industry to German identity, about the need for protective tariffs favored by the estate-owning and politically influential Junker landowners of eastern Prussia, and in the context of a naval arms race fueled by the Kaiser's desire to compete with Great Britain.[13]

Though unification in 1871 coincided with a gradual decline in the agricultural way-of-life and a rise in urbanization and industrialization, German conservatives from the nineteenth century to the Nazis held to the notion of the land as the basis of German cultural and spiritual integrity. The rural ideal served as a unifying principle in a rapidly changing world; its power was rhetorical and psychological, and it resisted the realities of industrial and commercial growth and two world wars. Farmers and farming represented German culture and German values, even if farmers' actual share of the population and of employed adults diminished steadily after 1900.[14] Germany long saw itself as uniquely self-sufficient among European nations, able to provide for itself agriculturally and industrially. Nationalists of the late nineteenth and early twentieth centuries could point to galloping industrial growth as evidence that the German course of development both politically and economically was inarguably successful, that an industrial nation with a strong agrarian sector behind it was the best means of establishing a formidable national power.

Germany was great not because it recapitulated and then outstripped the British commercial and industrial model of civilization, but because it rose to such heights of success without losing its connection to its heritage. Industry remained connected to the nation's pre-national spiritual values, and the rural way-of-life represented an important component of these historic traditions. The Reichstag debates over Germany's future in the late nineteenth and early twentieth centuries centered around the question of protective tariffs for German agriculture, then and through World War II dominated by the aristocratic Junkers of the eastern parts of the country. Conservative intellectuals, including the prominent economist and agriculturalist Adolf Wagner, spoke out in favor of the Junkers' cause.[15] For Wagner and his colleagues, what was at stake in the conflict between the Junkers and the up-and-coming industrialists was not merely economic, but cultural and spiritual; German identity hinged, in his estimation, on the patriarchal, quasi-feudal social organization of the Junker estates, which cultivated and embodied a particular, unique German spirit [Geist].

Wagner's student, Werner Sombart, revisited such characterizations of the German character during World War I, inverting the argument that the Allies fought for "the ideas of 1789" or "western European civilization" against German "barbarism and militarism."[16] Sombart argued, instead, that the war really pitted a nation of merchants—British traders, with their spiritually bankrupt "shopkeeper ideal" [Krämerideal]—against German heroes, the heroes who put duty before profit, and nation [Volk] before individual wants and desires.[17] Germany's spiritual strength lay in its agrarian roots, in its resistance to the industrial forms of social organization that left the British so self-centered and morally bereft. It was no accident, of course, that the same types of insults Sombart and others lobbed at the British—that they were acquisitive, individualistic capitalists with no real sense of nation or connection to a larger Volk—were and would continue to be applied to the Jews, another group of nationless non-farmers who lacked a sense of "duty" and connection.[18]

The First World War occasioned the introduction of rationing in Germany, a major "industrial" intercession in Germans' mythically spiritual connection to the land. The calorie's association with food energy is a late-nineteenth innovation, passing from mid-nineteenth-century French physics terminology to American food science through the medium of German physiology. While the French Nicolas Clément is often credited with first using the term "calorie" to describe a unit of heat, French scientists spoke of calories in reference to steam engines; German scientists, from the 1860s through the turn-of-the-century, began to use calorimetry and the calorie unit to measure and describe the units of energy contained in food, including in efforts to analyze livestock feed and to determine the least expensive sources of nutritionally balanced foods and animal feeds.[19] The conception of food as human energy arose, then, alongside the growth of German industry and in conjunction with projects to rationalize and maximize animal work output. Similar logic—maximal work output on minimal caloric input—would underpin the creation of ration scales in World War I and beyond.

While wartime civil rationing held up remarkably well initially, thanks in large part to a significant degree of public cooperation, it faltered as the British-led blockade wore on and gave way to considerable suffering and deprivation.[20] Germany's eventual leaders learned two lessons from the apparent failure of civil rationing: first, that reliable sources of food needed to be secured for German civilians and military alike in order to support a sustained war effort; and second, that apparent "self-feeding" could be turned to the service of nationalism, enhancing popular cooperation and cohesion. A spiritual connection to the land went hand-in-hand with apparent self-sufficiency; well-fed Germans would drive the national expansion the Nazis had in mind. Though the blockade ended in 1919, the lean inflationary years of 1921–1923 confirmed for a certain strain of nationalist a belief in the importance of maintaining autarkic agricultural policies—or at least, an official policy of autarky, however much that might rely on the militarized domination of continental Europe. A veneer of autarkic self-sufficiency, supported by the exploitation of conquered lands to the East, allowed the Nazis to hearken back to an earlier, pre-industrial era of German development, one characterized by agricultural plenty and a rural way-of-life.

ALIMENTARY SOVEREIGNTY IN THE THIRD REICH

In the interwar period, anxiety about international entanglements prompted a raft of protective tariffs in Europe and Japan and presaged a widespread mania for autarky.[21] Importation of everything from foodstuffs to raw materials to manufactured goods, even on the eve of World War II and after Hitler's protracted push for autarky, allowed most Germans to accept apparent success at self-sufficiency at face value. According to Nazi ideology, successful autarky implied that Germans were uniquely suited to rule over the rest of Europe and steward the land and resources that other, lesser peoples squandered. Successful agricultural stewardship marked the superior race; "From the Nazi perspective,

Slavic peasants (though not German farmers) were superfluous. German farmers would reclaim the fertile soil with their own sweat and the blood of others."[22] Nationalism always underpinned German commitment to and pride in self-sufficiency, and expansionism was the corollary to proper resource management at home.

The Nazis' enthusiasm for industrial war-making did not dampen their affection for the rural ideal, and the notion of the farmer's spiritual labor infused thinking about work in general. The Nazi concept of *Leistung* elevated individualistic, virtuous German labor above that of non-Germans. Germans were bound by blood, but also by their sense of duty and the "joy" with which they approached their work.[23] *Leistung* "invoked achievement, performance, and fulfillment of a duty or task; it carried connotations of both the virtue of high individual performance and the need to achieve it through personal sacrifice"; it also justified the use of Jewish, Soviet and other non-German forced and slave labor, as well as the insufficient food rations provided to these workers.[24] Foreign and Jewish laborers were not human beings, but tools to make life easier and more convenient for Germans. These labor-saving devices contrasted with the fully human Germans, who spiritually labored for Heimat even as they dug coal alongside Soviet slave laborers in the Ruhr mines.

Rationalization played a significant role in the Nazi project of coordinating the German economy, but the Nazis only applied such strict caloric efficiency to their victims and enemies—not to the racially pure German populace, beneficiaries of the spiritual connection between people and land and not, therefore, subject to such a dehumanizing calculus of caloric rationalization. Ordinary Germans were subject to rationing categories during the war, but rationed amounts were quite generous, to such an extent that some military observers pointed to "excessive" and "inflated" levels of food availability during the war as the cause of Germans' dissatisfaction with more "realistic" ration levels after it. The League of Nations, in an effort to keep abreast of the expected crisis in food supplies, produced a 1942 report on the food situation and rationing policies in twenty-five European countries—including Germany but excluding the Soviet Union. The report found that "…the quantities of calories rationed amounts to nearly 100 per cent in the Axis area, whereas, it is around 50 per cent for the United Kingdom and Switzerland"; occupied Europe enjoyed only about 50% of its prewar consumption levels, and malnutrition was observed in Italy, France,

Belgium, Norway, Finland and Spain. Germany, meanwhile, continued to consume about 80% of its prewar caloric intake.[25]

There was little indication that the "undernourishment and malnutrition" that affected other parts of Europe was a major problem under the Third Reich. While the Nazis subjected Germany to *some* rationing, its comparatively minimal impact on daily life undergirded claims about Germany's capacity for autarky and fueled considerable shock and suffering when such relatively generous food supplies dried up at war's end. Of course, so-called wartime autarky was more of a propagandistic illusion than a reality: In fact, the Germans continued to enjoy plentiful food supplies even as the German army laid waste to European economies because of the Nazis' ruthless exploitation of foreign labor and agricultural produce. In 1942–1943, "occupied Europe supplied Germany with more than a fifth of its grain, a quarter of its fats, and almost 30 per cent of its meat," most of it from the General Government in present-day Poland.[26] When difficulties on the eastern front forced the regime to cut the rations of ordinary Germans in the spring of 1942, they met widespread outrage; the regime responded rapidly, re-committing itself to a policy of eastern exploitation. By October 19, 1942, German rations could be (re)increased thanks to successful coordination of foreign food imports.[27] These measures lulled the German population, which imagined that Nazi claims of German self-sufficiency were true. Germany could, to a certain extent, feed its own population in peacetime, but the pressures of war made autarky sustainable only with the added element of brutal exploitation of foreign peoples and lands.

The Collapse of the Productive *Heimat*

The Nazi ideal of "autarky" depended heavily on the exploitation of resources and labor on the expanding eastern frontier. Indeed, the pressures of urbanization and the changing dietary habits of a less-rural population strained Germany's pre-World War II agricultural capacity and contributed to right-wing desire for an agrarian German hinterland in the East. While Germany possessed a great deal of fertile agricultural lands and had much more success in feeding its own population than did less agricultural countries like England or the Netherlands, Germany in the 1930s was not "self-sufficient" to the extent that Hitler might have liked.[28] The rural ideal was a useful illusion that allowed Germans to consider themselves an industrial people who had built the future without having to sacrifice their spiritual core. Rurality stood in for spirituality; as long as Germans maintained a mythical connection to the soil, they could count themselves as superior to those who would recklessly industrialize without an eye to the national soul.

An examination of postwar German responses to food shortage illuminates the moment of crisis in the ongoing balancing act between *Industriestaat* and *Agrarstaat* within Germany, a crisis which heralded the unseating of German supremacy within Europe, not to mention the demotion of German power globally. The loss of the war was not Germany's only source of shame and tension in 1945; rather, the splitting of Germany and the conditions of defeat reintroduced old anxieties about the weakness of a nation characterized by industry and urbanity— like, for example, that of their old foes, the British, who may have triumphed again but at great personal cost, and only with the help of their American (and Soviet) allies.

In 1945, Germanness based on a productive rurality could no longer prevail in a world in which Germans struggled to feed themselves and depended on Allied support and intervention to keep them from starving. Bountiful harvests and plentiful tables were the mark of self-sufficient nineteenth-century agrarian Germanness, and the lack of such indices of well-being combined with defeat to shake the foundations of German identity. Defeat after World War I had been psychologically crushing and economically devastating, but it had not undermined German identity in such a wholesale fashion; hunger in 1918 could be attributed directly to the British blockade, not to the collapse of an agricultural ideal on which Germany had always been able to rely.

The *Heimat* ideal facilitated popular cohesion based on a balance between urban and rural. Now, tensions arose between producers and consumers who each resented the other group's supposed privileged status in the new postwar order. Occupation authorities elevated rations in cities in an effort to stem acute hunger and weaken black markets. Ration calculations took into account rural access to fresh fruits and vegetables, which could be scavenged, grown at home or supplied by sympathetic farming friends. "Hamstering," which involved scavenging for extra food in fields and forests, required more time, energy and transportation access for city residents than it did for the rural folk who already lived in or near prime hamstering locations. British zone food authorities, for example, considered such privileged rural access when they elevated rations by 200 calories/day for urban residents in their zone of occupation in the summer of 1946.[29]

Many of the farmers and villagers who complained to the food ministry cited the seemingly preferential treatment of the city dwellers as evidence of a sea change, one characterized by German dependence on foreign aid and, more insidiously but no less ominously, by an industrialized, mechanized population alienated from the land and from the fruits of their own labor. Urban complainants expected miracles instead of acknowledging the practical nature of agriculture. The urgency of food production demands reflected a fundamental misunderstanding of "the soil," beleaguered farmers argued. They complained about pressure to increase agricultural yields from the occupation authorities, food administration, and fellow Germans, none of whom really understood either the usual processes of farming or the new difficulties engendered by the war. "The farmer spends all his time in close contact with nature," opined a newspaper columnist about the misunderstood agriculturalist. "One cannot expect rapid results in the rebuilding of a devastated agricultural industry. All things in nature require time. Despite all of these difficulties, results have been so far very promising. To the hungry city dweller, however, this may come as a surprise."[30]

Labor for farming remained in short supply, as it did in all sectors of the economy. Plans to put the eastern refugees to work on the land emerged gradually, but in the meantime the agricultural field suffered from the lack of labor power due to the repatriation of forced/foreign workers, the continued absence of many men and the diminished physical capacities of some farmers due to the limited availability of a wide variety of nutritious food.[31] In some areas, denazification efforts exacerbated labor shortages. An attorney from Schleswig-Holstein reported that many local farmers—particularly the leaders of farming organizations—had belonged to the Nazi Party, and their removal from administrative positions had badly impacted local food production.[32] Denazification, claimed Herr Skowronski, led to "the installation of ignorants… simply because once upon a time, they signed the right Party book."[33] The (temporary) elevation of anti-fascist political credentials over experience and education has been well-documented, as has the eventual reversion of western Allied policies to ones that re-established former Nazis in their old positions. For several years after the war, though, denazification did have an impact on agricultural output as it further complicated an already confused, cash-poor and materially bereft operation.

Farmers struggled to revivify their livelihood in the absence of the material and human inputs necessary to do so. The western food ministry labored to maximize agricultural output by continuing the consolidation of fragmented farmlands that had begun under the Nazis, but this project was arduous and time-consuming: By 1949, only 1/3 of fragmented farmlands had been consolidated, and the food ministry estimated that at the present rate, it would take 80 years to consolidate lands in Bavaria, 60 years in Baden-Württemberg and 40–50 years in the remaining western lands.[34] The officials who calculated these disappointing figures noted that nearly 2.5 million hectares of the 5.8 million hectares of fragmented land in the combined former Germany had been consolidated, and that much of this consolidation had occurred in and would benefit those who lived outside the 1945 borders. Optimistic experts still hoped that land consolidation and the diversification of crops would modernize German agriculture, as in any case, "German agriculture must participate in the world economy," warned Herr Kling in an agricultural trade journal.[35] Farming could not be considered the solution to native hunger problems so much as part of the industrial solution to western Germany's future. "Germany will be a farmers' land or it won't be," Kling wrote tellingly, "but if we don't rebuild our industry, we're lost. Farmers, have faith in God and in yourselves! The legacy of our fathers is entrusted to us, and we must maintain and cultivate it."[36] While the rural ideal and its associations with *Heimat* could not, perhaps, be salvaged, the livelihoods of farmers certainly could, provided they were willing to change.

The "agrarian" Soviet zone worried about the caloric needs of the urban populace, despite its local reserves. Relatively urbanized regions (Saxony, e.g., the most densely populated of regions in the eastern zone) scrambled to coordinate "imports" from elsewhere in the zone.[37] Emerging communist organizations in the East sought to resolve the tension between urban and rural areas by promoting farming programs for young people. Farming was a "point of honor for our youth," according to Soviet zone youth organization, the *Freie Deutsche Jugend* (FDJ), because it "secured for our people their daily bread."[38] Hunger was a problem in postwar Germany no matter how close one lived to the hinterlands, and the rhetoric surrounding farm work underlines its practical value and its connection to *Heimat*. "The German village," proclaimed the FDJ, "is the refuge of peace, democracy, and progress... When the youth of city and country [*Stadt- und Landjugend*] go hand-in-hand, then a new democratic order will prevail in all the villages of Germany."[39] The FDJ linked *Heimat* to agricultural productivity, attempting to revive the formula that had seemingly allowed for self-sufficiency.

The Expellees and the End of German "Self-Sufficiency"

The nexus of Germany's agricultural and spiritual/cultural crises was the loss of land in the east, seen most dramatically in the plight of the expellees. The expellees consciously understood their loss as spiritually and materially catastrophic for Germany at large. One expellee wrote to the food ministry, "Without the eastern lands there is no Germany, and without Germany there is no Europe!"[40] The eastern lands housed, too, the necessary processing facilities for agricultural products. Much of the potato industry lay beyond the Oder-Neisse; the western zones produced some wheat and rice, as well as potatoes of "inferior quality," but could hardly approach the vast amounts of staple potatoes Germans were used to consuming.[41] Expellees addressed the VELF, rather than, or in addition to, the food division of the Economic Office (*Wirtschaftsamt—Abteilung Lebensmittel*) because they framed their concerns in terms of their own capacity to contribute to agricultural production, squandered by division of Germany to the detriment of everyone.

Canny expellees pointed to their lost homelands as the source of German deprivation, and sometimes framed their arguments for restitution in terms of a need for increased food. The expellees refigured territorial loss in global terms: Loss of the *Ostgebiete* [eastern lands] did not merely imperil German food supplies, but endangered European and global food supplies at a time when "hunger zones" constituted much of the world. The expellees couched their efforts at repatriation in terms of the food-producing potential of their former homes. They appealed to the food ministry, not exclusively on the basis of their historical claims to the lands of eastern Europe, or their emotional connection to their longstanding *Heimat*, but on the need for a productive agricultural solution to Germany's food shortage. Pointing to the importance of territorial revision for Germany's nutritional future, the letter writer who previously connected German and European fortunes estimated that the "*Abtrennung*" [partition] of the eastern regions would result in a 30%

reduction in farmland, a 23% reduction in forestland, a 35.5% reduction in rye production, 31% reduction in potato production and a 25% reduction in feed grain and sugar beet production, respectively.[42] It is not clear if the letter writer was attempting to calculate loss of productivity minus the lands beyond the Oder-Neisse or without those "lost" to both East Germany and Poland, but if the latter, his estimates were conservative. In 1944, 12,556,000 hectares of Germany was dedicated to the cultivation of cereal crops including wheat, rye, barley, oats, potatoes and sugar beets; in 1949, West Germany cultivated 5,522,000 hectares of its land for a loss of farmland of 56%.[43] While German expansionism may have been discredited by double military defeat, surely the health and well-being of the *Volk* itself could not be so easily forgotten. Could access to land not be justified in terms of caloric needs?

Accordingly, the expellees sought to depict themselves as producers rather than consumers, provided they were given access to the means of contributing meaningfully. One displaced Pomeranian dairyman wrote movingly to the VELF, citing his experience and the eager readiness of his teenaged sons and son-in-law to get back to work on the land.[44] He hoped the ministry could help them find work, and even enclosed a letter from his pastor vouching for his experience, work ethic and anti-Nazi credentials.[45] The food ministry had nothing to offer and directed him to get in touch with the Bonn-area farmers' association, but sympathized with "the great loss endured by all the eastern expellees."[46] The dairyman and his family did not want to be burdens, but could not readily find a place for themselves in the western zones. Similarly, a "healthy 46-year-old… from the other side of the Oder" with experience in the fields and with horses sent two letters to the food ministry in 1948, seeking some kind of employment on one of the newly consolidated farms.[47] He, too, wanted a chance to support his family, but not did find immediate means of doing so. Letters came from wives and parents, too, all citing political credentials and farming experience and finding little more than sympathy and occasional recommendations from the food ministry administrators.[48]

German authorities, on the other hand, wanted to underline the burdens imposed by these refugee populations. The expellees, forced off their lands east of the Oder-Neisse, would need to be fed as well as accommodated by a truncated western German economy. The food ministry underlined this strain in an internal report on conditions in the western zones in 1947–1948, noting that the division of Germany had further exacerbated shortage: "...imagine how easy the feeding of western Germany would be if all of Germany was a unified economic zone, as foreseen at Potsdam... and the expelled population could return to their homeland."[49] A report out of Bremen suggested a Germany put upon by war loss and refugee populations, unable to feed itself without the support of the occupiers.[50]

Food and agricultural experts at the VELF agreed with the occupation authorities that putting eastern refugees to work "on the land" would both solve the problem of their parasitic status as well as increase the local food supply, but plans to promote such a program were slow to crystallize. While efforts to incorporate craftsmen and industrial workers from the expellee population into the German economy were largely successful, the integration of refugee farmers had yet to show fruitful progress by 1949.[51] Before the currency reform, the food ministry pointed to a lack of building material for the construction of farm buildings and adequate housing; after the currency reform, they blamed a lack of capital for their inability to find a productive place for refugee farmers. The food ministry was finally able, with the assistance of both Lutheran and Catholic charitable groups, farmers' associations [Bauernverbände], county associations and refugee representatives, to facilitate the passage of the "Law for the Integration of Refugees in Agriculture" [Gesetz zur Förderung der Eingliederung der Heimatvertriebenen in die Landwirtschaft] or the so-called Refugee Settlement Law [Flüchtlingssiedlungsgesetz] by the Federal Republic's Economic Advisory Group on June 24, 1949.[52] The law provided the organizational framework for establishing settlements of refugee farm families on estates whose owners had no heirs and on "barren" estates with poor soil. It did not, however, address capital shortages, and as such provided more of a guideline for further work than a comprehensive instrument of reform. The principle of "self-help" and voluntary participation continued to animate reform efforts in the new Federal Republic, as they had in the western zones since war's end.

While expellees sought to portray themselves as potential farmers, given access to territory, few of them had farming experience or the capacity to perform the kinds of heavy labor required by agriculture, so whether they returned to their lost land or integrated into the economy of the western zones was likely to have little impact on food outputs. Some dispute between German and Allied experts arose over whether the expellees were primarily women, children and the elderly, or whether they were working-aged men drawn from non-agricultural economic sectors, but both conditions undermined the capacity of the expellees to contribute meaningfully on the farm.[53] In the Soviet zone of occupation, the effort to increase food production by granting land to new farmers, most of whom were eastern expellees, underlined the fruitlessness of such projects. Though the eastern food administration was largely successful in promoting *"Junkerland in Bauernhand"* [*Putting Junker estates into farmers' hands*] through the breaking up of large estates in 1945 and 1946, the new farms and their new farmers were less successful in actually producing anything edible. Lack of fertilizer, seed, equipment and experience hampered new farmers' efforts.[54] The eastern agricultural officials struggled in vain to keep the new farmers on the land, but they, like their more seasoned fellows, balked at the low set prices offered for what they did produce and kept their foodstuffs off the market.

The industrial, commercial Volk of the future would need to be nourished, at least temporarily, by the support of occupying powers. Nonetheless, expellees made a case analogous to that made by many traditional farmers: The *Volk* could nourish if given the chance. Access to their lost lands would mitigate the burden on the western zones economically and nutritionally while addressing the global food problems the Allies had been so keen to underline.

Conclusion

Heimat became increasingly bereft of its connection to rurality, but hardly receded into the background; films and literature continued to explore the nature of Heimat—and of Germanness—in the wake of the Nazi period. Some expellees mounted a campaign to regain their homelands or at least secure reparations for their expulsion, a campaign that has continued to this day. Historians have certainly taken up the ongoing quest to define an elusive Germanness, especially in light of national division and now in the context of record numbers of non-European immigrants.

Postwar Germans east and west faced, among other hardships, an autarkic hangover. The experience of two World Wars and the deprivations entailed by each, coupled with the savvy machinations of Nazi leaders, helped to transform Germany's historical identity as an agricultural nation into an increasingly indispensable component of Heimat mythology. Heimat meant many things to many different Germans when it first became part of nationalist language in the era of unification, but by 1945 it stood in part for a lost sense of security: that Germans, no matter what, would always be able to feed themselves.

NOTES

1. BArch BL, DY 30/IV 2/2.022/63; SAPMO; Sozialistische Einheitspartei Deutschlands Zentralkommittee, Sekretariat Paul Merker: H. Lehmann, Parteivorstand der SED Zentralsekretariat, Abt. IV. Landwirtschaft. 22. May 1946.
2. BArch K, Z 6/I 234. "Welche Schwierigkeiten behindern die Ernährungspolitik im Vereinigten Witschaftsgebiet Deutschlands?" Zentralamt für Ernährung und Landwirtschaft in der britischen Zone und Verwaltung für Ernährung, Landwirtschaft und Forsten des Vereinigten Wirtschaftsgebiets: Büro des Direktors Dr. Schlange Schöningen, 1947–1948.
3. BArch BL, DY 30/ IV 2/ 2.022/ 63; SAPMO; Sozialistische Einheitspartei Deutschlands Zentralkommittee, Sekretariat Paul Merker: H. Lehmann, Parteivorstand der SED Zentralsekretariat, Abt. IV. Landwirtschaft to the Landes- (Provinzial-) Vorstände der SED, "Sicherung der Volksernährung (Unsere Aufgaben auf dem Lande)," 22. May 1946: 1.
4. BArch K, Z 6/I 234, "Welche Schwierigkeiten behindern die Ernährungspolitik im Vereinigten Witschaftsgebiet Deutschlands?" Zentralamt für Ernährung und Landwirtschaft in der britischen Zone und Verw. für Ern., Landwirtschaft und Forsten des Vereinigten Wirtschaftsgebiets: Büro des Direktors Dr. Schlange Schöningen, 1947–1948: 27. It is important to note that the western zone's food administration tended to elide the difference between lands in the Soviet zone of occupation [*sowjetische Besatzungszone*—SBZ] and those beyond the Oder in newly conceived Poland. These figures refer to the lands beyond the Oder, with the SBZ counted as part of "the West" in the food office's rhetorical reckoning.
5. Andrew Demshuk, *The Lost German East: Forced Migration and the Politics of Memory, 1945–1970* (New York: Cambridge University Press, 2012).
6. Alice Weinreb, "The Tastes of Home: Cooking the Lost *Heimat* in West Germany in the 1950s and 1960s," *German Studies Review* 34, no. 2 (2011); and Alice Weinreb, "'For the Hungry Have No Past Nor Do They Belong to a Political Party': Debates Over German Hunger After World War II," *Central European History* 45, no. 1 (2012): 50–78.

7. Atina Grossmann, "Grams, Calories, and Food: Languages of Victimization, Entitlement, and Human Rights in Occupied Germany, 1945–1949," *Central European History* 44 (2011): 118–148.
8. "The utility of *Heimat*," writes Celia Applegate, "lay in its capacity to obscure any chasms between small local worlds and the larger ones to which the locality belonged." Applegate, Celia, *A Nation of Provincials: The German Idea of Heimat* (Berkeley: University of California Press, 1990): 10.
9. The term is Helstosky's, in reference to fascist Italy. See Carol F. Helstosky, "Fascist Food Politics: Mussolini's Policy of Alimentary Sovereignty," *Journal of Modern Italian Studies* 9, no. 1 (2004): 1–26.
10. Assessments of *Heimat* as a literary and historical concept include Peter Blickle, *Heimat: A Critical Theory of the German Idea of Homeland* (Rochester, NY: Camden House, 2002); Elizabeth Boa and Rachel Palfreyman, eds., *Heimat—A German Dream: Regional Loyalties and National Identity in German Culture 1890–1990*, Oxford Studies in Modern European Culture (Oxford: Oxford University Press, 2000); and, of particular interest to this study, Gregory F. Schroeder, "Ties of Urban Heimat: West German Cities and Their Wartime Evacuees in the 1950s," *German Studies Review* 27, no. 2 (2004): 307–324.
11. Alon Confino, *The Nation as Local Metaphor: Württemberg, Imperial Germany, and National Memory, 1871–1918* (Chapel Hill and London: University of North Carolina Press, 1997).
12. The classic study of Germany's political development, itself critically linked to the question of industrial growth, is David Blackbourn and Geoff Eley, *The Peculiarities of German History: Bourgeois Politics and Society in Nineteenth-Century Germany* (Oxford and New York: Oxford University Press, 1984). Blackbourn and Eley argue that German political development, namely the "failure" to sustain a viable bourgeois revolution in 1848, cannot be appropriately compared to development in England or France. On the political program of industrialization in Soviet Russia, particularly under Stalin, see Stephen Kotkin, *Magnetic Mountain: Stalinism as a Civilization* (Berkeley: University of California Press, 1995).
13. Kenneth D. Barkin, *The Controversy Over German Industrialization, 1890–1902* (Chicago: University of Chicago Press, 1970) is helpful on the academic and political debates over tariff policies in the late nineteenth and earlier twentieth centuries.
14. Brian R. Mitchell, *International Historical Statistics: Europe 1750–2000* (Basingstoke: Palgrave Macmillan, 2007), 4, 153.
15. On the Reichstag debates of 1902, particularly the involvement of academic economists, see Kenneth D. Barkin, *The Controversy Over German*

Industrialization, 1890–1902 (Chicago: University of Chicago Press, 1970).
16. Werner Sombart, *Händler und Helden; Patriotische Besinnungen* (München and Leipzig: Duncker & Humbolt, 1915).
17. Sombart, 57.
18. Beginning in the nineteenth century, Jews were linked to a shifty statelessness tied to capitalism, urbanization and femininity. The Dreyfus case in France depicted the Jew as lacking in honor, manliness and patriotic fervor. See Otto Weininger's self-loathing treatise on Jewish male femininity and lack of character, Otto Weininger, Daniel Steuer, and Laura Marcus, *Sex and Character: An Investigation of Fundamental Principles* (Bloomington, IN: Indiana University Press, 2005), as well as Sander Gilman, *Freud, Race and Gender* (Princeton, NJ: Princeton University Press, 1993); and Ritchie Robertson, "Historicizing Weininger: The Nineteenth-Century German Image of the Feminized Jew," in *Modernity, Culture, and 'the Jew'*, edited by Bryan Cheyette and Laura Marcus, 23–29 (Stanford, CA: Stanford University Press, 1998).
19. James L. Hargrove, "History of the Calorie in Nutrition," *The Journal of Nutrition* 136, no. 12 (December 2006): 2959.
20. Keith Allen, "Sharing Scarcity: Bread Rationing and the First World War in Berlin, 1914–1923," *Journal of Social History* 32, no. 2 (1998): 371–393.
21. Nick Cullather, "The Foreign Policy of the Calorie," *The American Historical Review* 112, no. 2 (2007): 357.
22. Timothy Snyder, *Bloodlands: Europe Between Hitler and Stalin* (New York: Basic Books, 2010), 394.
23. Joan Campbell, *Joy in Work, German Work: The National Debate, 1800–1945* (Princeton, NJ: Princeton University Press, 1989).
24. Jennifer K. Alexander, "An Efficiency of Scarcity: Using Food to Increase the Productivity of Soviet Prisoners of War in the Mines of the Third Reich," *History & Technology* 22, no. 4 (2006): 395.
25. Arthur Schweitzer, "Review," *Southern Economic Journal* 10, no. 2 (1943): 169–171. See also Economic Intelligence Service, League of Nations, *Wartime Rationing and Consumption* (New York: Columbia University Press, 1942).
26. J. Adam Tooze, *The Wages of Destruction: The Making and Breaking of the Nazi Economy* (New York: Viking, 2007: 549).
27. Ibid.
28. David Schoenbaum's thesis on the Nazi social revolution highlights the pragmatism of Nazi agricultural policies, pointing to the replacement of the ideological Walther Darré with food expert Herbert Backe as evidence that Hitler sought to maximize food output in preparation

for war rather than just lionize the rural way-of-life for political gain. See David Schoenbaum, *Hitler's Social Revolution; Class and Status in Nazi Germany, 1933–1939* (Garden City, NY: Doubleday, 1966); and Gesine Gerhard, "Change in the European Countryside: Peasants and Democracy in Germany, 1935–1955," in *War, Agriculture, and Food: Rural Europe from the 1930s to the 1950s*, edited by Paul Brassley, Yves Segers, and Leen van Molle (New York, NY: Routledge, 2012), 198.

29. BArch Koblenz, Z 7/19: Pressemeldungen zu Ernährungsfragen [Geschäftsstelle des Ministers für Landwirtschaft und Ernährung in der französischen Zone], "Um das tägliche Brot," *Kölnische Rundschau*, August 9, 1946, 1.
30. BArch K, Z 7/19—Pressemeldungen zur Ernährungsfrage. "Die Deutsche Landwirtschaft in Vergangenheit, Gegenwart und Zukunft," *Kölnische Rundschau*, September 6, 1946.
31. To be clear: While a farmer might enjoy a relatively higher caloric intake due to access to his or her own produce, he or she might end up eating a lot of potatoes, rather than the protein and vitamins needed to sustain difficult work.
32. BArch K, Z 6/I 130: Günther Skowronski. 23. August 1948.
33. Ibid.
34. SzB, 4Q 137. *Die Überwindung des Hungers: Maßnahmen der Ernährungs- und Agrarpolitik seit dem Zusammenbruch* (Frankfurt am Main: Verwaltung für Ernährung, Landwirtschaft und Forsten der Vereinigten Wirtschaftsgebietes, 1949), 42.
35. BArch Koblenz, Z 6/I 118: H. Kling, "Die Zukunft der Deutschen Landwirtschaft," *Saat und Ernte: Zeitschrift für Arbeitstechnik und Betriebswirtschaft im Landbau - Mannheim*, August 8, 1947.
36. Ibid.
37. HSA Dresden, 11393: Landesregierung Sachsen, Ministerium für Handel und Versorgung Nr. 587, "Versorgung der Bevölkerung mit Lebensmitteln," Summer 1947.
38. BArch BL, DY 24/169: "Landjugendprogramm der FDJ," September 26, 1948.
39. Ibid.
40. BArch K, Z6/I 122: Dr. Maixner to Otto von John, September 20, 1948.
41. BArch Koblenz, Z6/I 122: Memorandum für eine Besprechung der Deutsche Maizena Werke A. G. mit dem Herrn Ernährungsminister Dr. Schlange-Schöningen. 28. November 1946.
42. BArch K, Z6/I 122: Dr. Maixner to Otto von John, September 20, 1948.
43. In 1944, 12,556,000 hectares of Germany was dedicated to the cultivation of cereal crops including wheat, rye, barley, oats, potatoes and sugar beets. In 1949, West Germany cultivated 5,522,000 hectares of its land

for a loss of productive territory of 56%. Some of this land was "lost" to East Germany, some to Poland. See Brian R. Mitchell, *International Historical Statistics: Europe 1750–2000*, 231–233.

44. BArch K, Z 6/I 122: Karl Manzke to Schlange-Schöningen, Celle, April 30, 1948.
45. BArch K, Z 6/I 122: Adolf Weimar to Schlange-Schöningen, Lüneberg, April 30, 1948.
46. BArch K, Z 6/I 122: O. von John to Karl Manzke, Frankfurt/Main, May 10, 1948.
47. BArch K, Z 6/I 132: von Schuckmann to Schlange-Schöningen, Bliestorf über Kastorf, August 29, 1948.
48. BArch K, Z 6/I 135: Irmgard Volkmer to Schlange-Schöningen, Stolzenau an der Weser, December 4, 1948.
49. BArch K, Z 6/I 234: *Welche Schwierigkeiten behindern die Ernährungspolitik im Vereinigten Witschaftsgebiet Deutschlands?* Zentralamt für Ernährung und Landwirtschaft in der britischen Zone und Verwaltung für Ernährung, Landwirtschaft und Forsten des Vereinigten Wirtschaftsgebiets: Büro des Direktors Dr. Schlange Schöningen, 1947–1948.
50. Ibid.
51. SzB, 4Q 137: *Die Überwindung des Hungers*, 46.
52. Ibid., 47.
53. Philip M. Raup, Marginalia, *Reparations Sozialprodukt Lebensstandard: Versuch einer Wirtschaftsbilanz*, vol. 3, Part 2 (Bremen, 1948), 15, Philip M. Raup Papers, University of Minnesota Libraries.
54. BArch BL, DY 30/IV 2/2.022/63: SAPMO, Sozialistische Einheitspartei Deutschlands Zentralkommittee, Sekretariat Paul Merker: H. Lehmann, Parteivorstand der SED Zentralsekretariat, Abt. IV. Landwirtschaft, "Sicherung der Volksernährung (Unsere Aufgaben auf dem Lande)," (May 22, 1946), 12.

Archives

Collection of Official Publications, 4Q. Staatsbibliothek zu Berlin, Berlin, Germany.

Ministerium für Handel und Versorgung Landesregierung Sachsen, 11393. Hauptstaatsarchiv Dresden, Germany (HSA Dresden).

Philip M. Raup Papers. University of Minnesota Libraries, Minneapolis, USA.

Stiftung Archiv der Parteien und Massenorganisationen der DDR im Bundesarchiv (SAPMO), DY 30/ IV. Bundesarchiv, Berlin-Lichterfelde, Germany (BArch BL).

Verwaltung für Ernährung, Landwirtschaft, und Forsten des Vereinigten Wirtschaftsgebietes - Büro des Direktor Dr. Schlange Schöningen, Z-6/I. Bundesarchiv, Koblenz, Germany (BArch K).

PUBLISHED

Alexander, Jennifer K. "An Efficiency of Scarcity: Using Food to Increase the Productivity of Soviet Prisoners of War in the Mines of the Third Reich." *History & Technology* 22, no. 4 (2006): 391–406.

Allen, Keith. "Sharing Scarcity: Bread Rationing and the First World War in Berlin, 1914–1923." *Journal of Social History* 32, no. 2 (1998): 371–393.

Applegate, Celia. *A Nation of Provincials: The German Idea of Heimat*. Berkeley: University of California Press, 1990.

Barkin, Kenneth D. *The Controversy Over German Industrialization, 1890–1902*. Chicago: University of Chicago Press, 1970.

Blackbourn, David, and Geoff Eley. *The Peculiarities of German History: Bourgeois Politics and Society in Nineteenth-Century Germany*. Oxford and New York: Oxford University Press, 1984.

Campbell, Joan. *Joy in Work, German Work: The National Debate, 1800–1945*. Princeton, NJ: Princeton University Press, 1989.

Confino, Alon. *The Nation as Local Metaphor: Württemberg, Imperial Germany, and National Memory, 1871–1918*. Chapel Hill and London: University of North Carolina Press, 1997.

Cullather, Nick. "The Foreign Policy of the Calorie." *The American Historical Review* 112, no. 2 (2007): 337–364.

Demshuk, Andrew. *The Lost German East: Forced Migration and the Politics of Memory, 1945–1970*. New York: Cambridge University Press, 2012.

Gerhard, Gesine. "Change in the European Countryside: Peasants and Democracy in Germany, 1935–1955." In *War, Agriculture, and Food: Rural Europe from the 1930s to the 1950s*, edited by Paul Brassley, Yves Segers, and Leen van Molle, 195–208. New York, NY: Routledge, 2012.

Grossmann, Atina. "Grams, Calories, and Food: Languages of Victimization, Entitlement, and Human Rights in Occupied Germany, 1945–1949." *Central European History* 44, no. 1 (2011): 118–148.

Hargrove, James L. "History of the Calorie in Nutrition." *The Journal of Nutrition* 136, no. 12 (December 2006): 2957–2961.

Helstosky, Carol F. "Fascist Food Politics: Mussolini's Policy of Alimentary Sovereignty." *Journal of Modern Italian Studies* 9, no. 1 (2004): 1–26.

Mitchell, Brian R. *International Historical Statistics: Europe 1750–2000*. Basingstoke [u.a.]: Palgrave Macmillan, 2007.

Schroeder, Gregory F. "Ties of Urban Heimat: West German Cities and Their Wartime Evacuees in the 1950s." *German Studies Review* 27, no. 2 (2004): 307–324.

Schweitzer, Arthur. "Review." *Southern Economic Journal* 10, no. 2 (1943): 169–171.

Snyder, Timothy. *Bloodlands: Europe Between Hitler and Stalin.* New York: Basic Books, 2010.

Sombart, Werner. *Händler und Helden; Patriotische Besinnungen.* München and Leipzig: Duncker & Humblot, 1915.

Tooze, J. Adam. *The Wages of Destruction: The Making and Breaking of the Nazi Economy.* New York: Viking, 2007.

Weinreb, Alice. "'For the Hungry Have No Past nor Do They Belong to a Political Party': Debates Over German Hunger After World War II." *Central European History* 45, no. 1 (2012): 50–78.

———. "The Tastes of Home: Cooking the Lost Heimat in West Germany in the 1950s and 1960s." *German Studies Review* 34, no. 2 (May 2011).

CHAPTER 8

Postwar Food Rumors: Security, Victimhood and Fear

Laura J. Hilton

In 1946, US occupation authorities in Bremen displayed three piles of food, highlighting the disparities between occupation forces, Displaced Persons (DPs) and Germans in stark detail, in both sheer amounts and types of food. US soldiers received 29,288 calories per week (almost 4200 per day), including such "luxuries" as whole milk, fruit, fruit juice, butter and lard. Overall, DPs received 12,950 calories per week (44% of the Army's allotment, 1850 calories per day), and the rationing system allocated Germans 7098 calories per week (24% of the Army's allotment, 1014 calories per day).[1] This display seems a curious choice, given the simmering resentment regarding access to adequate food, festering among the Germans since the occupation began. It is also a red herring, since official rations rarely matched actual consumption. In postwar Germany, the calorie stood for much more than actual projected food intake.[2] Occupation authorities used calories to define and rank the worthiness of populations, pegged to their wartime experiences as victims,

L. J. Hilton (✉)
Muskingum University, New Concord, OH, USA

© The Author(s) 2019
H. M. Benbow and H. R. Perry (eds.), *Food, Culture and Identity in Germany's Century of War*,
https://doi.org/10.1007/978-3-030-27138-1_8

perpetrators or bystanders. In the early years, this system privileged the occupiers and DPs; over time, it leveled these distinctions.[3]

Given its central place in the postwar discourse, food became a battleground, one transnational in its production, delivery and consumption. Food scarcity and the Germans' lack of control over it imbued food with immense meaning and power. Although it was a central issue within rumor culture, historians have not addressed the public's conceptions of food through this lens. This rumor culture, which swirled amid the rubble and reconstruction, filled the gap between official news and the population's desire for information. As one occupation official stationed in Berlin warned, "Rumor did not await the next morning's editions to reach the population. It fled as prairie wildfire across the darkened city, whispering grimly to factory workers who saw their jobs disappearing, to mothers who could visualize their babies starving, to the ill and aged for whom there would be no more help nor hope."[4] Within this charged atmosphere, rumors related to food churned. Claims acquired additional substance with each re-telling, regardless of their veracity. Control over food and access to it were both about power relations. Many rumors focused on why shortages existed and rarely were the war and the worldwide food scarcity the most common explanations. Instead, Germans wrote about and told one another, of corruption, favoritism, punishment and wastefulness. Analysis of the rumor culture demonstrates that Germans believed that the lack of food was due to vindictiveness, exploitation and mismanagement. They shifted responsibility for the food shortage from their shoulders, to the hands of others, mainly non-Germans within their midst and overseas. By constructing narratives that re-centered this responsibility and created alternative explanations for deprivations, Germans sought to re-establish both their sense of self and control over their country, cementing their victimhood in the wake of the Second World War.

Historiography and Methodology

Scholars have explored this issue, of Germans recreating their postwar identities often without grappling with their past, for decades. The writings of Theodor Adorno in the early 1960s are a key starting point, especially his fear that fascism and its values were lingering within the new West German democracy and his distinction between the Germans "mastering" their past and their lack of commitment to work through it.[5] One strand of this inquiry is the idea that Germans "forgot" their past. As the German literary critic and author W.G. Sebald stated, "I think there was certainly what has often been described as a conspiracy of silence. [...] One had tacitly agreed to leave this behind and developed an attitude which was entirely forward-looking, which was bent on not remembering."[6] However, studying rumors in the postwar period provides a different slant, one that probes not the individual "forgetting," but rather the collective re-remembering of the recent past. One of the most ubiquitous images of the postwar is the *Trümmerfrauen*, heroically clearing the rubble left in the war's wake. As historian Leonie Treber has proven, in fact, a tiny minority of women engaged in this work, and yet in the memories of the postwar period, their presence and efforts became magnified.[7] As the intense debates spurred by the publication of Jörg Friedrich's book on the Allied bombings, *The Fire*, published in 2002 demonstrate, the topic of German wartime and postwar miseries is an important focal point.[8]

If the remembered past is more real to those who lived it than what they actually experienced, how can historians navigate this murky picture? K. Michael Prince explains that the wartime experiences were the core of German identity, and as such, so was loss. He writes, "The Second World War acted like a black hole, sucking the German past – and soon all of Europe's as well – into a dimensionless plane of general suffering caused by the depredations of war."[9] Therefore, their memories and identity were about their own travails, rather than the woes that Germany had inflicted. In their research, Corning and Schuman demonstrate that for Germans who lived through the Second World War and the postwar period, their memories focused on "their own suffering under bombing, wartime shortages, and Allied occupation."[10] Robert Moeller's important work on expellees and German POWs returning from Soviet captivity invigorated scholarly discussion of this topic.[11] By analyzing the rumors that Germans told each other, many of which were not accurate, this chapter aims to engage in close examination of how this process of re-remembering occurred at the street level in the immediate postwar period.

Intertwining food and rumors offers a more complicated understanding of the power dynamics within postwar Germany. Drawing on a deep primary source base, including letters, intelligence reports and taped phone conversations, this chapter uses rumors to investigate patterns of beliefs, behaviors and fears. Reading food supply reports or endless tables of caloric values cannot provide these. It embeds the rumors within the theoretical framework provided by social psychologists and sociologists to probe the postwar zeitgeist. It also draws on the work of food scholars, such as Peter Jackson, who writes of the collective importance of food, given its measurable and symbolic significance, theorizing that concerns about food "have a wide sociological significance, acting as a vehicle for the expression of a range of other issues ....."[12] He explains, "the use of food in identity formation may also be a source of anxiety, through ... the processes of group identification and social regulation."[13] Postwar authorities were concerned enough about rumors to track and analyze them, continuing wartime practices. Unlike the surveys they conducted, rumors were, in a sense, more authentic than the canned responses that Germans believed the Allies wanted to hear.[14] Despite the ravages of the Allied bombing campaign, the lack of electricity and limited presses and access to paper, occupation authorities quickly controlled media outlets, as part of the processes of denazification and democratization.[15] However, Germans were skeptical of official information and into the void left by the absence of German-controlled news outlets swept rumors. As one description of the postwar period stated, "it was the hopeless feeling of being out of touch, living in an unreal world of rumours [*sic*]...."[16] Germans sought stability and closure and they utilized rumors to construct explanations for their current circumstances with which they were comfortable, in part because they diverted responsibility onto others.

Emerging during the Second World War, scholarly work on rumors sees them as a form of knowledge, wherein people attempt to make sense of uncertain circumstances, especially within the context of war, crisis and/or disaster. Rumors become more powerful when they reinforce pre-existing beliefs.[17] Allport and Postman, one of the initial teams of researchers hired by the US government during the war to track and analyze rumors, posit rumors as a society's collective effort to find meaning when facts are in short supply.[18] Their work, foundational in rumor theory, suggests that rumors circulate when people perceive something as important to them and seek to fill in the blanks to assure themselves, either confirming a fear or cementing a belief. If people consider the rumor and repeat it, they believe it could be possible. Fanciful or farfetched rumors often quickly run their course, because people do not want others to question their credibility.[19] The act of repeating a rumor is a form of cognitive closure; by repeating it, it becomes more believable, thereby reinforcing one's own fears or ideas.[20] In the 1960s, Shibutani refined this, defining rumor as a "collective problem – a solving transaction that develops as people trapped in an ambiguous situation try to construct some meaningful interpretation of it."[21] In this way, rumors are integral in understanding a society's collective beliefs. They demonstrate explicit concerns, are a site of discussing distressing issues and act as a vehicle to share one's own fears or desires while obscuring them as one's own.[22]

Since rumors claim to be both plausible and relevant, they stand as a critique of the social order and provide insight into the common discourse. As Gary Fine explains, "as collective talk, rumor is tied to how society should be properly constituted. When solidified into firm belief, what once was a topical rumor can enter into collective memory. Put another way, rumor is a form of mnemonic practice, a way of conceiving how the world is structured."[23] As DiFonzo and Bordia state: "rumors arise in situational contexts of threat or potential threat, both tangible and psychological, highlighting the psychological needs for control and self-enhancement, and leading to rumors that help to regain a sense of control and defend a threatened sense of self."[24] Even where information existed to disprove rumors, and when authorities directly refuted them, Germans further spread and believed them, thereby devising alternative explanations, by which they became the victims, rather than the perpetrators or bystanders.

FOOD SCARCITY AND RATIONING, 1939–1948

Food was a central element of Nazi economic policy, as it strove for autarky. The *Reichsnährstand* (RNS) controlled agrarian production initially under the leadership of Walther Darré, the Minister for Food and Agriculture. Unable to achieve self-sufficiency, the solution, according to Adolf Hitler, was to secure *Lebensraum* in the east through conquest.[25] As the war began, Germany remained more dependent on food imports than its European counterparts did. Pre-1939, Europe as a continent imported less than 10% of its food supply,[26] whereas Germany was only 83% self-sufficient.[27] As the war began, the RNS, now under the leadership of Herbert Backe, set initial rations in late September 1939 of 2570 calories per day for normal consumers and sought to increase imports.[28]

As both Götz Aly and Gesine Gerhard have argued, the Nazis' ability to feed its people was a sustaining element of the Third Reich.

By providing sufficient commodities, they solidified the *Volksgemeinschaft* (people's national community) and its sense of entitlement.[29] With increased purchasing power and the lack of customs barriers, Germans stationed abroad sent huge numbers of packages to relatives and friends at home.[30] However, most imports arrived via official, albeit ruthless, requisitioning. In 1942, Germany obtained 18% of its grain, 22% of its meat and 18% of its edible fats from occupied Europe.[31] The Third Reich exported between 10 and 20% of French agrarian production, and Backe's so-called Hunger Plan stripped enormous amounts from occupied Eastern Europe.[32] Göring's proclamation that, "if someone has to go hungry, let it be someone other than a German,"[33] exemplifies this brutal impact. In terms of grains, from Denmark, the Netherlands and France, the Germans requisitioned 21.4 million tons of grains, whereas from the occupied regions of the USSR, they took 14.7 million tons.[34] Between 1941 and 1943 from the USSR alone, the Third Reich collectively imported almost 1 million tons of grains, 60,000 tons of meat, more than 600,000 tons of oils and margarines and 15,000 tons of potatoes, which does not include food requisitioned and consumed by German troops.[35] Given this reality, it was completely plausible to postwar Germans that the Allied occupiers were exploiting their resources, as the Third Reich and its citizens had done the same for six years.

For many Germans, especially those in urban areas, by 1943, their food supply was in jeopardy. By 1943–1944, Germans consumed, on average, 40% less fat, 60% less meat and 20% less bread than they had prior to September 1939.[36] Yet, in many German memories of wartime, food was not a major concern. A student from Berlin recollected that the Party had always cared for its people and contrasted this with the winter of 1946, when people froze and starved to death, seeming to lack comprehension that the German food security during the war came at the expense of fellow Europeans. She reminisced, "I do not recall yearning for something that was not available … I do not recall anyone who said they were hungry during the war."[37] In 1947, a woman, while shopping, said that she would "kiss Hitler's hands and feet if he came back. Under him there was more to eat, and conditions such as now did not exist under his rule."[38] Aly shares similar recollections from German women, "During the war we didn't go hungry. Back then everything worked. It was only after the war that things turned bad."[39] While the Germans' access to food had been good until 1944–1945,[40] as the Third Reich began to collapse, its ability to produce or obtain sufficient food faltered.

Germans began to hoard food, black marketeering increased and farmers regularly circumvented the Nazis' centralized controls. Between bombing raids, ration reductions and German troops and refugees streaming into Germany, hunger was no longer a German export but a home front reality.[41] Yet, Germans mostly cast hunger as a postwar phenomenon.[42]

In May 1945, the German economy was at a standstill, due to its total mobilization for war and to constant Allied bombing raids. More than one hundred major urban areas lay in ruins, the communication systems were practically non-existent, and only about 10% of the railway network remained intact. In addition, damage to utilities was widespread, and the materials to rebuild them were in short supply.[43] Within the western zones, 400 million cubic meters of rubble stood as a stark reminder of what war had wrought.[44] As a whole, Europe was producing 64% less food in 1945 than in 1939.[45] Germany's agricultural production had plummeted from 200,000,000 tons in 1939 to 61,000,000 tons, by the end of 1944.[46] Germany's defeat also meant liberation for 22% of its agricultural workforce, forced and slave laborers.[47] Its agricultural sector could provide approximately 1000 calories per day for its urban population.[48] Given this scarcity, additional food had to be imported. However, the country best positioned to provide this food, the United States, instead lifted rationing the day after Japan's surrender.[49] Germany had lost the war and, with it, its status and ability to be satiated.

Once the Allied occupation began, Germans were no longer in control of their own food supply, raising the specter of starvation. The hunger that had confronted Germany in the First World War, due to the British blockade, helped to shape collective fears, as did the persistent warnings of the Third Reich of impending Allied punishment. Nazi propaganda had played up the punitive measures of the Morgenthau Plan, which suggested Germany's return to a pastoral society, calling it the "Jewish Murder Plan."[50] Postwar, Germans told one another, "British authorities are evolving a scheme for reallocation of land in the West and the resettlement of people in agriculture."[51] They asserted, "American occupation authorities purposely are cutting German food rations to a bare, subsistence level and will continue to do so for the next twenty years in order to completely weaken and exhaust the nation."[52] Fears of Allied reprisal, specifically a plan to starve Germans, abounded.[53] For example, Germans told one another that Americans were systematically starving the Germans "in retaliation for gas attacks targeting American troops,"[54] that the British and Americans had a systematic plan to "reduce the German population 50% by starvation"[55] and that British authorities were "pretending" to choose areas to construct RAF landing strips, and once they had eradicated the crops, that the British would move on and repeat the process elsewhere.[56] In Wiesbaden, a rumor circulated that "Occupation Authorities decided, that all small children between the age of one and three years have to die."[57] Anxieties, like rumors, thrive in times of uncertainty, especially where there is a chasm between official and public understanding.[58] Contrary to popular belief, the Allies were importing food as early as June of 1945; in the American Zone, the military imported 650,000 tons of wheat in June.[59]

Occupation authorities continued the Third Reich's system of allocating food through rationing, but now the Germans were at the bottom. One year before, their daily rations had been 1910 calories per day as compared to 1115 in occupied France and 1160 in the General Government.[60] German author Hans-Erich Nossack described the postwar hardships, lamenting the lack of vegetables in the German diet save the occasional turnip or cabbage, and saying, "It's a cruel life of starvation, I assure you."[61] When General Clay stated, "Conditions are going to be extremely difficult in Germany this winter [1945-1946] ... Some cold and hunger will be necessary to make the German people realize the consequences of a war which they caused,"[62] he gave a realistic assessment of the situation on the ground. In response, Germans told one another, "Fifteen million Germans will die this winter because of lack of fuel, food, and Allied assistance."[63] This evidences the serious distrust German harbored toward their occupiers. To Germans, Clay's statement fulfilled the fears embedded in Nazi propaganda that all Germans would suffer during peacetime, and it conflicted with their own understanding of who was responsible for the situation. From seldom feeling the pinch of hunger during the war, Germans were now literally hungry for food and craved a return to their previously superior social standing.

Responsibility for food supply straddled multiple authorities, but ultimately, the Allied occupiers were in charge. They authorized the United Nations Relief and Rehabilitation Administration (UNRRA) to provide relief and rehabilitation of DPs, while it worked with local German officials, to provide food for Germans. Initially, the US Zone was only between 60 and 70% self-sufficient, and it set daily rations for the German population at 1550 calories per day. To meet this, by June of 1945, the United States was importing 650,000 tons of wheat.[64] However, even with imports, supplies failed to meet this initial ration level even once by September 1945, so occupation officials lowered it to 1300.[65] In the British and French Zones, straits were even more dire, as Germans in the British Zone received 1014 calories per day officially,[66] while French officials estimated that Stuttgart's population had access to 793 calories a day.[67]

Occupation troops had the first claim on resources, then Displaced Persons and finally the local German population and expellees.[68] While the United States and Great Britain imported food to feed their troops, the French, in their zone, fed their troops from local supplies.[69] Despite the American and British commitments to import enough food for their troops, Germans steadfastly believed that troop demands and their callous wasting of food were two of the core reasons for the shortage.[70] In addition, Germans resented the rich food supply it believed existed in DP camps (due to the black market and the aid from voluntary agencies), some even labeling the flourishing trade within DP camps as a "wonderland."[71] However, given their local access to goods and connections, Germans were often better off than the DP and/or persecutee populations. They grumbled about the unequal distribution of food to the victims of the Third Reich, continuing Nazi stereotypes about Jews, as well fed and greedy. If they were going to have to do with less, so too should those deemed inferior to them. In this context, the assertion that so many people starve daily in Berlin that "the police have special cars which collect the bodies and take them to one of five special crematories" is startling.[72] Concerns about food supply and relations between occupation troops and German women were linked as well. In one such rumor, it claimed that mothers of illegitimate children, of American parentage, received double ration cards.[73]

Food and Postwar Earwitnesses

In my database of 3000+ discrete rumors, food is one of the most common subjects, cropping up in almost one-fifth of them. Given its scarcity and difficulties people had to go to in order to secure it, this is not surprising. Yet, historical explanation has not yet probed the public and collective sense of victimhood as formed and strengthened by rumors during the postwar period itself. German concerns about food shifted over time, increasingly viewing it as a serious problem. Whereas in 1945, 17% of respondents listed food as a "greatest care or worry," and by 1947, more than half (53%) named food as their chief concern.[74]

Germans based this transformative process, from the *Volksgemeinschaft* to a *Notgemeinschaft* (community in need), on the international community's responsibility for their well-being.[75] The Germans experienced hunger collectively, and therefore, their discussion of it through the flourishing rumor culture demonstrates their communal perceptions.

In 1946, the entire world experienced a severe grain shortage, not only of wheat but also of rice in India and China. Since 1939, Europe had experienced a 70% drop in the production of grains and a 50% drop in general agricultural production. The average caloric consumption for much of the European population was below 2000 calories per day.[76] Across Europe, Germany had the second-lowest average caloric intake as of September 1947; only Greece's was lower.[77] Between 1945 and 1947, German rations hovered between 1300 and 1600 calories per day in the US Zone, complicated by the Soviets reneging on their agreement to share food from their zone, which had supplied the vast majority of grains in Germany (see Table 8.1). Yet these numbers mask the reality on the ground, as Germans supplemented rations by growing their own food, receiving food from friends and relatives in the countryside and dealing on the black/gray markets.[78]

The system was rife with opportunities and motivation for exploitation. The Allies continued with a top-down model of food collection, echoing the Nazi's system of expecting farmers to hand over most food to authorities. Regional authorities did not comply with these directives, and this attitude cascaded down to the local level. In addition, tensions between rural and urban Germans continued.[79] German farmers refused both to hand over full production of crops and to reduce their

Table 8.1 Ration Scales for Normal Consumers, U.S. Zone of Occupation

Ration Period	Dates	Caloric Value
86	4 March–31 March 1946	1545 calories/day
93	16 September–13 October 1946	1300 calories/day
97	6 January–2 February 1947	1545 calories/day
105	18 August–14 September 1947	1555 calories/day
116	July 1948	1712 calories/day
118	September 1948	1846 calories/day
122	January 1949	1779 calories/day

Source Table created by author. Data compiled from the Office of the Military Government, United States (OMGUS), *Statistical Annex* Nos. 29 (Nov. 1947); 35 (May 1948); 39 (Sept. 1948); and 43 (Jan. 1943)

livestock holdings and profited from this. Between December 1945 and December 1946, the illegal slaughtering of animals removed 138,000 tons of meat and 9000 tons of fat from the official food distribution channels.[80] In addition, even when grain production increased, it was not all reaching the market. One estimate from 1948 charged that farmers still kept 12% of the grain for their own consumption, and millers and bakers siphoned off an additional 4% during production.[81] In addition, at the regional level, *Länder* (the federal states) refused to have portions of their agricultural output redistributed to other areas within Germany.

In the battle over the "crucial power level" that food became in this postwar world, Germans flattened the playing field between 1945 and 1948, until distinctions ceased to exist. The rumor culture was a major influence in this regard. A British relief worker noted, "Rumours [*sic*] spring up out of nothing and are rife in Germany as you know and spread all over the country as authentic facts."[82] During the spring of 1946, 41% of Germans surveyed by the occupation government believed that the food shortage was worldwide and/or that poor harvests were largely to blame. However, by November of 1946, 46% stated that the food shortage was due to overpopulation, specifically DPs, expellees and other foreigners; those blaming bad harvests worldwide dropped to just 10%.[83] Germans changed the power balance by spreading rumors about corruption, mismanagement and supposed Allied subterfuge.

Corruption within the food supply chain was rampant, and while recalcitrant farmers were partially responsible, German consumers railed against the alleged misuse or squandering of food by German and Allied officials. In October of 1945, a mayor supposedly refused to allocate a surplus of butter, preferring that it either be destroyed or be "used to polish the boots of British soldiers."[84] By spring of 1946, rumors circulated that the Americans were deliberately delaying US imports of food into Germany,[85] that the British were destroying "large quantities of preserved food"[86] and that American troops destroyed leftover food, especially bread, by pouring gasoline on it and setting it on fire rather than redistributing it. Analysis of this last rumor asserted, "German people are painfully touched when observing or hearing this, having starvation standing before their door."[87] In Regensburg, Germans believed that the American Army "burned a truck load of white bread at the garbage dump," and that this occurred frequently.[88] They alleged that the British were hoarding seed potatoes for their own use and had let them rot in air raid shelters. Supposedly, a British harbormaster ordered that an entire shipload of fish heads and pig's heads and feet be thrown overboard into the Kiel harbor, as "it was too good for the Germans."[89] Another iteration is that the British just sank ships containing fish deliberately in the harbor.[90] By spring of 1947, rumors spread that American troops were using powdered milk to put down lines on their baseball fields.[91] Embedded in each of these examples is the assertion that the Allies were deliberately punishing the German people, and in each instance, the commodity in question (bread, fish, meat, milk) was both prized and in short supply.

Germans also believed that the Allies were thwarting international efforts to assist them. The supposed countries and goods involved varied, from Norway and Denmark wanting to send fish or butter, to the International Red Cross wanting to distribute food parcels from South America, to banning any neutral ships from docking at German ports.[92] Even where imports did arrive, the Germans were skeptical of their veracity. This perception was so pervasive that jokes about it began to circulate, such as one starring classic characters from Köln puppet theater. "Tünnes is standing on the Rhine Bridge looking down the river. Schäl comes up and asks him, 'What are you looking for?' Tünnes: 'For the wheat ships from Canada.' Schäl – 'You blockhead, they don't come up the river, they come through the radio'."[93] In Aalen, military authorities documented multiple protests at the local theater in response to newsreel footage of international food shipments. According to their report, "They [the German audience] insist that these pictures are faked to create the impression that very large food allotments are being sent to starving Germany. If the food actually is unloaded, where does it go? They insist that the present rations consist of purely German food stuffs."[94] In addition to rumors, there is ample written evidence that Germans bitterly resented the shortages and did not believe the occupation-controlled media. Said one woman: "For months now we hear in the radio and we read in the newspapers, that the Americans send so much food to Germany, But does [*sic*] the people see any of it?"[95] The idea that the German economy had recovered, but that the Allies were squandering and/or hoarding goods and resources was so pervasive, scarcely a fortnight went by without such a rumor spreading.

One fascinating thread that runs through the rumor culture is that Germans believed that they were producing enough food to sustain themselves; it was the addition of all the foreigners in their midst and systematic exporting of German food that caused food shortages. In mid-July of 1945, Germans believed that the RAF was flying fresh fruit and vegetables out of Germany, destined for British consumers, and the following month, the rumor spread that dock workers in Hamburg were on strike because they refused to load German food on ships bound for Britain.[96] This rumor persisted, re-emerging multiple times, with the added details of Germans forced at gunpoint to load ships destined for Britain.[97] Berliners frequently asserted that the USSR was removing food to feed its own people and populations in Eastern Europe.[98] A returning German POW stated that shops in London were "full of butter labelled Deutsch Markenbutter."[99] Believable given the huge amount of food and other commodities received from occupied Europe, these types of rumors persisted, demonstrating the underlying sentiments that gave them legs. "In Potsdam, an acquaintance of mine kept back five tins of jam when unloading a lorry and discovered inside German butter for export."[100] Rather than confront the theft of the tins, the focus is on the supposed large-scale smuggling of German butter. A slew of rumors in June of 1946 charged that the Allies were taking all of the following from Germany and exporting them: butter, vegetables (specifically spinach and asparagus) and strawberries.[101] In the British Zone, a rumor circulated that the occupation authorities were eliminating the meat ration because it was shipping 90,000 head of cattle to France.[102] Letters from Germans in Bavaria in July 1946 asserted that they had received mail from people in Britain and the United States, writing about how the conditions in Germany could not be too terrible, since they were eating butter and/or eggs from Germany.[103] In one example, Germans in Wiesbaden, the capital of Hesse, stated that authorities were exporting German sugar, disguised in bags labeled cement.[104] In 1947, rumors charged that the French were exporting food (specifically coffee, wheat and sugar) from their zone to France and Algeria[105] and that the British were exporting German cattle to the Netherlands.[106] The idea that Germans were able to support themselves if not for the rapacious acquisition and export of their resources stretched into every corner of the economic realm.

In addition to believing that the Allies were exporting large amounts of key foods, Germans repeated a variety of concerns that the Allies were taking German food and re-labeling it, to convince them that the food had been imported. For example, in June of 1946, word spread that the Allies were marking German-produced butter, sugar and flour as if it originated in Canada or the Netherlands.[107] In a phone conversation, one caller shared that "our butter, wrapped in American paper, is being exported to Austria as American butter and the whole thing is a swindle."[108] According to the rumor mill, the British stored German wheat in bags marked Canada and then distributed it as relief supplies,[109] and American troops were taking German potatoes and putting them in American sacks, to mask that they were requisitioning food for themselves.[110] Persistent rumors that the Allies were shipping German grain to Austria were, in fact, true, in one instance, in order to head off catastrophic starvation there. Although authorities replenished the German supply from their own stocks and publicized this fact, the rumor continued to circulate.[111] Similar rumors re-emerged in 1947, with German wheat placed in American sacks and German meat placed in tins with American labels.[112]

In 1947, the amount of foodstuffs produced globally fell well short of global demands. The FAO estimated that food supplies would decrease in Western and Central Europe by 5–10%, unless additional food imports occurred.[113] By then, urban German consumers had access officially to 25% less meat and fats.[114] The American and British zones combined produced only 886 calories per day per person, now distributed evenly across DPs and Germans.[115] That spring as the economic situation worsened, hunger protests in the Ruhr spread to the Rhineland and Westphalia, and more than 300,000 miners went on strike. Germans continued sporadic strikes, equated their hunger with that of concentration camp victims, appealed to international law to assuage their hunger and leveled their most fearsome threat, to be seduced to the side of Communism.[116] One woman warned that unstable conditions were pushing Germans toward their "worst and cunning enemy," namely Communism.[117] General Clay was cognizant of this threat, stating that "There is no choice between becoming a Communist on 1,500 calories and a believer in democracy on 1,000 calories. It is my sincere belief, that our proposed ration allowance in Germany will not only defeat our objective in middle Europe but will pave the road to a Communist Germany."[118]

In this heated atmosphere, the United States conducted a poll in May of 1947, in which 46% of respondents believed that the food situation in Germany was so dire due to "overpopulation, too many refugees, influx of expellees, too many foreigners."[119] In Augsburg, someone placed a sign at the entrance to its cemetery, saying, "Entrance to the 102nd ration period."[120] By June of 1947, rumors swirled that the rations would drop to 750 calories per day.[121] Using the federal state of Hesse as one example, its agricultural output could produce only sufficient bread for 50% of its inhabitants, meat for 56%, potatoes for 70% and fats for 20%.[122] In response, the American and British governments imported a staggering amount of food into their zones: 4,334,350 metric tons, valued at $516,412,500 during 1947 alone.[123] CARE (Cooperative for American Remittances to Europe) packages also supplemented official rations, especially welcome given that they contained "preserved meat, margarine and lard, dried fruit, chocolate, milk powder, coffee, and other food items."[124] No longer were DPs the main beneficiaries of charitable donations of food from abroad. However, rumors circulated that the Western powers would cease all food imports into Germany at the end of the year, reviving claims that the Allies sought to starve the Germans as punishment.[125] In response, US Generals Adcock and Macready reiterated that Germany received the second-largest amount of food imports worldwide, that it received the largest amount of food exported from America and that until the population received, on average, 2000 calories per day, the United States would not reduce food imports.[126]

The battle over food supplies continued even after the occupation forces introduced the Deutschmark in June of 1948. Food supply remained a serious issue, despite an initial flurry of scarcer goods and luxury goods appearing on store shelves. However, black marketeering, while it lessened in volume, did not immediately disappear.[127] For the United States, 1948 saw the infusion of enormous amounts of food and agricultural materials into Europe, through the European Recovery Program (ERP).[128] Within Germany, by the harvest of 1949, grain production was 105% of 1938 levels, potatoes were at 107% and farmers were delivering more of their goods to market. For 1949, the average caloric intake per German civilian was 2780, almost doubling ration levels from 1946.[129] Europe, as a whole, did not reach pre-war levels of agricultural output until 1951.[130]

Conclusion

As Prince queries, once the tree has fallen in the forest and those who heard it are gone, will anyone remember that the tree fell or what it sounded like as it descended and thumped to the ground? He states, "Many experiences are only lived and never remembered, recalled by no one."[131] The Third Reich fell, and we know it hit the ground. But, how did Germans explain how it wound up on the ground and the repercussions thereof? In this case, the postwar deprivations in terms of food have been remembered, but remembered in a different way than they occurred. Rumors help scholars see the actual process of re-remembering in action.

Although occupation officials controlled the flow of information and food, the German population sought to undermine their power in both respects. Rumors, when used as tools of analysis, illuminate the divisive nature of the postwar period, the differences between perceptions and reality of German wartime and postwar experiences and post-1945 anxieties about hunger and scarcity. Germans developed an alternative discourse to make sense of their circumstances, one that imbued food with tremendous meaning and, therefore, became a central element of their postwar identities. They downplayed the food shortages that had occurred during the Third Reich, magnified the postwar scarcities while displacing responsibility for them onto outsiders and then linked the greater food stability post-1948 with the resumption of their control over their own economy. Hunger became one of the primary ways that Germans re-wrote their recent past, through the collective rumor culture that imagined different explanations of postwar scarcity. As Germans told and re-told these rumors centered on food, they created a world that laid claim to a different past, one in which they bore little responsibility.

Notes

1. Food Exhibit, Office of Military Government (OMG), Bremen, 1946.
2. Nick Cullather, "The Foreign Policy of the Calorie," *The American Historical Review* 112, no. 2 (April 2007): 337–364.
3. Atina Grossmann, "Grams, Calories, and Food," *Central European History* 44 (March 2011): 118–148, 122–123; and Alice Weinreb, *Modern Hungers* (Oxford: Oxford University Press, 2017), 100–101.
4. Lowell Bennett, *Berlin Bastion* (Frankfurt am Main: Fred Rudl, 1951), 40.
5. Theodor Adorno, Jeffrey Olick, and Andrew Perrin (eds. and trans.), *Guilt and Defense* (Cambridge: Harvard University Press, 2010), 4–9.
6. W.G.Sebald, "W.G. Sebald," in Christopher Bigsby, *Writers in Conversation*, vol. II (Norwich: Pen and Press, 2001), 139–165, 142–143.
7. Leonie Treber, *Mythos Trümmerfrauen* (Essen: Klartext Verlag, 2014).

8 POSTWAR FOOD RUMORS: SECURITY, VICTIMHOOD, AND FEAR   193

8. For a thorough examination of the impact of Friedrich's book, see Aleida Assman, *Shadows of Trauma*, trans. Sarah Clift (New York, NY: Fordham University Press, 2016), Chapter 7.
9. K. Michael Prince, *War and Germany Memory: Excavating the Significance of the Second World War in German Cultural Consciousness* (Lanham: Rowman and Littlefield, 2009), 4.
10. Amy Corning and Harold Schuman, *Generations and Collective Memory* (Chicago: University of Press, 2015), 107.
11. Robert Moeller, *War Stories: The Search for a Usable Past in the Federal Republic of Germany* (Berkeley: University of California Press, 2001).
12. Peter Jackson, *Anxious Appetites* (London: Bloomsbury, 2015), 2–4.
13. Jackson, *Anxious Appetites*, 5.
14. Olick and Perrin, *Guilt and Defense*, 17–18.
15. See Rebecca Boehling, *A Question of Priorities* (New York, NY: Berghahn, 1996), 80–81, 90–91, 105–106.
16. Audrey Duchesne-Cripps, *The Mental Outlook of the Displaced Persons* (self-published, 1955), 73.
17. Gary Fine and Bill Ellis, *The Global Grapevine* (Oxford: Oxford University Press, 2010), 5.
18. G.W. Allport and L.J. Postman, *The Psychology of Rumor* (New York, NY: Holt, Rinehart & Winston, 1947), ix.
19. The key study, often cited in literature, is a survey of an introductory Psychology course, whereby researchers deliberately inserted a rumor into the class population of 180 students and then analyzed its spread. See Marianne Jaeger et al., "Who Hears What from Whom and with What Effect?" *Personality and Social Psychology Bulletin* 6, no. 3 (1980): 473–478.
20. F.H. Allport and M. Lepkin, "Wartime Rumors of Waste and Special Privilege: Why Some People Believe Them," *Journal of Abnormal and Social Psychology* 40 (1945): 3–36.
21. Tomatsu Shibutani, *Improvised News: A Sociological Study of Rumor* (Indianapolis: Bobbs-Merrill, 1966).
22. Fine and Ellis, *The Global Grapevine*, 9.
23. Gary Fine, "Rumor, Trust and Civil Society: Collective Memory and Cultures of Judgment," *Diogenes* 54, no. 1 (February 2007): 5–6, 5–18, 15–17.
24. Nicholas Di Fonzo and Prashant Bordia, "Rumor, Gossip, and Urban Legends," *Diogenes* 54, no. 1 (February 2007): 19–35, 31.
25. Lizzie Collingham, *The Taste of War: World War II and the Battle for Food* (New York, NY: Penguin, 2012), 29–31.
26. Hein Klemann with Sergei Kudryashov, *Occupied Economies* (London: Berg, 2012), 375.

27. Joachim Lehmann, "Agrarpolitik und Landwirtschaft in Deutschland 1939 bis 1945," in *Agriculture and Food Supply in the Second World War*, edited by Alan S. Milward and Bernd Martin (Ostfildern: Scripta Mercaturae, 1985), 29–49, 30.
28. Adam Tooze, *The Wages of Destruction: The Making and Breaking of the Nazi Economy* (New York: Penguin, 2008), 361.
29. Gesine Gerhard, *Nazi Hunger Politics* (Lanham: Rowman & Littlefield, 2015), 45.
30. Götz Aly, *Hitler's Beneficiaries*, trans. Jefferson Chase (New York: Metropolitan Books, 2005), 94–99.
31. Klemann, *Occupied Economies*, Table 9.5, 106; Tooze, *Wages of Destruction*, 539, 548. Tooze's figures include foodstuffs requisitioned and consumed by the German military within occupied territory: more than 20% of its grain; 25% of its fats; and close to 30% of its meat.
32. Klemann, *Occupied Economies*, 378. This does not include foodstuffs Germany also seized to feed its troops stationed in France.
33. As quoted in Aly, *Hitler's Beneficiaries*, 170.
34. Collingham, *Taste of War*, 165. See also Tooze, *Wages of Destruction*, Table A5, 686.
35. Aly, *Hitler's Beneficiaries*, 176. See also, Mark Mazower, *Hitler's Empire* (New York, NY: Penguin, 2008), 274–277, 284–290.
36. Collingham, *Taste of War*, 164. Both the quantity that Germans ate had dropped, as had the quality of what they consumed. See John Farquharson, *The Western Allies and the Politics of Food* (London: Berg, 1985), 22–23.
37. Collingham, *Taste of War*, 218.
38. BSHA, OMGB, RG 260, 10/87–3/5, IIR, Darmstadt, 8/5/1947.
39. Aly, *Hitler's Beneficiaries*, 179.
40. Some estimates range as high as approximately 3000 calories per day, including an astonishing 106 grams of fat. See Grossmann, "Grams, Calories, and Food," 124.
41. Gerhard, *Nazi Hunger Politics*, 121–122.
42. Weinreb, *Modern Hungers*, 100.
43. Report of Military Governor. July 1945. No. 1, 8/20/1945. Tooze estimates that British and American bombers dropped more than 1,000,000 tons of bombs on Germany between June 1944 and April 1945. Tooze, *Making and Breaking*, 649.
44. "Aus Trümmern zum Wiederaufbau," in *Hessen: Kultur und Wirtschaft*, edited by Georg August Zinn (Wiesbaden: Erasmusdruck Max Krause, 1952), 167.
45. Collingham, *Taste of War*, 469.
46. Lehmann, "Agrarpolitik und Landwirtschaft," 29–49, 39.

47. Ibid., 37.
48. Collingham, *Taste of War*, 467.
49. Ibid., 478–479.
50. Weinreb, *Modern Hungers*, 93.
51. PRO, FO 1012/97, Intelligence Summary (IS), Berlin, 1/14/1946.
52. NARA, RG 260, Entry A2B3C1, Box 170, OMGB, Political Intelligence Report, 5/25/1946.
53. See NARA, RG 260, Box 903, CIC Report, Berlin, 10/26/46, and PRO, FO 1005/1863, RR, 6/12/1947. These spurious claims gained traction again in the 1990s with the publication of James Bacque's *Crimes and Mercies: The Fate of German Civilians Under Allied Occupation, 1944–1950* (New York, NY: Little, Brown, 1997).
54. PRO, FO 1005/1714, WIR, Third Army, No. 60, 7/17/1946.
55. PRO, FO 1005/1753, WIR, 8/7/1946.
56. NARA, RG 407, Entry 368, Box 1168, WPIS, 7/4/1945 and Strang Report, 7/7/1945.
57. PRO, FO 1005/1723, WIR, Wiesbaden, 8/31/1946.
58. Jackson, *Anxious Appetites*, 49.
59. Earl Ziemke, *The U.S. Army in the Occupation of Germany, 1944–1946* (Washington, DC: Center of Military History, 1975), 275.
60. Klemann, *Occupied Economies*, Table 17.1, 380.
61. In Manfred Malzahn, *Germany 1945–1949* (London: Routledge, 1991), 109–111.
62. James Smith, ed., *The Papers of General Lucius D. Clay*, vol. 1 (Bloomington: Indiana University Press, 1974), 24.
63. NARA, RG 407, Entry 368, Box 1199, Office of Military Government, United States (OMGUS), ODI, 1/4/1946.
64. Earl Ziemke, *US Army in the Occupation of Germany, 1944–1946* (Washington, DC: CMI US Army, 1975), 274–275.
65. Military Government in Germany, Monthly Report of the Military Governor (MRMG), U.S. Zone, September 20, 1945, No. 2, 6.
66. Collingham, *Taste of War*, 468.
67. Gerhard, *Nazi Hunger Politics*, 127.
68. USFET. Military Government Regulations, Title 20, Displaced Persons, February 1946.
69. Gerhard, *Nazi Hunger Politics*, 133.
70. See for example, NARA, RG 407, Entry 368, Box 1204, IS, British Army of the Rhine (BAR), No. 14, 11/2/1945 and NARA, RG 407, Entry 368, Box 1186, FIS, BAR, 11/11/1945.
71. Grossmann, "Grams, Calories, and Food," 136.
72. PRO, FO 1005/1714, WIR, Third Army, No. 60, 7/17/1946.
73. PRO, FO 1005/1723, Monthly Trend Report (MTR), 9/17/1946.

74. ICD, *Trends in German Public Opinion*, Report Number 100, March 1948.
75. Weinreb, *Modern Hungers*, 102–104.
76. UNRRA, *Monthly Review*. No. 19, March 1946 and No. 22, June 1946.
77. See OMGUS. *Economic Data on Potsdam Germany*. Special Report of the Military Governor. September, 1947: 89
78. Malte Zierenberg, *Berlin's Black Market, 1939–1950* (Houndmills: Palgrave Macmillan, 2015), especially Chapter 4; Paul Steege, *Black Market, Cold War* (Cambridge: Cambridge University Press, 2007); and Laura J. Hilton, "The Black Market in History and Memory: German Perceptions of Victimhood from 1945 to 1948," *German History* 28, no. 4 (December 2010): 479–97.
79. Farquharson, *Agricultural and Food Supply*, 50–68, 60–61.
80. Ibid., 57–59.
81. NARA, RG 260, 8-1/1-5, Folder: Information Reports, Memo from Bad Schwalbach Officer to OMGH, April 20, 1948.
82. UNA, PAG 004, 3.0.11.0.1.6, Box 7, Letter from Carl H. Martini to Sir Michael Creagh, 8/20/1946.
83. NARA, RG 260, 8/120-3/21, ICD Opinion Survey No. 70, "German Understanding of Reasons for the Food Shortage."
84. NARA, RG 407, Entry 368, Box 1199, IS, Headquarters, BAR, No. 12, 10/6/1945.
85. NARA, RG 407, Entry 368, Box 1199, WIR, No. 42, 3/13/1946.
86. NARA, RG 407, Entry 368, Box 1199, SHIOFS, 4/1/1946.
87. NARA, RG 260, Entry A2B3C1, Box 170, WIR, Gelnhausen, 5/16/1946.
88. NARA, RG 260, Entry A2B3C1, Box 170, Political Round-Up, Regensburg Area, 5/28/1946.
89. NARA, RG 260, Entry A2B3C1, Box 158, SHIOFS, 6/15/1946. This exact rumor re-emerged in Hamburg the following spring. See NARA, RG 260, Entry A2B3C1, Box 677, MSIS, Hamburg, 5/1/1947.
90. NARA, RG 260, Entry 893(A1), Box 111, SHIOFS, 5/15/1946.
91. NARA, RG 260, Entry A2 B1 C3, Box 340, Weekly Intelligence Summary (WIS), OMG Bavaria, 6/18/1947.
92. NARA, RG 407, Entry 368, Box 1199, RIOS, Hamburg, 2/191/946; NARA, RG 260, Entry A2B3C1, Box 158, RIOS, 6/15/1946; PRO, FO 371, 3086, RIOS, Hamburg, 6/29/1946 and NARA, RG 260, Entry 1250, Box 144, RIOS, 6/1/1946.
93. PRO, FO 1005/1713, WPS, 8/17/1946.
94. PRO, FO 1005/1753, WIR, Aalen, 2/17/1947.
95. NARA, RG 260, 8-119/3-13&14, Folder: Correspondence from German Civilians, Letter from Henriette Notrott to OMGH, 1/4/1948.

8 POSTWAR FOOD RUMORS: SECURITY, VICTIMHOOD, AND FEAR   197

96. NARA, RG 407, Entry 368, Box 1168, WPIR, July 14, 1945 and NARA, RG 260, Entry A2B3C1, Box 170, 21st Army, Sit-Rep, 8/11/1945.
97. NARA, RG 407, Entry 368, Box 1204, RIOS, 1/24/1946.
98. NARA, RG 407, Entry 368, Box 1199, IS, No. 36, Headquarters, British Troops, Berlin, 3/21/1946.
99. NARA, RG 260, Entry 893 (A1), Box 109, RIOS, 4/5/1946.
100. PRO, FO 1005/1863, RR, 8/12/1947.
101. NARA, RG 260, Entry A2B3C1, Box 158, RIOS, 6/15/1946; NARA, RG 466, Entry 274, Box 29, SHIOFS, 6/15/1946; PRO, WO 205/1078, SHIOFS, 6/21/1946.
102. PRO, WO 205/1078, SHIOFS, 6/21/1946.
103. PRO, FO 1032, 419, Letter from Lentze to Langhead, 7/9/1946; PRO, FO 1012/97, Letter from Recke to Jung, 7/15/1946. See also PRO, FO 1005/1713, OMG (Bavaria), ICD, Political Affairs Section, 15 August 1946.
104. PRO, FO 1005/1753, WIR, 11/19/1946.
105. NARA, RG 260, Entry A2B3C1, Box 663, IIR, 4/14/1947.
106. PRO, FO 1005/1721, MIS, 11/27/1947.
107. PRO, FO 1005/1707, IS, Berlin, 6/21/1946. Another rumor in this vein spread in October of 1946 that the food eaten by the British Army all came from German supplies. See PRO, FO 1005/1707, IS, Berlin.
108. NARA, RG 466, Entry 274, Box 14, Phone tap, 5/17/1946.
109. NARA, RG 260, Entry A2B3C1, Box 170, SHIOFS, 5/17/1946 and NARA, RG 260, Entry 893(A1), Box 104, SHIOFS, 6/15/1946.
110. NARA, RG 260, Entry A2B3C1, Box 170, WIR, Usingen, 5/23/1946. This exact rumor re-circulated in September of 1946. PRO, FO 1005/1713, WIR, Untertaunus, 9/5/1946.
111. NARA, RG 466, Entry 274, Box 21, OMG (Bavaria), ICD, Political Affairs Section, 8/15/1946.
112. PRO, FO 1005/1715, Daily Brief, Political Branch, OMGB, 8/9/1947; NARA, RG 466, Entry 274, Box 5, WIR Aalen, 9/29/1947; NARA, RG 260, Entry A2 B1 C3, Box 340, Report No. 45 on Rumors, Präsidium der Landpolizei von Bayern, 11/5/1947.
113. FAO, *The State of Food and Agriculture: 1947* (Geneva: United Nations, 1947), 5.
114. John Farquharson, "The Management of Agriculture and Food Supplies in Germany, 1944–1947," in *Agriculture and Food Supply in the Second World War*, edited by Alan S. Milward and Bernd Martin (Ostfildern: Scripta Mercaturae, 1985), 50–68, 61.
115. R. L. Fisher, "The Army and Displaced Persons," *Military Government Journal*, April 1948.

116. Grossmann, "Grams, Calories, and Food," 130.
117. NARA, RG 260, 8–119/3–13–14, Folder: Correspondence from German Citizens, Letter from Gisela Walther to OMGH, May 1948.
118. James Smith, *The Papers of General Lucius D. Clay*, 184.
119. NARA, RG 260, 8/215–1/4, Folder: Executive Office, ICD, Research Branch, Special Report No. 32, German Reactions to the Food Situation, 5/1947.
120. NARA, RG 466, Entry 274, Box 59, Weekly Intelligence Summary, OMG Bavaria, 5/7/1947.
121. PRO, FO 1005/1753, MSIS, Hamburg, 6/1/1947.
122. HSA, Record Group 509, Folder 2029, Letter, 11/29/1947.
123. OMGUS, *Monthly Report of the Military Governor*, No. 30, December 1947: 40–41. In comparison, the total food imports into Bizonia in 1946 totaled 3,177,800 metric tons, valued at $476,000,000.
124. Gerhard, *Nazi Hunger Politics*, 128.
125. PRO, FO 1005/1753, RR, Berlin, 6/12/1947.
126. NARA, RG 260, Folder: Radio Broadcasts, Radio Broadcast regarding food, 1/20/1948.
127. Zierenberg, *Berlin's Black Market*, 187–194.
128. Weinreb, *Modern Hungers*, 120.
129. Hubert G. Schmidt, *Food and Agricultural Programs in West Germany, 1949–1951* (Frankfurt: OMGUS, 1952), 14–15, 93, 97.
130. Alan Milward, "Second World War and Long-term Change in World Agriculture," in *Agriculture and Food Supply in the Second World War*, edited by Alan S. Milward and Bernd Martin (Ostfildern: Scripta Mercaturae, 1985), 5–15, 8.
131. Prince, *War and Germany Memory*, 8.

Bibliography

Allport, G.W., and L.J. Postman. *The Psychology of Rumor.* New York, NY: Holt, Rinehart & Winston, 1947.
Aly, Götz. *Hitler's Beneficiaries.* Translated by Jefferson Chase. New York, NY: Metropolitan Books, 2005.
Assman, Aleida. *Shadows of Trauma.* Translated by Sarah Clift. New York, NY: Fordham University Press, 2016.
Bennett, Lowell. *Berlin Bastion.* Frankfurt am Main: Fred Rudl, 1951.
Bigsby, Christopher. "W.G. Sebald." In *Writers in Conversation*, vol. II. Norwich: Pen and Press, 2001.
Boehling, Rebecca. *A Question of Priorities: Democratic Reform and Economic Recovery in Postwar Germany.* New York, NY: Berghahn, 1996.

Collingham, Lizzie. *The Taste of War: World War II and the Battle for Food*. New York, NY: Penguin, 2012.
Corning, Amy, and Harold Schuman. *Generations and Collective Memory*. Chicago: University of Chicago Press, 2015.
Cullather, Nick. "The Foreign Policy of the Calorie." *The American Historical Review* 112, no. 2 (2007): 337–364.
Di Fonzo, Nicholas, and Prashant Bordia. "Rumor, Gossip, and Urban Legends." *Diogenes* 54, no. 1 (2007): 19–35.
Duchesne-Cripps, Audrey. *The Mental Outlook of the Displaced Persons*. Self-published, 1955.
Farquharson, John. *The Western Allies and the Politics of Food*. London: Berg, 1985.
Fine, Gary. "Rumor, Trust and Civil Society: Collective Memory and Cultures of Judgment." *Diogenes* 54, no. 1 (2007): 5–18.
Fine, Gary, and Bill Ellis. *The Global Grapevine*. Oxford: Oxford University Press, 2010.
Fisher, R. L. "The Army and Displaced Persons." *Military Government Journal*, 1948.
Gerhard, Gesine. *Nazi Hunger Politics: A History of Food in the Third Reich*. Lanham: Rowman & Littlefield, 2015.
Grossmann, Atina. "Grams, Calories, and Food." *Central European History* 44 (2011): 118–148.
Hilton, Laura J. "The Black Market in History and Memory." *German History* 28, no. 4 (2010): 479–497.
Jackson, Peter. *Anxious Appetites: Food and Consumer Culture*. London: Bloomsbury, 2015.
Klemann, Hein with Sergei Kudryashov. *Occupied Economies: An Economic History of Nazi-Occupied Europe, 1939–1945*. London: Berg, 2012.
Malzahn, Manfred. *Germany 1945–1949*. London: Routledge, 1991.
Mazower, Mark. *Hitler's Empire: How the Nazis Ruled Europe*. New York: Penguin, 2008.
Martin, Bernd, and Alan Milward, eds. *Agriculture and Food Supply in the Second World War*. Ostfildern: Scripta Mercaturae Verlag, 1985.
Moeller, Robert. *War Stories: The Search for a Usable Past in the Federal Republic of Germany*. Berkeley: University of California Press, 2001.
Olick, Jeffrey, and Andrew Perrin. *Guilt and Defense*. Cambridge: Harvard University Press, 2010.
Prince, K. Michael. *War and German Memory: Excavating the Significance of the Second World War in German Cultural Consciousness*. Lanham: Rowman and Littlefield, 2009.
Schmidt, Hubert. *Food and Agricultural Programs in West Germany, 1949–1951*. Frankfurt: OMGUS, 1952.

Smith, James, ed. *The Papers of General Lucius D. Clay*, vol. 1. Bloomington: Indiana University Press, 1974.

Steege, Paul. *Black Market, Cold War: Everyday Life in Berlin, 1946–1949*. Cambridge: Cambridge University Press, 2007.

Tooze, Adam. *The Wages of Destruction: The Making and Breaking of the Nazi Economy*. New York, NY: Penguin, 2008.

Treber, Leonie. *Mythos Trümmerfrauen*. Essen: Klartext Verlag, 2014.

Weinreb, Alice. *Modern Hungers: Food and Power in Twentieth-Century Germany*. Oxford: Oxford University Press, 2017.

Ziemke, Earl. *US Army in the Occupation of Germany, 1944–1946*. Washington, DC: CMI, US Army, 1975.

Zierenberg, Malte. *Berlin's Black Market, 1939–1950*. Houndmills: Palgrave Macmillan, 2015.

Zinn, Georg August, ed. *Hessen: Kultur und Wirtschaft*. Wiesbaden: Erasmusdruck Max Krause, 1952.

CHAPTER 9

The Taste of Defeat: Food, Peace and Power in US-Occupied Germany

Kaete O'Connell

In the first published account of the occupation, Julian Bach presented the "grim" facts facing America's Germany, facts that demanded recognition and action, but not sympathy.[1] Bach, whose book was excerpted in *Life* on the one-year anniversary of VE Day, commented extensively on the growing food crisis in the US Zone, debunking sensational rumors but emphasizing the very real consequences of existing American policy. Lessons of World War I informed the decision to enforce a punitive occupation, including the prohibition of food shipments and a refusal to allow voluntary aid agencies to assist German civilians. But could the terms of a hard peace guarantee a bright future? For Bach, the food problem was never black and white: "Some Germans are starving, millions are suffering from malnourishment, while other millions are neither starving nor suffering."[2] With food supplies dwindling, a growing number of non-governmental organizations and religious aid societies pushed the question of German food relief. In early 1946, President Truman reversed course and permitted food imports for German civilians. Truman also publicly endorsed the Council of Relief Agencies Licensed

---

K. O'Connell (✉)
Center for Presidential History, Southern Methodist University, Dallas, TX, USA

© The Author(s) 2019
H. M. Benbow and H. R. Perry (eds.), *Food, Culture and Identity in Germany's Century of War*,
https://doi.org/10.1007/978-3-030-27138-1_9

to Operate in Germany (CRALOG), allowing the organization to solicit charitable donations for civilian relief.[3]

American postwar humanitarian action is often remembered fondly in Germany and for good reason. US food aid to the defeated nation restored stability, improved nutrition and boosted morale at a pivotal moment. This chapter explores the origins of that story by examining the relationships forged by food in conquered and early occupied Germany. There is excellent scholarship on hunger and identity in postwar Germany, but little that examines food's role in civil-military relations—the emotional and cultural consequences of food exchange.[4] What role did food play in fraternization? Were American "gifts" of food warmly embraced or begrudgingly accepted? How did images of hunger and deprivation compromise Military Government's enforcement of the hard peace? Postwar Germany was the site of elaborate food negotiations, with food utilized as both a weapon of war and tool of peace. In the final weeks of the conflict, and extending for many months after, food served as a conduit between conqueror and conquered. Ultimately, this chapter argues that food offers an alternative measure of power and a lens to appreciate how the occupation was experienced and understood by American soldier and German civilian alike.

In 1943, Margaret Mead, an anthropologist serving on the National Research Council's Committee on Food Habits, published an article advocating for greater research into the feeding practices of occupied areas. Mead believed relief efforts "had to respect local cultures in order to be effective and to lay the appropriate foundation for postwar development."[5] In her article, she emphasized the psychological aspects of feeding, noting the frequent association of provisioning with parental actions toward children: "thus whenever a people feels that its food supply is in the hands of an authority, it tends to regard that authority as to some degree parental." The giving of this food not only "prov[ed] to an anxious and disturbed people that the powers that be … have their welfare at heart," but also highlighted the benevolence inherent in American occupation policy.[6] Historian Atina Grossmann took this metaphor one step further in her analysis of rations and shifting standards of victimization in occupied Germany, writing, "the allied 'parents' discriminated among their … dependent 'children,' who in turn squabbled over who was more entitled or deprived."[7] The paternalist mission inherent in US military action abroad has been well documented and analyzed by historians, but more can be done to assess how these acts of official and unofficial food sharing contributed to the emergence of new ideas about victor and vanquished, friend and foe and villain and victim, exploring how various forms of food dispersal illustrate contrasting images of control and discipline with support and guidance.[8]

Discussing war through the lens of a daily, transcendent commodity allows for the atypical experience to be normalized. Food exemplified the experience of war for soldier and civilian alike—its presence necessary for maintaining morale and preventing disease on both the home and war fronts and in conquered territory. But food offered emotional sustenance as well, never a "purely biological act," eating lies "at the core of our most intimate social relationships."[9] Writing about the British Army in World War I, historian Rachel Duffet states that food was the site of complex and contradictory emotional responses, "each and every day it provided a locus where the men were confronted with both the disturbing breaks and the reassuring continuities of their new environment."[10] The same can be said of food experiences in occupied Germany, where consumption became "a form of self-identification and of communication."[11] The symbolism ascribed to food and feeding during war persisted in the postwar era and was laden with new meaning during the occupation. Food lay at the heart of numerous conflicts and debates over occupation policy both within and beyond the offices of Military Government (OMGUS).[12] Relying on military and civilian sources, this chapter explores both positive and negative relationships with food in postwar Germany, including looting by occupied forces, the black market, fraternization, the brewing ban, differences in taste and the military's role in food dispersal following the decision to allow aid in early 1946. These early food relationships provide an opportunity to examine inconsistencies in American policy, exploring the many ways official policy was confronted, contradicted and circumvented during the interregnum between war and peace.

"We Took What We Wanted": Food and Punishment

Writing to his mother in April 1945, Clifford Shirley relayed a macabre story about German cats and dogs "used for food," echoing earlier rumors drifting out of Berlin and other large cities.[13] Shirley did not question the veracity of such reports, explaining, "I can believe it after seeing them go thru the garbage we dumped."[14] Shirley's account betrays neither disgust nor empathy at what would become a common sight in US-conquered territory. American forces accustomed to the cheers of liberated populations crossed the Rhine to meet somber faces of defeat, "the women didn't smile and they didn't throw flowers at us and blow kisses. Only the kids were happy to see us ... with happy squeals of terror."[15] Arriving in Germany, the category "enemy" now extended to civilians, demanding that hostility "underlie all the casual little contacts."[16] Many GIs found it difficult "to stifle compassion for an old woman rummaging in the remains of her bombed house, or to resist the appeal of a four year old boy ... who waves and laughs and cries '*Soldaten, Soldaten!*' as one walks by." This led Leo Bogart to tartly write that it would be easier to recognize the enemy had all Germans "grown horns and turned blue."[17]

The first food relationships to develop in enemy territory were rarely rooted in commensality, but instead emerged from Americans' often visceral reactions to scenes of Nazi orchestrated genocide and destruction. GIs' earliest encounters with images of deprivation and malnourishment at the hands of Nazis occurred in liberated territory, specifically the Netherlands. During the winter of 1944–1945, the German military prohibited all food transports into western Holland in retaliation for rail strikes organized by the Dutch resistance, leaving 500,000 Dutch to subsist on tulip bulbs and beets.[18] Watching a fight unfold between starving Dutchmen over garbage, one American soldier wrote with disgust, "what untold suffering those dumb, non-thinking, egotistical, goose-stepping klouts have inflicted needlessly on untold innocent thousands."[19] Food was unquestionably a cause of war, but it was also a weapon of war perfected by Herbert Backe, Reich Minister of Food and Agriculture, the mastermind behind the *Hungerplan* in the Soviet Union, devised to divert Ukrainian food supplies to Germany and systematically starving millions of Slavs.[20] In addition to half-starved civilian populations, American GIs were embittered by the appearance of their brothers-in-arms liberated from German POW camps. Food shortages throughout Germany in 1944–1945 resulted in starvation level rations in POW camps, including "soup with maggots in it, bread with sawdust, and ... other horrible concoctions."[21] Although Red Cross parcels were shipped to the camps, their dispersal was frequently erratic, with the Tenth Armored Division discovering a cache of Red Cross packages addressed to Allied prisoners of war.[22] Encountering hunger among their fellow soldiers was a punch to morale and served to validate desires for punitive action.

The most gruesome images of starvation, however, confronted those US troops responsible for liberating the work camps. On April 12th, Generals Dwight D. Eisenhower and George S. Patton toured Ohrdruf Nord, a forced labor camp near Gotha discovered by Allied forces a week prior. Eisenhower was left sick by "the visual evidence and the verbal testimony of starvation, cruelty and bestiality."[23] Patton recorded in his diary that it was "one of the most appalling sights" he had ever seen.[24] The *Washington Post* attributed most of the deaths at Belsen to starvation, describing meager rations of "watery soup made with meal and a few vegetables" and again reporting undistributed Red Cross packages.[25] From Buchenwald came Margaret Bourke-White's brutal photographs of "living corpses" and Edward R. Murrow's unapologetically grim national broadcast, describing the "evil-smelling stink" as he stood surrounded by a mass of starving men while "well-fed Germans" plowed the green fields beyond the fence.[26] The following week Eisenhower requested that members of Congress and prominent journalists visit the camps "to leave no doubt in their minds about the normal practices of the Germans."[27] The images haunted those who saw them firsthand and hardened public opinion in an unprecedented fashion, especially when contrasted with early reports on the seemingly high German standard of living. Soldiers frequently commented on the number of "surprisingly healthy" blond youngsters they encountered, while papers like the *New York Times* reported Germans "look[ed] fat and well fed."[28] Margaret Bourke-White's photos from Frankfurt included an image of German housewives modeling hats looted from a railcar, noting "good teeth show they did not suffer dietary deficiencies during the war," their smiles offering visual proof of their supposed health and well-being at the expense of the rest of Europe.[29]

Anticipating fierce civilian resistance, soldiers were warned not to accept food or drink for fear it was poisoned, with a Civil Affairs Division memo identifying Nescafe, sugar and chocolate used "in connection with the terrorist phase of the German resistance program."[30] Newspapers informed readers that retreating Germans purposefully left behind contaminated food stocks, while GIs reported canned fruit and preserves mixed with crushed glass and left in cupboards.[31] Suspicions lingered throughout the summer, with the Second Armored Division reporting several casualties, including three deaths, which the Division surgeon attributed to poisoned cognac.[32] Raymond Gantter acknowledged the seriousness of sabotage, but still accepted cough syrup from an elderly woman: " ... you had to make a decision one way or another and then take your chances ... I guess I was right each time."[33] Not every food encounter, however, was met with suspicion. Sgt. Francis Mitchell described his unit's arrival in Cologne, where residents "tossed Americans loaves of bread and brought out jam, preserved cherries, beer and pretzels," hosting a spontaneous party in the midst of rubble.[34] Private Elmer Jones documented German goodwill in letters home, writing, "a woman slipped us a bowl of potatoe [sic] salad through the window of our room ... The last place we were at the woman offered us milk and boiled potatoes."[35] The further his unit marched into Germany, the better civilians treated them, particularly when it came to sharing food.

American soldiers embraced German gifts of food and drink, but also felt empowered to take what they pleased. Writing to his parents in April 1945, Emanuel Lamb apologized for the recent lack of communication, explaining that his unit was embarking on their own *blitzkrieg* across Germany. The 83rd Division, he wrote, had a reputation for moving quickly and frequently outpaced their supplies; thus, rations were difficult to acquire. Quick to address parental concern about his well-being, Lamb assured them "we didn't starve," explaining that when he and his comrades stopped at a German home, "we took the food we wanted, slept in the rooms and beds we wanted and did what we wanted ... on Germany we have no pity."[36] Soldiers had grown bored of the rations that accompanied them on their march into Germany and sought fresh food wherever they could find it, often helping themselves to eggs from local farms. One German girl noted in her diary that Americans always seemed to carry steel helmets filled with eggs on their way to new quarters.[37] Eggs were particularly popular due to the ease in which they could be cooked and digested. They also, according to Phillip Rutherford, served a psychological function, reminding young soldiers of home, "embody[ing] the safety and security of faraway civilian life and the tranquility of a prelapsarian innocence."[38] Regardless of the seeming "innocence" behind the eggs, the young German girl feared being alone and risking an encounter with foraging Americans.

The real prize for GIs, however, was German beer. Military facilities in the United States and overseas began selling Army Beer (limited to 3.2%) in 1942 but demand unsurprisingly outpaced supply. With military supplied alcohol running scarce, soldiers indulged in local fare, liberating champagne and wine from cellars in the Rhineland and later embracing the *Biergärten* (beer gardens) and the *Festhalle* (festival hall) drinking culture. Writing to his parents in the summer of 1945, Earl Bailey raved about the "endless quantity of (8%) beer" admitting that German beer was "pretty good."[39] Robert Greivell recalled his assignment to the company *Biergärten* fondly. The position came with a number of perks, including an apartment, but with great power came great responsibility. Supplying the *Biergärten* was seldom an easy task, forcing managers to rely on unconventional methods of procurement. Greivell recalled one such visit to a nearby distillery, flashing forged documents and emptying the facility, "We must have taken a thousand bottle of cognac."[40] Military Government enforced strict regulations regarding the manufacture and sale of beer, but soldiers often circumvented these rules when obtaining alcohol or selling it to civilians.

American GIs were awash in German beer, but Germans suffered the fate of prohibition. The use of food grains for brewing was initially banned during the early months of the occupation. Newspapers in the US critical of the occupation had printed reports that Germans were using grain to brew beer rather than bake much-needed bread. General Lucius D. Clay allowed some breweries to remain open as suppliers for the army of occupation, but not the civilian population. Stanley Andrews, Clay's man in charge of Food and Agriculture, considered this to be "the hardest blow of all against the civilian population ... taking ... the last shred of respectability away from the German people."[41] The problem was particularly acute in Bavaria where "beer is not only a beverage but a nutrient like bread."[42] Plain water was an insufficient substitute, requiring fuel to boil it and eliminate the threat of typhoid. Speaking with John Dos Passos, one German woman gave a "deprecatory smile" as she explained there was "no use forbidding beer ... When the German farmer couldn't get beer, he just drank his milk."[43] This tendency to drink milk as a substitute negatively impacted the production of much-needed fats in the form of milk, butter and cheese products, further exacerbating the existing shortages.[44] June Lorenz of Bremerhaven told a reporter that "my children do not know what it is to drink a glass of milk with their meals."[45] Cognizant of the negative "psychological effect" the reopening of breweries may have on US public opinion, Clay wrote the War Department in February 1946 and announced he was permitting breweries in the US Zone to produce a weak beer. Acknowledging beer's place as a "native drink" in Bavaria, he argued that controlled brewing "will prevent widespread home brewing, bootlegging, and black market operations which would in fact consume larger quantities of grain."[46]

"The Science of Fratting": Food and Survival

The rapid growth of black markets was of serious concern in late 1945 and early 1946.[47] Black markets in Germany, "one of the most shameful and degrading aspects of the military occupation" according to Stanley Andrews, cropped up immediately following VE Day, providing an opportunity to barter both personal possessions and looted goods.[48] Russian soldiers flooded the market with freshly printed occupation *Marks*, which could then be taken to US Military Post Offices where they were converted into a postal money order transferred to the United States in US dollars. Andrews wrote that "millions upon millions were converted" before occupation authorities stepped in, the "racket" involving not only the military, but even Truman's civilian staff who accompanied him to the Potsdam Conference, "many of them boarded their planes home with everything sold but the shirts on their backs and their pants – even shoelaces and neckties were absent."[49] The law forbade Allied soldiers from selling PX rations and their personal possessions, but many did so anyway and made a killing, with a 5 cent candy bar bringing in $5 and a bottle of whiskey or gin selling for $75–$100. Julian Bach estimated that prior to the November 1945 crackdown on black market activity, an officer selling his cigarette, candy bar and liquor rations could make a minimum yearly profit of $11,726.20, and that was before factoring in the sale of items shipped to soldiers from family and friends in the States.[50]

Germans were similarly forbidden from participating in black market activities, but for many, these food exchanges offered the only means of supplementing the official ration. In the fall of 1945, "obtaining food was as much a matter of having contacts as it was having a ration card," and while the official ration was set at 1500 calories a day per normal consumer, actual consumption varied greatly.[51] Hunger persisted, and malnutrition remained a threat, but starvation was less common. As Gertrud B. succinctly put it, "We are healthy, only both quite tired and always getting thinner."[52] Personal possessions soon flooded the market, with Germans trading their furniture, porcelain and cameras for coffee, cigarettes and food. "Everybody," Wolfgang Samuel remembered, "at one time or another had to fall back on the black market to obtain something to keep a family functioning, it was not a frivolous choice."[53] The economy of postwar Germany was rooted in an elaborate barter system, with chocolate, alcohol and cigarettes serving as currency. Arnim Krüger played the piano for a Russian soldier in Berlin and received four bars of chocolate which he traded for cigarettes on the black market. These cigarettes were worth more than the chocolate and allowed him to trade for something even more valuable: butter.[54] Military Government struggled to control black market activities throughout late 1945 and 1946, but it was currency reform in 1948 that finally put an end to the barter system.

The exchange of food items was also ensnared in debates over the military's enforcement of non-fraternization, a policy that proved overwhelmingly ineffective, "by banning Yankee-Kraut dalliances, the 'furlines' become forbidden fruit, thus making them in the minds of many men all the tastier." Bach explained the science of "fratting" as follows: "I. Soldier Sees Girl and Whistles II. Soldier Gives Girl a Hershey Bar (from the PX) and Fanny Farmer taffy (sent by mother, but not for this purpose) III. Soldier Goes to Bed with Girl (while girl tries to steal the rest of his candy)."[55] It is important to remember that while "connections between food and sex are primal," for many women, especially those with children, these relationships were a matter of survival.[56] The pack of cigarettes or can of coffee a woman received from a GI could be bartered on the black market for "the food she needed for her children or aged parents."[57] Krüger recalled in July 1945, when the Americans arrived in Berlin for the Potsdam Conference, that his mother left and when she returned the next day, "she was loaded down with food, including lots of chocolate," but "she didn't talk about how she got the food."[58] Still, *Life* magazine chided young German women who "flaunt[ed] themselves partly to taunt the Americans but chiefly in order to get 'frau bait' of candy, gum, and cigarets [*sic*]."[59] This trope was so widely known that it appeared in popular culture, including Billy Wilder's comedy on denazification, *A Foreign Affair* (1948). Two American GIs entreat a German girl to accompany them on their bicycle, singing: "Fraulein, Fraulein, / willst Du ein Candy bar. / Schön fein, Fraulein. / You like G.I.s, nicht war?"[60] Historian Werner Sollors reminds readers that the working title of the film was *Operation Candybar*.[61] Elisabeth C. recounted walking home and being approached by an American for the first time, asking where she was headed alone. Indignant that this was an attempt to pick her up, she responded in English that she was on her way to visit her mother and was stunned when the soldier gifted her chocolate to share with her mother.[62]

Writing in March 1945, Jakob B. noted that fellow Germans spoke well of the "Ami," with children especially looking forward to chocolate and other sweets.[63] Candy was an icebreaker, initiating interactions between soldiers and young Germans. Trudy Miller remembered when US forces marched into her town, "All of a sudden one soldier came right under the balcony and threw a Hershey bar up to me, and I threw it back!" Surprised, the soldier tried again, this time the sway of the chocolate overpowered Miller's pride, and she could not throw it back.[64] Sweets were scarce in postwar Germany, but abundant in the pockets of American GIs. Once considered a feminine indulgence, candy consumption by men was "culturally sanctioned" around the turn-of-the-century, with male consumption "characterized by endurance and power."[65] The War Department aided this transition, commissioning candy companies to supply troops around the globe, with GIs and sailors appearing in advertising campaigns throughout the 1920s. Candy bars offered "concentrated carbohydrates, portable and palatable calories, [and] quick energy … candy wasn't just delicious food; candy was essential food."[66] Chocolate, candy and chewing gum were not life essentials, but they were considered important for upholding troop morale. Perhaps more importantly, sweets also served as universal symbols of American abundance, "GIs looked rich, and they had a swagger and a mouth full of gum."[67] In many ways, candy was at the fore of a deluge of American processed foods that flooded European markets after the war, "foods that, like candy, were convenient, portable, palatable, and cheap."[68]

Hershey bars and chewing gum were prized among German children, although not without some confusion. Wolfgang Samuel recalled the first piece of chewing gum gifted him by an American soldier, finding that while it "tasted strangely refreshing," he could not understand why he would want to chew rubber over food.[69] Chocolate and chewing gum were not the only novelty items gifted German children, although they were arguably the most sought after. Dieter Hahn recalled the moment he learned the difference between an orange and a grapefruit. On that particular day, American soldiers passing through his village tossed the children "giant oranges," which they scrambled after and brought home, discovering "the first taste was as disappointing as their size had been impressive, bitter."[70]

"Believers in Democracy": Food Aid and Friendship

As early as May 1945, Clay acknowledged the severity of the food situation in Germany. At the time Eisenhower's chief deputy in governing Germany, he maintained that food policy in Germany was to be dictated by the American people and Congress.[71] He wrote, "Some cold and hunger will be necessary to make the German people realize the consequences of a war which they caused," but believed a thin line existed between the hunger deemed necessary and that which posed a threat to military security.[72] For many officials, discussions on food relief were guided by military necessity, not humanitarian impulse. Clay reiterated this concern later in the summer, conceding that "suffering should not extend to the point where it results in mass starvation and sickness."[73] He believed food imports were necessary for a successful occupation and was not alone in this line of thinking. Clay was pragmatic; he warned that in addition to the negative physical and psychological effects, ration decreases risked damaging American "prestige."[74] Patton shared similar views, writing a few days prior to his removal as Military Governor of Bavaria, "If we let Germany and the German people be completely disintegrated and starved, they will certainly fall for Communism."[75] Earlier in the summer, he openly criticized the deindustrialization of Germany, believing it "patently impossible for Germany to be an agricultural state." Raging in his personal diary, the general asserted that not only was this "undemocratic," but it "follow[ed] practically Gestapo methods."[76] Clay and others in Military Government recognized the psychological currency of food relief in occupied Germany, "There is no choice between becoming a Communist on 1500 calories and a believer in democracy on 1000 calories."[77]

At a press conference held at the end of August, Eisenhower confirmed that food imports were necessary to feed Germany through the winter, remarking that it was "inescapable."[78] He reiterated that the Germans would only receive what was necessary to stave off malnutrition and disease, explaining that he understood this to be 2000 calories daily, but the exact amount was to be set in accord with the other occupying powers. Any food imports would be calculated as an occupation expense with Germany held responsible for those costs. In October, British authorities revised food policies in their zone, motivated by a belief that increased rations would stabilize control of the region and make the occupation more "palatable" for Britons and Germans alike.[79]

While the British decision signaled a shift, many Americans continued to voice disgust that the occupation had gone "soft." Writing for the *New York Times*, Raymond Daniell placed the blame firmly within the large numbers of civilian and military personnel arriving in the US Zone who never experienced combat or witnessed firsthand the extent of Nazi destruction in liberated Europe. He was angered by the "new arrivals" who voiced concerns that German women queued for upwards of nine hours waiting for rations or that German children were collecting acorns to eat, reminding readers that shoppers wait in long lines at grocery stores across the continent and in London. And the acorns were not used for food, but ersatz coffee, something devised years earlier to accommodate coffee shortages "while the Germans were hoarding foreign credits to build their war machine."[80] For Daniell, American sympathy was "our Achilles heel," and he warned that the shipment of food on credit was the "first step" toward repeating the errors of the last peace.[81]

Military interest in nutrition extended beyond economic and public health concerns and was directly connected to efforts at reeducation, because "empty stomachs did not make youngsters more receptive to democratic teachings."[82] German Youth Activities (GYA), organized by the American military to show German children the benefits of democracy, actively sought to improve the welfare of German children and provided food at all events. Food's importance was acknowledged in the official military history of GYA which noted how in the early days of the occupation small children frequently clustered around American GIs: "soldiers enjoyed the smiles which came to the faces of the children when they were given candy, chewing gum, and bits of food from the military rations."[83] In October 1946, American military personnel were authorized to donate food to German children, provided the food was consumed in their presence. In Heidelberg, for example, cooked and perishable foods from the Army mess hall that could not be used in leftover menus were distributed to local orphanages.[84] The military, alongside humanitarian agencies like CRALOG and the American Friends Service Committee, worked to supply and distribute food to schools throughout the American Zone. Sabina de Werth Neu remembered the confusion lining up in the schoolyard before American soldiers, armed with canteens and spoons rather than guns.[85] Gradually, images of German children rummaging through refuse were replaced by those depicting children queued for school feedings.

Military officials worked tirelessly to prevent malnutrition and stabilize rations throughout the winter and spring of 1946 but were foiled by a decrease in global wheat supplies. The only alternative was corn, a source of anxiety for OMGUS officials culturally attuned to German food habits: "To the Germans outside Bavaria the use of maize for human consumption was wholly unacceptable."[86] Referring to corn as "cattle food," one young German prisoner of war recuperating in an American military hospital lamented that corn must be prisoner food, "I am nauseated when I think of it … In Germany, we feed it to the pigs. But now it is being served to us."[87] General John Hilldring, the Secretary for Occupied Areas, had the foresight to organize a special mission designed to educate Germans on the proper use of corn prior to its arrival and distribution. Bakers developed new ratios of corn to wheat flour resulting in bread that was dense and unpopular, but edible and filling. The Corn Mission enlisted the aid of scientists and nutritionists from the University of Heidelberg and popular food writers to educate the public on the proper use of corn. Recipes were shared, and volunteer groups in the United States shipped seeds to support *Kleingärten*, small garden plots.[88] The Corn Mission also devised new methods of dehydration for preserving non-root vegetables after learning that a shortage of glass jars and rubber rings limited vegetable preservation.[89]

The food situation in Germany slowly improved, but many Americans felt Germans did not fully appreciate the American "gift" of food, "higher-ups somewhere along the line thought that the individual German buying a loaf of bread at the local bakery should be told that he was receiving a gift from the American people."[90] The Commanding General in Bavaria instructed his agricultural staff to correct this "lack of information." The solution was a "series of charts which showed the journey of a bushel of wheat in Kansas to the loaf of bread picked up by the hausfrau at the corner bakery in Bavaria."[91] Military Government held mandatory meetings in villages across Bavaria, where they explained bread was a gift from America. Stanley Andrews, Deputy Director of Food and Agriculture in the US Zone, recounts how "bewildering" this was for German housewives who could not see how bread they paid for was a gift.[92]

Conclusion

Military officials calculated the success of food relief strictly in numbers, but the human response to US food and feeding offers an alternative measure. This chapter explored the physical and psychological dimensions of food and feeding in conquered Germany, juxtaposing policymakers' desire for a hard peace and the military's concern over security with the day-to-day realities of occupation. The food shortage and resulting images of hunger, deprivation and malnourishment that American forces encountered on a regular basis undermined many preconceived notions of the German foe. As the US military transitioned to a force of occupation, soldiers' individual involvement with food and feeding contributed to the erosion of a hard peace, forgone in favor of a lasting peace reliant upon the relationships fostered by food in the American Zone. Food's prevalence in the historical record offers a unique vantage point for a closer examination of the relationship between Germans and Americans. Official and spontaneous acts of feeding altered the character of the occupation while simultaneously transforming the relationship between the occupying forces and German civilians.

This essay underscores the symbolic significance of food in the pursuit of American wartime and postwar objectives. The diplomatic and cultural consequences of food sharing in the US Zone were manifold. In many instances, the sharing of food fostered a sense of fraternity and normalcy that made wartime and postwar conditions bearable for both conqueror and defeated. The act of breaking bread bridges cultures through a "common source of experience," and offers a "medium for cultural engagement" while simultaneously contributing to the establishment of new social hierarchies.[93] Food creates a tangible, emotional connection that can transcend language barriers; the act of eating is about more than sustenance, it is conditioned by meaning.[94] Scarce in postwar Germany, chocolate was an American luxury that conveyed the affluence of the victors and the rewards of democracy. Beer, however, was withheld, with concerns for troop morale outweighing the nutritional needs of German civilians, while bread, regardless of its flavor or lack thereof, demanded appreciation as a gift from a benevolent power.

In January 1946, John Dos Passos wrote in *Life* that he feared the United States had lost the peace, "the taste of victory had gone sour in the mouth of every thoughtful American I met."[95] The taste of victory, however, was nothing compared to the taste of defeat. The war was a turning point for food diplomacy, with food becoming as important in the postwar years as it was during the conflict. Food could be used for trade, it could be withheld for punishment or it could be gifted as a symbol of goodwill. As both weapon of war and tool of peace, food had the power to improve relations and escalate tensions, a quality that would be exploited by both sides in the ensuing Cold War.

NOTES

1. Julian Bach covered the occupation in Germany as a correspondent for *Army Talks* and served in Europe during the war. Julian Bach, Jr., *America's Germany* (New York: Random House, 1946).
2. Bach, "America's Germany: An Account of the Occupation," *Life*, May 13, 1946, 104.
3. This decision paved the way for the work of numerous humanitarian aid organizations operating under the umbrella of CRALOG and CARE (Cooperative for American Remittances in Europe).
4. See Atina Grossmann, "Grams, Calories, and Food: Languages of Victimization, Entitlement, and Human Rights in Occupied Germany, 1945–1949," *Central European History* 44, no. 1 (March 2011): 118–148; Alice Weinreb, "For the Hungry Have No Past Nor Do They Belong to a Political Party: Debates Over German Hunger After World War II," *Central European History* 45 (March 2012): 50–78; and Weinreb, *Modern Hungers: Food and Power in Twentieth Century Germany* (New York: Oxford University Press, 2017), 88–121.
5. Peter Mandler, *Return from the Natives: How Margaret Mead Won the Second World War and Lost the Cold War* (New Haven: Yale University Press, 2013), 144.
6. Margaret Mead, "Food and Feeding in Occupied Territory," *Public Opinion Quarterly* 7, no. 4 (1943): 619. Petra Goedde includes Mead in her discussion of the Berlin Airlift, writing that "food became the most important instrument with which Americans pledged their commitment toward Berlin." Goedde, *GIs and Germans: Culture, Gender, and Foreign Relations, 1945–1949* (New Haven, CT: Yale University Press, 2003), 180.
7. Grossmann, "Grams, Calories, and Food," 123.
8. For more on American occupations and paternalism see Susan Carruthers, *The Good Occupation: American Soldiers and the Hazards of Peace* (Cambridge: Harvard University Press, 2016); Goedde, *GIs and Germans*; Kristin Hoganson, *Fighting for American Manhood: How Gender Politics Provoked the Spanish-American and Philippine-American Wars* (New Haven: Yale University Press, 1998); Alan McPherson, *The Invaded: How Latin Americans and Their Allies Fought and Ended U.S. Occupations* (New York: Oxford University Press, 2014); Mary Renda, *Taking Haiti: Military Occupation and the Culture of U.S. Imperialism 1915–1940* (Chapel Hill: University of North Carolina Press, 2001); and Naoko Shibusawa, *America's Geisha Ally: Reimagining the Japanese Enemy* (Cambridge: Harvard University Press, 2007). Studies of food and World War II are increasingly exploring the symbolism behind food.

See for example Bruce Makato Arnold, "'Your Money Ain't No Good O'er There': Food as Real and Social Currency in the Pacific Theater of World War II," *Food and Foodways* 25, no. 2 (April 2017): 107–122.
9. Sidney Mintz, *Tasting Food, Tasting Freedom: Excursions into Eating, Power, and the Past* (Boston: Beacon Press, 1996), 7; and Warren Belasco, *Food: The Key Concepts* (Oxford: Berg, 2008), 1.
10. Rachel Duffet, *The Stomach for Fighting: Food and the Soldiers of the Great War* (Manchester: Manchester University Press, 2015), 21.
11. Mintz, *Tasting Food*, 13.
12. Office of Military Government, United States.
13. *Stars and Stripes* reported food shortages in Berlin, but quickly dismissed sensationalized accounts, remarking, "the supply situation is not that acute but the increasing difficulties are reflected in the black market." "Very Little Meat (if Any) and No Potatoes Top Berlin's Food Woes," *Stars and Stripes*, February 26, 1945, 2.
14. Clifford Shirley to Gladys Shirley, April 11, 1945, Clifford B. Shirley Papers, Institute on WWII and the Human Experience, Florida State University, Tallahassee, FL (hereafter IWWII).
15. Raymond Gantter, *Roll Me Over: An Infantryman's World War II* (New York: Ballantine Books, 1997), 293.
16. Leo Bogart, *How I Earned the Ruptured Duck: From Brooklyn to Berchtesgaden in World War II* (College Station: Texas A&M University Press, 2004), 122.
17. Ibid., 91.
18. For more on the hunger situation in Holland see William Hitchcock, *The Bitter Road to Freedom: A New History of the Liberation of Europe* (New York: Free Press, 2008), 98–122.
19. Orval Eugene Faubus, *In This Faraway Land: A Personal Journey of Infantry Combat in World War II* (Conway, AR: River Road Press, 1971), 545.
20. For more on Backe see Gesine Gerhard, *Nazi Hunger Politics: A History of Food in the Third Reich* (Lanham, MD: Rowman & Littlefield, 2015).
21. Ralph Sirianni and Patricia Brown, *POW #3959: Memoir of a World War II Airman Shot Down Over Germany* (Jefferson: McFarland & Company, Inc., 2006), 93.
22. "Red Cross Packages in a Pit," *New York Times*, May 18, 1945, 11.
23. #2418 Eisenhower to Marshall, April 15, 1945, in *The Papers of Dwight David Eisenhower*, edited by Alfred D. Chandler, Jr., et al. (Baltimore: Johns Hopkins University Press, 1970), 4:2616 (hereafter *PDDE*).
24. George S. Patton, *George S. Patton Papers: Diaries, 1910–1945*, April 12, 1945, Digital Collection, Library of Congress, Washington, DC (hereafter LOC), accessed June 2, 2018, https://www.loc.gov/item/mss35634038/.

25. "Disease Ridden Prison Littered with Corpses," *Washington Post*, April 19, 1945, 2.
26. "Atrocities," *Life*, May 7, 1945; Edward R. Murrow, "They Died 900 a Day in 'the Best' Nazi Death Camp," *OTR*, April 16, 1945, accessed August 20, 2018, http://www.otr.com/ra/450415%20CBS%20Edward%20Murrow%20On%20Buchenwald.mp3. For more on atrocity images from the liberated camps see Mark Philip Bradley, *The World Reimagined: Americans and Human Rights in the Twentieth Century* (New York: Cambridge University Press, 2016), 70–91.
27. #2424 Eisenhower to Marshall, April 19, 1945, in *PDDE*, 4: 2623.
28. Malcolm Fleming, *From War to Peace in 1945 Germany: A GI's Experience* (Bloomington: Indiana University Press, 2016), 153; and Virgil Pinkley, "Ruhr Area Aglow from Explosives," *New York Times*, April 12, 1945, 5.
29. Margaret Bourke-White, *"Dear Fatherland, Rest Quietly": A Report on the Collapse of Hitler's "Thousand Years"* (New York: Simon and Schuster, 1946), n.p.
30. Memorandum for Op-13-2 (Capt. L.S. Sabin, USN), April 25, 1945, Records of the War Department General and Special Staffs, Civil Affairs Division, General Records, Security Classified General Correspondence, 1943–July 1949, RG 165, Entry 463, Box 25, National Archives and Records Administration, Archives II, College Park, MD (hereafter NARA).
31. Gene Currivan, "Poisoned Food Left by Fleeing Enemy," *New York Times*, April 1, 1945, 3; and Wilbur J. Myers, *Memories to Cherish*, typescript memoir, p. 60, Wilbur J. Myers Papers, IWWII.
32. "Poison Liquor Kills 3 Men," *Hell on Wheels*, July 11, 1945, p. 2, Clippings [scrapbook] (MS03), Hugh D. Matheson Collection (AFC 2001/001/54411), Veterans History Project Collection, American Folklife Center, LOC.
33. Gantter, *Roll Me Over*, 292.
34. "Americans Ignore Army Ban on Fraternizing as 'They Feel Sorry' for Cologne Civilians," *New York Times*, March 9, 1945, 3.
35. Elmer D. Jones to Family, April 6, 1945, in *Infantry Incidents (Excerpts from Letters Home by Private Elmer D. Jones)*, 28, Elmer D. Jones Papers, IWWII.
36. Emanuel Lamb to Parents, April 11, 1945, Emanuel Lamb Papers, IWWII.
37. Käthe G., *Über unser Leben in der Zeit des Zusammenbruches Deutschlands*, Rg. Nr. 3583 2, Deutsches Tagebucharchiv, Emmendingen, Germany (hereafter DTA).
38. Phillip T. Rutherford, "On Arms and Eggs: GI Egg Mania on Battlefields of World War II," *Food and Foodways* 25, no. 2 (April 2017): 123.

39. Earl Bailey, "June 25, 1945 (Letter to Folks)," June 25, 1945, Earl Bailey Papers, Digital Collections, IWWII, accessed May 25, 2018, http://digital-collections.ww2.fsu.edu/scripto/items/show/431.
40. Robert Greivell, interview by Eric Tenbus, transcript, April 13, 2001, 39–40, Collection #1164, Reichelt Program for Oral History, IWWII.
41. Stanley Andrews, *Journal of a Retread*, vol. II, p. 526, Box 30, Stanley Andrews Papers, Harry S. Truman Library (hereafter HSTL).
42. "Military Government Ansbach," August 22, 1945, Records of United States Occupation Headquarters, World War II, Office of Military Government for Germany, Records of the Office of Military Govt Bavaria, Records of the Food, Agriculture, & Forestry Div, RG 260, Entry 1046, Box 7, NARA.
43. John Dos Passos, *Tour of Duty* (Boston: Houghton Mifflin, 1946), 257.
44. "Manufacture of Beer," October 18, 1945, Records of United States Occupation Headquarters, World War II, Office of Military Government for Germany, Records of the Office of Military Govt Bavaria, Records of the Food, Agriculture, & Forestry Div, RG 260, Entry 1046, Box 7, NARA.
45. Larry Rue, "Finds Pallor of Hunger Common among Germans," *Chicago Daily Tribune*, October 26, 1945, 14.
46. "90. Reopening German Breweries," Letter from Clay for Hilldring, February 16, 1946, in *The Papers of General Lucius D. Clay, Germany 1945–1949*, vol. 1, ed. Jean Edward Smith (Bloomington: Indiana University Press, 1974), 161.
47. For a more detailed discussion of Black Markets see Paul Steege, *Black Market, Cold War: Everyday Life in Berlin, 1946–1949* (New York: Cambridge University Press, 2008).
48. Andrews, *Journal of a Retread*, vol. III, p. 672, Box 31, Stanley Andrews Papers, HSTL.
49. Ibid., 674.
50. Bach, *America's Germany*, 57–59.
51. Wolfgang Samuel, *German Boy: A Refugee's Story* (Jackson, MS: University Press of Mississippi, 2000), 235.
52. Gertrud B., "Sonntag, d. 10. Juni," *Tagebuch für die Kinder aus schwerer Zeit 1945*, Reg-Nr. 1200 I, DTA.
53. Samuel, *German Boy*, 346.
54. Arnim Krüger, "Arnim Krüger~Potsdam, Brandenburg," in *The War of Our Childhood: Memories of World War II*, reported by Wolfgang W.E. Samuel (Jackson, MS: University Press of Mississippi, 2002), 256, Kindle.
55. Bach, *America's Germany*, 73, 76.
56. Belasco, *Food*, 35.
57. Samuel, *German Boy*, 346.

58. Krüger, "Arnim Krüger," in Samuel, *The War of Our Childhood*, 256, Kindle.
59. "German Girls," *Life*, July 23, 1945, 36.
60. This song is satirical, the lyrics a mix of broken German and English: "young lady, young lady, do you want a candy bar? Beautiful, you like GIs, no?" *A Foreign Affair*, directed by Billy Wilder (1948; Universal City, CA: Universal Studios, 2013), DVD.
61. Werner Sollors, *The Temptation of Despair: Tales of the 1940s* (Cambridge: The Belknap Press of Harvard University Press, 2014), 169.
62. Elisabeth C., *Wie ich das Kriegsende erlebte*, 9, Reg. Nr. 474/I, DTA.
63. Ami was German slang for *Amerikaner* (American). Jakob B., "25.3.1945," *Tagebücher und Briefe*, Reg. Nr. 664 1-3, DTA.
64. Trudy Miller, interview by Robin Sellers, transcript, April 2–3, 2001, 7, Collection #1222, Reichelt Program for Oral History, IWWII.
65. Jane Dusselier, "Bonbons, Lemon Drops, and Oh Henry! Bars: Candy, Consumer Culture, and the Construction of Gender, 1895–1920," in *Kitchen Culture in America: Popular Representations of Food, Gender and Race*, edited by Sherrie Inness (Philadelphia: University of Pennsylvania Press 2001), 34, 40.
66. Samira Kawash, *Candy: A Century of Panic and Pleasure* (New York: Farrar, Straus and Giroux, 2013), Chapter 9, Kindle.
67. James J. Cooke, *Chewing Gum, Candy Bars and Beer: The Army PX in World War II* (Columbia: University of Missouri Press, 2009), 2.
68. Kawash, *Candy*, Chapter 1, Kindle.
69. Samuel, *German Boy*, 152–153. For more on candy's role in the relationship between American servicemen and German children see Kaete O'Connell, "'Uncle Wiggly Wings': Children, Chocolates, and the Berlin Airlift," *Food and Foodways* 25, no. 2 (2017): 142–159.
70. Dieter Hahn, "Dieter Hahn~Posen, Wartheland (Poland)," in Samuel, *The War of Our Childhood*, 242, Kindle.
71. "'Starving' in Reich Is Put Up to U.S.," *New York Times*, May 17, 1945, 4.
72. "14. Conditions in Germany," Letter from Clay for McCloy, June 16, 1945, in Smith, *Papers*, vol. 1, 24.
73. "17. Conditions in Germany," Letter from Clay for McCloy, June 29, 1945, in Smith, *Papers*, vol. 1, 42.
74. "118. Food Situation in U.S. Zone," Letter from Clay for Echols, May 18, 1946, in Smith, *Papers*, vol. 1, 208.
75. Patton, *Diaries*, September 22, 1945, Digital Collection, LOC, accessed June 2, 2018, https://www.loc.gov/item/mss35634039/.
76. Patton, *Diaries*, August 27, 1945, Digital Collection, LOC, accessed June 2, 2018, https://www.loc.gov/item/mss35634039/.

77. "103. Food Situation in U.S. Zone," Letter from Clay for Echols and Petersen, March 27, 1946, in Smith, *Papers*, vol. 1, 184.
78. Gladwin Hill, "Must Feed Reich, Eisenhower Says," *New York Times*, August 31, 1945, 9.
79. For more on the British decision see Johannes-Dieter Steinert, "Food and the Food Crisis in Post-War Germany, 1945–1948: British Policy and the Role of British NGOs," in *Food and Conflict in Europe in the Age of the Two World Wars*, ed. Frank Trentmann and Flemming Just (New York: Palgrave Macmillan, 2006), 266–288.
80. Raymond Daniell, "Pity for Germans Grows in U.S. Ranks," *New York Times*, October 5, 1945, 6.
81. Raymond Daniell, "'We Talk Tough, but We Act Soft,'" *New York Times*, October 7, 1945, SM3.
82. Dana Adams Schmidt, "Youth of Germany Eagerly Joins U.S. Sports-Educational Program," *New York Times*, September 26, 1946, 5.
83. U.S. Army Historical Division, *The U.S. Armed Forces German Youth Activities Program 1945—1955* (Headquarters Europe: n.p., 1956), 1.
84. Ibid., 26.
85. Sabina de Werth Neu, *A Long Silence: Memories of a German Refugee Child, 1941—1958* (Amherst, NY: Prometheus Books, 2011), 86.
86. Ibid., 110.
87. Walter Krause, *So I Was a Sergeant: Memoirs of an Occupation Soldier* (Hicksville, NY: Exposition Press, 1978), 109.
88. Popular before the war, German municipalities assigned garden plots on tracts of land near railroads or factories.
89. Jane Ebbs, *The Hidden War* (Edinburgh: Pentland Press, 1991), 110–111.
90. Andrews, *Journal of a Retread*, vol. III, p. 650, Box 31, Stanley Andrews Papers, HSTL.
91. Ibid.
92. Ibid., 651.
93. Tanfer Emin Tunc and Annessa Ann Babic, "Food on the Home Front, Food on the Warfront: World War II and the American Diet," *Food and Foodways* 25, no. 2 (April 2017): 104; Paul Rockower, "The State of Gastrodiplomacy," *Public Diplomacy Magazine*, March 2, 2014, accessed May 31, 2018, http://www.publicdiplomacymagazine.com/the-state-of-gastrodiplomacy/.
94. Mintz, *Tasting Freedom*, 7.
95. John Dos Passos, "Americans are Losing the Victory in Europe," *Life*, January 7, 1946, 24.

Bibliography

"Americans Ignore Army Ban on Fraternizing as 'They Feel Sorry' for Cologne Civilians." *New York Times*, March 9, 1945. Proquest Historical Newspapers.
Andrews, Stanley. *Journal of a Retread*, 1934–1950. Stanley Andrews Papers. Harry S. Truman Presidential Library, Independence, MO.
Arnold, Bruce Makato. "'Your Money Ain't No Good O'er There': Food as Real and Social Currency in the Pacific Theater of World War II." *Food and Foodways* 25, no. 2 (April 2017): 107–122. http://dx.doi.org/10.1080/07409710.2017.1311160.
"Atrocities." *Life*, May 7, 1945. Google Books.
B., Gertrud. *Tagebuch für die Kinder aus schwerer Zeit 1945*, 1945. Deutsches Tagebucharchiv, Emmendingen, Germany.
B., Jakob. *Tagebücher und Briefe*, 1945–1946. Deutsches Tagebucharchiv, Emmendingen, Germany.
Bach, Jr., Julian. *America's Germany*. New York: Random House, 1946.
Bach, Jr., Julian. "America's Germany: An Account of the Occupation." *Life*, May 13, 1946. Google Books.
Bailey, Earl. Letter to Folks, June 25, 1945. Earl Bailey Papers. Digital Collections, Institute on WWII and the Human Experience, Florida State University, Tallahassee, FL. http://digital-collections.ww2.fsu.edu/scripto/items/show/431.
Belasco, Warren. *Food: The Key Concepts*. Oxford: Berg, 2008.
Bogart, Leo. *How I Earned the Ruptured Duck: From Brooklyn to Berchtesgaden in World War II*. College Station: Texas A&M University Press, 2004.
Bourke-White, Margaret. *"Dear Fatherland, Rest Quietly": A Report on the Collapse of Hitler's "Thousand Years."* New York: Simon and Schuster, 1946.
Bradley, Mark Philip. *The World Reimagined: Americans and Human Rights in the Twentieth Century*. New York: Cambridge University Press, 2016.
C., Elisabeth. *Wie ich das Kriegsende erlebte*, 1944–1946. Deutsches Tagebucharchiv, Emmendingen, Germany.
Carruthers, Susan. *The Good Occupation: American Soldiers and the Hazards of Peace*. Cambridge, MA: Harvard University Press, 2016. Kindle.
Chandler, Jr., Alfred D., Stephen E. Ambrose, Louis Galambos, Daun van Ee, Joseph P. Hobbs, Elizabeth S. Hughes, and others, eds. *The Papers of Dwight David Eisenhower*. Online edition. 21 vols. Baltimore: Johns Hopkins University Press, 2003. https://eisenhower.press.jhu.edu.
Cooke, James J. *Chewing Gum, Candy Bars and Beer: The Army PX in World War II*. Columbia: University of Missouri Press, 2009.
Currivan, Gene. "Poisoned Food Left by Fleeing Enemy." *New York Times*, April 1, 1945. Proquest Historical Newspapers.

Daniell, Raymond. "Pity for Germans Grows in U.S. Ranks." *New York Times*, October 5, 1945. Proquest Historical Newspapers.
Daniell, Raymond. "We Talk Tough, but We Act Soft." *New York Times*, October 7, 1945. Proquest Historical Newspapers.
"Disease Ridden Prison Littered with Corpses." *Washington Post*, April 19, 1945. Proquest Historical Newspapers.
Dos Passos, John. "Americans Are Losing the Victory in Europe." *Life*, January 7, 1946. Google Books.
Dos Passos, John. *Tour of Duty*. Boston: Houghton Mifflin, 1946.
Duffet, Rachel. *The Stomach for Fighting: Food and the Soldiers of the Great War*. Manchester: Manchester University Press, 2015.
Dusselier, Jane. "Bonbons, Lemon Drops, and Oh Henry! Bars: Candy, Consumer Culture, and the Construction of Gender, 1895–1920." In *Kitchen Culture in America: Popular Representations of Food, Gender and Race*, edited by Sherrie Inness, 13–49. Philadelphia: University of Pennsylvania Press, 2001.
Ebbs, Jane. *The Hidden War*. Edinburgh: Pentland Press, 1991.
Faubus, Orval Eugene. *In This Faraway Land: A Personal Journey of Infantry Combat in World War II*. Conway, AR: River Road Press, 1971.
Fleming, Malcolm. *From War to Peace in 1945 Germany: A GI's Experience*. Bloomington: Indiana University Press, 2016.
G., Käthe. *Über unser Leben in der Zeit des Zusammenbruches Deutschlands*, 1945. Deutsches Tagebucharchiv, Emmendingen, Germany.
Gantter, Raymond. *Roll Me Over: An Infantryman's World War II*. New York: Ballantine Books, 1997.
Gerhard, Gesine. *Nazi Hunger Politics: A History of Food in the Third Reich*. Lanham, MD: Rowman & Littlefield, 2015.
"German Girls." *Life*, July 23, 1945. Google Books.
Goedde, Petra. *GIs and Germans: Culture, Gender, and Foreign Relations, 1945–1949*. New Haven, CT: Yale University Press, 2003.
Greivell, Robert. Interview by Eric Tenbus, Transcript, April 13, 2001. Collection #1164. Reichelt Program for Oral History, Institute on WWII and the Human Experience, Florida State University, Tallahassee, FL.
Grossmann, Atina. "Grams, Calories, and Food: Languages of Victimization, Entitlement, and Human Rights in Occupied Germany, 1945–1949." *Central European History* 44, no. 1 (March 2011): 118–148. https://doi.org/10.1017/S0008938910001202.
Hahn, Dieter. "Dieter Hahn~Posen, Wartheland (Poland)." In *The War of Our Childhood: Memories of World War II*, reported by Wolfgang W.E. Samuel, 239–249. Jackson, MS: University Press of Mississippi, 2002. Kindle.
Hill, Gladwin. "Must Feed Reich, Eisenhower Says." *New York Times*, August 31, 1945. Proquest Historical Newspapers.

Hitchcock, William. *The Bitter Road to Freedom: A New History of the Liberation of Europe.* New York: Free Press, 2008.

Hoganson, Kristin. *Fighting for American Manhood: How Gender Politics Provoked the Spanish-American and Philippine-American Wars.* New Haven: Yale University Press, 1998.

Jones, Elmer. *Infantry Incidents (Excerpts from Letters Home by Private Elmer D. Jones),* n.d. Elmer D. Jones Papers. Institute on WWII and the Human Experience, Florida State University, Tallahassee, FL.

Kawash, Samira. *Candy: A Century of Panic and Pleasure.* New York: Farrar, Straus and Giroux, 2013. Kindle.

Krause, Walter. *So I Was a Sergeant: Memoirs of an Occupation Soldier.* Hicksville, NY: Exposition Press, 1978.

Krüger, Arnim. "Arnim Krüger~Potsdam, Brandenburg." In *The War of Our Childhood: Memories of World War II,* reported by Wolfgang W.E. Samuel, 250–263. Jackson, MS: University Press of Mississippi, 2002. Kindle.

Lamb, Emanuel. Letter to Parents, April 11, 1945. Emanuel Lamb Papers. Institute on WWII and the Human Experience, Florida State University, Tallahassee, FL.

Mandler, Peter. *Return from the Natives: How Margaret Mead Won the Second World War and Lost the Cold War.* New Haven: Yale University Press, 2013.

McPherson, Alan. *The Invaded: How Latin Americans and Their Allies Fought and Ended U.S. Occupations.* New York: Oxford University Press, 2014.

Mead, Margaret. "Food and Feeding in Occupied Territory." *Public Opinion Quarterly* 7, no. 4 (1943): 618–628. JSTOR.

Miller, Trudy. Interview by Robin Sellers, transcript, April 2–3, 2001. Collection #1222. Reichelt Program for Oral History, Institute on WWII and the Human Experience, Florida State University, Tallahassee, FL.

Mintz, Sidney. *Tasting Food, Tasting Freedom: Excursions into Eating, Power, and the Past.* Boston: Beacon Press, 1996.

Murrow, Edward R. "They Died 900 a Day in 'the Best' Nazi Death Camp." OTR, April 16, 1945. http://www.otr.com/ra/450415%20CBS%20Edward%20Murrow%20On%20Buchenwald.mp3.

Myers, Wilbur J. *Memories to Cherish,* n.d. Wilbur J. Myers Papers. Institute on WWII and the Human Experience, Florida State University, Tallahassee, FL.

Neu, Sabina de Werth. *A Long Silence: Memories of a German Refugee Child, 1941–1958.* Amherst, NY: Prometheus Books, 2011.

O'Connell, Kaete. "'Uncle Wiggly Wings': Children, Chocolates, and the Berlin Airlift," *Food and Foodways* 25, no. 2 (2017): 142–159. http://dx.doi.org/10.1080/07409710.2017.1311163.

Patton, George S. *George S. Patton Papers: Diaries, 1910 to 1945,* 1945. Manuscript Division, Library of Congress, Washington, DC. https://www.loc.gov/collections/george-s-patton-diaries/.

Pinkley, Virgil. "Ruhr Area Aglow from Explosives." *New York Times*, April 12, 1945. Proquest Historical Newspapers.

"Poison Liquor Kills 3 Men." *Hell on Wheels*, July 11, 1945. Hugh Mattheson/54411 (AFC 2001/001/54411). Veterans History Project Collection, American Folklife Center, Library of Congress, Washington, DC.

Records of the U.S. Occupation Headquarters, World War II. Office of Military Government for Germany. RG 260, Entry 1046, National Archives and Records Administration, Archives II, College Park, MD.

Records of the War Department General and Special Staffs. Civil Affairs Division. RG 165, Entry 463, National Archives and Records Administration, Archives II, College Park, MD.

"Red Cross Packages in a Pit." *New York Times*, May 18, 1945. Proquest Historical Newspapers.

Renda, Mary. *Taking Haiti: Military Occupation and the Culture of U.S. Imperialism 1915–1940*. Chapel Hill: University of North Carolina Press, 2001.

Rockower, Paul. "The State of Gastrodiplomacy." *Public Diplomacy Magazine*, March 2, 2014.

Rue, Larry. "Finds Pallor of Hunger Common Among Germans." *Chicago Daily Tribune*, October 26, 1945.

Rutherford, Phillip T. "On Arms and Eggs: GI Egg Mania on Battlefields of World War II." *Food and Foodways* 25, no. 2 (April 2017): 123–141. http://dx.doi.org/10.1080/07409710.2017.1311161.

Samuel, Wolfgang. *German Boy: A Refugee's Story*. Jackson, MS: University Press of Mississippi, 2000. Kindle.

Schmidt, Dana Adams. "Youth of Germany Eagerly Joins U.S. Sports-Educational Program." *New York Times*, September 26, 1946. Proquest Historical Newspapers.

Shibusawa, Naoko. *America's Geisha Ally: Reimagining the Japanese Enemy*. Cambridge: Harvard University Press, 2007.

Shirley, Clifford B. Letter to Gladys Shirley, April 11, 1945. Clifford B. Shirley Papers. Institute on WWII and the Human Experience, Florida State University, Tallahassee, FL.

Sirianni, Ralph and Patricia Brown. *POW #3959: Memoir of a World War II Airman Shot Down Over Germany*. Jefferson: McFarland & Company, 2006.

Smith, Jean Edward, ed. *The Papers of General Lucius D. Clay, Germany 1945–1949*. 2 vols. Bloomington: Indiana University Press, 1974.

Sollors, Werner. *The Temptation of Despair: Tales of the 1940s*. Cambridge: The Belknap Press of Harvard University Press, 2014.

"'Starving' in Reich Is Put Up to U.S." *New York Times*, May 17, 1945. Proquest Historical Newspapers.

Steege, Paul. *Black Market, Cold War: Everyday Life in Berlin, 1946–1949.* New York: Cambridge University Press, 2008.

Steinert, Johannes-Dieter. "Food and the Food Crisis in Post-War Germany, 1945–1948: British Policy and the Role of British NGOs." In *Food and Conflict in Europe in the Age of the Two World Wars*, edited by Frank Trentmann and Flemming Just, 266–288. New York: Palgrave Macmillan, 2006.

Tunc, Tanfer Emin, and Annessa Ann Babic. "Food on the Home Front, Food on the Warfront: World War II and the American Diet." *Food and Foodways* 25, no. 2 (April 2017): 101–106. http://dx.doi.org/10.1080/07409710.2017.1311159.

U.S. Army Historical Division. The U.S. Armed Forces German Youth Activities Program 1945–1955. Headquarters Europe: n.p., 1956.

"Very Little Meat (if Any) and No Potatoes Top Berlin's Food Woes." *Stars and Stripes*, February 26, 1945.

Weinreb, Alice. "For the Hungry Have No Past Nor Do They Belong to a Political Party: Debates Over German Hunger After World War II." *Central European History* 45 (March 2012): 50–78. https://dx.doi.org/10.1017/S0008938911000987.

———. *Modern Hungers: Food and Power in Twentieth Century Germany.* New York: Oxford University Press, 2017.

Wilder, Billy, dir. *A Foreign Affair.* 1948; Universal City, CA: Universal Studios, 2013. DVD.

CHAPTER 10

Cold (Beer) War: The German *Volksgetränk* in East German Rhetoric (1945–1971)

John Gillespie

On November 14, 1958, Albert Norden took the stage of the Berlin *Sportspalast* (sports palace) in the city's western zone. This speech in front of several thousand supporters was entirely unusual for this time and place, because Albert Norden sat on the Politburo of East Germany's Socialist Unity Party (SED). As such, he represented the most powerful group of decision-makers in the socialist German Democratic Republic (GDR) and now he stepped up to make a campaign speech in the capitalist West. The SED had chosen to participate in West Berlin's municipal elections for the first time since the two German states separated a decade before. According to transcripts of the speech, Norden's point came through clearly: A vote for the West German political parties was a vote for war and militarism, as opposed to the SED's promises of peace and disarmament. The East German leader hammered his message home repeatedly; he attacked the western politicians as warmongering bourgeois American puppets and took every opportunity to strike at flaws in their country.

J. Gillespie (✉)
Vanderbilt University, Nashville, TN, USA

© The Author(s) 2019
H. M. Benbow and H. R. Perry (eds.), *Food, Culture and Identity in Germany's Century of War*,
https://doi.org/10.1007/978-3-030-27138-1_10

Toward the end of his speech, Norden evoked disconcerting recent events in Berlin. Just a few weeks earlier, youthful western "*Rowdys*" attending a Bill Haley concert at the *Sportspalast* had been so overcome by the music's frenzied energy that a full-scale riot ensued. Norden verbally bashed his opponents by drawing a clear contrast between the values and culture promoted by East Germany and those of the "Americanized" Federal Republic (FRG). "Perhaps Lemmer and Brandt [the West German mayoral candidates] fear that we want to get the West Berliners drunk with our outstanding Radeberger Pilsner... The individuals who recently vandalized this *Sportspalast* had not drunk any Radeberger, but rather were intoxicated by the fleeting and minor art culture of Rock'n Roll imported from America."[1]

Norden's words highlight an evocative trend among the East German leadership and media during the early decades of the Cold War. Beer had become a political weapon. The unassuming everyday drink of so many Germans, a true *Volksgetränk* (people's drink), now served as a cultural battlefield in the war of words between competing social and economic systems. This chapter tracks the role of beer in East German politics and rhetoric through the lens of the government and press during the first two decades after World War II, ending with Erich Honecker's takeover of the SED from Walter Ulbricht in 1971. I argue that the East German regime claimed beer as a cultural commodity better suited to their new, socialist vision of German life than to West German capitalism, thus making the socialist state the rightful heir to Germany's beer heritage. From their leaders and newspapers, GDR citizens received narratives of beer as a symbol of worker comradery and proletarian solidarity. When discussing West Germany, however, the GDR's media consistently presented visions of an over-indulgent, backward and exclusionary culture of beer consumption.

Unwilling to concede that the capitalists had more successfully revived German beer culture, the state-directed media largely ignored conditions in the industry and instead focused on an idealized conception of the beverage's role in German society, emphasizing its moderating and convivial part in blue-collar social life. Starting from this notion, which conveniently reflected the worldview of the SED, East German newspapers arrived at the conclusion that their country had realized a truly virtuous relationship to beer. This allowed them to circumvent consideration of the disappointing material reality in the GDR's breweries. As the state's leaders pushed a rapid modernization of the brewing infrastructure in the 1950s and 1960s, economic struggles forced them to accept an "alternate modernity" for East German beers compared to their western counterparts. In concrete terms, this meant that much of the beer produced in the GDR failed to meet the state's standards, which were more permissive than definitions of "quality" in the West. East Germany's economic planners faced the further embarrassment of depending on "non-socialist economies" for brewing supplies and equipment. Thus, the rhetoric claiming socialism's superiority in this inter-German beer war became increasingly disconnected from any semblance of the reality on the ground.

This chapter utilizes East German government records and three leading GDR newspapers to reconstruct the SED's handling of the brewing industry as well as its attempts to manipulate beer and beer culture into tools for Cold War propaganda. It shows the symbolic importance and power of this beverage for the socialist regime. Moreover, these messages were disseminated widely among the GDR's population. As Anke Fiedler and Michael Meyen point out in their edited volume on this subject, distribution of GDR print media grew throughout the state's history until, by the end of the 1980s, its collective circulation per capita was double that in the FRG. "Three out of four households had a subscription to an SED district newspaper, and the *Neue Deutschland*... achieved a circulation of over one million."[2] An individual reader's personal beliefs and place in society heavily influenced their views on the state-controlled press, but a variety of groups found the information presented there valuable and important. "True-believers" may have thought that the East German print media presented the most accurate and honest account of events, but many others read these papers to get a clear indication of the views and policies of the SED leadership.[3] This chapter draws source material from the *Neue Deutschland*, the *Berliner Zeitung* (largest of the SED district newspapers) and the *Neue Zeit* (daily paper of the East German CDU).[4]

A great deal of research has recently emerged exploring issues of consumption in socialist states and its importance in understanding the broader history of the Cold War. Mark Landsman argues that consumption played a critical role in shaping East German politics during the "long 1950s." He and other scholars emphasize the role of supply problems in pushing major events such as the 1953 Workers Uprising. Their works also remind audiences that the most immediate crisis facing the GDR's leaders in the 1950s came from the flight of their own citizens, often out of frustration with supply failures. This tendency of East Germans to "vote with their feet" and head toward the supposed bounty of the FRG's "miracle-economy" served as the immediate motivation for significant economic reforms in the GDR in the late 1950s. In turn, the inadequacy of those reforms in answering consumer demands led to the construction of the Berlin Wall in 1961.[5] Other studies addressing a range of goods, from clothing to automobiles, further solidify the centrality of consumption within East German politics. Works by Ina Merkel and Katherine Pence reveal the power of the populace to communicate their demands to the regime and the often-surprising level of consideration they received, even if that attention usually resulted in a dismissive or disappointing response.[6]

Out of all the consumer issues that states have to contend with, there is likely none more poignant than the demand for sufficient and quality foodstuffs, which during this period centered around one of the most clearly articulated issues of socialist consumption: economic modernity.[7] The GDR emerged in a moment of extreme food insecurity quickly followed by a period of rapid modernization and rising food production among the world's wealthier nations, a trend which the SED felt compelled to match. Indeed, Alice Weinreb makes precisely the point that hunger did not represent a counterpoint to projects of modernization in Germany, but rather was integral to them.[8] As real-existing problems or remembered crises, moments of widespread hunger acted as a common topic of refrain for every German government during the early- to mid-twentieth century, including East Germany. Both postwar German states sought to build modern food supplies that would put the people's nightmares of starvation to bed once and for all. Of course, they disagreed about how that task should be accomplished, who should bear the burden for feeding German families (women in their "traditional" place in the home or the state through mass distribution programs), and any number of other points.[9] Yet arguments regarding modernity and plentitude extended beyond everyday necessities such as bread, meat and dairy products and included items with a uniquely cultural value, such as beer. Regardless of any debate over the dietary or utilitarian worth of such items, ordinary citizens viewed them as indispensable. That alone made these goods worth fighting over for German politicians.

Beer and Modernity in the Postwar World

Modernity became the critical word in the worldwide beer industry after World War II. The drive to "modernize" production and distribution surrounded and impacted the beverage's fate in the two German states. Artificial refrigeration, mechanized bottling, motor-powered equipment and improved transportation had transformed the industry in the late nineteenth century. This brought commercial beer production and consumption to an all-time high in Europe, its colonies, and the United States around the turn of the century. The bright future of beer offered by these developments suffered setbacks from the 1910s to the 1940s as wars, economic depression, and "noble experiments" left the global brewing industry reeling.[10] Finally, after 1945, the stage reset for a new "golden age" of beer. Worldwide production and consumption skyrocketed and did not begin to plateau until the 1970s. Previously untapped markets for European-style beer suddenly flourished with growth, particularly in Eastern Europe and Asia where Russia, Japan and China started importing and producing hundreds of times more beer than before.[11]

The postwar years of booming growth also saw the emergence of more ambivalent trends that some commentators have harshly criticized in recent decades for their impact on the worldwide market. For good or ill, this period produced undeniable shifts toward extreme consolidation of the industry and increasing uniformity of its products. In the United States, for one example, thousands of breweries that operated in the late nineteenth century gave way to just a few hundred after World War II. By 1977 that number shrank to 50 beer companies running less than 100 actual breweries.[12] Similar developments played out in other major markets, including Great Britain and Belgium.[13] In most places, the emergent brewing conglomerates thrived by greatly expanding their advertising budgets and producing consistent, highly uniform, relatively bland variations on the same style: adjunct lagers. These beers had several advantages for companies looking to produce on a massive scale with low cost. Chemical additives sped up the brewing process by reducing fermentation and maturation time. Manufacturers increasingly substituted cheaper ingredients such as corn and rice for a portion of the more expensive malted barley, giving the beer a drier, more neutral flavor. With less of the sweetness produced by barley, the breweries could use a smaller portion of hops to flavor their product and still produce a hint of bitterness. The neutral flavor helped spread the popularity of these beers. Their mild and refreshing nature (especially when served very cold) coupled with a still-appreciable alcohol content appealed to a wide consumer base. Mass-produced adjunct lagers became the hammer that massive breweries used to flatten their smaller competition.[14]

Yet, beer production in West Germany remained relatively decentralized and still adhered to a "traditional" standard of production fiercely defended by powerful interest groups who successfully championed beer quality and "purity" as a popular issue of German cultural pride.[15] West Germans proved unusually attached to local and regional breweries, which may have stemmed, in part, from the fact that they also retained a strong affinity for local and regional styles of beer.[16] Perhaps the single largest divergence between West Germany's beer market and the rest of the world, however, was its continued adherence to a much-mythologized Bavarian "Purity Law" from 1516, known since 1918 as the *Reinheitsgebot*. Officially adopted as national law in the early 1900s and reconfirmed by the FRG as an element of the tax code in the 1950s, the *Reinheitsgebot* stipulates that only four ingredients: Barley, hops, water and yeast may be used in the production of lager beer. This denied the possibility of adjunct lagers gaining a foothold in West Germany until 1987, which likely contributed to the slower pace of industry consolidation and, by extension, preserved a market characterized by regional variation and production.[17]

In East Germany, the history of the beer market more closely resembled larger global trends, but the combination of solidifying Cold War boundaries and unrealistic demands placed on the planned economy created a host of additional challenges. Here too, beer manufacturing and per capita consumption grew steadily in the 1950s and 1960s. However, while the GDR maintained a higher number of small and regional-sized breweries than the United States or UK, consolidation proved an attractive option for the SED. The entire industry came under control of the state, which sought to build "rationalized" markets. As a result, the government increasingly centralized the management of smaller brewing facilities at the regional or district level.[18] Moreover, the GDR's brewing industry joined in the worldwide movement toward increasing use of adjuncts in its products. Early in its existence, the East German government abandoned the *Reinheitsgebot* as an official measure of quality in order to economize beer production and make it easier to meet rising demand. Nevertheless, some industry leaders and professional brewers in the GDR continued to look on it as an ideal and a marker of quality. Until the state's collapse, a number of premium, export-quality beers brewed in the East remained in compliance with the stipulations of the Purity Law.[19] Regardless of definition GDR breweries struggled to maintain even basic quality standards on a regular basis.[20]

The East German leadership displayed two primary goals in its treatment of beer and the brewing industry. Both involved a certain vision of modernity, and both played a critical role in shaping the government's use of beer in Cold War polemic against the West. On the one hand, the SED regime had a vision of advanced technological and industrial development that would allow the GDR to catch up to the FRG in beer production while eliminating the exploitative practices of an industrial economy. The government-prescribed Scientific and Technical Revolution of the early 1960s included plans for a new era of beer production, which would liberate workers from the difficult and tedious tasks required to make and package beer.[21] In that area, East Germany did make some progress during this period. For example, a number of breweries received automated bottling lines that (when they functioned correctly) removed the need for a great deal of monotonous labor.[22] In terms of production during Ulbricht's leadership, the GDR never caught up to the FRG, and its attempts to artificially stretch the volume of brewery output with its available resources contributed to quality issues.[23] As a result, the East German media, while more than happy to criticize West German breweries, bar owners and beer patrons, tended to avoid any comparative description of the product itself.

On the other hand, state newspapers suggested the proper role that beer could play in a kind of social modernity, in keeping with the ideal vision of a "new socialist person."[24] The media, and by extension the government, made clear that it had "nothing against a glass of beer."[25] Still, the regime did have a certain understanding of how one should properly enjoy that beer. Particularly in the 1960s, once alcohol consumption had returned to a relatively high level by international standards, nearly all mentions of beer in the print media included some form of the injunction, "but remember, drink responsibly comrades."[26] A good German socialist could drink beer, but only in a healthy, moderate and politically acceptable manner. This idealized concept of the "proper" socialist relationship to beer, which very often did not reflect reality, served as a kind of template against which the East German media would compare the supposedly decadent and corrupt West.

Their narratives employed beer as one clear sign of the fact that the GDR was striding forward into a bright new future of mankind, while the "other Germany" slipped further and further into degradation on the inevitable path to collapse.

Beer, the Worker's Drink

The intersection of beer and politics was nothing new in the history of unified Germany. In 1906, Bavaria successfully lobbied within the *Kaiserreich* to extend a modified version of the 1516 Purity Law to all of Imperial Germany. It similarly demanded that the Weimar Republic adopt a form of the law in 1918 and that the Federal Republic do the same in 1949.[27] Arguably beer's largest political role, however, came from its adoption as the de facto drink of the proletariat in the late nineteenth century and early twentieth century. Workers' demands for access to affordable and quality beer sparked conflicts in the bloody "Beer Riot" of 1873 in Frankfurt am Main and the "Beer War" of 1909. The latter event helped convince Germany's largest socialist party, the SPD, to embrace beer as the drink of the working classes.[28] Manfred Hübner's book on the German Worker's Movement during these years identifies beer as "*sozialdemokratischer Saft*" (social-democrat juice), borrowing a phrase from the time.[29] In short, the earnest importance of the *Volksgetränk* within blue-collar German society regularly made it a point of contention. Though class identity and interests always proved more amorphous than a strict Marxist interpretation would suggest, on this particular issue the battle lines often saw non-socialist politicians, publicans and brewery owners pitched against the masses of urban industrial workers and their advocates.[30]

The East German media appropriated this connection between beer and the proletariat to reaffirm the state's claim to Germany's brewing heritage and its commitment to building a socialist future. In the vision of the GDR press, beer represented one of the quintessential consumer goods of the "*werktätigen*" (workers).[31] A 1951 article in East Berlin's daily *Berliner Zeitung* reported that "on the same day as the living conditions of the workers in the GDR have been further improved by a new price reduction, the British *World* reported from Hamburg that the situation of the little man [*kleinen Mannes*] in West Germany is continuing to get worse." To prove the deteriorating circumstances of workers in Hamburg, the article identified a 50% decline in beer consumption as a clear indicator.[32] An opinion piece in the same publication two years later called for a joint effort between East Berlin restaurants and breweries to reintroduce the tradition of outdoor beer gardens where people could meet and relax in the fresh air. It noted that "the families of the workers lack these spaces for relaxation and recovery."[33] The qualification here that the families "of workers" lacked the spaces served to reassure readers that the author intended these beer-centered locales to specifically serve the greater cause of building socialism.

The East German media emphasized how beer acted as a common thread for blue-collar workers of both East and West. A 1954 article reported on a gathering of table-makers from East and West Berlin at a pub in the city's center. The men met at their *Stammtisch* (regular table) and passed a merry evening of beer drinking and cigarette smoking in comradery. The West Berliners complained of the poor conditions in their zone and the burden of West German government policies on the working class. In reply, the East German participants proudly exclaimed how much better their government treated them and how the system in the East supported their work and their way of life. The message in this story clearly reflected the Marxist notion that class interests should rise above all other considerations. The workers have so much in common as they sit in brotherhood around a traditional space of blue-collar gathering, drinking the beverage of the working man (beer-related content was most often, though not exclusively, male-oriented).[34] Why then would the poor and exploited West German craftsmen not support the GDR in its mission to uplift the proletariat?

Beer and Capitalism

The East German press portrayed the government as striving to provide the people with beer because beer represented a commodity of special importance to the "workers and farmers" that the SED claimed to represent. Within the logic of that paradigm, West Germany would inevitably disappoint the beer-drinking masses, because the interests of their leaders lay elsewhere. Unsurprisingly, associations of the FRG with poor supplies of beer began almost immediately after the war as East German newspapers accused the Western Allies of neglecting the *Volksgetränk*. The GDR press painted business confiscations in the British zone as property grabs by the occupying forces. Hard facts and consistent reasoning came second to a resounding judgment that the people's desire for beer was subject to the greed of business owners.[35] Thus, when breweries in the West German cities of Hamburg and Bremen requested to export their beer two years after the war, the East German *Neue Zeit* newspaper reported that the dreadful conditions under Anglo-American administration made it impossible.[36] One year later, following currency reform, the same newspaper denounced beer exports on the grounds that the Western Allies had fixed prices to encourage producers to send desperately needed agricultural goods abroad rather than sell them locally.[37]

The ordinary West German drinker regularly appeared as a victim of the vicious trends and swings in the market economy. Another *Neue Zeit* column from 1952 described increasing beer prices in Bavaria as an "antisocial price spiral," and approvingly reported calls for "beer strikes" among the population there.[38] However events transpired, reporters in the Soviet Zone, and later the GDR, used beer to remind their readers that the western economy and government offered nothing but disappointment and exploitation.[39] A 1957 *Berliner Zeitung* article offers a good example of the direct connection made between capitalism and beer. The author reported that breweries in Austria falsely complained about their profit margins being squeezed by rising utility prices, when in fact they simply wanted an excuse to raise the consumer price of beer and stuff the wallets of their shareholders.[40]

The GDR's journalists aimed their sharpest critiques at West German brewery owners and managers, sometimes including charges of Nazism in their diatribes. Shortly after the war, a story appeared in the East German press regarding the former head of the brewery administrative organization under the Third Reich, Dr. Ernst Röhm. In 1947, a Munich-area court remunerated him for personal financial damages caused by the war even though he had been a member of the Nazi party since 1938. The article implied that the Western Allied authorities excused the businessman's political affiliation based on his reputation as a good Christian and his participation in the well-loved enterprise of brewing. The columnist did not buy the man's story that he had only joined the Nazi Party to "save Germany's breweries." The article states: "translated into sober German, that means he wanted to save himself, or even to secure some capitalist profit."[41]

The most common polemics against West German brewery owners involved conspiracy and political intrigue.[42] The East German media often described brewing concerns in the FRG as "monopolistic."[43] The practice of allowing "tied pubs" served as proof of unscrupulous business practices in the capitalist system.[44] This arrangement allowed beer producers to own retailers and thereby require that only their products be sold in the pub, tavern or store. Perhaps the most prominent scandal (from the perspective of the GDR) involving beer directly affected the first chancellor of the Federal Republic, Konrad Adenauer. Adenauer's wife, according to the state newspapers, came from a wealthy family that had owned more than a dozen large breweries in East Germany. Eastern journalists and prominent politicians reveled in accusing Adenauer of wanting to reunify Germany under a capitalist system simply to regain property and increase his own personal wealth.[45] In another pithy line, again recorded by the *Berliner Zeitung*, Albert Norden announced in a speech that "now that these [breweries] are owned by the people and their profits flow to the Worker's and Farmer's State, the beer tastes much better to us."[46]

The GDR media found plenty to dislike about the social environment that surrounded beer in West Germany. Even while they portrayed beer as a unifying tradition for workers and a potential vehicle of socialist progress, East German press members identified the *Volkgetränk* as a magnet for backward social attitudes and regressive politics under capitalism. Bavaria, viewed as the most conservative region in the FRG and perhaps the most entrenched beer culture in the world, often bore the brunt of these attacks.[47] One 1954 report from *München* critiqued "the traditional separatism of Bavarian citizens" in the region's beer halls, where men wanted to be left in peace at their *Stammtisch* with their beer and their traditional foods and not be concerned with the problems of society.[48] These images of negligent or even reactionary public spheres involved copious consumption of beer to the point of excess coupled with crude or even violent behavior evoking traditions of patriarchy, political corruption and bourgeois social dominance. One 1956 article reported on a Bavarian man from a small village who reluctantly traveled to West Berlin to bury his recently deceased brother. Finding the beer somewhat stronger there than in his hometown, the rustic character, depicted in *Lederhosen* in an adjacent drawing, accidentlly got drunk. The story took a dark turn when the man returned to his hotel and found a woman in his bed. The author suggests that the man thought she was a prostitute and felt entitled to assault her. Only later when he was arrested and charged with attempted rape did the man discover that he had entered the wrong room.[49] Violence by drunk men against women recurred frequently as a theme in East German polemics against drinking culture in the FRG.

The *Stammtisch*, a social tradition in German drinking culture, neatly encapsulated all the potential problems of unenlightened alcohol-fueled gatherings. The continuing affinity for these regular meetings in West German society received regular condemnation from the GDR press. For them, the *Stammtisch* served as the archetype for "anti-social" spaces involving alcohol. While bad behavior fueled by drunkenness certainly played a role, the most pernicious danger from the *Stammtisch* was the circulation of unacceptable ideas. The media depicted these spaces as a support network for misogynistic behavior toward women as well as political conservatism or recidivism, including meetings of former or unrepentant Nazis.[50] One 1953 article stated directly that Hitler started the Nazi Party with the help of thirty liters of beer and seven acolytes at "the *Stammtisch* of a smoky Munich beer cellar."[51]

The Growing Gap Between Rhetoric and Reality

These unsubtle digs deflected attention from an East German beer industry struggling to overcome widespread difficulties and dependent on western trade. Attacks on the capitalist system of beer production failed to mention the state of the industry in the GDR. When complaints or issues did appear in the media, blame always fell on an individual brewery or on the population itself. Put simply, when disruptions emerged in the West German beer industry, the problem was the capitalist system of economy. When similar issues occurred in the East, the root cause was anything but the socialist model of production. The fact that East Germany relied upon an exchange of goods and ideas across the Iron Curtain to sustain and improve its beer supply never appeared in these articles. Despite repeated efforts to steer all such trade toward fellow socialist states, the Ulbricht government authorized trade of equipment and materials, as well as finished beer, with capitalist countries, including the FRG, throughout his leadership.

As early as 1949, brewery officials in the GDR warned their political superiors of the serious threat of competition from FRG beer. The fear of being undersold by western brewers formed a core part of the argument for reducing East German beer taxes in the early 1950s.[52] Thereafter, industry leaders and economic functionaries regularly acknowledged that the FRG's breweries outproduced their eastern counterparts.[53] When forced to compare the beer from the two states in terms of quality, GDR officials showed reluctance to admit that their beer was not as good but, reading between the lines, their recognition of that fact becomes obvious. One report by a special committee in 1960 stated "beer quality is, in general, equivalent to the West." Immediately following this assertion was an admission that East German beer "sometimes" showed poor standards because of rushed production during the summer months. The following sentence then claimed equal quality based on a comparison of "top brands," such as Radeberger, with beers from the FRG, even though such beers were hardly representative of quality in the general industry.[54] Four years later, the State Planning Commission reported that 78 percent of beer in the GDR did not meet quality standards.[55]

Cold War tensions also contributed to the inferiority of the GDR's beer supply by limiting the state's access to critical sources of raw goods, basic supplies and high-quality imports.[56] Eastern breweries depended on shipments of hops from the FRG for a large quantity of their demand in the 1950s. By the end of the decade, the GDR's economic planners began pushing harder and harder to reduce the state's dependence on western hops even though domestic cultivation remained inferior in terms of both quality and quantity.[57] The East German media blamed hop shortages in the late 1950s on a dastardly attempt by the West German and American governments to hamper GDR beer production by reducing the hop supply. A 1959 article reported, "[s]ince 1956 the Bonn Government [West Germany] has reduced the hop supply in order to cause difficulties in GDR beer production. Bonn received help in this effort from the USA, which built huge supply hoards and bought-up almost the entire export capacity of West Germany."[58] Once again, the press deflected attention from issues in the East German brewing industry by putting the blame on corrupt politicians and greedy capitalists in the West.

Conclusion

Nikita Khrushchev remarked in a 1958 speech to an East German audience that "Germans absolutely cannot live without sausage and beer."[59] His words, as an outsider looking in at life in East Germany, reflect precisely why the GDR's leadership felt incentivized, and indeed compelled, to bring the issue of beer into the fray of Cold War competition with the "other Germany." The state's ability to properly furnish such a mainstay of cultural consumption reflected directly upon its claims to be building socialism that was truly German in nature. With open archives and the gift of hindsight, it has become clear that little in the regime's public rhetoric on this issue reflected truth. The history of German beer culture cannot be split between the positive aspects that the GDR media claimed to find in its state and the negative traditions that it associated with the West. In terms of production, quality and efficiency, conditions and government policy in the East resulted in an objectively inferior beer supply, even if one sets aside the question of the *Reinheitsgebot*. More importantly, combining the available evidence on this matter makes clear the considerable attention that this Cold War of beer received from East German officials. It mattered enough that they created a media-wide mask of false narratives, lies and misinformation to disguise the reality of a seemingly trivial issue. War, cold or otherwise, has a way of emphasizing the significance of what might otherwise seem to be the commonplace of everyday life, and that certainly includes the *Volksgetränk*.

Notes

1. "Ganz Berlin deutsche Hauptstadt des Friedens: Aus der Rede des Genossen Albert Norden auf der großen Kundgebung im Westberliner Sportpalast; Störenfriedpolitik endet schlect; Wir drohen mit Milch und Gemüse, mit Weizen und Bier," *Neues Deutschland*, November 14, 1958.
2. Anke Fiedler and Michael Meyen, eds., *Fiktionen für das Volk: DDR-Zeitungen als PR-Instrument* (Berlin: LIT Verlag, 2011), 8.
3. Fiedler and Meyen, *Fiktionen*, 13.
4. Though I hope to address both subjects in future research, it is not within the purview of this chapter to comment on public reception of the government's beer rhetoric, nor is a comparative study of West German discourse possible at this stage of research.
5. Mark Landsman, *Dictatorship and Demand: The Politics of Consumerism in East Germany* (Cambridge, MA: Harvard University Press, 2005); Katherine Pence, "'You as a Woman Will Understand': Consumption, Gender and the Relationship Between State and Citizenry in the GDR's Crisis of 17 June 1953," *German History* 19, no. 2 (June 2001): 218.
6. Ina Merkel, *Utopie und Bedürfnis: die Geschichte der Konsumkultur in der DDR* (Köln: Böhlau, 1999); Pence, "You as a Woman Will Understand"; Eli Rubin, "The Trabant: Consumption, Eigen-Sinn, and Movement," *History Workshop Journal* 68 (2009): 27–44.
7. See Katherine Pence and Paul Betts, eds., *Socialist Modern: East German Everyday Culture and Politics* (Ann Arbor: The University of Michigan Press, 2008); Dagmar Herzog, "East Germany's Sexual Evolution," in *Socialist Modern: East German Everyday Culture and Politics*, edited by

Katherine Pence and Paul Betts (Ann Arbor: The University of Michigan Press, 2008), 71–95.
8. Alice Autumn Weinreb, *Modern Hungers: Food and Power in Twentieth-Century Germany* (New York: Oxford University Press, 2017), 2.
9. Weinreb, *Modern Hungers*, 124–131.
10. The "Noble Experiment" was a term coined by American president Herbert Hoover to describe the nationwide prohibition of alcohol in the United States starting in 1919.
11. Johan F.M. Swinnen, ed., *The Economics of Beer* (Oxford and New York: Oxford University Press, 2011), 17.
12. Randy Mosher, *Tasting Beer: An Insider's Guide to the World's Greatest Drink* (North Adams, MA: Storey Publishing, 2017), 24.
13. Gavin Smith, *Beer: A Global History* (London: Reaktion Books, 2014), 32–34.
14. Mosher, *Tasting Beer*, 22–24.
15. Robert Terrell, "The People's Drink: Beer, Bavaria, and the Remaking of Germany, 1933–1987" (PhD diss., University of California San Diego, 2018), 168–232; Frank von Tongeren, "Standards and International Trade Integration: A Historical Review of the German 'Reinheitsgebot,'" in *The Economics of Beer*, edited by Johan F.M. Swinnen (Oxford and New York: Oxford University Press, 2008), 58; see also *Statistisches Jahrbuch der Deutschen Demokratischen Republik* (SJDDR) *1972*, 120.
16. von Tongeren, "Standards and International Trade Integration," 59.
17. Ibid., 51–61.
18. SJDDR 1969, 118–119.
19. With beers exported to the FRG this was a legal requirement.
20. Dr. Lothar Fröhlich and Dr. Peter Lietz, "12.3 Der Erlass neuer lebensmittelrechtlicher Bestimmungen in der DDR und ihre Auswirkungen für die Bier- und Malzherstellung," in *Die Brau- und Malzindustrie in Deutschland-Ost zwischen 1945 und 1989: Ein Beitrag zur Geschichte der deutschen Brau- und Malzindustrie im 20. Jahrhundert*, edited by Peter Lietz and Hans-J. Manger (Berlin: VLB Berlin, 2016), 446–447.
21. Peter Grieder, *The German Democratic Republic* (Houndmills, Basingstoke, Hampshire and New York: Palgrave Macmillan, 2012), 12; n.a., "Technische und technologische Forderungen bei grundlegender Beachtung der technologischen Einrichtungen und der Maschinen der Brauindustrie, unter besonderer Berücksichtigung des Bedürfnissses an Einrichtungen für die Periode bis zum Jahre 1965," 1960, BArch, DE 4/23562; Report from Stako to Rat des Bezirkes Dresden, Abt. Industrie, VA Lebensmittelindustrie, "Ermittlung des Maschinenbedarfs für sämtliche Gruppen der Lebensmittelindustrie für die Jahre 1962 bis 1965," 23 May 1961, BArch, DE4 23552.

22. See individual entries for different GDR breweries in Peter Lietz and Hans-J. Manger, eds., *Die Brau- und Malzindustrie in Deutschland-Ost zwischen 1945 und 1989: Ein Beitrag zur Geschichte der deutschen Brau- und Malzindustrie im 20. Jahrhundert* (Berlin: VLB Berlin, 2016).
23. n.a.—SPK, Abt. LMI, "Hauptrichtung der wissenschaftlich-technischen Entwicklung," n.d., BArch, DE 1/51636, n.p; Matthies, Direktor—SG, "Protokol über die Tagung der Zentralen Kommission für Warenbilanzierung am 30.7.1962," 31 July 1962, BArch, DE 4/24531 Bd. 2, pg. 4; "Jahresanalyse 1962," 18 January 1963, BArch, DE 4/7408, pg. 2; Lemmel, Abteilungsleiter—SG FA Koordinierung, Grundsatzfragen und Getränkeversorgung, "Protokoll über die Arbeitsaung der Leiter der Leitlaboratorien und der TKO-Bearbeiter der Bezirke am 26.2.1963 im Kulturraum des Betriebsteils Engelhardt-Brauerei Berlin," 7 March 1963, BArch, DE 4/7596, pg. 1.
24. Greg Eghigian, "'Homo Munitus:' The East German Observed," in *Socialist Modern: East German Everyday Culture and Politics*, edited by Katherine Pence and Paul Betts (Ann Arbor: The University of Michigan Press, 2008), 45.
25. Ihre Diätassistentin Monika, "Nichts gegen ein Gläschen Bier: Organische Schäden durch größere Mengen Alkohol," *Neue Zeit*, October 1, 1966.
26. See Na., "'Pils' aus Berline," *Berliner Zeitung*, October 12, 1965; Wolfgang Hasse, "Zwischen Warnow-Kal und Banquereau-Bank (10), Nachts tagt das Heringskollegium; Kulinarische Probleme auf hoher See – Pro Fangreise elf Tonnen Fleisch und Wurst – Frische 'Milche vom Block,'" *Neue Zeit*, March 18, 1969.
27. Horst Dornbusch and Karl-Ullrich Heyse, "Reinheitsgebot," in *The Oxford Companion to Beer*, edited by Garrett Oliver (Oxford: Oxford University Press, 2012), 692–693.
28. James S. Roberts, *Drink, Temperance, and the Working Class in Nineteenth-Century Germany* (Boston: Allen & Unwin, 1984), 96–99.
29. Manfred Hübner, *Zwischen Alkohol und Abstinenz: Trinksitten und Alkoholfrage im deutschen Proletariat bis 1914* (Berlin: Dietz, 1988), 74.
30. Hübner, *Zwischen Alkohol und Abstinenz*; David Blackbourn, *The Long Nineteenth Century: A History of Germany 1780–1918* (New York: Oxford University Press, 1998), 359.
31. See also Nie., "Unsere aktuelle Untersuchung zur Versorgungslage: Durstig Kehlen hoffen auf Berliner Bier: 130 000 hl werden zusätzlich gebraut / Die Bierniederlagen müssen ausgebaut werden / Flaschenproblem lösen," *Berliner Zeitung*, May 24, 1954.
32. "Und die andere Seite," *Berliner Zeitung*, December 11, 1951.
33. "Wo findet Hans seine Liesel? Glück im Berliner Kaffeegarten / Warum ist das heute so schwer?" *Berliner Zeitung*, April 3, 1953.

34. "Um den goldenen Boden: Handwerker am Stammtisch / Rechnung mit ++ // auf dem Bierdeckel," *Berliner Zeitung*, November 24, 1954.
35. Lietz, "Die politischen und wirtschaftlichen Ausgangsbedingungen in der sowjetischen Besatyungszone," 25; G. H., "Anglo-amerikanische Reparationen aus Deutschland," *Neues Deutschland*, September 18, 1946.
36. Hwg. "Brauereien wollen exportieren," *Neue Zeit*, March 12, 1947.
37. "Rund um die Agrarkrise," *Neue Zeit*, July 27, 1948.
38. "Hiobsbotschaft für Bayerns Biertrinker," *Neue Zeit*, June 26, 1952.
39. "… und ohne Bier," *Berliner Zeitung*, July 24 1947; "Kein Starkbier in der Bizone," *Neues Deutschland*, October 14, 1948; G.K., "Ein Budget gegen das Volk," *Berliner Zeitung*, May 5, 1949; AP, "Unverschämte Handelsspannen," *Berliner Zeitung*, February 26, 1950; "Und die andere Seite," *Berliner Zeitung*, December 11, 1951; Hako, "Der 'selbstständige' Unternehmer der 'freien Welt': Mittelständler werden zu Angestellten der Konzerne degradiert," *Neues Deutschland*, March 26, 1957.
40. "In Österreich illustriert: Volkskapitalismus: Verschiedene Seiten des 'gesegneten Zeitalters' / Bier auch teurer / Entlassungen als Druckmittel," *Berliner Zeitung*, May 25, 1957.
41. "Religion und Bayrisch Bier: Nazi zur "Rettung des Braugewerbs" / Auch Beichtvater half nicht," *Berliner Zeitung*, August 15, 1947.
42. For further examples, see "Strauß würgt SPD-Zeitungen ab: Bonns Kriegsminister greift mit Polizeistaatmethoden in den Wahlkampf / Terrorwelle ausgedehnt," *Neues Deutschland*, November 8, 1958; G. Fl., "Krieg & Bier en gros," *Neues Deutschland*, April 23, 1960.
43. "60 Millionäre im Nacken der Westberliner: Immer schärfere Gegensätze zwischen Reichtum und Armut / Hemmungslose Prasserei der Neureichen," *Berliner Zeitung*, December 2, 1954.
44. Hako, "Der 'selbstständige' Unternehmer der 'freien Welt': Mittelständler werden zu Angestellten der Konzerne degradiert," *Neues Deutschland*, March 26, 1957; see also "Und Schwarz," *Berliner Zeitung*, February 18, 1960.
45. "Albert Norden, Sekretär des Zentralkomitees: Unsere Republik ist das Leben und die Zukunft," *Berliner Zeitung*, July 15, 1958; Herald Feudenberg, "Das wahre Gesicht eines Rosenzüchters," *Berliner Zeitung*, August 13, 1960; Albert Norden, "Repräsentant einer untergehenden Zeit: Das kapitalistische Königreich einer Familie," *Neues Deutschland*, November 8, 1961.
46. "Albert Norden, Sekretär des Zentralkomitees: Unsere Republik ist das Leben und die Zukunft," *Berliner Zeitung*, July 15, 1958.

47. "München hat keine Zeit für politischen Krakeel: Oktoberfest mit schäumenden Maßkrügen," *Neue Zeit*, September 25, 1949; Jurgen Ruhle, "München bleibt bei Weißwurst: Kulturreportage aus Bayern (II)," *Berliner Zeitung*, May 12, 1954; Günther Fuchs, "Begegnungen in Westdeutschland: "Anna-Seghers-Ensemble" besuchte Hessen," *Neues Deutschland*, October 26.
48. Ruhle, "München bleibt bei Weißwurst."
49. Cobra, "Beerdigung eines alten Bayern: Abenteuer eines Trauergastes, der das Banner der Moral verteidigte," *Berliner Zeitung*, July 12, 1956; see also Paule Panke, "Sorgen am Stammtisch," *Berliner Zeitung*, March 11, 1956; Jaroslav Hasek, "Der lila Blitz und andere Geschichten: Erzählt von Jaroslav Hasek, deutsch von Rudolf Feige, Wir drucken mit freundlicher Genehmigung des ARTIA-Verlag Prag.," *Berliner Zeitung*, October 23, 1960.
50. Paule Panke, "Sorgen am Stammtisch," *Berliner Zeitung*, March 11, 1956; Cobra, "Bester Diplomat: Der Chauffeur," *Berliner Zeitung*, May 21, 1959; "Pierrot," *Neue Zeit*, September 3, 1960; Kochan, *Blauer Würger*, 18; Helmut Oelschiegel, "Wie Krieg entsteht," *Neue Zeit*, July 1, 1951; Hans Marchwitza, "Die Heimkehr der Kümiaks," *Neues Deutschland*, January 24, 1953; F.C. Weiskopf, "Die Versuchung," *Berliner Zeitung*, July 28, 1953; Jurgen Ruhle, "München bleibt bei Weißwurst: Kulturreportage aus Bayern (II)," *Berliner Zeitung*, May 12, 1954; Max Kretzer, "Der Millionenbauer," *Neue Zeit*, May 12, 1957.
51. Cobra, "Alter Nazi auf großer Fahrt: Provokation in der S-Bahn / Unter der Maske des Biedermannes," *Berliner Zeitung*, November 5, 1953; see also Cobra, "Im Stuhlgewitter der Brautzeit: Der Bräutigam zwischen Bacchus und Venus / Das Versprechen," *Berliner Zeitung*, May 12, 1957; Prof. Dr. med. habil. F. Lickint, "Butter, Brot und Barrenturnen: Aus einem Diskussionsbetrag," *Neues Deutschland*, July 11, 1959.
52. gez. Sack und gez. Baum, "Abschrift der im Sekretariat veränderten und angenommenen Vorlage," 11 October 1949, BArch, DA 4/1171, 2.
53. n.a., "Protokoll über die Leitbetriebstagung der Brauereien am 30. 3. 1960 in der Diamant-Brauerei Magdeburg," 30 March 1960, BArch, DE 4/5176, 6; n.a., "Jahresanalyse 1960," n.d., BArch, DE 4/7408; Dipl. rer.oec. B. -D.Schimizek und Dr.rer.oec. W. Dlouhy, "Berichtsreihe: Internationale Entwicklungstendenzen bei Nahrungs- und Genußmitteln, Bericht 4: Die Entwicklung des Bierverbrauchs im internationalen Maßstab," September 1966, BArch, DL 102/224; Dipl. Oec. J. Hawemann, "Internationaler Vergleich: Pro-Kopf-Verbrauch einiger Nahrungs-u. Genußmittel in ausgewählten RGW - u. kapitalistischen Industrieländern im Jahre 1976," 30 November 1977, BArch, DZ 30/25124.
54. n.a., "Jahresanalyse 1960," n.d., BArch, DE 4/7408.
55. n.a.—SPK, Abt. LMI, "Hauptrichtung der wissenschaftlich-technischen Entwicklung," n.d., BArch, DE 1/51636, n.p.

56. Ulrich, Werkleiter—Köstritzer Schwarzbierbrauerei und Lemmel, Mitarbeiter—SG, "Niederschrift über eine Beratung in Export-Angelegenheiten im VEB Köstritzer Schwarzbierbrauerei - Bad Köstritz," 16 March 1961, BArch, DE 4/780, 2; Matthies, Geschäftsleiter—VLK Getränke, "Entwicklung des VE-Versorgungs- und Lagerungskontors der Lebensmittelindustrie Getränke," n.d., BArch, DE 4/24528, n.p.
57. Message from Hillebrad, Werkleiter; Weber, Planungsleiter; Beutler, Leiter der Abteilung Arbeit; und Schmidt, Sekretär der B P O der SED—VEB Brauerei Dessau to z. Hd. der Kollegin Hölterhof - SPK, Abt. LMI, Gruppe Genußmittelindustrie, "Niveauvergleich im Rat der gegenseitigen Wirtschaftshilfe, Erzeugnis Bier und Malz," 25 July 1961, BArch, DE 4/28135; Bosewitz / Schaak, "Volkswirtschaftsplan 1961 Plan Forschng und Technik Themenblatt: Einfluss des Austausches von Hopfen aus Westdeutschland durch Hopfen aus sozialistischen Ländern," 30 August 1961, BArch, DE 4/5176; Wozny, Leiter d. Techn. Büros—SG, "Protokoll über die Sitzung des Techn. Büros des Staatlichen Getränkekontors zur Störfreimachung der Getränkeindustrie der DDR von Westdeutschland und dem kapitalistischen Ausland am 28. 11. 1961, 10.00 Uhr," 2 March 1962, BArch, DE 4/24530.
58. W.R., "ND Kommentiert: Bonn ruiniert Hopfenbauern," *Neues Deutschland*, September 21, 1959.
59. "Weite Perspektive durch sozialistische Zusammenarbeit," *Neues Deutschland*, July 25, 1958. 5. Original quote: "Mias ist Wurst, und der Deutsche kann doch ohne Wurst und Bier nicht leben."

BIBLIOGRAPHY

PRIMARY SOURCES

Archives
Bundesarchiv Berlin – Lichterfelde (BArch – BL).
Stiftung Archiv Parteien und Massenorganisationen (BArch – SAPMO).
Periodicals
Berliner Zeitung. Accessed online via *Staatsbibliothek zu Berlin - Preußischer Kulturbesitz*.
Neue Zeit. Accessed online via *Staatsbibliothek zu Berlin - Preußischer Kulturbesitz*.
Neues Deutschland. Accessed online via *Staatsbibliothek zu Berlin - Preußischer Kulturbesitz*.
Online Archive
Statistischen Jahrbücher der Deutsche Demokratische Republik. Accessed online via DigiZeitschriften, Das Deutsche Digitale Zeitschriftenarchiv.

Secondary Sources

Blackbourn, David. *The Long Nineteenth Century: A History of Germany 1780–1918*. New York: Oxford University Press, 1998.

Dornbusch, Horst, and Karl-Ullrich Heyse. "Reinheitsgebot." In *The Oxford Companion to Beer*, edited by Garrett Oliver, 692–693. Oxford: Oxford University Press, 2012.

Eghigian, Greg. "'Homo Munitus:' The East German Observed." In *Socialist Modern: East German Everyday Culture and Politics*, edited by Katherine Pence and Paul Betts, 37–70. Ann Arbor: The University of Michigan Press, 2008.

Fiedler, Anke, and Michael Meyen, eds. *Fiktionen für das Volk: DDR Zeitungen als PR-Instrument*. Berlin: LIT Verlag, 2011.

Fröhlich, Dr. Lothar, and Dr. Peter Lietz. "12.3 Der Erlass neuer lebensmittelrechtlicher Bestimmungen I der DDR und ihre Auswirkungen für die Bier- und Malzherstellung." In *Die Brau- und Malzindustrie in Deutschland-Ost zwischen 1945 und 1989: Ein Beitrag zur Geschichte der deutschen Brau- und Malzindustrie im 20. Jahrhundert*, edited by Peter Lietz and Hans-J. Manger, 443–446. Berlin: VLB Berlin, 2016.

Grieder, Peter. *The German Democratic Republic*. Houndmills, Basingstoke, Hampshire and New York: Palgrave Macmillan, 2012.

Hübner, Manfred. *Zwischen Alkohol und Abstinenz: Trinksitten und Alkoholfrage im deutschen Proletariat bis 1914*. Berlin: Dietz, 1988.

Landsman, Mark. *Dictatorship and Demand: The Politics of Consumerism in East Germany*. Harvard Historical Studies. Cambridge, MA: Harvard University Press, 2005.

Merkel, Ina. *Utopie und Bedürfnis: die Geschichte der Konsumkultur in der DDR*. Köln: Böhlau, 1999.

Mosher, Randy. *Tasting Beer: An Insider's Guide to the World's Greatest Drink*, 2017.

Pence, Katherine. "'You as a Woman Will Understand': Consumption, Gender and the Relationship Between State and Citizenry in the GDR's Crisis of 17 June 1953." *German History* 19, no. 2 (June 2001): 218–252.

Roberts, James S. *Drink, Temperance, and the Working Class in Nineteenth-Century Germany*. Boston: Allen & Unwin, 1984.

Rubin, Eli. "The Trabant: Consumption, Eigen-Sinn, and Movement." *History Workshop Journal* 68 (2009): 27–44.

Smith, Gavin. *Beer: A Global History*. London: Reaktion Books, 2014.

Swinnen, Johan F.M. *The Economics of Beer*. Oxford and New York: Oxford University Press, 2011.

Weinreb, Alice Autumn. *Modern Hungers: Food and Power in Twentieth-Century Germany*, 2017.

CHAPTER 11

Brewing Global Relations During the Cold War: Coffee, East Germans and Southeast Asia, 1978–1990

Andrew Kloiber

In December 1986, the East German newspaper *Berliner Zeitung* published an article about Vietnam's expanding coffee industry, informing readers that the country's previously "untouched" highland region had experienced "fundamental change" in the name of building a coffee industry over the previous five years.[1] The article described the enormous effort involved in this undertaking, from constructing roads, clearing and irrigating thousands of acres of land, to building power plants and living quarters for the thousands of Vietnamese who were migrating to the region in search of work.[2] The project reflected "the ingenuity and spirit of the Vietnamese people," who "welcome[d] assistance" from brother socialist nations, above all the German Democratic Republic (GDR).[3] East Germany hoped its investments in the Vietnamese coffee industry—including materials, equipment and technical expertise—formed a partial solution to an ongoing "coffee crisis" at home, where the state's attempts to stretch coffee supply through an adulteration of available blends had backfired on state planners.

A. Kloiber (✉)
Independent Scholar, Hamilton, Canada

© The Author(s) 2019
H. M. Benbow and H. R. Perry (eds.), *Food, Culture and Identity in Germany's Century of War*,
https://doi.org/10.1007/978-3-030-27138-1_11

247

The public rejected the state's coffee measures, insisting that the state maintains a consistent quality in the products it provided its people. The GDR required partners to forego payment for coffee in hard currency, which it found in the developing world. In tracing the causes of a coffee crisis, and the GDR's efforts to solve it, foods like coffee help illustrate the GDR's global entanglements and the interconnectedness of the socialist world late in the Cold War. Indeed, East Germany's efforts to mitigate the effects of a domestic "coffee crisis" by leveraging its relationship with countries like Vietnam reveal that, far beyond signing a mere goods-for-goods trade negotiation, East Germany and Vietnam entered into a long-term development project to bring a nearly non-existent coffee industry to a level of production that could satisfy the GDR's needs over the next twenty years.[4]

In many ways, the Cold War determined the rigid structures of power in which East Germany could manoeuver and created the very domestic crises it faced. As well, East and West Germany's political rivalry came to embody a sort of microcosm of the global ideological war being fought between the two superpowers, the Soviet Union and the United States. When the Federal Republic of Germany (FRG) introduced the Hallstein Doctrine in 1955, it attempted to isolate East Germany from the international community by claiming sole right to represent Germans on German soil and threatening to cease diplomatic and trade relations with any nation (save the Soviet Union) that granted East Germany official recognition.[5] Until the two German states signed the Basic Treaty in 1972, which nullified Hallstein by granting East Germany official recognition, the GDR's options for trade partners were extremely limited, leaving East Germany to spend most of its diplomatic efforts seeking—though not receiving—international recognition.[6]

Yet the rivalry also had a direct impact on East Germany's domestic policies—and its political strife, as the GDR perceived an increasing need to compete directly with West Germany's growing economic prosperity. Over the course of the 1950s, general food supply increased in the East, and by 1958, the GDR could adequately meet citizens' basic nutritional needs, bringing an end to twenty years of domestic rationing.[7] Pressure to compete with the West increased over the 1950s, in part as a means to counter the Federal Republic's claims to be the sole representative of all Germans, but even more significant was the ruling Socialist Unity Party's (*Sozialistische Einheitspartei Deutschlands*, SED) desire to combat the growing perception that East Germany was rapidly falling behind the

West in terms of quality of life. Whether from living in border regions, having contacts in the West, or hearsay, East Germans themselves could draw direct comparisons between their own material conditions and those in the West, as they bore witness to the prosperity of West Germany's "Economic Miracle."[8] Perceiving the opportunity for better job prospects, greater material wealth and political freedom, many East Germans chose to flee to the Federal Republic, leading to a mass exodus—the so-called *Republikflucht*-literally, "Flight from the Republic"—of nearly 3.5 million East Germans to the West over the course of the 1950s, most of whom represented the GDR's youngest professionals.[9] In response, at the 5th Party Congress in July of 1958 SED chairman Walter Ulbricht proclaimed the new "Main Economic Task" of the Party, which called for per-capita consumption to overtake West German general consumption by 1961.[10] Improving the supply of foodstuffs like coffee was one way in which the regime could try to make the GDR a more attractive place to live and thus improve the morale of workers—who in the view of the SED formed the front line in the global—*cultural*—Cold War. However, this strategy also tied the SED's political legitimacy to its capacity to fulfill those promises.[11] Yet maintaining this supply was a massive undertaking for a country which relied so utterly on international markets for coffee, especially when prices sat at nearly four times their normal rate in 1977.

The GDR's search for coffee brought it into contact with producing countries in the developing world, and the resulting trade deals reveal as much about the GDR's intended form of engagement with those coffee-producing countries as they do about its own self-image as a modern state in a divided, yet globalizing world. These trade deals, in turn, offer a complication to a metanarrative of global bipolarity which still dominates in historical discussions of the Cold War and has tended to emphasize the global "contest of power" between the superpowers. Beyond showing East Germany's commitment to supplying coffee to its own people, this trade agreement provides an example of the GDR's capacity to successfully foster constructive bilateral relationships with other countries who themselves were marginalized within the power structures of the late Cold War. Furthermore, this case also shows how East Germany used these deals to cultivate a specific self-image *vis-à-vis* its Vietnamese partner. Likewise, studies of East Germany's Cold War experience tend to overemphasize the GDR's *place within* this global political order, as a passive participant in a game played between much larger players.

A majority of historical accounts tend to emphasize the ways in which the GDR was at the mercy of capitalist markets for the raw materials and finished goods it needed—a familiar narrative that highlights the GDR's failures. But is this all there is to say about East Germany's place in that global economy? A growing number of scholars have begun to challenge this narrative, such as Young-Sun Hong's comparative study of East and West German humanitarian projects, in which she argues that "'local events' were not merely a side stage for the proxy wars of the global cold war, but must be seen on a much larger global canvas."[12] Scholarship should move beyond considering merely East Germany's *place within* a global order and instead ought to examine the GDR's global *engagement* more closely, because East Germany was never merely a passive participant in the process of globalization in the twentieth century.

Drinking Socialism: Coffee and Socialist Society in East Germany

While reflecting on their experience in "Espresso Hungaria," a small café on Berlin's Stalinallee, in fall 1961, one East German journalist wrote "I can fully relate to the barista who succumbed to the graceful seduction of this dearly beloved drink," agreeing with an entry in the café's guest book describing the coffee as "the best in Berlin."[13] The author depicted the mood at Espresso Hungaria, drawing the reader into an evening scene:

> There you sit with me at a small table inside Espresso Hungaria. It's evening. The stores are closed. Across the street the neon sign for 'Möbel-Passage' [a furniture store] invites you over. Outside on the asphalt median of Stalinallee, parked cars reflect the colourful neon light. The café is full; the tables are occupied. Girls nibble biscuits, four young men spoon ice cream with cherries, a mother rocks a stroller with her left hand, while her right brings a cup to her mouth. A young man writes – a love poem? Modern sociability [*Gemütlichkeit*], entertaining relaxation, sweet reflection...[14]

By noting the café's location on Stalinallee and the affordable prices of its menu items, the article celebrated the café as an achievement of socialism. At the same time, the overall tone of the piece clearly emphasized the café as a pleasurable experience; East Germans were meant to view coffee drinking as an enjoyable experience which depended on comfort, relaxation and "the best coffee" available. Although this article encouraged East Germans to imagine themselves enjoying a cup of coffee in the ambiance of a modern café, the supply of coffee was hardly guaranteed in 1961. In a front-page article earlier that year, the same newspaper asked readers "do you like to drink a cup of coffee? Surely. But have you put any thought into where the coffee comes from?" This article explained the delicate balance between imports and exports on which the GDR relied for such goods, emphasizing that the GDR's ability to import goods like coffee required German export goods to be of the highest quality "on which our international reputation depends."[15]

Together, these two *Berliner Zeitung* articles exemplify the story of coffee drinking in the GDR in a number of ways. First, each tied coffee drinking to the achievements of socialism, in terms of both workers' equal access to consumer goods and the domestic production on which that access relied. Coffee was not a given, but it was a product to which the regime committed resources, tying its political legitimacy to fulfilling its promise to improve living standards. Second, both articles took it for granted that Germans enjoyed their coffee. Coffee was best consumed for pleasure, in relaxing surroundings, whether alone or with companions—and above all, coffee was meant to taste *good*. Yet, while scholars agree that the regime's inability to maintain the supply of consumer goods challenged its political legitimacy, coffee's importance lay in more than simply its availability.[16]

Coffee—and the activities related to its consumption—had a role to play in the building of socialism. Through the 1960s, the design journal *Kultur im Heim* published photos displaying new furniture for the "socialist" apartment, featuring the simple lines and clean, clutter-free spaces that in part characterize mid-century modernism. Coffee sat in the middle of these utopian visions; in almost every image of a kitchen or living room, a coffee service made of gleaming East German porcelain sat atop the table, inviting readers to imagine entertaining guests in just such a room.[17] Household etiquette books discussed coffee as a lubricant for social gatherings, tying it to notions of sociability, civility and hosting etiquette.[18] Consider, for example, the advice given by *Festlich Gedeckte Tisch* that an engagement party "is best celebrated with coffee … nowhere else can two unfamiliar families get together more easily than with the fragrance of a delicious coffee!"[19] State-run periodicals also ran frequent articles about particular factories and firms, and these stories would usually include a picture of the featured worker or brigade group during their coffee break. As Katherine Pence has pointed out, the portrayal of workers enjoying coffee together in restful scenarios conveys a significant idea: Coffee could foster solidarity between citizens through idle relaxing in the break room, not necessarily through work.[20]

In its January 1967 issue, the women's magazine *Für Dich* asked its readers, "Can you manage to go without coffee for a day? For weeks, months, years—your entire life?" The reality, according to the article, was in fact the reverse: "every year we import around 31,000 tons. ... Every day – in homes, offices and factory cafeterias – 15 million cups of this 'daily jolt' are drunk."[21] This figure corresponded to about one cup per capita per day, and the article's implication was clear: East Germans enjoyed their coffee as a regular component of everyday life. The article placed coffee into a longer European history, noting the first German coffee houses that opened in Leipzig. As inheritors of this café culture, East Germans could partake in an older European heritage every time they enjoyed a cup of coffee in a place like Espresso Hungaria. Emphasizing East Germans' participation in this longer cultural heritage, however, would prove politically volatile when world prices challenged the state's ability to keep coffee flowing.

BITTER GROUNDS: THE "COFFEE CRISIS" OF 1977

From July 17–20, 1975, a massive cold front swept through Brazil's coffee-producing regions of Minas Gerais, São Paulo and Parana, destroying two-thirds of these regions' coffee trees and jeopardizing over half of the 1976–1977 crop.[22] Supplying roughly one-third of the world's coffee at the time, such a devastating environmental disaster had serious implications for the international coffee market. The real coffee price doubled between 1975 and 1976, nearly quadrupling by 1977.[23] This dramatic rise placed the currency-poor GDR in a financial quandary, as state import plans for 1977 called for 51,900 tons of raw coffee, an increase of 1,900 tons over the previous year's coffee imports.[24] Industry and government officials viewed this problem as a genuine "coffee crisis" and decided that if the state was to have any hope of maintaining supply and thus fulfilling the Party's 1973 claims that East Germans now lived in "real existing socialism," they needed to stretch remaining coffee reserves through adulteration.[25] On June 28, the Council of Ministers approved the cessation in production of the most affordable coffee brand, *Kosta*, which would be replaced by *Kaffee-Mix*, a blend made of 51% roasted coffee and 49% "surrogate" products: chicory, sugar beet and rye.[26]

Public reaction to *Kaffee-Mix* was overwhelmingly negative and focused above all on the poor quality of *Kaffee-Mix*. In the coming weeks, citizens wrote fourteen thousand petition letters to roasting firms and retailers, as well as to state and party officials from the local to the national levels.[27] A group letter from Erzgebirge complained, "the coffee we had in the war didn't taste so miserable!"[28] In one of the most striking examples, a self-identified "coffee drinker collective" in Karl-Marx-Stadt wrote a cheeky letter containing what they called the "test results" of a probe they conducted on *Kaffee-Mix*. Among their (many) findings, the group suggested *Kaffee-Mix* could improve workers' discipline, as "avid coffee drinkers would avoid their coffee breaks."[29] Some citizens also identified the political ramifications of the coffee measures, such as Frau M., who asked: "Do you think that pensioners can afford more expensive coffee? Do you even know, *with your great salaries*, what it takes to make ends meet with 300 marks a month? And you want to be a workers' government?"[30] Her letter pointed to a larger political problem: The coffee crisis threatened the official narrative of "living in real existing socialism" because it could exacerbate social differentiation in a social system that was supposed to provide equal access to goods.[31] The coffee crisis challenged both the supposed superiority of the planned economy and the regime's claims to legitimacy when it struggled to keep coffee flowing into East Germans' expectant cups.

When East Germans rejected *Kaffee-Mix* on account of its poor taste and quality, they resolved to purchase *Rondo* and *Mona* instead, despite the higher costs resulting from these brands' higher coffee content.[32] The Ministry for State Security [*Ministerium für Staatssicherheit*, Stasi] reported a number of strikes and, above all, a general boycott of the brand: Several districts reported that customers refused to purchase the new brand, to the extent that in Karl-Marx-Stadt, retailers faced a stockpile of over 11.6 tons of *Kaffee-Mix* by August 15.[33] This behavior guaranteed the rapid depletion of coffee reserves, not only jeopardizing the state's plans to save hard currency, but effectively rendering the state's conservation measures a complete loss. If East Germans were only going to purchase brands with high coffee content, the regime had no alternative but to find new sources of raw coffee without increasing hard currency expenditures. By 1979, world prices still sat more than twice as high as their pre-1975 levels, leaving barter-based trade as the only alternative.[34] Traders intensified their negotiations in East Asia, specifically in Vietnam, in the hopes of establishing long-term import lines.

Trade Rather Than Aid: East German Relations with Vietnam

Since gaining official autonomy from the Soviet Union in 1955, East German foreign policymakers sought to establish the GDR as a viable alternative to the "revival of imperialism" of which it accused West Germany.[35] In its relations with developing countries, East Germany aimed to foster meaningful relationships based on a commitment to solidarity through socialism. Central to this strategy was the GDR's attempt to differentiate its own forms of humanitarian and development aid from those offered by the West, demonstrating the extent to which development projects contributed to the GDR's Cold War political strategy. Western humanitarian aid, according to GDR spokesmen, targeted only select industries or regions of specific economic value to the imperialist powers. In its report on the 1964 United Nations conference for trade and development, the SED's official newspaper, *Neues Deutschland*, argued that Western development aid was most often used "to exert political pressure" and to secure "new cheaper sources of raw materials for Western companies."[36] According to the women's magazine *Für Dich*, Western aid did nothing to "help against hunger, but rather against '*Revolution* from hunger.'"[37] By contrast, the SED claimed to support the demands of developing nations for "equal trade, not aid [*Handel statt Hilfe*]."[38] At the core of "socialist aid" lay the principle of mutually beneficial cooperation in the economic and political spheres, which concentrated on "constructing and modernizing" these nations' industry and agriculture.[39] Through its commitment to socialist solidarity, the GDR would assist developing countries in their struggle for independence, as well as their economic and social development.[40]

Driven by the need for coffee, but guided by these principles, East Germany recognized Vietnam a logical—and indeed, ideal—candidate for a cooperative coffee development program. Vietnam represented a perfect ally and the war a perfect propaganda opportunity, as it could be easily portrayed as a socialist "victim" of an aggressive American invasion which came under increasing scrutiny and criticism as the war dragged on. West Germany openly supported America's intervention and thus could be vilified alongside the United States. East Germany's early and fervent opposition to the war eventually provided the GDR with considerable international clout, particularly as worldwide public opinion turned against American intervention. As Gerd Horten points out as well, the Vietnam War was an "organic" opportunity, in that East Germany had no need to invent or "stubbornly defend [its position] against the better knowledge of an ever skeptical East German population."[41] This anti-war stance also contributed to the GDR's domestic stability: As anti-war sentiment grew among the East German public during the 1960s as it did around the globe, the SED's anti-war stance appeared to bolster the party's legitimacy in the eyes of its citizens, something Horten has called the GDR's "Vietnam bonus."[42]

Despite the massive destruction visited upon Vietnam throughout that war, including the devastating effects of napalm and Agent Orange, Vietnam's coffee fields—first cultivated under French colonial rule—remained largely intact and untouched by the time the war ended in 1975. Yet the war had exacted an enormous toll, including approximately 700,000 casualties and the destruction of 45% of the country's towns.[43] The war had destroyed much of the country's industrial and agricultural infrastructure, and famine threatened to take hold in a number of regions. With the exception of rice, production had fallen well below pre-war levels.[44] Keenly aware of the need to provide employment, and the need to feed the population, the government launched a widespread program of collectivization throughout the south, bringing farms and factories into the centrally planned economy. The country—now renamed the Socialist Republic of Vietnam (SRV)—joined the Council for Mutual Economic Assistance (COMECON) in 1978, seeking to alleviate some of its economic woes and secure lines of trade.[45] American-led embargos severely limited the SRV's ability to acquire finished goods or raw materials on the world market. Meanwhile, Hanoi's relationship with Beijing had deteriorated throughout the war as the Vietnamese drew closer to the Soviets and only worsened after reunification.[46]

Faced with an acute need after the war for economic development, the Vietnamese Communist Party recognized the potential of coffee as a cash crop and, during its Fourth Party Congress in 1976, the regime began an ambitious project to increase Vietnam's coffee exports.[47] The French had introduced coffee to Vietnam during colonization, but the industry did not experience any large-scale growth before decolonization in the mid-twentieth century. The Vietnam War interrupted all coffee cultivation so that by 1973, the industry had sat dormant for more than a decade. In 1975, Vietnam possessed approximately 20,000 hectares of coffee fields, scattered throughout the country and produced a meager five to seven thousand tons per year.[48]

Growing Coffee in Vietnam, 1978–1986

When SED General Secretary Erich Honecker visited Hanoi in December 1977, as stockpiles of *Kaffee-Mix* continued to grow, he signed a general treaty of friendship and economic cooperation which specifically noted a mutual desire to "intensify the export" to the GDR of products like fruits, rubber and coffee.[49] Vietnam represented a perfect coffee partner for a number of reasons, chief among which was the fact that Vietnam was not a member of the International Coffee Organization (ICO), a regulatory body comprised of producing and consuming nations headed by Brazil, which had set world coffee prices as well as import and export quotas since 1963.[50] Since neither country was beholden to the ICO's rules and regulations, they were able to negotiate a bilateral agreement that suited their own respective needs and ambitions. Negotiations continued until August 1980, when both countries agreed to jointly establish a coffee plantation in the province of Dac Lac.[51] The treaty adopted the language of socialist solidarity, writing that the coffee agreement served the interests of continued development and "strengthening of mutually beneficial economic cooperation."[52] East Germany would provide equipment and materials for planting and fostering coffee plants, as well as fertilizers and pesticides.[53] The GDR would also send specialists to train Vietnamese workers in the use of this equipment, as well as to help organize and supervise coffee cultivation. In exchange for German assistance, Vietnam agreed to prepare and cultivate an additional 10,000 hectares of fields by the end of the five year plan and to deliver coffee to East Germany in ten annual installments, beginning in 1986 and increasing by 700 tons per year until 1991, after which payments would continue at 3000 tons per year.

Extensive measures were necessary to carry out the expansion of the coffee industry. For instance, acquiring seeds from the world market was impossible due to existing trade embargoes against Vietnam, so seeds had to be handpicked from those few trees that were still viable.[54] With a population density of 20 inhabitants per square kilometer, Dac Lac was a very thinly populated area. Although people began migrating to the region when the regime first initiated a coffee program after 1975, the regime also forcibly relocated a great number of families; by 1977, between 60,000 and 75,000 people now lived in the region.[55] These new arrivals required housing, access to medicine and educational materials. Coffee cultivation would also require the construction of irrigation systems and therefore power plants.[56]

Providing aid for Vietnam's coffee industry also served the SED's goal of improving Germans' belief in socialism, as it could use such agreements to show the population that East Germany was contributing to large-scale development projects around the world. The *Berliner Zeitung* told readers that Vietnamese state farms hoped to triple existing coffee fields to 73,000 hectares—an exaggeration that anticipated the potential of this agreement.[57] East German assistance allowed Vietnam to "productively utilize its large labor reserves," according to *Neues Deutschland*, emphasizing East Germany's contributions to this effort.[58] By 1985, the coffee project witnessed some measurable success, as farmers doubled the annual rate at which they planted new fields.[59] German observers increasingly claimed responsibility for these developments. For instance, in a report from 1986, the Center for Information and Documentation of Foreign Trade (*Zentrum für Information und Dokumentation der Außenwirtschaft*, ZIDA) claimed that assistance from the GDR over the previous years "puts Vietnam in the position to intensify production of important export goods" for socialist countries, especially the GDR.[60]

By framing the developments in Vietnam as part of a modernizing enterprise that relied on East German assistance, GDR state media promoted a vision of East Germany actively engaged in a globalizing economy, directly improving the lives of thousands of people over 9000 kilometers away. These messages encouraged Germans to internalize the idea that the GDR was in a position to offer this aid and guidance because it belonged to the modern industrial world. If the regime could not fully convince its population of socialism's superiority over capitalism in material prosperity, its humanitarian efforts abroad could deliver this message another way.

Between 1986 and 1990, Vietnam agreed to expand the coffee fields by another 5000 hectares.[61] Estimates for future production were promising, as German experts reported improved yields, and Vietnamese plans to increase acreage to 50,000 hectares by 1990.[62] Progress reports for the period 1986–1990 are scarce, but from 1986 onward, Vietnam had exported about five thousand tons of coffee beans to the GDR, and by 1989, the Kombinat Viet-Duc (Combine Vietnam-GDR) plantation had grown in size from 600 to 8000 hectares, becoming the largest coffee plantation in the country.[63] Of the ten thousand hectares planned for the period, 7272 hectares had been planted between 1986 and 1988, though less than half the planned volume of raw beans was delivered to the GDR in the same period.[64]

To the extent that the search for coffee led to a number of barter-based trade agreements that did not reflect standard international practice of direct purchase, and to large-scale development projects affecting thousands of lives, the coffee projects reveal the GDR's global footprint, as well as its lasting legacy in a post-Cold War era.[65] During the 1990s, Vietnam emerged as the world's second largest producer of Robusta coffee next to Brazil, jumping from 1.2% of world production in 1989 to 12.4% by the turn of the century.[66] The ICO feared the impact East Germany's cooperative partnerships with the developing world—in particular, the coffee project in Vietnam—would have on the world market. These projects had introduced new competitors, and the ICO felt the long-term implications of these developments were too uncertain in 1990. The ICO argued "there is no real way to determine what the value of Vietnamese coffee beans really is as yet."[67] Thus, it would be difficult for the ICO to effectively formulate policy and strategies to cope with the emergence of these new coffee markets, especially if major producers like Brazil (which held a majority interest in the ICO) would now have to compete with new producing countries.

Cultivating Connections: Coffee Culture and an East German "Legacy" in Vietnam

The coffee crisis and the trade deals to which it led illustrate the interconnectedness of consumer socialism, commodity culture and the GDR's place in the global economy. Planners found themselves increasingly dependent on a global market dominated by capitalist producing countries, but also increasingly unable to pay for a commodity that had become a staple of East German diets. In many ways, the cooperative relationships East Germany formed with coffee-growing countries did in fact lead to meaningful and mutually beneficial exchanges. The GDR's efforts to help Vietnam build their local coffee industry proved successful and had lasting effects well beyond the GDR's dissolution. The interpersonal connections between Germans and locals in developing countries also led to cultural exchange and understanding, as well as a genuine belief that both sides were involved in an important humanitarian project, a belief that anthropologist Christina Schwenkel has called "affective solidarity." For the East Germans helping to rebuild the North Vietnamese city of Vinh, she argues, solidarity meant more than a vague connection with the Third World, and the Vietnamese were more than "mere tokens of racial otherness." In fact, East German specialists' "humanist ethics and political values coalesce[d] in the collective work of rebuilding a devastated city."[68]

Concepts of mutual respect and benefit were central to the ideological makeup of East German relations with the developing world, especially Vietnam. Following these principles often proved more difficult than the GDR had initially anticipated, however. When delays in production or logistics prevented East Germany from making timely deliveries of the goods it had promised, trade partners used these failings to claim the GDR was not honoring their commitments to a mutually beneficial trade agreement. East German efforts to foster a global community of socialist brotherhood did not always bear fruit in the way the SED had hoped, but failure—or at least limited impact—of these projects should not negate the effort to foster global alternatives.

Yet socialism's collapse left legacies around the world, in this case, a thriving coffee industry in Vietnam. Coffee provided an opportunity for collaboration, demonstrating that relatively marginalized countries found ways to maneuver the complicated geopolitical and economic circumstances brought about by both decolonization and the global Cold War conflict. These connections cannot be understood as mere trade agreements arranged for the sake of political or economic efficiency. Geopolitics certainly played a large role in shaping the framework in which the coffee projects discussed here were formed, and economic realities placed considerable limits on the conditions of those endeavors. But these partnerships also came about because of the SED's political choice to uphold a set of cultural values and traditions associated with coffee drinking and must be understood as the culmination of these considerations. East Germans formed their own conceptions of the global divisions of the Cold War world, and furthermore, the GDR had its *own* ambitions, self-image and approach to what constituted "socialism." Through these projects, the GDR played an active role in *shaping* the process of globalization in the second half of the twentieth century, and its contributions had effects lasting well beyond the fall of state socialism in Germany.

Notes

1. I would like to thank like the German Academic Exchange Service (Deutsche Akademische Austauschdienst, DAAD), as well as McMaster University, for the generous funding which facilitated the research used for this paper. I would also like to thank Heather Benbow and Heather Perry for their feedback and encouragement on this paper. All translations are the author's.
2. Bernd Findeis, "Kaffee aus dem Zentralen Hochland," *Berliner Zeitung*, 12 December 1986, 4.
3. Ibid.
4. Some scholars have already examined elements of the coffee crisis and the GDR's attempts to find new sources of coffee through trade deals with Angola and Ethiopia, where the GDR traded small arms for coffee. See Hans Joachim Döring, *Es geht um unsere Existenz: Die Politik der DDR gegenüber der Dritten Welt am Beispiel von Mosambik und Äthiopien* (Berlin: Ch links Verlag, 1999); Anne Dietrich, "Kaffee in der DDR – 'Ein Politikum ersten Ranges'," in *Kaffeewelten: Historische Perspektiven auf eine globale Ware im 20. Jahrhundert*, edited by Christiane Berth, Dorothee Wierling, and Volker Wünderich (Göttingen: Vandenhoeck and Ruprecht, 2015), 225–247.
5. Helga Haftendorn, *Coming of Age: German Foreign Policy Since 1945* (Toronto: Rowman & Littlefield, 2006), 126; William Glenn Gray, *Germany's Cold War: The Global Campaign to Isolate East Germany, 1949–1969* (Chapel Hill: University of North Carolina Press, 2003).
6. Michael Scholz, "East Germany's North European Policy Prior to International Recognition of the German Democratic Republic," *Contemporary European History* 15, no. 4 (November 2006): 553–571, here 553.
7. Katherine Pence, "Grounds for Discontent? Coffee from the Black Market to the Kaffeeklatsch in the GDR," in *Communism Unwrapped: Consumption in Cold War Eastern Europe*, edited by Paulina Bren and Mary Neuburger (New York: Oxford University Press, 2012), 207.
8. Jeffrey Kopstein, *The Politics of Economic Decline in East Germany, 1945–1989* (Chapel Hill: The University of North Carolina Press, 1997), 42.
9. Mary Fulbrook, *The People's State: East German Society from Hitler to Honecker* (New Haven: Yale University Press, 2005), 36.

10. Eli Rubin, *Synthetic Socialism: Plastics & Dictatorship in the German Democratic Republic* (Chapel Hill: University of North Carolina Press, 2008), 33; Mark Landsman, *Dictatorship and Demand: East Germany Between Productivism and Consumerism, 1948–1961* (Cambridge, MA: Harvard University Press, 2005), 173; and André Steiner, *The Plans That Failed: An Economic History of East Germany, 1945–1989* (Berlin: Berghahn Books, 2010), 81–100.
11. The 1960s also saw important shifts in the tone of Cold War rhetoric both at the highest political levels and among the general public, which linked matters of political and economic conflict with culture and everyday life. Culture came to sit at the heart of the broader global conflict, as exemplified by the infamous "kitchen debate" between then American Vice President Richard Nixon and Soviet leader Nikita Khrushchev on 24 July 1959. Stood before a physical recreation of a "typical" American kitchen, the two politicians argued over which economic system offered better convenience for the modern family. The event has been described by historians as a key turning point in the broader Cold War because of the ways in which the American and Russian public interpreted that "debate." The exchange revealed the fact that at its core, the Cold War was about far more than direct military or political conflict, but rather represented a deeper cultural question: Which economic system offered its citizens the superior lifestyle, and which could sustain improvements to living standards into the future? See Greg Castillo, *Cold War on the Home Front: The Soft Power of Midcentury Design* (Minneapolis: University of Minnesota Press, 2010).
12. Young-sun Hong, *Cold War Germany, the Third World, and the Global Humanitarian Regime* (New York: Cambridge University Press, 2015), 319.
13. Jupp, "Espresso Hungaria," *Berliner Zeitung*, 4 November 1961, 3.
14. Ibid. Other possible definitions for *Gemütlichkeit* include 'comfort,' or 'coziness.'
15. Lothar Görne, "Kontrolle und Hilfe," *Berliner Zeitung*, 8 April 1961, 1.
16. Ina Merkel argues that consumption played a vital role in shaping expectations about improving living standards, a goal to which the SED committed itself, thus tying their political legitimacy directly to their ability to improve those living conditions. See *Utopie und Bedürfnis*; Mark Landsman argues that while consumerism proved a constant thorn in the regime's side, "the maintenance of power required periodic concessions to consumerism." See his *Dictatorship and Demand: East Germany Between Productivism and Consumerism, 1948–1961* (Cambridge, MA: Harvard University Press, 2005), particularly 222; and Monika Sigmund, *Genuss als Politikum: Kaffeekonsum in beiden deutschen Staaten* (Berlin: De Gruyter Oldenbourg, 2014).

17. See for example "Drei neue Küchenmodelle," *Kultur im Heim*, no. 2 (1957): 32; "Die Küche der Zukunft," *Für Dich*, no. 51 (3 December 1963): 40–41; "Ein Essplatz ist notwendig," *Guter Rat*, no. 3 (1967): 16–18.
18. Household advice books are a rich source of material on everyday life in the GDR. For examples of their use, see Paul Betts, *Within Walls: Private Life in the German Democratic Republic* (New York: Oxford University Press, 2010); Donna Harsch, *Revenge of the Domestic: Women, the Family, and Communism in the German Democratic Republic* (Princeton: Princeton University Press, 2007), especially her discussion of these books as a means to reinforce bourgeois gender roles within East German households on 191–193.
19. *Festlich Gedeckte Tische für viele Gelegenheiten*, Bestellung nummer 607. Leipzig: Verlag für die Frau (no date); Kloiber, "Brewing Relations: Coffee, East Germany, and Laos," 64.
20. Katherine Pence, "Grounds for Discontent? Coffee from the Black Market to the Kaffeeklatsch in the GDR," in *Communism Unwrapped: Consumption in Cold War Eastern Europe*, edited by Paulina Bren and Mary Neuburger (New York: Oxford University Press, 2012), 211.
21. "Kaffee Kaffee das muss ich haben," *Für Dich* 5 (January 1967): 24.
22. The state coffee firm, the *Instituto Brasileiro do Café* (IBC) announced on 23 July that over half of the 1976/77 crop had been destroyed, and it suspended all coffee exports on 19 July as a protective measure, a risky move as coffee "account[ed] for 20 to 25 per cent of the country's total exports." See John Talbot, *Grounds for Agreement: The Political Economy of the Coffee Commodity Chain* (New York: Rowman & Littlefield, 2004), 68; "Frost Damages Next Year's Crop of Brazil Coffee." On use of reserves, see "Frost in Brazil Said to Ruin Half of Coffee Crop and Peril Herds," *The New York Times*, 24 July 1975, 10.
23. International Coffee Organization, "Comparative Analysis of World Coffee Prices and Manufactured Goods," International Coffee Council, 112th session, March 3–7, 2014, London, 3.
24. BArchBL-SAPMO, DY 3023/1218, Rüscher to Mittag, 20 April 1977, 1.
25. Dietrich, "Kaffee in der DDR – 'Ein Politikum ersten Ranges'"; Pence, "Grounds for Discontent?"; Sigmund, *Genuss als Politikum*; Pavel Szobi, "Konsumsozialismus in den 1970er und 1980er Jahren am Beispiel der DDR und der ČSSR," in *Die ČSSR und die DDR im historischen Vergleich: Gemeinsamkeiten und Unterschiede zweier staatssozialistischer Systeme in Mitteleuropa*, edited by Miloš Řezník and Katja Rosenbaum, 49–62 (Leipzig and Berlin: Kirchhof & Franke, 2013), 51; and Volker Wünderich, "Die 'Kaffeekrise' von 1977: Genussmittel und Verbraucherprotest in der DDR," *Historische Anthropologie* 11, no. 2 (2003): 248.

26. BArchB, DY 30 J IV 2/2 1680, "Anlage Nr.6 zum Protokoll nr. 26/77 der Sitzung des Politbüros des ZK der SED vom 28. Juni 1977," 52–55.
27. BArchB, DY 3023/1218, Wange to Mittag, "Entwicklung der Importe von Rohkaffee und der Qualität der Röstkaffeemischungen," 10 August 1978, 480–481, here 481.
28. BArchB, DL 1- VA, 22954b, Erzgebirge, *Eingabe* 1517/7.
29. BArchB, DY 30/25310, Bericht an Genossen Hermann Pöschel ..., Das "Kaffeetrinker-Kollektiv" (*Eingaben*).
30. BArchB, DY 30/9069, Frau M. "Betrifft Kaffee!" (*Eingabe*), 23 September 1977 (emphasis added).
31. Ina Merkel. *Utopie und Bedürfnis*; Monika Sigmund. *Genuss als Politikum*. See also Ina Merkel and Felix Mühlberg, "Eingaben und Öffentlichkeit," in *"Wir sind doch nicht die Mecker-Ecke der Nation:" Briefe an das DDR-Fernsehen*, edited by Ina Merkel (Köln: Böhlau, 1998), 19; Jonathan Zatlin, *The Currency of Socialism: Money and Political Culture in East Germany* (Washington: Cambridge University Press, 2008). "Weltmarktpreise und Kaffeeversorgung," *Berliner Zeitung*, 23 September 1977, 2; "Preisregulierung bei Kaffee," *Neue Zeit*, 23 September 1977, 2; "Mitteilung des Ministeriums für Handel und Versorgung," *Neues Deutschland*, 23 September 1977, 2.
32. The Germans' continued boycott sparked shortages in *Rondo* in late September and early October, as customers scrambled to buy up limited supplies of the better brands. BArchB, DL 1- VA, 22954b, *Eingabe* from Manfred Popp, Naunhof, 3 October 1977.
33. Foundation Archives of Parties and Mass Organizations of the GDR in the Federal Archives (hereafter BArchBL-SAPMO), DY 30-IV B 2-5-999, "Information über Meinungen und Äußerungen der Bevölkerung über *Kaffee-Mix*," Karl-Marx-Stadt, 3 August 1977, 3.
34. In 1978 world prices had declined, allowing the GDR to increase its coffee imports from its traditional sources, principally Brazil and Colombia, beginning in 1978 and 1979 respectively. "Ausfuhr und Einfuhr ausgewählter Erzeugnisse nach Ländern," *Statistisches Jahrbuch der Deutschen Demokratischen Republik* (Zeitschriftenband 1983), Log 68, 235–246, accessed July 21, 2016, www.digizeitschriften.de/dms/img/?PID=PPN514402644_1982|log68&physid=phys262#navi.
35. Ingrid Muth, *Die DDR-Außenpolitk 1949–1972: Inhalte, Strukturen, Mechanismen* (Berlin: Ch links Verlag, 2000), 17. East German autonomy was nonetheless always limited, and the country remained heavily influenced by Soviet trajectories throughout its existence. The GDR followed the Soviet Union's commitment to 'peaceful coexistence' in the 1950s and 1960s. Wherever Soviet and East German interests collided, primacy fell to Soviet considerations. Nonetheless, in many respects, the

GDR practiced its foreign policy independently—including in its humanitarian projects in the Third World. See Hope Harrison, *Driving the Soviets Up the Wall: Soviet-East German Relations, 1953–1961* (Princeton: Princeton University Press, 2005); and Michael Scholz, "East Germany's North European Policy Prior to International Recognition of the German Democratic Republic," *Contemporary European History* 15, no. 4 (November 2006): 553–571.

36. Rolf Gutermuth, "Freier Welthandel setzt friedliche Koexistenz voraus," *Neues Deutschland* 19, no. 82 (22 March 1964), 7.
37. "Hat die Erde Brote für Alle?" *Für Dich* 41, no. 2 (October 1968), 26–27 (emphasis added).
38. Rolf Gutermuth, "Freier Welthandel setzt friedliche Koexistenz voraus," *Neues Deutschland* 19, no. 82 (22 March 1964), 7. Hans Joachim Döring also discusses the GDR's conceptualization of 'Handel statt Hilfe' in his *Es geht um unser Existenz: Die Politik der DDR gegenüber der Dritten Welt am Beispiel von Mosambik und Äthiopien*. Berlin: Ch links Verlag, 1999. Also, at the 1955 Bandung conference, a range of third world countries founded the 'Third World Movement', which sought to create a united front against the exploitation of colonial and neo-colonial forces, to level the terms of trade. See Young-sun Hong, *Cold War Germany*, especially Chapter 1.
39. "Hat die Erde Brote für Alle?" *Für Dich* 41, no. 2 (October 1968), 26–27.
40. Hans Joachim Döring, "*Es geht um unsere Existenz*," 41.
41. Gerd Horten, "Sailing in the Shadow of the Vietnam War," *German Studies Review* 36, no. 3 (2013): 558.
42. Ibid., 557–578.
43. Brown, *The Rise and Fall of Communism*, 345.
44. Schaefer, "Socialist Modernization in Vietnam: The East German Approach, 1976–89," in *Comrades of Color: East Germany in the Cold War World*, edited by Quinn Slobodian (New York: Berghahn Books, 2015), 96.
45. Ibid., 100.
46. Even here, Vietnam's relationship with the USSR was also "relatively distant and difficult," as Vietnam continuously proved its willingness to pursue its own policy initiatives. For more on this strained relationship, see Céline Marangé, "Les relations politiques de l'Union soviétique avec le Vietnam de 1975 à 1995," *Outre-Mers. Revue d'histoire* 94, no. 354 (2007): 147–171, here 148.
47. BStU MfS HA XVIII, Nr 8641, "Vietnam - Ökonomische Einschätzung zu den Beziehungen der SR Vietnam zur UdSSR und den anderen sozialistischen Ländern, den kapitalistischen Industrieländern und Entwicklungsländern," 1979.

48. Doan Trieu Nhan, "Orientations of Vietnam Coffee Industry," Speech at International Coffee Conference May 17–19, 2001 in London, UK, accessed June 7, 2017, http://www.ico.org/event_pdfs/nhan.pdf.
49. BArchB, DC 20/I/4/3998, "Beschluß über die Entwicklung der Wirtschaftsbeziehungen zwischen der DDR und Vietnam (Anlage: Konzeption für die Koordinierung der Volkswirtschaftspläne der DDR und der SRV für den Zeitraum 1981–1985)," 9 February 1978, 182–199, here 187.
50. See "International Coffee Agreements, 1962–1968," The International Coffee Organization, London, accessed January 1, 2014, http://www.ico.org/icohistory_e.asp?section=About_Us#sthash.XLTFrgT2.dpuf.
51. BArchB, DC 20 I/4/4615 Bd.5, "Beschluss über den Entwurf des Abkommens zwischen der Regierung der Deutschen Demokratischen Republik und der Regierung der Sozialistischen Republik Vietnam über die Lieferung von Rohkaffee aus der Sozialistischen Republik Vietnam in die Deutsche Demokratische Republik," 26 August 1980, 69.
52. BArchB DE 1 56153, Memo from Lietz to Schürer, 10 March 1980. Appendix: "Abkommen zwischen der Regierung der DDR und der Regierung der SRV über die Zusammenarbeit bei der Produktion von Rohkaffee, (Draft)," 1.
53. Ibid., 2.
54. Siegfried Kaulfuss, "Die Entwicklung des Kaffeeanbaus in Vietnam," in *Die DDR und Vietnam: Berichte, Erinnerungen, Fakten*, edited by Ilona Schleicher (Berlin: Verband für Internationale Politik und Völkerrecht e.V., Schriften zur internationalen Politik. Band I u. II. 2011), 43.
55. Ibid.
56. Bernd Schaefer, "Socialist Modernization in Vietnam: The East German Approach, 1976–89," 100.
57. "Mehr Kaffee in Vietnam," *Berliner Zeitung*, 20 January 1981, 5. See also "DDR und Vietnam schlössen langfristige Abkommen ab," *Neues Deutschland*, 5 November 1980, 2; "Handelsabkommen DDR-SRV unterzeichnet," *Neue Zeit* 36 (5 November 1980): 2.
58. Hartmut Kohlmetz, "Von der Solidarität zum beiderseitigen Vorteil der Partner," *Berliner Zeitung*, 14 March 1981, 4.
59. BArchB, DY 3023/1003, "Information über den Stand der Realisierung mit der SRV getroffener Vereinbarungen zur Zusammenarbeit auf dem Gebiet der Lebensmittelindustrie, insbesondere bei der Produktion von Rohkaffee, und Schlußfolgerungen für die weitere Arbeit," 21.
60. BArchB, DL2/6424, "Information für den Außenhandel: SR Vietnam," Zentrum für Information und Dokumentation der Außenwirtschaft (ZIDA), Nr. 2/86. 1986, 414–429, here 419.

61. BArchB, DK1/28475, "Abkommen zwischen der Regierung der Deutschen Demokratischen Republik und der Regierung der Sozialistischen Republik Vietnam über die Fortführung der Zusammenarbeit bei der Produktion von Rohkaffee und die Lieferung von Rohkaffee aus der Sozialistischen Republik Vietnam in die Deutsche Demokratische Republik," 27 February 1986, 3.
62. BArchB, DL 2/6220, "Information zur Wirtschaft der DDR im Monat April 1986," 64.
63. Schaefer, "Socialist Modernization in Vietnam: The East Germany Approach, 1976–89," 108.
64. BArchB, DQ 4/5303, "Protokoll der 14th Tagung des Ausschusses für wirtschaftliche und wissenschaftlich-technische Zusammenarbeit zwischen der DDR und der SRV," 24 Januar 1988, 8.
65. See Young-Sun Hong, *Cold War Germany*; Michael Scholz, "East Germany's North European Policy Prior to International Recognition of the German Democratic Republic"; Gerd Horten, "Sailing in the Shadow of the Vietnam War"; Eli Rubin, *Synthetic Socialism*; Greg Castillo, *Cold War on the Home Front*; and Mike Dennis, "Working Under Hammer and Sickle: Vietnamese Workers in the German Democratic Republic, 1980–89," among others.
66. Mark Pendergrast, *Uncommon Grounds: The History of Coffee* (Basic Books, 2010), 363; Q. Luong and L.W. Tauer, "A Real Options Analysis of Coffee Planting in Vietnam," *Agricultural Economics* 35, no. 49 (November 2006): 57. Cited in: Sylvie Doutriaux, Charles Geisler, and Gerald Shively, "Competing for Coffee Space: Development-Induced Displacement in the Central Highlands of Vietnam," *Rural Sociology* 73, no. 4 (2008): 528–554, here 528.
67. Hartmut Brandt, *The Formulation of a New International Coffee Agreement* (Berlin: German Development Institute (GDI), 1991), 97.
68. Christina Schwenkel, "Affective Solidarities and East German Reconstruction of Postwar Vietnam," in *Comrades of Color: East Germany in the Cold War World*, edited by Quinn Slobodian (New York: Berghahn Books, 2015), 270.

Bibliography

BArchB, DL 1- VA, 22954b, *Eingabe* from Manfred Popp, Naunhof, 3 October 1977.

BArchBL-SAPMO, DY 30-IV B 2-5-999, "Information über Meinungen und Äußerungen der Bevölkerung über *Kaffee- Mix*," Karl Marx Stadt, 3 August 1977, 3.

BArchB, DY 3023/1003, "Information über den Stand der Realisierung mit der SRV getroffener Vereinbarungen zur Zusammenarbeit auf dem Gebiet der Lebensmittelindustrie, insbesondere bei der Produktion von Rohkaffee, und Schlußfolgerungen für die weitere Arbeit," 21.

BArchB, DL2/6424, "Information für den Außenhandel: SR Vietnam," Zentrum für Information und Dokumentation der Außenwirtschaft (ZIDA), Nr. 2/86. 1986, 414–429, here 419.

BArchB, DK1/28475, "Abkommen zwischen der Regierung der Deutschen Demokratischen Republik und der Regierung der Sozialistischen Republik Vietnam über die Fortführung der Zusammenarbeit bei der Produktion von Rohkaffee und die Lieferung von Rohkaffee aus der Sozialistischen Republik Vietnam in die Deutsche Demokratische Republik," 27 February 1986, 3.

BArchB, DL 2/6220, "Information zur Wirtschaft der DDR im Monat April 1986," 64.

BArchB, DQ 4/5303, "Protokoll der 14th Tagung des Ausschusses für wirtschaftliche und wissenschaftlich-technische Zusammenarbeit zwischen der DDR und der SRV," 24 Januar 1988, 8.

BArchBL-SAPMO, DY 3023/1218, Rüscher to Mittag, 20 April 1977, 1.

BArchB, DY 30 J IV 2/2 1680, "Anlage Nr.6 zum Protokoll nr. 26/77 der Sitzung des Politbüros des ZK der SED vom 28. Juni 1977," 52–55.

BArchBL-SAPMO, DY 42/2437, Fengler to the Bezirksvorstand Berlin, August 3, 1977, p. 1; BArchB, DY 30/25310, "Bericht über die Erfüllung der Produktion prodution von und die Versorgung mit Kaffee," 8 August 1977, 1.

BArchB, DY 3023/1218, Wange to Mittag, "Entwicklung der Improte Importe von Rohkaffee und der Qualität der Röstkaffeemischungen," 10 August 1978, 480–481, here 481.

BArchB, DL 1- VA, 22954b, Erzgebirge, *Eingabe* 1517/7.

BArchB, DY 30/25310, Bericht an Genossen Hermann Pöschel ..., Das "Kaffeetrinker- Kollektiv" (*Eingaben*).

BArchB, DY 30/9069, Frau M. "Betrifft Kaffee!" (*Eingabe*), 23 September 1977 (emphasis added).

BArchB, DC 20/I/4/3998, "Beschluß über die Entwicklung der Wirtschaftsbeziehungen zwischen der DDR und Vietnam (Anlage: Konzeption für die Koordinierung der Volkswirtschaftspläne der DDR und der SRV für den Zeitraum 1981–1985)," 9 February 1978, 182–199, here 187.

BArchB DE 1 56153, Memo from Lietz to Schürer, 10 March 1980. Appendix: "Abkommen zwischen der Regierung der DDR und der Regierung der SRV über die Zusammenarbeit bei der Produktion von Rohkaffee, (Draft)," 1.

BStU MfS HA XVIII, Nr 8641, "Vietnam - Ökonomische Einschätzung zu den Beziehungen der SR Vietnam zur UdSSR und den anderen sozialistischen

Ländern, den kapitalistischen Industrieländern und Entwicklungsländern," 1979.
Betts, Paul. *Within Walls: Private Life in the German Democratic Republic.* New York: Oxford University Press, 2010.
Brandt, Hartmut. *The Formulation of a New International Coffee Agreement.* Berlin: German Development Institute (GDI), 1991.
Brown, Archie. *The Rise and Fall of Communism.* Toronto: Doubleday, 2009.
Castillo, Greg. *Cold War on the Home Front: The Soft Power of Mid-Century Design.* Minneapolis: University of Minnesota Press, 2010.
"DDR und Vietnam schlössen langfristige Abkommen ab," *Neues Deutschland* (5 November 1980), 2.
Dennis, Mike. "Working Under Hammer and Sickle: Vietnamese Workers in the German Democratic Republic, 1980–89." *German Politics* 16, no. 3 (2007): 339–357.
Dietrich, Anne. "Kaffee in der DDR – 'Ein Politikum ersten Ranges'." In *Kaffeewelten: Historische Perspektiven auf eine globale Ware im 20. Jahrhundert*, edited by Christiane Berth, Dorothee Wierling, Volker Wünderich, 225–247. Göttingen: Vandenhoeck & Ruprecht, 2015.
Döring, Hans-Joachim. *‚Es geht um unsere Existenz.' Die Politik der DDR gegenüber der Dritten Welt am Beispiel von Mosambik und Äthiopien.* Forschungen zur DDR-Gesellschaft. Berlin: Christoph Links Verlag, 1999.
Doutriaux, Sylvie, Charles Geisler, and Gerald Shively. "Competing for Coffee Space: Development-Induced Displacement in the Central Highlands of Vietnam." *Rural Sociology* 73, no. 4 (2008): 528–554.
Federal Commissioner for the Records of the State Security Service of the former German Democratic Republic (Behörde des Bundesbeauftragten), Central Evaluation and Information Group (Die Zentrale Auswertungs- und Informationsgruppe), no. 4120, "Hinweise auf erste Reaktionen der Bevölkerung der DDR zur Mitteilung des Ministeriums für Handel und Versorgung am 23.9.1977 zur Kaffeesituation."
Festlich Gedeckte Tische für viele Gelegenheiten, Bestellung Nnummer 607. Leipzig: Verlag füur die Frau (no date).
Findeis, Bernd. "Kaffee aus dem Zentralen Hochland." *Berliner Zeitung* 42 (12 December 1986).
Görne, Lothar. "Kontrolle und Hilfe." *Berliner Zeitung* (8 April 1961): 1.
Gray, William Glenn. *Germany's Cold War: The Global Campaign to Isolate East Germany, 1949–1969.* Chapel Hill: University of North Carolina Press, 2003.
Gutermuth, Rolf. "Freier Welthandel setzt friedliche Koexistenz voraus." *Neues Deutschland* 19, no. 82 (22 March 1964): 7.
Haftendorn, Helga. *Coming of Age: German Foreign Policy Since 1945.* Toronto: Rowman & Littlefield, 2006.

"Handelsabkommen DDR-SRV unterzeichnet," *Neue Zeit* 36 (5 November 1980), 2.
Harrison, Hope. *Driving the Soviets Up the Wall: Soviet-East German Relations, 1953–1961.* Princeton: Princeton University Press, 2005.
Harsch, Donna. *Revenge of the Domestic: Women, the Family, and Communism in the German Democratic Republic.* Princeton: Princeton University Press, 2007.
"Hat die Erde Brote für Alle?" *Für Dich* 41, no. 2 (October 1968), 26–27 (emphasis added).
Hong, Young-Sun. *Cold War Germany, the Third World, and the Global Humanitarian Regime.* Cambridge: Cambridge University Press, 2015.
Horten, Gerd. "Sailing in the Shadow of the Vietnam War: The GDR Government and the 'Vietnam Bonus' of the Early 1970s." *German Studies Review* 36, no. 3 (2013): 557–578.
International Coffee Organization. "Comparative Analysis of World Coffee Prices and Manufactured Goods." International Coffee Council, 112th session, March 3–7, 2014, London, 3.
Jupp. "Espresso Hungaria." *Berliner Zeitung* (4 November 1961): 3.
"Kaffee Kaffee dass muss ich haben." *Für Dich* 5 (January 1967): 24.
Kaulfuss, Siegried. "Die Entwicklung des Kaffeeanbaus in Vietnam." In *Die DDR und Vietnam: Berichte, Erinnerungen, Fakten,* Teil I, edited by Hannelore Bock and Ilona Schleicher, 39–51. Berlin: Verband für Internationale Politik und Völkerrecht, c.V., 2011.
Kohlmetz, Hartmut. "Von der Solidarität zum beiderseitigen Vorteil der Partner." *Berliner Zeitung* 37 (14 March 1981): 4.
Kwon, Hoenik. *The Other Cold War.* New York: Columbia University Press, 2010.
Landsman, Mark. *Dictatorship and Demand: East Germany Between Productivism and Consumerism, 1948–1961.* Cambridge, MA: Harvard University Press, 2005.
Marangé, Céline. "Alliance ou interdépendance inégale? Les relations politiques de l'Union soviétique avec le Vietnam de 1975 à 1991." *Outre-mers* 94, no. 354 (2007): 147–171.
"Mehr Kaffee in Vietnam." *Berliner Zeitung* (20 January 1981), 5.
Merkel, Ina. *Utopie und Bedürfnis. Die Geschichte der Konsumkultur in der DDR.* Cologne: Böhlau, 1999.
Merkel, Ina, and Felix Mühlberg. "Eingaben und Öffentlichkeit." In *"Wir sind doch nicht die Mecker- Ecke der Nation:" Briefe an das DDR-Fernsehen,* edited by Ina Merkel, 9–32. Köln: Böhlau, 1998.
Muth, Ingrid. *Die DDR-Außenpolitik 1949–1972. Inhalte, Strukturen, Mechanismen.* Berlin: Ch. Links, 2001.

Nhan, Doan Trieu. "Orientations of Vietnam Coffee Industry." Speech at International Coffee Conference, May 17–19, 2001 in London, UK. Accessed 7 June 2017. http://www.ico.org/event_pdfs/nhan.pdf.

Pence, Katherine. "Grounds for Discontent? Coffee from the Black Market to the Kaffeeklatsch in the GDR." In *Communism Unwrapped: Consumption in Cold War Eastern Europe*, edited by Paulina Bren and Mary Neuburger, 197–225. New York: Oxford University Press, 2012.

Pendergrast, Mark. *Uncommon Grounds: The History of Coffee*. New York: Basic Books, 2010.

Rubin, Eli. *Synthetic Socialism: Plastics & Dictatorship in the German Democratic Republic*. Chapel Hill: University of North Carolina Press, 2008.

Schaefer, Bernd. "Socialist Modernization in Vietnam: The East German Approach, 1976–1989." In *Comrades of Color: East Germany in the Cold War World*, edited by Quinn Slobodian, 95–116. New York: Berghahn Books, 2015.

Scholz, Michael. "East Germany's North European Policy Prior to International Recognition of the German Democratic Republic." *Contemporary European History* 15, no. 4 (November 2006): 553–571.

Schwenkel, Christina. "Affective Solidarities and East German Reconstruction of Postwar Vietnam." In *Comrades of Color: East Germany in the Cold War World*, edited by Quinn Slobodian, 267–292. New York: Berghahn Books, 2015.

Sigmund, Monika. *Genuss als Politikum: Kaffeekonsum in beiden deutschen Staaten*. Berlin: De Gruyter Oldenbourg, 2014.

Szobi, Pavel. "Konsumsozialismus in den 1970er und 1980er Jahren am Beispiel der DDR und der ČSSR." In *Die ČSSR und die DDR im historischen Vergleich: Gemeinsamkeiten und Unterschiede zweier staatssozialistischer Systeme in Mitteleuropa*, edited by Miloš Řezník and Katja Rosenbaum, 49–62. Leipzig and Berlin: Kirchhof & Franke, 2013.

Talbot, John. *Grounds for Agreement: The Political Economy of the Coffee Commodity Chain*. New York: Rowman & Littlefield, 2004.

Valentine, John. "Frost Damages Next Year's Crop of Brazil Coffee: Half of Output May Be Lost." *The Wall Street Journal* (21 July 1975): 14.

"Weltmarktpreise und Kaffeeversorgung," *Berliner Zeitung*, 23 September 1977, 2; "Preisregulierung bei Kaffee," *Neue Zeit*, 23 September 1977, 2; "Mitteilung des Ministeriums für Handel und Versorgung," *Neues Deutschland*, 23 September, 1977, 2.

Wünderich, Volker. "Die 'Kaffeekrise' von 1977. Genußmittel und Verbraucherprotest in der DDR." *Historische Anthropologie* 11 (2003): 240–261.

Zatlin, Jonathan R. *The Currency of Socialism: Money and Political Culture in East Germany*. Washington: Cambridge University Press, 2008.

Index

A
Abderhalden, Emil, 33, 38
Abraham, Herrmann, 78, 80, 81, 89, 90, 95, 98, 99
Adcock, Clarence, 191
Adenauer, Konrad, 237
Adorno, Theodor, 178, 192
advertisements, 131–134, 140
agricultural production, 38, 165, 183, 186
Aknaszlatina ghetto, 117
Alabama, 9, 125, 131, 132, 135, 139, 142, 148
Algeria, 189
Aliceville POW camp, 9, 125, 126, 132, 134, 135, 138–144, 146–148
alimentary sovereignty, 155, 170. See *also* self-feeding
Allied Forces, 205
Alsatia, 59
Andrews, Stanley, 207, 208, 213, 218, 220
apiaries, 139, 141
Armen-Speisungs-Anstalt (Food Relief Centre for the Poor), 78

asparagus, 189. See *also* vegetables
Austria, 190, 236
Austrian-Prussian War, 78

B
Backe, Herbert, 171, 181, 182, 204, 216
baking, 24, 139, 140
  and housewives, 7, 25, 27–30, 32, 34, 205
  and POWs, 9, 125–127, 135–141, 145, 146
barley, 23, 24, 166, 172, 231, 232. See *also* grain
Bäumer, Gertrude, 25, 39, 49, 97
Bavaria, 11, 30, 164, 189, 207, 213, 234, 236, 237, 241
  and beer, 11, 207, 234, 236, 237
beer
  and capitalism, 11, 157, 228, 236–239
  and production in the FRG, 11, 229, 232, 233, 235–239
  and production in the GDR, 229, 232, 233, 237–239, 250, 251

and production in the UK, 232
and production in the US, 127, 128, 135, 207, 231
and regional production, 232
and socialism, 229, 235, 240
and US soldiers, 11
consumption in the GDR, 11, 228–230, 234, 239, 251
Beer Riot, 234
Belgium, 161, 231
Berlin, 8, 10, 14, 17, 20, 22, 24, 25, 28, 29, 33, 34, 36–38, 76–79, 81–87, 89–96, 98, 99, 178, 182, 185, 203, 209, 216, 227, 228, 230, 234, 235, 237, 252
Berliner Tageblatt, 79, 97
Berliner Zeitung, 229, 234, 236, 237, 242–244, 249, 253, 259, 262, 263, 265, 267
bio-science, 18. See also nutritional science
black market, 112, 113, 162, 185, 196, 203, 207–209, 216, 218, 262, 264
Brazil, 254, 258, 260, 264, 265
bread, 14, 22, 23, 36, 50–52, 54–57, 59–62, 83, 105, 111, 113–115, 138, 139, 164, 171, 182, 187, 188, 191, 204, 206, 207, 213, 214, 230
breastfeeding, 24
British blockade, 21, 24, 162, 183
British occupation of Germany, 162, 185, 189
Budapest, 107
Bürgerküche, 89
Bürgerspeisehalle, 89
butter, 23, 56, 177, 187–190, 207, 209, 244

C
cabbage, 140, 184. See also vegetables
calories, 22, 24, 28, 107, 111, 116, 140, 158, 160, 163, 170, 171, 177, 181, 183–186, 190–192, 194, 195, 198, 208, 210, 211, 215
candy, 112, 208–210, 212, 219
cannibalism, 9, 116
capitalism, 11, 157, 171, 228, 236–239, 259
and beer, 11, 228, 230, 235–239
carbohydrates, 22, 23, 28, 210
care packages (food packages to soldiers on the front by their families), 53, 56
CARE packages (US hunger relief for German civilians after WWII), 191
cattle, 11, 189. See also livestock
censorship, 7, 51, 126, 143. See also Feldpressestelle
chewing gum, 210, 212
China, 186, 231
chocolate, 52, 55, 59, 61–63, 115, 137, 191, 205, 208–210, 214, 219
Christianity, 236
Christian values, 236
Christmas, 55, 129, 130, 136, 137. See also holidays
Chust ghetto, 108
civil-military relations, 202
Clay, Lucius D., 184, 190, 207, 211
Clément, Nicolas, 158
Coca-Cola, 2, 131, 132, 134, 135, 145. See also drink
coffee
and cafés, 110, 112
and development aid, 256
and GDR, 11, 12, 250–254, 258–261

INDEX   273

and Vietnam, 11, 12, 249, 250, 256–261
crisis, 11, 249, 250, 254, 255, 260, 262
prices, 87, 251, 252, 254, 255, 258, 264
surrogates, 11, 12, 255. *See also* Ersatz coffee
colonialism, 255, 264
Cold War, 4, 5, 11, 12, 214, 228, 229, 232, 233, 239, 240, 250–252, 256, 261, 263. *See also* Iron Curtain
communism, 190, 211
concentration camps, 104, 111, 113, 116, 117, 190. *See also* labor camps
cookbooks, 30, 39
  war, 7, 25, 30, 32
cooking, 24. *See also* kitchen technology
  and mothers, 24, 111, 130
  and POWs, 133, 138, 142, 146, 147, 155
  and women, 7, 18, 24, 25, 27, 29, 30, 32, 86, 130, 132
  home, 7, 25, 27, 32, 111
corn, 11, 23, 213, 231. *See also* maize
Council for Mutual Economic Assistance (COMECON), 257
Council of Relief Agencies Licensed to Operate in Germany (CRALOG), 201, 212, 215
cucumber, 139. *See also* vegetables
culinary habits, 18

D
decolonization, 257, 261
democracy, 165, 178, 190, 211, 212, 214
Der Ruf, 127, 143

Der Zaungast, 9, 126–129, 133–135, 137, 141, 144–147, 149
Deutscher Hausfrauenbund (League of German Housewives), 25
developing countries, 256, 261
development aid, 256
Die Gutsfrau, 34
Die Sappe, 61, 63
dietary restrictions, 115
Displaced Persons (DPs), 115, 177, 178, 184, 185, 187, 190, 191, 195. *See also* DP Camps
Dos Passos, John, 207, 214, 218, 220
DP Camps, 185
Dresden, 77, 92–95, 100, 172, 241
drink, 7, 8, 11, 12, 24, 45–50, 54, 59, 63–65, 78, 111, 127, 128, 130, 132, 134, 135, 145, 205–207, 228, 233, 234, 252, 253. *See also* beer; Coca-Cola; coffee; milk; soda; wine

E
Easter, 137. *See also* holidays
East Germany, 166, 173, 228–230, 232, 233, 237–240, 249–252, 256–262, 264, 266, 268. *See also* German Democratic Republic (GDR)
East Prussia, 32, 157
economic insecurity, 18
eggs, 56, 110, 137, 189, 206
Eisenhower, Dwight D., 205, 211, 216, 217, 220
emergency kitchens, 76, 79, 82–84, 86–90, 95, 99. *See also* public kitchens
Entente Blockade, 5
Ersatz coffee, 12, 115, 212
European Recovery Program (ERP), 191
expellees (Volksvertriebene), 154

F

Fassbender, Martin, 27–29, 39
fats, 22, 23, 27, 29, 33, 57, 112, 161, 182, 187, 190, 191, 194, 205, 207
Federal Republic of Germany (FRG), 11, 228–230, 232, 233, 235–239, 241, 250. *See also* West Germany
   and beer, 11, 229, 232, 233, 235, 237–239, 241
   and coffee, 11, 250
Feldpressestelle, 48
Festlich Gedeckte Tische, 253, 264
Finland, 161
fish, 24, 30, 188
food
   and communication, 46, 56, 141, 203, 206
   and emotional sustenance, 203
   and gender, 2, 3, 8, 18, 19, 46, 48
   and identity, 46, 128, 156, 180, 202
   and intimacy, 49, 64
   and memory, 5, 19
   and power relations, 178
   and religious restrictions, 106
   and science, 18, 32, 33, 35, 158
   and sexual relations, 64
   as weapon of war, 11, 12, 202, 204, 214
   coupons, 86, 88
   deprivation, 5, 7, 17–19, 52, 104, 114, 115, 118, 159, 165, 178, 192, 202, 204, 214. *See also* food scarcity; food shortage; hunger
   fantasies, 8, 48, 114, 116, 122
   food-sharing, 49, 53, 203, 206, 214
   hoarding, 187, 188, 212
   kosher, 9, 115
   processing, 18, 114, 165
   production, 5, 10, 18, 24, 37, 91, 110, 116, 153, 163, 168, 178, 181, 186, 187, 191, 207, 230, 232, 233, 257
   quality of, 140, 194, 251, 255
   rationing, 20, 33, 34, 75, 76, 104, 139, 158–161, 177, 183, 184, 250
   requisitioning of, 182, 190
   rumours, 180, 187
   self-sufficiency, 86, 154, 156, 159–161, 165, 181
   shortage, 4, 8–10, 18–21, 24, 25, 29, 35, 36, 55, 75, 76, 83, 91, 103, 128, 139, 141, 156, 162, 165, 167, 178, 185, 187, 188, 192, 196, 204, 207, 212–214, 216. *See also* food deprivation; food scarcity; hunger
   supply, 12, 19, 22, 27, 34, 75–77, 79, 81, 83, 87, 90, 91, 93, 94, 107, 110, 118, 167, 179, 181–185, 187, 191, 202, 250
   theft, 110, 115, 116
   trade (exports and imports), 5, 8, 110, 113, 155, 209, 214, 238, 250, 256, 262
food scarcity, 19–21, 24, 37, 46, 50, 52, 114, 178
Fort McClellan POW camp, 9, 125–128, 131, 134–136, 138, 139, 142, 143, 146
France, 157, 160, 170, 171, 182, 184, 189, 194
Freie Deutsche Jugend (FDJ), 164, 165, 172
French occupation of Germany, 185
fresh fruit, 129, 162, 189
fruit, 23, 33, 59, 132, 163, 177, 191, 205, 209, 258, 261. *See also* fresh fruit; melons; peaches; strawberries
Für Dich, 254, 256, 264, 266
Fürth, Henriette, 30, 39

G

gardening, 63. *See also* market gardening
German Democratic Republic (GDR), 11. *See also* East Germany
and beer, 11, 228, 229, 232–240
and cold war, 11, 12, 228, 229, 232, 233, 239, 240, 250–252, 256, 260, 261
and print media, 229, 233
and relations with developing countries, 256
German *Hausfrau*, 18, 24, 28. *See also* kitchen soldiers
German unification 1871, 157
Germany, 3–6, 8–12, 17–25, 27–30, 32–35, 46, 49, 50, 55, 57, 64, 75–77, 93, 104, 130, 132, 137, 138, 140, 153–162, 164–168, 177, 179, 181–184, 186–191, 201–204, 206, 208, 210, 211, 213, 214, 228, 230, 234, 236, 237, 262. *See also* Federal Republic of Germany (FRG); German Democratic Republic (GDR); Kaiserreich; Nazi Germany
German Youth activities (GYA), 212
Gestapo, 211
globalization, 12, 252, 262
globalizing economy, 259
Göring, Hermann, 182
grain, 22, 23, 38, 161, 166, 182, 186, 187, 190, 191, 194, 207. *See also* barley; oats; rye; wheat
Goulaschkanonen, 81, 90

H

Hallstein doctrine, 250
Hamburg, 29, 37, 77, 92–95, 119, 189, 196, 234, 236
hamstering, 162
health, 5, 7, 17, 18, 21, 22, 24, 28, 29, 33–36, 40, 87, 166, 205
Heimat, 9, 10, 144, 145, 147, 148, 154–156, 160, 162, 164, 165, 168–170
loss of, 156
Heyl, Hedwig, 24, 34, 38, 96
Hilldring, John, 213
Hitler, Adolf, 181
holidays, 57, 106, 130, 136, 137, 144. *See also* Christmas, Easter, Passover
home economy schools, 7
Honecker, Erich, 228, 258, 262
humanitarian aid, 215, 256
Hungary, 105
hunger, 3, 4, 6–10, 12, 18–20, 22, 36, 45–55, 57, 58, 61, 65, 67, 104, 105, 109, 111, 112, 114, 116, 117, 119, 154, 155, 162, 164, 183, 184, 186, 190, 192, 202, 204, 208, 211, 214–216, 230, 256. *See also* food, deprivation; food scarcity
and civilians, 5, 6, 8–10, 18, 46, 48, 55, 58, 64, 202, 204, 214
and soldiers, 6–8, 45–48, 50–52, 54–58, 61, 64, 67, 204, 214
in Jewish ghettos, 104

I

ice cream, 134, 135, 252
India, 186
indigence, 88–90, 92–94, 97
industrialization, 5, 157, 170
International Coffee Federation, 258, 260, 264
intoxication, 49
Iron Curtain, 238. *See also* Cold War
Italy, 160, 170

J

Japan, 159, 183, 231
Jewish ghettos, 104, 107, 108, 117
Jews, 9, 61, 65, 103–111, 113, 115–118, 120, 158, 171, 185
Joint Distribution Committee, 105, 120
Jünger, Ernst, 60, 71

K

Käber, Ernst, 91, 97, 100
Kaiserreich, 234
   and beer, 234
Kaiser-Wilhelm-Institut für Arbeitsphysiologie (Kaiser-Wilhelm-Institute for Work Physiology), 22
Kassa ghetto, 106
Khrushchev, Nikita, 239, 263
kitchen soldiers, 7, 18, 32, 34, 35
kitchen technology, 18
Kleingarten, 213
kosher, 9, 65, 71, 115
Kovno ghetto, 111
Krakow ghetto, 113, 115, 120
Kriegsernährungsamt (War Foods Office), 34
Kriegsorganisation Dresdner Vereine (Wartime organization of associations in Dresden), 92
Kriegsrohstoffabteilung (KRA), War Raw Materials Office, 21
Kultur im Heim, 253, 264

L

labor camps, 116, 205. *See also* concentration camps
Land und Frau, 34
Lang, Helene, 25
lard, 177, 191
League of Nations, 160, 171
Libya, 127
Life Magazine, 209
livestock, 24, 159, 187
living conditions/standards, 82, 94, 205, 234, 253, 263
   in the FRG, 11
   in the GDR, 234, 253
Łódź ghetto, 109, 111, 113–115, 121
Lokal-Anzeiger, 89, 97
looting, 106, 203. *See also* food, theft
Lvov ghetto, 107, 110, 112, 113, 117, 120

M

Macready, Gordon, 191
maize, 213
malnourishment, 201, 204, 214
margarine, 23, 182, 191
Marxism, 234, 235
   and beer, 234, 235
masculinity, 49, 66
Mateszalka ghetto, 111, 113
matzah, 115
Mead, Margaret, 202, 215
meal pass, 82–88, 99
meat, 23, 24, 30, 56, 83, 112, 114, 115, 161, 182, 187–191, 194, 230. *See also* cattle; livestock; pork
melons, 128. *See also* fruit
milk, 24, 61, 62, 134, 177, 188, 191, 206, 207
   skim, 24
Ministry for State Security (*Ministerium für Staatssicherheit*, Stasi), 255
Minsk ghetto, 114
modernity, 11, 12, 50, 230, 231, 233
   and food production, 230
Morgenstern, Lina, 78
Morgenthau Plan, 183

N

Nagyvarad ghetto, 106
Nationaler Frauendienst NFD (National Women's Service), 29, 33, 76, 80
national identity, 18, 35, 128, 156
National Research Council's Committee on Food Habits, 202
Nazi Germany, 8–10, 103–105, 107, 109, 116–119, 155, 157, 159–161, 163, 164, 168, 172, 181, 183–186, 204, 212, 236, 238. *See also* Third Reich
and agricultural policies, 157, 159
and attitudes to beer, 48
and food policies, 8, 11, 104, 119, 211
Netherlands, 161, 182, 189, 204
Neues Deutschland, 240, 243–245, 256, 259, 265–267
Neue Zeit, 229, 236, 242–244, 265, 267
New York Times, 205, 212, 216, 217, 219, 220, 264
non-commissioned officers (NCO), 125, 126, 146
Norden, Albert, 227, 228, 237, 240, 243
North Africa, 125, 146
Norway, 161, 188
nutrition, 7, 13, 17, 18, 22–24, 27, 30, 32–35, 37, 38, 40, 47, 51, 57, 58, 65, 75, 134, 202, 212. *See also* food
nutritional advice manuals, 7
balance, 159
science, 18, 27, 32, 33, 35. *See also* bio-science
nutritional science, 21
Nutrition Exhibition 1928, 17, 35
nuts, 33, 136

O

oats, 48, 166, 172. *See also* grain
overpopulation, 187, 190

P

Passover, 106, 115. *See also* holidays
Patton, George S., 205, 211
peaches, 134, 139
Poland, 108, 120, 154, 156, 161, 166, 169, 173, 219
pork, 115
potatoes, 22, 23, 57, 62, 83, 165, 166, 172, 182, 187, 190, 191, 206, 216
POW-Oase, 9, 126–129, 131, 132, 136, 141, 144–148
preserved fruit and vegetables, 25
Prisoners of War (POWs), 6, 9, 125–128, 130–132, 134–142, 179, 204
and baking, 9, 125–127, 135–141
and cooking, 133, 138, 142, 146, 147
and plant cultivation, 139
processed foods, 112, 210. *See also* food processing
prohibition, 201, 207, 241
prostitution, 8, 121
protein, 21–24, 172
Prussia, 154
public health, 17, 34, 35, 212
public kitchens, 4, 8, 76–79, 83–96, 98, 99
Purity Law, 11, 134, 232–234. *See also* Reinheitsgebot

R

Red Cross (International Red Cross), 81, 83, 84, 89, 97, 136, 137, 139, 188, 204, 205

Red Cross Society (German), 80, 97
Reichsnährstand (RNS), 181
Reinheitsgebot, 232, 240–242. *See also* Purity Law
Remarque, Erich Maria, 45, 46, 49, 52, 65, 67
Röhm, Ernst, 236
Romania, 62, 63, 65, 66
Rubner, Max, 22–24, 33, 37, 38
rurality, 156, 162, 168
Russia, 13, 170, 231. *See also* Soviet Union; USSR
rutabaga, 32, 33
rye, 23, 166, 172, 255. *See also* grain
Rymanow ghetto, 109

S
Schlange-Schöningen, Dr., 154, 169, 172, 173
school feedings, 212
Sebald, W.G., 179, 192
self-feeding, 155, 159. *See also* alimentary sovereignty
sexual violence, 63, 64, 121
smuggling, 8, 110, 112, 113, 189
socialism, 229, 235, 239, 252–256, 259–262
social reform, 7, 28
soda, 131, 134, 135. *See also* drink
Sombart, Werner, 158, 171
Somme-Wacht, 47, 50
Soviet occupation of Germany, 153, 168, 169
Soviet Union, 154, 160, 204, 250, 256, 265. *See also* Russia; USSR
Sozialdemokratische Partei Deutschlands (SPD), 39, 234, 243
Sozialistische Einheitspartei Deutschlands (SED), 154, 169, 173, 227–230, 232, 233, 235, 245, 250, 251, 256–259, 261, 263, 265
Spain, 161
Speiseausschuss der Hamburgischen Kriegshilfe (Public feeding committee of Hamburg's wartime welfare), 93
spinach, 189. *See also* vegetables
Stammtisch, 235, 237, 238, 243. *See also* beer
Starachowice Ghetto, 111, 117
starvation, 5, 11, 19, 22, 27, 104, 107, 116, 117, 119, 183, 184, 187, 190, 204, 205, 208, 211, 230. *See also* hunger
stollen, 136
strawberries, 189. *See also* fruit
sugar, 23, 59, 189, 205
sugar beet, 166, 172, 255
Switzerland, 160

T
Tacova ghetto, 117
Theresienstadt ghetto, 111, 121
Third Reich, 161, 171, 181–185, 191, 192, 236. *See also* Nazi Germany
tomatoes, 140
Truman, Harry S., 201, 208, 218
Tunisia, 127, 129
turnips, 50, 51, 57, 184. *See also* vegetables

U
Ukraine, 108
Ulbricht, Walter, 228, 233, 238, 251
United Economic Zone, 154
United Nations (UN), 197, 256
United Nations Relief and Rehabilitation Administration (UNRRA), 184, 196

INDEX

United States (US), 2, 11, 25, 34, 40, 119, 125, 127, 130–132, 140, 142, 143, 180, 183–187, 189–191, 195, 201, 202, 204–208, 210, 212–214, 216, 218, 231, 232, 241, 250, 257
urbanity, 162
US-occupation of Germany, 177, 207
USSR, 182, 189, 266. *See also* Russia; Soviet Union

V
van Noorden, Carl, 23
vegetables, 23, 32, 57, 83, 86, 112, 114, 139, 148, 162, 184, 189, 205, 213. *See also* asparagus; cabbage; cucumber; potatoes; spinach; tomatoes; turnips
VELF Verwaltung der Ernährung, Landwirtschaft und Forsten des Vereinigten Wirtschaftsgebietes (Administration for Food, Agriculture, and Forests in the United Economic Zone), 153, 165–167
Verein der Berliner Volksküchen von 1866 (Berlin's Society for Public Kitchens since 1866), 78
Verein für Kindervolksküchen und Volkskinderhorte (Society for the Care and Feeding of Children), 78
Verein zur Errichtung von Arbeiterinnenheimen (Society for the Support of Female Workers Homes), 81
Vietnam, 266–268
  and coffee, 11, 12, 249, 250, 256–261, 267

Vietnam War, 258, 266, 268
vitamins, 34, 134, 140, 172
Volks-Kaffee- und Speisehallen-Gesellschaft (People's Coffee and Dining Hall Society), 78, 81, 96
Volkskrieg, 46, 52, 58
Volksküche, 89
Volksspeisehalle, 89
von Bethmann-Hollweg, Theobald, 90
von Voit, Carl, 21

W
Wagner, Adolf, 158
Warsaw, 108, 109
Warsaw ghetto, 109, 111, 113, 116, 121
Washington Post, 205, 217
Weimar Republic, 19, 25, 234
Wermuth, Adolf, 90, 91, 95, 97–100
West Germany, 166, 169, 172, 228, 232, 234, 235, 237, 239, 250, 251, 256. *See also* Federal Republic of Germany (FRG)
wheat, 23, 24, 165, 166, 172, 184, 186, 188–190, 213. *See also* grain
wine, 24, 48, 49, 54, 62, 206. *See also* drink
Wirtschaftsfräulein, 34, 40
work camps, 205. *See also* concentration camps
working class, 38, 234, 235
  and beer consumption, 234, 235
The World, 9, 35, 98–100, 128, 135, 143, 155, 164, 165, 181, 230, 232, 237, 254, 257–261
World War I, 7, 45–48, 51, 54, 61, 64, 76, 77, 158, 159, 162, 201, 203
World War II, 9, 11, 118, 158, 159, 228

Y
Yalta conference, 156

Z
Zentrale Einkaufs-Gesellschaft (ZEG), Central Purchasing Agency, 21, 30

Zentrale für private Fürsorge (Center for Private Welfare), 79, 96, 99
Zentrum für Information und Dokumentation der Außenwirtschaft (ZIDA), 259